ASIAN POLITICAL, ECONOMIC AND SECURITY ISSUES

POLITICAL AND ECONOMIC DEVELOPMENTS IN ASIA

ASIAN POLITICAL, ECONOMIC AND SECURITY ISSUES

Additional books in this series can be found on Nova's website under the Series tab.

Additional E-books in this series can be found on Nova's website under the E-books tab.

Asian Political, Economic and Security Issues

Political and Economic Developments in Asia

Felix Chin
Editor

Nova Science Publishers, Inc.
New York

Copyright ©2011 by Nova Science Publishers, Inc.

All rights reserved. No part of this book may be reproduced, stored in a retrieval system or transmitted in any form or by any means: electronic, electrostatic, magnetic, tape, mechanical photocopying, recording or otherwise without the written permission of the Publisher.

For permission to use material from this book please contact us:
Telephone 631-231-7269; Fax 631-231-8175
Web Site: http://www.novapublishers.com

NOTICE TO THE READER

The Publisher has taken reasonable care in the preparation of this book, but makes no expressed or implied warranty of any kind and assumes no responsibility for any errors or omissions. No liability is assumed for incidental or consequential damages in connection with or arising out of information contained in this book. The Publisher shall not be liable for any special, consequential, or exemplary damages resulting, in whole or in part, from the readers' use of, or reliance upon, this material. Any parts of this book based on government reports are so indicated and copyright is claimed for those parts to the extent applicable to compilations of such works.

Independent verification should be sought for any data, advice or recommendations contained in this book. In addition, no responsibility is assumed by the publisher for any injury and/or damage to persons or property arising from any methods, products, instructions, ideas or otherwise contained in this publication.

This publication is designed to provide accurate and authoritative information with regard to the subject matter covered herein. It is sold with the clear understanding that the Publisher is not engaged in rendering legal or any other professional services. If legal or any other expert assistance is required, the services of a competent person should be sought. FROM A DECLARATION OF PARTICIPANTS JOINTLY ADOPTED BY A COMMITTEE OF THE AMERICAN BAR ASSOCIATION AND A COMMITTEE OF PUBLISHERS.

Additional color graphics may be available in the e-book version of this book.

LIBRARY OF CONGRESS CATALOGING-IN-PUBLICATION DATA

Political and economic developments in Asia / editors, Felix Chin.
 p. cm.
 Includes index.
 ISBN 978-1-61209-783-1 (hardcover)
 1. Asia--Foreign relations--United States. 2. United States--Foreign
relations--Asia. 3. Asia--Foreign economic relations--United States. 4.
United States--Foreign economic relations--Asia. 5. Asia--Strategic
aspects. 6. Asia--Politics and government--21st century. 7. Asia--Economic
conditions--21st century. I. Chin, Felix, 1962-
 DS33.4.U6P63 2011
 337.51--dc23
                        2011029482

Published by Nova Science Publishers, Inc. † New York

CONTENTS

Preface		vii
Chapter 1	Asia Pacific Economic Cooperation (APEC) and the 2008 Meetings in Lima, Peru *Michael F. Martin*	1
Chapter 2	The Proposed U.S.-South Korea Free Trade Agreement (KORUS FTA): Provisions and Implications *William H. Cooper, Mark E. Manyin, Remy Jurenas and Michaela D. Platzer*	29
Chapter 3	North Korea's Nuclear Weapons Development and Diplomacy *Larry A. Niksch*	79
Chapter 4	Burma and Transnational Crime *Liana Sun Wyler*	101
Chapter 5	China's Currency: A Summary of the Economic Issues *Wayne M. Morrison and Marc Labonte*	119
Chapter 6	China-U.S. Trade Issues *Wayne M. Morrison*	131
Chapter 7	Assistance to North Korea *Mark E. Manyin and Mary Beth Nikitin*	161
Chapter 8	Taiwan-U.S. Relations: Developments and Policy Implications *Kerry Dumbaugh*	179
Chapter 9	U.S.-China Military Contacts: Issues for Congress *Shirley A. Kan*	209
Index		271

PREFACE

This new book presents and discusses various political and economic developments in Asia. Topics discussed include the Asia Pacific Economic Cooperation (APEC); the Proposed U.S.-South Korea Free Trade Agreement (KORUS FTA); North Korea's nuclear weapons development and diplomacy; Burma and transnational crime; China's currency; China-U.S. trade issues; Taiwan-U.S. relations and U.S.-China military contacts.

Chapter 1 - Congress and the Executive Branch have historically identified the Asia Pacific Economic Cooperation (APEC) as an important organization to help promote the U.S. goal of liberalizing international trade and investment in Asia, and possibly the rest of the world. APEC's commitment to the goal of trade and investment liberalization is embodied in its Bogor Goals, in which APEC members pledged to free and open trade and investment in the Asia-Pacific by 2010 for industrialized economies and 2020 for developing economies.

However, several alternative avenues for the promotion of trade integration in Asia have emerged, challenging the past U.S. focus on APEC. The Association of Southeast Asian Nations (ASEAN) is promoting the creation of various forms of an all-Asian free trade association that would exclude the United States. In addition, during its last few months, the Bush Administration indicated its intention to enter into negotiations with the Trans-Pacific Strategic Economic Partnership Agreement (TPP), an existing free trade agreement between Brunei Darussalam, Chile, New Zealand, and Singapore.

In November 2008, APEC held its annual Leaders' Meeting in Lima, Peru. Although the official theme for the meeting was "A New Commitment to Asia-Pacific Development," global economic events overshadowed the event, focusing discussion on resisting protectionist pressures and expediting economic recovery. In their joint meeting statement, the APEC leaders stated that they thought their economies would recover within 18 months. They also expressed their support for the G20 commitment to refrain from erecting new trade barriers for at least 12 months.

The next three years may be a critical period for APEC and its achievement of the Bogor Goals. The 2009 meetings are to be held in Singapore, traditionally a strong supporter of APEC and trade and investment liberalization. Japan is scheduled to be the host of the 2010 meetings—the target year for APEC's industrialized members to achieve the Bogor Goals. The United States will host the 2011 meetings.

Historical trade data is consistent with the premise that APEC has been successful in promoting greater trade within its member economies and with the rest of the world. Both the exports and imports of APEC members have grown faster than global trade since the creation of APEC. However, APEC's greater trade growth may be attributable to other factors than the liberalization of trade and investment policies among its members.

The 111th Congress has an opportunity to reexamine U.S. policy towards APEC. It has already increased APEC-related funding in FY2009, in part to provide for the preparations for the 2011 APEC meetings to be held in the United States. In addition, there are other actions Congress may chose to take with respect to APEC, depending on its determination of APEC's role for trade promotion initiatives in Asia. Congressional attitudes and actions may also be influenced by the Obama Adminstration's trade policies in Asia—and the role APEC plays in those policies.

Chapter 2 - On June 30, 2007, U.S. and South Korean trade officials signed the proposed U.S.-South Korean Free Trade Agreement (KORUS FTA) for their respective countries. If approved, the KORUS FTA would be the largest FTA that South Korea has signed to date and would be the second largest (next to North American Free Trade Agreement, NAFTA) in which the United States participates. South Korea is the seventh-largest trading partner of the United States and the United States is South Korea's third largest trading partner. Various studies conclude that the agreement would increase bilateral trade and investment flows. The final text of the proposed KORUS FTA covers a wide range of trade and investment issues and, therefore, could have substantial economic implications for both the United States and South Korea.

The agreement will not enter into force unless Congress approves implementation legislation. The negotiations were conducted under the trade promotion authority (TPA), also called fast-track trade authority, that the Congress granted the President under the Bipartisan Trade Promotion Act of 2002 (P.L. 107-2 10). The authority allows the President to enter into trade agreements that receive expedited congressional consideration (no amendments and limited debate). The Bush Administration did not send draft implementing legislation to Congress.

The Obama Administration has not indicated if and when it will send the draft implementing bill to Congress The Administration has stated that it is developing "benchmarks for progress" on resolving "concerns" it has with the KORUS FTA, particularly over market access for U.S. car exports. While U.S. Trade Representative Ron Kirk has called attention to the economic opportunities the KORUS FTA presents, he also has said that if the Administration's concerns are not resolved, "we'll be prepared to step away....".

In South Korea, however, the politics of the KORUS FTA likely will make it difficult for the government of President Lee Myung-bak to appear to accede to new U.S. demands. This is particularly due to memories of events in 2008, when Lee reached an agreement with the United States to fully lift South Korea's ban on U.S. beef imports, triggering massive anti-government protests that forced the two governments to renegotiate the beef agreement. Lee lifted the ban to make it easier for the George W. Bush Administration to submit the KORUS FTA to Congress. The South Korean National Assembly has yet to vote on the KORUS FTA, and is debating whether or not to do so before the U.S. Congress acts. It is expected that the Assembly would pass the agreement, at least in its current version.

While a broad swath of the U.S. business community supports the agreement, the KORUS FTA faces opposition from some groups, including some auto and steel manufacturers and labor unions. Agricultural groups and some Members of Congress are monitoring the flow of U.S. beef to South Korea to judge whether and to what extent to support the agreement. Some U.S. supporters view passage of the KORUS FTA as important to secure new opportunities in the South Korean market, while opponents claim that the KORUS FTA does not go far enough. Other observers have suggested the outcome of the KORUS FTA could have implications for the U.S.- South Korean alliance as a whole, as well as on U.S. trade policy and Asia policy. This report will be updated as events warrant.

Chapter 3 - Since August 2003, negotiations over North Korea's nuclear weapons programs have involved six governments: the United States, North Korea, China, South Korea, Japan, and Russia. Since the talks began, North Korea has operated nuclear facilities at Yongbyon and apparently has produced weapons-grade plutonium. Various estimates place North Korea's plutonium production at between 30 and 50 kilograms, enough for five to eight atomic weapons.

After North Korea tested a nuclear device in October 2006, the six party talks served as a framework for bilateral negotiations between the Bush Administration and North Korea, with significant Chinese influence on these bilateral talks. The Bush Administration negotiated four agreements with North Korea between February 2007 and October 2008; two were issued as six party accords. The agreements produced the initiation of a disablement of North Korean nuclear installations at Yongbyon, including a nuclear reactor and plutonium reprocessing plant; Bush Administration lifting of Trading With the Enemy Act sanctions against North Korea and removal of North Korea from the U.S. list of state sponsors of terrorism; a North Korean declaration of nuclear programs limited to known nuclear installations at Yongbyon and reportedly a plutonium stockpile of 31 kilograms; and a commitment by the five non-North Korean governments in the six party talks to provide North Korea with one million tons of heavy fuel oil or equivalent forms of energy assistance. The fourth of these agreements, negotiated in October 2008, established a system of verification and inspections but limited to the declared facilities at Yongbyon and not including the taking of samples by inspectors. The Bush Administration and North Korea disputed the contents of this agreement, especially over sampling.

As of early 2009, full implementation of the agreements requires a completion of deliveries of one million tons of heavy fuel oil to North Korea and North Korean completion of the disablement of the Yongbyon facilities. Oil deliveries are about 200,000 tons short, and the Yongbyon facilities are about 80% disabled. The Bush Administration took the position that full implementation also would require North Korean Korean acceptance of inspection sampling at Yongbyon.

Completing the implementation of the agreement is one challenge facing the Obama Administration. A second challenge will be to develop a negotiating strategy for the next phase of nuclear negotiations, including decisions on how to respond to tough negotiating positions, which North Korea set forth at the start of 2009, which include a call for normalization of U.S.-North Korean relations prior to a final agreement to denuclearize the Korean peninsula and a demand that a final agreement include elimination of the "U.S. nuclear threat" to North Korea.

These agreements did not cover important components of North Korea's nuclear programs: the apparent production of a few atomic bombs; a highly enriched uranium program known to the United States since the late 1990s; and alleged nuclear collaboration with Iran and Syria. According to U.S. officials, collaboration with Syria involved the construction of a nuclear reactor, which Israel bombed in September 2007. Collaboration with Iran reportedly involves development of high enriched uranium, development of a nuclear warhead that could be mounted on a jointly developed intermediate range ballistic missile (North Korean Nodong, Iranian Shahab missile), collaboration in developing long-range missiles, and North Korean assistance in constructing deep underground installations to house part of Iran's nuclear program.

Chapter 4 - Transnational organized crime groups in Burma (Myanmar) operate a multi-billion dollar criminal industry that stretches across Southeast Asia. Trafficked drugs, humans, wildlife, gems, timber, and other contraband flow through Burma, supporting the illicit demands of the region and beyond. Widespread collusion between traffickers and Burma's ruling military junta, the State Peace and Development Council (SPDC), allows organized crime groups to function with impunity. Transnational crime in Burma bears upon U.S. interests as it threatens regional security in Southeast Asia and bolsters a regime that fosters a culture of corruption and disrespect for the rule of law and human rights.

Congress has been active in U.S. policy toward Burma for a variety of reasons, including combating Burma's transnational crime situation. At times, it has imposed sanctions on Burmese imports, suspended foreign assistance and loans, and ensured that U.S. funds remain out of the regime's reach. Most recently, the 110th Congress passed P.L. 110-286, the Tom Lantos Block Burmese JADE Act of 2008 (signed by the President on July 29, 2008), which imposes further sanctions on SPDC officials and prohibits the indirect importation of Burmese gems, among other actions. On the same day, the President directed the U.S. Department of Treasury to impose financial sanctions against 10 Burmese companies, including companies involved in the gem- mining industry, pursuant to Executive Order 13464 of April 30, 2008. The 111th Congress may choose to conduct oversight of U.S. policy toward Burma, including the country's role in criminal activity.

This report analyzes the primary actors driving transnational crime in Burma, the forms of transnational crime occurring, and current U.S. policy in combating these crimes. This report will be updated as events warrant. For further analysis of U.S. policy to Burma, see CRS Report RL33479, *Burma-U.S. Relations*, by Larry A. Niksch.

Chapter 5 - Many Members of Congress charge that China's policy of accumulating foreign reserves (especially U.S. dollars) to influence the value of its currency constitutes a form of currency manipulation intended to make its exports cheaper and imports into China more expensive than they would be under free market conditions. They further contend that this policy has caused a surge in the U.S. trade deficit with China in recent years and has been a major factor in the loss of U.S. manufacturing jobs. Although China made modest reforms to its currency policy in 2005, resulting in a gradual appreciation of its currency (about 19% through June 3, 2009), many Members contend the reforms have not gone far enough and have warned of potential punitive legislative action. Although an undervalued Chinese currency has likely hurt some sectors of the U.S. economy, it has benefited others. For example, U.S. consumers have gained from the supply of low-cost Chinese goods (which helps to control inflation), as have U.S. firms using Chinese- made parts and materials (which helps such firms become more globally competitive). In addition, China has used its abundant foreign exchange reserves to buy U.S. securities, including U.S. Treasury securities, which are used to help fund the Federal budget deficit. Such purchases help keep U.S. interest rates relatively low. For China, an undervalued valued currency has boosted exports and attracted foreign investment, but has lead to unbalanced economic growth and suppressed Chinese living standards.

The current global economic crisis has further complicated the currency issue for both the United States and China. Although China is under pressure from the United States to appreciate its currency, it is reluctant to do so because that could cause further damage to export sector and lead to more layoffs. China has halted its gradual appreciation of its currency, the renminbi (RMB) or yuan to the dollar in 2009, keeping it relatively constant at about 6.83 yuan per dollar. The federal budget deficit has increased rapidly since FY2008, causing a sharp increase in the amount of Treasury securities that must be sold. The Obama Administration has encouraged China to continue purchasing U.S. debt. However, if China were induced to further appreciate its currency against the dollar, it could slow its accumulation of foreign exchange reserves, thus reducing the need to invest in dollar assets, such as Treasury securities. Legislation has been introduced in the 111th Congress to address China's currency policy.

China's currency policy appears to have created a policy dilemma for the Chinese government. A strong and stable U.S. economy is in China's national interest since the United States is China's largest export market. Thus, some analysts contend that China will feel compelled to keep funding the growing U.S. debt. However, Chinese officials have expressed concern that the growing U.S. debt will eventually spark inflation in the United States and a depreciation of the dollar, which would negatively impact the value of China's holdings of U.S. securities. But if China stopped buying U.S. debt or tried to sell off a large portion of those holdings, it could also cause the dollar to depreciate and thus reduce the value of its remaining holdings, and such a move could further destabilize the U.S. economy. Chinese concerns over its large dollar holdings appear to have been reflected in a paper issued by the governor of the People's Bank of China, Zhou Xiaochuan on March 24, 2009, which called for replacing the U.S. dollar as the international reserve currency with a new global system controlled by the International Monetary Fund. China has also signed currency swap agreements with six of its trading partners, which would allow those partners to settle accounts with China using the yuan rather than the dollar. This report will be updated as events warrant.

Chapter 6 - U.S.-China economic ties have expanded substantially over the past three decades. Total U.S.- China trade has risen from $5 billion in 1980 to $409 billion in 2008. In 2008, China was the second largest U.S. trading partner, its third largest export market, and its biggest source of imports. About 12% of total U.S. global trade is now with China. According to U.S. data, U.S. firms have invested around $28 billion in China (through 2007), some of which is aimed at the Chinese domestic market, while other investment has gone into export-oriented manufacturing facilities.

With a huge population and a rapidly expanding economy, China is a potentially huge market for U.S. exporters. However, bilateral economic relations have become strained over a number of issues, including large and growing U.S. trade deficits with China ($266 billion in 2008), China's failure to fully implement its World Trade Organization (WTO) commitments (especially in regards to protection of intellectual property rights), its refusal to adopt a floating currency system, its use of industrial policies (such as subsidies) and other practices deemed unfair and/or harmful to various U.S. economic sectors, and its failure in some cases to ensure that its exported products meet U.S. health and safety standards.

Further complicating the bilateral economic relationship is China's large holdings of U.S. debt, such as Treasury securities. In September 2008, China overtook Japan to become the largest foreign holder of such securities. Some analysts welcome China's purchases of U.S.

debt securities, which help fund U.S. budget deficits, while others have expressed concerns that growing Chinese holdings of U.S. debt may increase its leverage over the United States.

The current global economic crisis could further challenge China-U.S. economic ties. Many analysts have expressed concern that the Chinese government may, in an effort to help its sagging export industries, implement new trade barriers, boost industrial subsidies, and/or depreciate its currency, which could harm some U.S. firms and workers. Many U.S. policymakers have urged China to lessen its reliance on exports for its economic growth and instead implement policies to promote domestic consumption. Central to this position is the belief that China should appreciate its currency and eventually adopt a floating exchange rate system, which would boost its imports.

Several Members of Congress have urged the Obama Administration to take a more assertive approach in dealing with Chinese economic practices, including increasing the use of U.S. antidumping, countervailing, and safeguard provisions; bringing more dispute resolution cases against China to the WTO; and continuing pressure on China to appreciate its currency. Others have warned against using "protectionist" measures to block imports of Chinese goods and have advocated using high-level bilateral talks (such as the Strategic Economic Dialogue that began during the Bush Administration in 2006) to resolve major trade disputes.

Economic and trade reforms (begun in 1979) have helped transform China into one of the world's fastest growing economies. China's economic growth and trade liberalization, including comprehensive trade commitments made upon entering the World Trade Organization (WTO) in 2001, have led to a sharp expansion in U.S.-China commercial. Yet, bilateral trade relations have grown increasingly strained in recent years over a number of issues, including a large and growing U.S. trade deficit with China, the refusal by China to adopt a floating currency, its failure to fully implement many of its WTO obligations, especially in regards to protection of intellectual property rights (IPR), and problems relating to the health and safety of Chinese-made products. Several Members of Congress have called on the Obama Administration to take a tougher stance against China to induce it to eliminate economic policies deemed harmful to U.S. economic interests and/or are inconsistent with WTO rules.

This report provides an overview of U.S.-China economic relations, surveys major trade disputes, and lists bills introduced in the 111th Congress that would impact bilateral commercial ties.

Chapter 7 - Since 1995, the United States has provided North Korea with over $1.2 billion in assistance, about 60% of which has paid for food aid and about 40% for energy assistance. U.S. aid fell significantly in the mid-2000s, bottoming out at zero in 2006.

The Bush Administration resumed energy aid in the fall of 2007, after progress was made in the Six-Party Talks over North Korea's nuclear program. The Six-Party Talks involve North Korea, the United States, China, South Korea, Japan, and Russia. The United States and other countries began providing heavy fuel oil (HFO) in return for Pyongyang freezing and disabling its plutonium-based nuclear facilities in Yongbyon. By the second week of December 2008, the United States had provided all of the 200,000 MT of HFO it had promised under this "Phase Two" of the Six-Party Talks process. The talks themselves have been at a standstill since a December 2008 meeting failed to achieve agreement on verification procedures. Russia completed its promised shipments of energy aid in January 2009. China and South Korea appear to be calibrating their Six-

Party-related assistance to progress in disabling Yongbyon, which was slowed by North Korea in early 2009. Plans for a "satellite launch" by North Korea, reportedly to take place in early April, further complicated progress in the Six Party Talks.

The United States also provides technical assistance to North Korea to help in the nuclear disablement process, a role that could be expanded should North Korea move to dismantle its nuclear facilities. In 2008, Congress took legislative steps to legally enable the President to give expanded assistance for this purpose.

For over a decade, North Korea has suffered from chronic, massive food deficits. Food aid – largely from China, the United States, and South Korea – has been essential in filling the gap. In 2008, United Nations officials issued calls for international donations of food to avert a "serious tragedy" in North Korea. In May 2008, the Bush Administration announced it would resume food assistance to North Korea by providing 500,000 metric tons (MT) of food, 80% of which was to be channeled through the United Nations World Food Programme (WFP). The rest was to be sent through a consortium of U.S. non-governmental organizations (NGOs). The United States has shipped nearly 170,000 MT of food under the program. In December 2008, U.S. shipments to the WFP were suspended due to differences between the U.S. and North Korean governments over implementing the agreement. Food shipments via the NGOs continued. In March 2009, however, North Korea shut down the NGO portion of the U.S. program.

Food aid to the DPRK has been scrutinized because Pyongyang has resisted making the economic reforms that many feel would help the country distribute food more equitably and pay for food imports to make up for its domestic shortfall. Additionally, the North Korean government restricts the ability of donors to operate in the country. In the past, various sources have asserted that some of the food assistance going to North Korea is routinely diverted for resale in private markets or other uses. Compounding the problem, China, North Korea's largest source of food aid, has little to no monitoring systems in place. The Bush Administration's May 2008 food aid pledge came after Pyongyang agreed to loosen its restrictions on access and monitoring.

Finally, in 2008, the Bush Administration began a new, $4 million program to provide assistance to several rural and provincial hospitals in North Korea.

Chapter 8 - Policy toward and support for Taiwan are a key element in U.S.- relations with the People's Republic of China (PRC) and an important component of U.S. policy in Asia. Official U.S. relations with the Republic of China (ROC) government on Taiwan became a casualty of the U.S. decision to recognize the PRC government as China's sole legitimate government. Since then, unofficial U.S. relations with Taiwan have been built on the framework of the 1979 Taiwan Relations Act (TRA – P.L. 96-8) and shaped by three U.S.-PRC communiques. Under these, the United States maintains official relations with the PRC, but continues to have unique and critical interests in Taiwan, including significant commercial ties, objections to PRC threats to use force against Taiwan, arms sales and security assurances, and support for Taiwan's democratic development. U.S. policy today remains rooted in a general notion of maintaining the "status quo" between Taiwan and the PRC. But other factors have changed dramatically since 1979, including growing PRC power and importance, Taiwan's democratization, and the deepening of Taiwan-PRC economic and social linkages. These changes have led to periodic discussions about the efficacy of current U.S. policy and whether or not it should be reviewed or changed.

Taiwan's current president, Ma Ying-jeou, elected in March 2008, moved quickly to jump start Taiwan-PRC talks that had been stalled since 1998. The talks to date have yielded a number of agreements, including agreements to establish regular direct weekend charter flights, direct sea and air transportation, postal links, and food safety mechanisms. Taiwan also has lifted long-standing caps on Taiwan investment in the PRC and lowered the profile of its bids for participation in U.N. agencies. These and other initiatives are welcomed by many as having contributed to greater regional stability. More pessimistic observers see growing PRC-Taiwan ties eroding U.S. influence, strengthening PRC leverage and, particularly in the face of expanding economic links, jeopardizing Taiwan autonomy and economic security.

The changing dynamic between Taiwan and the PRC poses increasingly difficult, competing policy challenges for the United States. Along with new policy challenges – such as what U.S. policy should be if Taiwan should continue to move closer to or even align with the PRC – the Obama Administration will be faced with other challenges familiar from past years, including decisions on new arms sales to Taiwan, which are anathema to the PRC; how to accommodate requests for visits to the United States by President Ma and other senior Taiwan officials; the overall nature of U.S. relations with the Ma government; whether to pursue closer economic ties with Taiwan; what role, if any, Washington should play in cross-strait relations; and more broadly, what form of defense assurances to offer Taiwan. In addition, the Taiwan government also is seeking to raise its international profile in other ways involving the United States. Taiwan is seeking to be removed from the U.S. Special 301 "Watch List" for intellectual property rights violations, and is seeking to qualify for the U.S. Visa Waiver Program (VWP), which eliminates some visa requirements for qualified countries. The Taiwan government also continues to ask for a U.S.-Taiwan Free Trade Agreement (FTA), which would broaden the current avenue for U.S.- Taiwan trade discussions, the 1994 Trade and Investment Framework (TIFA).

Legislation in the 111th Congress concerning Taiwan includes H.Con.Res. 18, urging that the United States resume diplomatic relations with Taiwan; and H.Con.Res. 55, expressing U.S. support for and commitment to Taiwan.

Chapter 9 - This CRS Report, updated as warranted, discusses policy issues regarding military-to-military (mil-to-mil) contacts with the People's Republic of China (PRC) and provides a record of major contacts and crises since 1993. The United States suspended military contacts with China and imposed sanctions on arms sales in response to the Tiananmen Crackdown in 1989. In 1993, the Clinton Administration re-engaged with the top PRC leadership, including China's military, the People's Liberation Army (PLA). Renewed military exchanges with the PLA have not regained the closeness reached in the 1980s, when U.S.-PRC strategic cooperation against the Soviet Union included U.S. arms sales to China. Improvements and deteriorations in overall bilateral relations have affected military contacts, which were close in 1997-1998 and 2000, but marred by the 1995-1996 Taiwan Strait crisis, mistaken NATO bombing of a PRC embassy in 1999, the EP- 3 aircraft collision crisis in 2001, and aggressive naval confrontations (including in March 2009).

In early 2001, the Bush Administration continued the policy of engagement with China, but the Pentagon skeptically reviewed and cautiously resumed military-to-military contacts. Secretary of Defense Donald Rumsfeld, in 2002, resumed the Defense Consultative Talks (DCT) with the PLA (first held in 1997) and, in 2003, hosted General Cao Gangchuan, a Vice Chairman of the Central Military Commission (CMC) and Defense Minister. General Richard

Myers (USAF), Chairman of the Joint Chiefs of Staff, visited China in January 2004, as the highest ranking U.S. military officer to do so since November 2000. Visiting Beijing in September 2005 as the Commander of the Pacific Command (PACOM), Admiral William Fallon sought to advance mil-to-mil contacts, including combined exercises. Secretary Rumsfeld visited China in October 2005, the first visit by a defense secretary since William Cohen's visit in 2000. Fallon invited PLA observers to the U.S. "Valiant Shield" exercise that brought three aircraft carriers to waters off Guam in June 2006. In July 2006, a CMC Vice Chairman, General Guo Boxiong, made the first visit to the United States by the highest ranking PLA commander after 1998.

Issues for the 111th Congress include whether the Obama Administration has complied with legislation overseeing dealings with the PLA and has pursued a program of contacts with the PLA that advances a prioritized list of U.S. security interests. Oversight legislation includes the Foreign Relations Authorization Act for FY1990-FY1991 (P.L. 101-246); National Defense Authorization Act for FY2000 (P.L. 106-65); and National Defense Authorization Act for FY2006 (P.L. 109-163). Skeptics and proponents of military exchanges with the PRC have debated whether the contacts have significant value for achieving U.S. objectives and whether the contacts have contributed to the PLA's warfighting capabilities that might harm U.S. security interests. Some have argued about whether the value that U.S. officials have placed on the contacts overly extends leverage to the PLA. U.S. interests in military contacts with China include communication, conflict prevention, and crisis management; transparency and reciprocity; tension reduction over Taiwan; weapons nonproliferation; strategic nuclear and space talks; counterterrorism; and accounting for POW/MIAs.

Despite U.S. pursuit of mil-to-mil dialogues, U.S. defense officials have reported inadequate cooperation from the PLA, including denials of port visits at Hong Kong by U.S. Navy ships around Thanksgiving 2007. Also, the PLA has tried to use its suspensions of exchanges (the latest in October 2008) to demand cessations of U.S. arms sales to Taiwan, U.S. legal restrictions on contacts with the PLA, the Pentagon's report to Congress on PRC Military Power, etc. The PRC's aggressive harassment of U.S. surveillance ships (including the Impeccable in March 2009) have shown the limits to the value of mil-to-mil talks and PLA restraint now and the future.

In: Political and Economic Developments in Asia
Editor: Felix Chin

ISBN: 978-1-61209-783-1
©2011 Nova Science Publishers, Inc.

Chapter 1

ASIA PACIFIC ECONOMIC COOPERATION (APEC) AND THE 2008 MEETINGS IN LIMA, PERU[*]

Michael F. Martin

ABSTRACT

Congress and the Executive Branch have historically identified the Asia Pacific Economic Cooperation (APEC) as an important organization to help promote the U.S. goal of liberalizing international trade and investment in Asia, and possibly the rest of the world. APEC's commitment to the goal of trade and investment liberalization is embodied in its Bogor Goals, in which APEC members pledged to free and open trade and investment in the Asia-Pacific by 2010 for industrialized economies and 2020 for developing economies.

However, several alternative avenues for the promotion of trade integration in Asia have emerged, challenging the past U.S. focus on APEC. The Association of Southeast Asian Nations (ASEAN) is promoting the creation of various forms of an all-Asian free trade association that would exclude the United States. In addition, during its last few months, the Bush Administration indicated its intention to enter into negotiations with the Trans-Pacific Strategic Economic Partnership Agreement (TPP), an existing free trade agreement between Brunei Darussalam, Chile, New Zealand, and Singapore.

In November 2008, APEC held its annual Leaders' Meeting in Lima, Peru. Although the official theme for the meeting was "A New Commitment to Asia-Pacific Development," global economic events overshadowed the event, focusing discussion on resisting protectionist pressures and expediting economic recovery. In their joint meeting statement, the APEC leaders stated that they thought their economies would recover within 18 months. They also expressed their support for the G20 commitment to refrain from erecting new trade barriers for at least 12 months.

The next three years may be a critical period for APEC and its achievement of the Bogor Goals. The 2009 meetings are to be held in Singapore, traditionally a strong supporter of APEC and trade and investment liberalization. Japan is scheduled to be the host of the 2010 meetings—the target year for APEC's industrialized members to achieve the Bogor Goals. The United States will host the 2011 meetings.

---

[*] This is an edited, reformatted and augmented version of CRs Report R40495, dated March 31, 2009.

Historical trade data is consistent with the premise that APEC has been successful in promoting greater trade within its member economies and with the rest of the world. Both the exports and imports of APEC members have grown faster than global trade since the creation of APEC. However, APEC's greater trade growth may be attributable to other factors than the liberalization of trade and investment policies among its members.

The 111th Congress has an opportunity to reexamine U.S. policy towards APEC. It has already increased APEC-related funding in FY2009, in part to provide for the preparations for the 2011 APEC meetings to be held in the United States. In addition, there are other actions Congress may chose to take with respect to APEC, depending on its determination of APEC's role for trade promotion initiatives in Asia. Congressional attitudes and actions may also be influenced by the Obama Adminstration's trade policies in Asia—and the role APEC plays in those policies.

This report will be updated as circumstances warrant.

INTRODUCTION

Congress and the Executive Branch have historically identified the Asia Pacific Economic Cooperation (APEC) as an important organization to help promote the U.S. goal of liberalizing international trade and investment in Asia, and possibly the rest of the world. In addition, because of the unique nature of APEC's membership [1] and organization, the association provides a forum at which the United States can hold bilateral discussions on non-economic matters, such as international security and human rights.

One indicator of previous congressional interest in APEC is the National Defense Authorization Act for Fiscal Year 2006 (P.L. 109-163). That legislation called for the President to develop a comprehensive strategy to address the "emergence of China economically, diplomatically, and militarily; promote mutually beneficial trade relations with China; and encourage China's adherence to international norms in the areas of trade, international security, and human rights" [2]. It continues by specifying that this comprehensive strategy should "identify and pursue initiatives to revitalize United States engagement in East Asia." The act then states, *"The initiatives should have a regional focus and complement bilateral efforts. The Asia Pacific Economic Cooperation forum (APEC) offers a ready mechanism for pursuit of such initiatives"* [3] [emphasis added].

The notion that APEC may be an effective forum for advancing U.S. interests in Asia was shared by the Bush Administration. During a White House pre-trip press briefing on August 30, 2007, National Security Council Senior Director Dennis Wilder stated, "The importance that the President attaches to APEC is demonstrated by the fact that he has not missed an APEC leaders meeting since taking office [4]. U.S. Ambassador to APEC Patricia Haslach has indicated that Obama Administration views relations with APEC as important for U.S. foreign policy in Asia.

It is unclear, however, what role APEC will play in future U.S. trade policy in Asia. The Bush Administration saw APEC as a vehicle for regional economic integration in the Asia Pacific under the concept of a Free Trade Area of the Asia-Pacific (FTAAP). This was widely seen as a counterforce to the efforts of some members of the Association of Southeast Asian Nations (ASEAN) [5] to pursue an alternative "Asian only" models for regional economic development that would exclude the United States. On September 22, 2008, then-U.S. Trade Representative Susan Schwab formally announced the United States would launch negotiations with Brunei Darussalam, Chile, New Zealand, and Singapore about joining the

Trans-Pacific Strategic Economic Partnership Agreement (TPP). At the time, it was uncertain if U.S. interest in the TPP represented a shift of focus from APEC to the TPP as the preferred forum for advancing trade integration in Asia, or if the TPP initiative was to complement the FTAAP initiative in APEC.

The uncertainty about the future role of APEC in U.S. trade policy comes just a year before the target deadline for the first of APEC's Bogor Goals—open trade and investment among the industrialized APEC members by 2010—and two years before the United States is scheduled to host the association's annual meetings in 2011. According to some analysts, the next three years could a critical time for APEC's development.

The 111th Congress could take action on APEC in several ways. First, Congress may choose to consider the level of direct and indirect financial support provided to APEC. Second, Congress may take into account U.S. commitments to APEC when considering legislation on various trade and non-trade issues. Third, Congress may increase oversight of APEC-related activities and programs of the U.S. Trade Representative, the Department of State and other federal departments and agencies.

Although the U.S. government in the past has considered APEC as important, it is uncertain that APEC has proven a reliable mechanism for advancing U.S. interest in Asia and if Congress and the White House shared a common view of what the U.S. interests in Asia are. In particular, the organizational and operational structure of APEC is unusual among multilateral associations, reflecting an atypical approach to trade liberalization. As a result, APEC's approach, organization, and operations may make it difficult for the United States to promote its positions on various issues through its activities in APEC.

APEC'S APPROACH TO TRADE LIBERALIZATION

APEC began in 1989 as an Australian initiative—backed by Japan and New Zealand—in recognition of the growing interdependence among Asia-Pacific economies and in response to the free-trade areas that had developed in Europe and North America. From that initiative, APEC has grown into an association of 21 "member economies" bordering the Pacific Ocean that are working cooperatively to promote economic growth and prosperity in the Asia-Pacific region. It is the only international trade organization, besides the World Trade Organization, in which China, Hong Kong, and Taiwan are members.

During the 1994 meetings in Bogor, Indonesia, APEC established the "Bogor Goals" of "free and open trade and investment in the Asia-Pacific by 2010 for industrialized economies and 2020 for developing economies" [6] These goals have been reaffirmed at the Leaders' Meeting each subsequent year.

In contrast to most other multilateral organizations, APEC is a cooperative forum in which members arrive at decisions via consensus. All commitments made by members are voluntary; APEC has no formal enforcement mechanisms to compel members to comply with any trade liberalization policies previously declared at APEC meetings—an approach often referred to as "open regionalism" [7]. Point 9 of the 1994 "APEC Economic Leaders' Declaration of Common Resolve" states, "APEC economies that are ready to initiate and implement a cooperative arrangement may proceed to do so while those that are not yet ready to participate may join at a later date." [8]

The underlying notion of the APEC approach to trade liberalization is that voluntary commitments are easier to achieve and more likely to be implemented than obligatory commitments derived from agreements negotiated by more traditional—and potentially, confrontational—methods. By establishing a common vision or goal for the organization, the belief is that future APEC discussions can make more rapid progress towards the organization's goals by seeking consensus views with which members are willing to comply.

By contrast, trade agreements negotiated according to more traditional approaches tend to foster confrontation and expectations of reciprocal concessions. Lacking a shared goal or objectives, it may be difficult to resolve differences among the parties and complete a trade agreement. Later on, if any party to the agreement feels that it was inequitable, they may fail to comply with the terms of the agreement, or withdraw from the agreement in its entirety, even if there are formal sanction or grievance provisions within the agreement.

APEC strives to meet the Bogor Goals in three "broad areas" of cooperation. First, members consult with each other to formulate individual and collective actions to liberalize merchandise and service trade, as well as international investment. Second, members discuss their domestic regulations and procedures to find ways of facilitating international business. Third, the members engage in "Economic and Technical Cooperation," or ECOTECH, to provide training and foster greater cooperation among APEC members.

In 1995, APEC created a template to achieve the Bogor Goals in its "Osaka Action Agenda" [9]. The Osaka Action Agenda emphasizes APEC's "resolute opposition to an inward-looking trading bloc that would divert from the pursuit of global free trade" by accepting a set of fundamental principles for APEC's trade and investment liberalization and facilitation. These principles include comprehensiveness; WTO consistency; comparability; non-discrimination; transparency; flexibility; and cooperation.

APEC ORGANIZATION AND OPERATION

APEC's unusual approach to trade liberalization is reflected in its organization and operation. APEC's organization consists of a small Secretariat in Singapore, which reports to the constituents of five separate groups: the preeminent Leaders' Meeting, the APEC Business Advisory Council, the Ministerial Meeting, the Sectoral Minister Meetings, and the Senior Officials Meetings. The Secretariat, in turn, supervises the work of six different groups: the Committee on Trade and Investment, the Economic Committee, the Steering Committee on ECOTECH, the Budget and Management Committee, Special Task Groups, and Working Groups.

Each member of APEC seconds representatives to work on the Secretariat's staff to serve as program directors [10].

The focal point of APEC activities is the annual Leaders' Meeting in which the APEC leaders set goals, publicize them, and provide momentum for the process [11]. This is usually held in October or November of each year, and is customarily attended by heads of state except for Taiwan which, because of China's objections, sends a special representative [12]. The first Leaders' Meeting was held in 1993 on Blake Island, near Seattle, Washington.

Major decisions are generally affirmed and/or announced at the Leaders' Meeting [13]. Although APEC confines its agenda primarily to economic issues, the leaders often hold bilateral meetings during the Leaders' Meeting to discuss international security, human rights, and other issues.

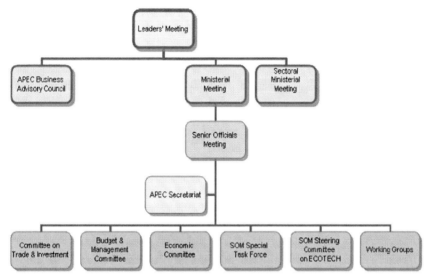

Source: APEC website, http://www.apec.org/apec/about_apec/structure.html.

Figure 1. APEC Organization.

Most of the decisions announced at the Leaders' Meeting are first considered in a series of Ministerial Meetings held throughout the year. These include the respective ministers dealing with trade, finance, transportation, telecommunications, human resources development (education), energy, environment, science and technology, and small and medium-sized enterprises. The largest ministerial is the annual Joint Ministerial Meeting which immediately precedes the Leaders' Meeting. It usually is attended by foreign trade or commerce ministers from member states. The various Ministerial Meetings make recommendations to the Leaders' Meeting; they do not have the authority to act independently on behalf of APEC.

Working under the direction of the various APEC ministers, the Senior Officials coordinate the activities of the various committees, working groups and task forces within APEC. Senior Officials Meetings are held three or four times a year. The current U.S. Senior Official for APEC is U.S. Ambassador to APEC Patricia M. Haslach.

The APEC Business Advisory Council (ABAC) consists of up to three individuals appointed by each APEC member. It provides advice on implementing the APEC agenda and other specific business-related issues [14]. ABAC also can make comments on the recommendations of the various Ministerial Meetings.

Most of the specific tasks before APEC are addressed in committees, working groups, or expert groups that deal with economic issues of importance to the region. For implementing the Bogor goals, the Committee on Trade and Investment plays the key role. APEC has ten working groups that work on specific areas of cooperation and facilitation: (1) Trade and Investment Data, (2) Trade Promotion, (3) Industrial Science and Technology, (4) Human Resources Development, (5) Energy Cooperation, (6) Marine Resource Conservation, (7)

Telecommunications, (8) Transportation, (9) Tourism, and (10) Fisheries. Each working group has one or more shepherds (members) who take responsibility for coordinating the work of the group.

The APEC chair rotates annually and since 1989 has been held by (in order): Australia, Singapore, South Korea, Thailand, the United States, Indonesia, Japan, the Philippines, Canada, Malaysia, New Zealand, Brunei, People's Republic of China, Mexico, Thailand, Chile, South Korea, Vietnam, Australia, and Peru, which was the APEC chair in 2008. The APEC chair for 2009 is Singapore. Japan is to be the chair in 2010, and the United States is to be chair in 2011.

Decisions within APEC's various organizational bodies are based on the consensus approach of APEC. Most committees, working groups, and special task groups have representatives from all 21 members, and select their leadership from amongst themselves. Members may delay or refrain from any action recommended or approved by a meeting, committee, working group or special task force without facing sanctions or recriminations from other members. However, all decisions and agreements of the various meetings, committees, and working groups must be implemented in accordance with the Osaka Action Agenda.

APEC actions take place at three levels: actions by individual members; actions with the confines of APEC; and collective APEC actions with respect to other multinational organizations. The primary form of individual member actions are the "Individual Action Plans," or IAPs. Each year, APEC members submit at the Ministerial Meeting an IAP that spells out what steps the member has taken and/or will take to advance their trade regime towards the achievement of the Bogor Goals. IAPs typically are organized along both sectoral (e.g., architectural services) and topical (e.g., customs procedures) lines. Although members cannot impose changes on each other's IAPs, the Osaka Action Agenda calls on each member to consult, submit, and review the IAPs to foster comparability, transparency, and cooperation amongst the IAPs.

The internal actions of APEC generally involve research on topics related to trade liberalization, the exchange of best practices, and the standardization of policies and procedures related to international trade and investment. In some cases, APEC will create a working group on a particular topic, with the goals of generating a "collective action plan," or CAP. In some cases, the CAPs are little more than a topical summary of the member IAPs; in other cases, the working group plays a more active role in promoting trade liberalization and facilitation via the CAPs.

Another example of an APEC's internal action is the "APEC Business Travel Card," an idea advanced by the ABAC. Business travelers possessing an APEC Business Travel Card (ABTC)) are allowed fast-track entry and exit through special APEC lanes at major airports, and multiple, visa-free entry amongst members that recognize the card. In September 2007, the United States became a "transitional member" to the ABTC scheme, providing possessors expedited visa appointments at U.S. embassies and consulates, and expedited immigration processing through airline crew lanes upon arrival at any U.S. international airport port of entry [15].

Collective actions of APEC usually involve joint or coordinated efforts to advance trade and investment liberalization in other multilateral organizations. APEC's collective actions have recently focused on helping complete the Doha Round of the WTO. For example, following the 2006 Leaders' Meeting in Hanoi, APEC released a statement on the "Doha

Development Agenda of the WTO" that affirmed the members' "collective and individual commitments to concluding an ambitious and balanced WTO Doha agreement" by each member "moving beyond our current positions in key areas of the Round." The key areas mentioned were "trade-distorting farm support," "market access in agriculture," "real cuts in industrial tariffs," and "new openings in services trade."

RESULTS OF THE 2008 MEETINGS IN LIMA

There was concern about the prospects for the 2008 APEC meetings well before the senior officials arrived in Lima. The decision to hold the meetings in Peru was allegedly met with some disinterest by some Asian members. Some observers speculated that some members may send alternative representatives rather than their top officials to the Leaders' Meeting held on November 22 and 23, 2008.

These concerns were exacerbated by the growing global financial crisis. As the ripple effects of the U.S. financial crisis began to be felt in international trade flows and real economic growth, there was a growing possibility that senior officials of the APEC members might decide that they could not afford politically or economically to attend the APEC meetings. The convening of a G20 [16]. Summit in Washington, DC, on November 15, 2008—just a week before the 2008 APEC Economic Leaders' Meeting—added fuel to the speculation that the Lima meetings would be anticlimactic.

By tradition, the host member selects a theme for the annual APEC meeting. In 2008, Peru chose the theme, "A New Commitment to Asia-Pacific Development." As described in the post-meeting economic leaders' statement, the 2008 theme "highlights the importance of reducing the gap between developed and developing member economies" [17].

Outcomes of the Major Meetings

In the end, while the concerns about attendance at the Lima meetings proved unfounded, the global financial crisis overshadowed the planned theme for the meetings. At both the 16th APEC Economic Leaders' Meeting and the preceding 20th APEC Ministerial Meeting, there was no discernible decline in the profile of the attending representatives. Then-President George W. Bush and then-Secretary of State Condoleezza Rice attended the meetings as representatives of the United States. However, as reflected in the joint statements issued after each meeting, the global financial crisis dominated the content of the meetings.

20th APEC Ministerial Meeting
The 20th APEC Ministerial Meeting was held on November 19 & 20, 2008 in Lima, Peru. Heading the U.S. delegation was then-Secretary Rice. The Ministerial Meeting, which by tradition is held a few days before the Leaders' Meeting, generally provides a preview of the main agenda items for the Leaders' Meeting. It also usually issues a joint statement following the two days of meetings.

The importance of the global financial crisis for the APEC meetings was made apparent by the ministers' joint statement [18]. After its general introductory section, the joint statement proceeds by stating:

We met during the most difficult set of economic conditions we have seen since APEC was created in 1989. All APEC economies are being affected by the global financial crisis and we are likely to experience a significant fall in the high rates of regional growth seen over the past decade.

The joint statement continues with a separate section on the global financial crisis, indicating that a "rapid, coordinated and effective response" to the global financial crisis is APEC's "highest priority" and will be the "focus of attention" for the Leaders' Meeting. The ministers also agreed to "stand firm against any protectionist sentiment arising out of the crisis." They recommended that the Leaders' Meeting support the pledge made at the recent G20 meeting to refrain from erecting new trade barriers. Later on in the joint statement, the ministers called for more efforts to strengthen financial markets in Asia.

Another major subject of discussion at the Ministerial Meeting was the future of regional economic integration. After reaffirming their commitment to the Bogor Goals, the ministers indicated that they "made significant progress this year in examining the options and prospects for an FTAAP through a range of practical and incremental steps." The joint statement also pointed out the progress made in the development of model measures for regional trade agreements (RTAs) or free trade agreements (FTAs). The model measures are intended to promote the creation of "high-quality, consistent, and comprehensive" RTAs and FTAs.

The ministers welcomed APEC's progress in trade facilitation. Besides promoting the greater acceptance of e-trade within APEC, the ministers' joint statement noted the value of aligning domestic standards with relevant international standards to simplify the flow of trade. In addition, the full implementation of the APEC Business Trade Card (ABTC) program by Mexico and the progress by Canada and the United States in adopting the system were commended.

Other important economic and trade issues addressed in the Ministers' joint statement include the protection of intellectual property rights, corporate social responsibility, food safety, and food security.

Leaders' Meeting

The Leaders' Meeting was held in Lima on November 22 & 23, 2008. Chairing the meeting was Peru's President Alan Garcia. Leading the U.S. delegation was President Bush. In contrast to the 2007 APEC meetings in Sydney, Australia, President Bush attended both days of the Leaders' Meeting [19]. Prior to the President's arrival in Lima, the White House held a press briefing on the U.S. priorities for the APEC meetings. Daniel Price, assistant to the President for international economic affairs, stated that the United States had five priorities for the APEC meetings:

1. Advancing the work of the G20 meeting in Washington on the global financial crisis;
2. Deepening regional economic integration;
3. Enhancing competitiveness of the APEC region;
4. Addressing "a range of human security needs;" and
5. Discussing the issues of energy security and climate change.

Of the five priorities, Price indicated that advancing the work of the G20 meeting was the President's top priority. Price also stated that the United States would use the Leaders' Meeting as an opportunity to explain the decision to open negotiations about joining the TPP.

As the White House desired, the global financial crisis was the highest priority of the Leaders' Meeting. The topic was reportedly the first issue addressed during the meeting. Following their first day of discussions, the APEC leaders released a statement concerning the global financial crisis [20]. Their statement made six main points. First, the APEC leaders "are convinced that we can overcome this crisis in a period of 18 months." Second, the crisis "highlights the importance of ongoing financial sector reform in our economies." Third, the APEC leader "welcome" the G20's declaration and they "strongly support" the G20's "action plan." Fourth, they recognized the "critical role" of the International Monetary Fund, the World Bank, the Asian Development Bank, the Inter-American Development Bank, and other multilateral development banks in the global economic recovery. Fifth, the APEC leaders "strongly support" the G20 pledge to refrain from raising new trade barriers during the next 12 months. Sixth, they recommitted to the Bogor Goals as "a key and organizing principle and driving force for APEC."

The usual joint statement issued at the completion of the Leaders' Meeting continued the focus on the global financial crisis and echoed the themes raised in the Ministerial joint statement [21]. Following an introductory paragraph, the APEC Leaders write, "The current global financial crisis is one of the most serious economic challenges we have ever faced." They stated they "will act quickly and decisively to address the impending global economic slowdown," and "will take all necessary economic and financial measures to resolve this crisis."

After addressing the global economic crisis, the joint statement turned to the issue of advancing regional economic integration. The APEC leaders indicated their commitment to APEC's Regional Economic Integration (REI) Agenda, which was endorsed at the Leaders' Meeting in Sydney, Australia in September 2007, and the Bogor Goals. They also noted that while a proposed Free Trade Area of the Asia-Pacific (FTAAP) would "likely be of economic benefit to the region as a whole, there would also be challenges in its creation," possibly reflecting some ambivalence within APEC over the merits of the proposed FTAAP. The APEC leaders welcomed the completion of five new model measures for RTAs and FTAs, bringing the total to 15 completed chapters [22].

The rest of the joint statement covered on a variety of issues, including improving food security in the region; promoting corporate social responsibility (SCR); combating corruption; strengthening cooperation; combating terrorism and securing regional trade; reducing disaster risk and enhancing disaster preparedness; confronting the challenges of climate change; and strengthening APEC.

Bilateral Meetings

As usual, President Bush utilized the APEC meeting for several bilateral meetings with heads of state of other APEC members. In 2008, there were bilateral meetings with Peruvian President Garcia, China's President Hu Jintao, Japan's Prime Minster Taro Aso, Russia's President Dmitry Medvedev, and South Korea's President Lee Myung-bak. In addition, there was a brief, three-way meeting between Prime Minister Aso, President Bush, and President

Lee. Below are brief summaries of each of the bilateral meetings. In addition, in a break with past practice, there was a bilateral meeting between Hu Jintao and the head of the Taiwan delegation, former vice president and honorary chairman of the Kuomintang Lien Chan.

President Garcia

President Bush met with President Garcia on the morning of November 23. Besides expressing his gratitude to Peru for hosting the APEC meetings, President Bush stated his intention to guide the proposed U.S.-Peru FTA through Congress.

President Hu

The meeting with President Hu took place on November 21, soon after President Bush's arrival in Lima. The meeting covered a wide-ranging set of issues, including China's participation in the recent G20 meeting, the status of the six-party talks on the denuclearization of the Korean Peninsula, and the importance of Sino-U.S. economic and trade relations. President Bush also called on China to continue its dialogue with the Dalai Lama.

Prime Minister Aso

Prime Minister Aso met with President Bush on November 22. Prime Minister Aso reportedly praised President Bush for strengthening the alliance between the two nations. The two leaders apparently agreed on the desirability of a resumption of the six-party talks.

President Medvedev

Prior to the start of the APEC meetings, the date for the bilateral talks between Russia and the United States had not been set. After further discussion, the meeting was held on November 22. It was the first meeting between President Bush and President Medvedev since Medvedev assumed office in May 2008. The meeting occurred at a time when relations between the two nations were relatively tense, in part due to the military conflict in Georgia [23]. According to then-White House press secretary Dana Perino, the leaders had a "cordial but direct and frank exchange" on a variety of issues during their meeting.

President Lee

The two presidents met on November 22. The discussion covered a range of issues, including the status of the proposed bilateral free trade agreement (FTA). President Bush reportedly told President Lee that Congress had delayed consideration of the FTA because of an "anti-trade backlash."24 Following the meeting, a White House official stated that President Lee did not provide any indication if and when the Korean parliament would take up the proposed trade pact [25]. The two presidents also discussed the status of the six-party talks and the global financial crisis.

Hu-Lien Meeting

The respective leaders of the Chinese and Taiwanese delegations to the APEC Leaders' Meeting met on November 21, 2008. President Hu and Chairman Lien had met twice before in 2008, but it was the first time that the two delegation leaders had held met at an APEC event, perhaps a signaling of improved bilateral relations [26]. President Hu indicated that he saw the meeting as an opportunity to build on the four agreements signed between the Mainland's Association for Relations Across the Taiwan Straits (ARATS) and Taiwan's Straits Exchange Foundation (SEF) [27]. Chairman Lien also pointed to the four agreements as a sign of improving cross-strait relations. Both officials stated that they hoped their meeting would help foster peaceful development and cooperation in the future.

Outlook for Future APEC Meetings

The official theme for the 2008 APEC meetings in Lima was not only overshadowed by the global financial crisis, it also was superseded by thoughts about the impending milestone for the Bogor Goals in 2010. As previously mentioned, the APEC members pledged in 1994 that the "industrialized economies" would achieve free and open trade and investment in the Asia-Pacific by 2010 [28]. Japan, the host of the 2010 meetings, has indicated an interest in using the event to take stock of APEC's progress on achieving the Bogor Goals. By contrast, the United States, which will host the 2011 meetings, appears to favor a more "forward looking" orientation for APEC meetings over the next few years. This year's host, Singapore, has selected "Sustaining Growth, Connecting the Region," for the 2009 theme. According to the web page for the 2009 APEC meetings, the theme "reflects the continuing efforts of APEC to facilitate trade and investment in the Asia-Pacific region, efforts which have gained even greater importance in the face of a challenging global economic environment."

APEC's Role in Regional Integration

Possibly the premier issue facing future meetings of APEC is its relevance for the possible creation of some form of open trade and investment association in the region. At present, there are several competing models for trade and investment integration in the Asia-Pacific, including ASEAN+3, ASEAN+6 (also known as the East Asia Summit), and the TPP. Although it has been presented by both the Bush and the Obama Administration as an initiative designed to complement APEC, the TPP has the potential to supplant APEC as a vehicle for trade and investment liberalization in the region. In addition, the United States may find TPP's obligatory administrative process easier to understand than APEC's consensus-based "open regionalism."

APEC and the Global Financial Crisis

Another major issue that will most likely remain one of APEC's top priorities for the foreseeable future is the ongoing effects of the global financial crisis. According to an International Monetary Fund's economic forecast released in March 2009, global economic activity is projected to decline by 0.5-1.0% in 2009, before gradually recovering in 2010 [29]. It is quite likely that when the APEC meetings are in Singapore the week of November 8-15, 2009, the global economy will still be in a recession. To what extent APEC may provide a forum for discussing the development of a coordinated response in Asia to the region's economic problems remains to be seen.

APEC Meetings in Singapore

For the 2009 meetings, one specific issue of concern is Singapore's announced plan to toughen its restrictions on the right of assembly [30]. The proposed legislation, according to Singapore's Ministry of Home Affairs, is necessary to enhance the ability of the police to ensure security during major events. Under the terms of the bill, the police could prevent an individual from leaving her or his home if the police knew the person was going to attend a political rally. The police could also order people to leave a public area if they police believed that a law was about to be broken. In addition, the legislation would prohibit the filming of law enforcement officials if it could place the officers in danger. Finally if passed, the law would require a police permit for all "cause-related" outdoor activities regardless of how many people were participating. Opposition politicians and activists in Singapore have been highly critical of the proposed legislation.

APEC AND INTERNATIONAL TRADE

The primary goal of APEC is to foster international trade by means of trade and investment liberalization and facilitation. Since its inception in 1989 and the adoption of the Bogor Goals in 1994, APEC members have lowered their trade restrictions to varying degrees. With nearly two decades of history, one question is whether or not there has been a corresponding rise in APEC members' foreign trade accompanying their liberalization and facilitation efforts.

Assessing APEC's Impact on Exports and Imports

Figure 2 compares the growth of intra-APEC and total APEC exports to the growth of global exports from 1970 to 2005. Starting in 1981, total APEC exports begin growing faster than global exports, and intra-APEC exports are outstripping total APEC exports. However, the pace of export growth slows for all three categories in 1995, with noticeable downturns in APEC exports occurring in 1998 and 2001, corresponding to the Asia financial crisis and the attacks on the World Trade Center and the Pentagon.31 Since the downturn in 2001, the pace of world export growth has increased, and the pace of APEC export growth has increased even more.

Import statistics reveal a similar pattern to exports (see Figure 3). From 1970 to 1980, there is little difference in the import growth rate for intra-APEC, total APEC, and the world. Starting in 1981, APEC's imports—both from amongst its members and from the world—begin to increase faster than world imports. The divergence between APEC import growth and world imports continues until 1997, when the Asian financial crisis precipitates a sharp decline in APEC's imports and global imports in 1998. For the next two years—1999 and 2000—global imports and APEC's imports recover, only to drop once again following the attacks on September 11, 2001. Import levels grew modestly in 2002 for both APEC and the world, and then accelerated starting in 2003, with APEC's import growth rate outstripping that of the world.

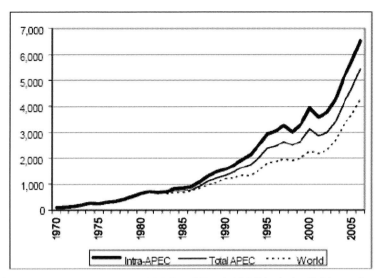

Source: Data from UNCTAD. Note: Intra-APEC and Total APEC include all 21 members regardless of date of membership.

Figure 2. APEC and World Export Growth (1970=100).

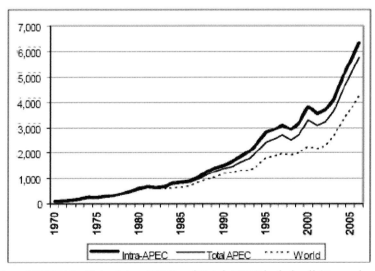

Source: Data from UNCTAD. Note: Intra-APEC and Total APEC include all 21 members regardless of date of membership.

Figure 3. APEC and World Import Growth (1970=100).

While the trade data appear to support the notion that APEC has promoted trade growth for its members, the results are not conclusive. Although APEC's exports and imports have grown at a faster rate than world trade figures since the creation of APEC, it is uncertain if its trade growth is the result of trade liberalization and facilitation, or caused by other economic factors. During the time period in question, APEC's members included several of the fastest growing economies in the world—for example, China and Vietnam—so the average economic growth rate for APEC members was higher than the global average. APEC's greater economic growth rate could be sufficient to explain most of its better trade performance compared to global figures.

The higher growth rate of trade among APEC members may also reflect changes in the global supply chain.32 The production of consumer goods is increasingly driven by major retailers and multinational corporations who source products from manufacturers and sourcing companies around the world. In turn, these companies subcontract out the production of subcomponents and parts to several other companies who may operate in several different countries. The subcomponents and parts are then shipped to possibly another country for final assembly. As a result, the initial order from the major retailer may initiate a chain of international trade flows that greatly exceed the total value of the final goods produced [33]

Such multinational supply chain networks are fairly common among the Asian members of APEC. Some may have been intentionally established among APEC members because of the association's relatively low trade barriers. For certain product categories—including clothing, textiles, consumer electronics, and toys—many of these supply chains depend on orders from U.S., European, or Japanese retailers or brand name distributors to initiate the multinational manufacturing of the consumer products. Also, a large percentage of these supply chains have their final assembly operations in China, but source the parts and components from several different Asian nations.

However, the fact that intra-APEC exports and imports are growing at a faster rate than total APEC trade raises concerns about possible trade diversion. On the one hand, the greater growth of intra-APEC trade could be the result of lower intra-APEC trade barriers stemming from the members' actions via their IAPs and CAPs, and the spread of RTAs and FTAs amongst APEC members. On the other hand, the higher intra-APEC trade expansion could represent the diversion of trade from other nations as APEC members form preferential bilateral trade agreements that siphon off trade from non-APEC members.

If APEC members have indeed benefited from more rapid trade and economic growth during the past few decades, they may also suffer more from the decline in trade and economic growth precipitated by the global financial crisis. As orders from Europe, Japan and the United States decline, so to the network of trade in intermediate goods associated with the Asian supply chains will decline even more quickly.

APEC as a Vehicle for Liberali%ing Trade

Even with its "open regionalism" approach to trade and investment liberalization, APEC has been seen since its inception as a possible vehicle for liberalizing both regional and global trade. In general, observers focus on two methods by which APEC may help foster greater trade and investment liberalization. The first method is by forming a coalition during WTO negotiations. The efforts of the APEC Geneva Caucus during the recent Doha discussions are often cited as an example of how APEC can help promote trade and investment liberalization. There is little disagreement among experts that APEC has been a positive force for trade and investment liberalization within the WTO.

The second method is more controversial. Over the last decade, the number of Asia-Pacific bilateral trade agreements (BTAs) has grown dramatically [34]. However, according to one observer, "The result is a competitive form of liberalization. As occurred within APEC itself, there are competing models of FTAs that cannot be integrated" [35]. A reporter described the phenomena as follows:

> The trade diplomacy of east Asia has become so blindingly complex that even the metaphors are getting muddled. The subtitle of one academic paper on free trade agreements (FTAs) suggests using "spaghetti bowls as building blocks." Another describes a "patchwork of bilateral hub-and-spoke FTAs in a noodle bowl."

According to some experts, the growth of bilateral trade agreements (BTAs) amongst APEC members represents an unsystematic process that could lead to the formation of an APEC-wide regional trade agreement (RTA) much like the proposed FTAAP. According to this view, the actions of APEC—via the IAPs, CAPs, model measures, and the various committee reports— form a commonality of perspective on issues, thereby permitting some members to conclude limited BTAs. The idea is that over time, the network BTAs will form the basis for the creation of a RTA.

However, other experts view the proliferation of BTAs as forming a barrier to trade and investment liberalization. As described by one scholar, "The resulting web of agreements and negotiations is fragmented, uncoordinated, and uneven in content and coverage" [36]. Because many BTAs are politically (not economically) motivated, the emerging BTAs in Asia generally suffer from several problems—WTO-incompatibility; narrow sector focus; discriminatory rules of origin (ROOs)—that make future amalgamation of the BTAs nearly impossible. As one expert describes it:

> The predictable results of foreign policy-driven FTA negotiations light on economic strategy are bitty, quick-fix sectoral deals. Politically sensitive sectors in goods and services are carved out.... Little progress is usually made in tackling domestic regulatory barriers.... Finally, the sway of power politics can result in highly asymmetrical deals, especially when one of the negotiating parties is a major player [37]

Even if the merger of the various BTAs into an Asia-Pacific RTA were accomplished, there are concerns that the resulting agreement would institutionalize a number of tariff and non-tariff trade barriers in the region. A U.S. trade official was quoted as saying, "Bilateral FTAs being pursued by China, and Japan, and Korea to some extent, risk falling to the lowest common denominator. As one commentator once quipped, 'they are neither F, nor T, nor A'" [38]

Some observers go on to argue that the rising number of BTAs in the region is generating dynamics that are preventing the formation of a FTAAP and progress in the Doha Round, despite the best efforts of APEC. One scholar writes:

> I note how the current discussions with the Asia-Pacific Economic Cooperation (APEC) forum to establish a Free Trade Area of the Asia-Pacific (FTAAP)," writes one scholar, "was also proposed at APEC's Santiago summit just two years ago. It failed then as it will probably fail now because of the immense political and technical challenge of harmonizing a large number of heterogeneous bilateral FTAs into a unified regional agreement." [39]

Another scholar is even more dismissive of APEC's potential, writing, "It cannot be expected to contribute anything serious to regional economic integration" [40].

Others see a slightly different effect of the BTAs on prospects for the creation of a FTAAP [41]. In this view, the stalled Doha Round is fostering the further disintegration of the global trading system, generating a rising number of BTAs, and increasing the risk of the creation of a discriminatory and undesirable East Asia Free Trade Area (EAFTA). The fear is that the EAFTA would become another barrier to the completion of the Doha Round, and possibly generate protectionist reactions from the European Union and the United States.

To counteract these trends, some experts say APEC should push for the creation of a more inclusive and comprehensive FTAAP. In this view, advancing the idea of a FTAAP, APEC might improve the prospects for the Doha Round, as non-APEC members may prefer to see progress at the WTO over the creation of a FTAAP. However, even if Doha talks remain stalled, discussion of the creation of a FTAAP could limit the growth of BTAs in Asia, and/or help insure that any new BTAs are less discriminatory and WTO-compatible. In summary, supporters of this view see APEC "playing four roles in this new regional dynamic" [42]. Those roles are:

1. Organizing regular meetings of regional trade and finance ministers and political leaders to advance the process at the multilateral and bilateral levels;
2. Reinforcing the 'Bogor Goal' of free and open trade and investment by 2010/2020 and authenticating neoliberal trade policies;
3. Developing "model measures" for FTAs and RTAs to achieve "high quality" liberalization and consistency; and
4. Promoting WTO-plus FTAs that are consistent with the policy agenda of the international and regional financial institutions.

APEC AND "HUMAN SECURITY"

Initially, APEC was viewed as a purely economic forum. APEC carefully kept its distance from political matters for fear that such issues would cause divisions within the group—particularly among China, Japan, Russia, Taiwan, and the United States. Such divisions could thwart cooperation in achieving economic goals. Consideration of non-economic issues was confined to bilateral meetings held before and after the Leaders' Meeting.

In 1995, the issue was raised of whether APEC should be expanded to include consideration of regional security issues. The consensus in 1995 among APEC members seemed to be that regional security issues should be discussed in the ASEAN Regional Forum and other fora rather than in APEC [43]

Starting in 2001, however, security was added to the official agenda of the Leaders' Meeting. At the October 2001 meetings in Shanghai, the attacks on the World Trade Center and the Pentagon overshadowed the economic agenda. The Leaders issued a joint statement condemning the attacks—APEC's first joint statement on non-economic issues. Since 2001, the agenda for the Leaders' Meeting has included issues related to "human security," with a focus on three topics: terrorism, disease, and disasters.

Counterterrorism and Secure Trade

Among APEC members, there are four principal areas of concern about terrorism. First, some member economies face domestic extremists who episodically conduct acts of violence targeted at the civilian population. Second, there is some evidence suggesting that international terrorist networks, including Al Qaeda, are utilizing financial institutions in the Asia-Pacific region to funnel money across international borders. Third, APEC member economies wish to restrict the movement of suspected terrorists through the region. Fourth, APEC has made the security of trade one of its key priorities. Over the last five years, APEC has developed programs to respond to each of these concerns.

To oversee its efforts on terrorism, APEC established the Counter-Terrorism Task Force (CTTF) in October 2002. The CTTF reports directly to the APEC's Senior Officials. Its mission "is to identify and assess counter-terrorism needs, coordinate capacity building and technical assistance programs, cooperate with international and regional organizations and facilitate cooperation between APEC fora on counter-terrorism issues." [44]. The CTTF generally meets quarterly, in coordination with the Senior Officials Meetings. At a meeting held in Cairns, Australia, in July 2007, the CTTF set up a study group to develop a plan to facilitate trade recovery in the aftermath of a major terrorist event. In addition to the work of the CTTF, each APEC member has created a Counter-Terrorism Action Plan (CTAP) [45]

Much of APEC's counterterrorism efforts have focused on the issue of secure trade. In 2002, APEC created the "Secure Trade in the APEC Region (STAR) Initiative." The STAR Initiative is "focused on policies and procedures to enhance security and efficiency in the APEC region's seaports, airports and other access points, including port and airport security; shipping container security; coastal patrol; capacity building; financial assistance, and private sector initiatives." [46]. The most recent STAR Conference, held in Lima on August 20 & 21, 2008, focused on enhancing security and safety while containing costs.

Diseases

In 2003, APEC established its ad hoc Health Task Force (HTF) to deal with the threats posed by emerging infectious diseases. In part, the HTF was created in response to the February 2003 outbreak of Severe Acute Respiratory Syndrome (SARS) in several APEC member economies. Not only did the people of several APEC members suffer serious health problems due to SARS, the economies of both SARS-infected and non-infected members were harmed by the loss of tourism [47]. The value of having the HTF was confirmed in 2004, with the outbreak of avian influenza H5N1 in 2004. Besides its responses to SARS and avian influenza, APEC is also concerned about the threat posed by HIV/AIDS. During the second Senior Officials Meeting in 2007, APEC endorsed the transformation of the Health Task Force to the Health Working Group (HWG) in 2008. The first and second meetings of the HWG were held in Lima in February and August 2008 respectively.

Most of APEC's efforts on disease have focused on the exchange of medical information and research, building a rapid-response and containment program, and the exchange of "best practices." For SARS and avian influenza, APEC has held a series of meetings to discuss means of more rapidly identifying and responding to possible outbreaks, and sharing "best practices" in areas such as passenger screening techniques and safeguarding measures for poultry. Regarding HIV/AIDS, APEC's HTF is fostering the exchange of information on members' programs to prevent the spread of the disease, and improving workplace management of HIV/AIDS.

Natural Disasters

The third form of threat to human security of great concern to APEC are natural disasters. In December 2004, a 9.3 earthquake off the coast of Indonesia propagated a devastating tsunami that killed thousands of people in several nations bordering the Indian Ocean. Although there was a tsunami warning system in place, many people were not warned of the impending natural disaster and fell victim to the tsunami.

In response to the Indian Ocean tsunami, APEC Senior Officials adopted in March 2005 an "APEC Strategy on Response to and Preparedness for Natural Disasters and Emergencies." They also established APEC's "Task Force for Emergency Preparedness (TFEP)." Working with APEC's Industrial Science and Technology Working Group (ISTWG), the TFEP has held a number of seminars and training sessions to help APEC members improve their seismic monitoring systems, disaster response infrastructure, building and infrastructure construction codes, and public education systems to reduce their exposure to natural disasters.

APEC members are also providing additional funding to natural disaster warning systems. In December, Congress passed P.L. 109-424, the "Tsunami Warning and Education Act." The act, signed by the President on December 20, 2006, authorizes additional funding to "enhance and modernize the existing Pacific Tsunami Warning System to increase coverage, reduce false alarms, and increase the accuracy of forecasts and warnings...." [48]. It authorizes $25 million in FY2008, and then authorizes an increase in funding by $1 million each year until FY2012.

IMPLICATIONS FOR CONGRESS

Past Congresses and the Bush Administration identified APEC as the primary regional institution in the Asia-Pacific for promoting open trade and practical economic cooperation. APEC is also seen as a useful forum for advancing U.S. concerns on issues related to human security.

Since APEC's inception in 1989, congressional interest and involvement with APEC has focused on two areas: (1) direct and indirect financial support for APEC; and (2) oversight of U.S. participation in APEC.

Previous Congressional Actions on APEC

Section 424 of the Foreign Relations Authorization Act, Fiscal Years 1994 and 1995, authorized the President to maintain United States membership in the Asia-Pacific Economic Cooperation and provided for U.S. contributions of APEC out of appropriations for "Contributions to International Organizations." The level of direct U.S. financial support for APEC for FY2009 is $900,000 per year.49 In addition, $2.3 million is included under the State Department's Office of International Conferences of the Diplomatic & Consular Programs for preparation work for the 2011 APEC meetings.

Section 2540 of the National Defense Authorization Act for Fiscal Year 1996 made "a noncommunist country that was a member nation of the Asia Pacific Economic Cooperation (APEC) as of October 31, 1993" eligible to participate in a loan guarantee program "arising out of the financing of the sale or long-term lease of defense articles, defense services, or design and construction services." [50]

The Federal Agriculture Improvement and Reform Act of 1996 (P.L. 104-127) included a finding by Congress that:

> ... during the period 1996 through 2002, there will be several opportunities for the United States to negotiate fairer trade in agricultural products, including further negotiations under the World Trade Organization, and steps toward possible free trade agreements of the Americas and Asian-Pacific Economic Cooperation (APEC); and the United States should aggressively use these opportunities to achieve more open and fair opportunities for trade in agricultural products [51]

In the Intelligence Reform and Terrorism Prevention Act of 2004 (P.L. 108-458), Congress finds:

> ... other economic and regional fora, such as the Asia-Pacific Economic Cooperation (APEC) Forum, and the Western Hemisphere Financial Ministers, have been used to marshal political will and actions in support of combating the financing of terrorism (CFT) standards [52]

Finally, the National Defense Authorization Act for Fiscal Year 2006 (P.L. 109-163) included as the sense of Congress:

> that the President should present to Congress quickly a comprehensive strategy to—
> (1) address the emergence of China economically, diplomatically, and militarily;
> (2) promote mutually beneficial trade relations with China; and
> (3) encourage China's adherence to international norms in the areas of trade, international security, and human rights.

To be included in that strategy are "[a]ctions to encourage United States diplomatic efforts to identify and pursue initiatives to revitalize United States engagement in East Asia. The initiatives should have a regional focus and complement bilateral efforts. The Asia-Pacific Economic Cooperation forum (APEC) offers a ready mechanism for pursuit of such initiatives."

Issues for the 111th Congress

For the 111th Congress, issues related to APEC could arise in a variety of direct and indirect ways. In addition to the issue of U.S. financial support for APEC, Congress may choose to express its sense on different policy issues. Also, there are oversight issues raised by U.S. participation in various APEC activities and, in particular, with respect to the 2011 APEC meetings to be held in the United States.

Proposed Legislation

No legislation has been introduced in the 111th Congress that explicitly refers to APEC, but one Senate resolution—S.Res. 76—does refer to APEC. The resolution, introduced by Senator Maria Cantwell on March 18, 2009, expressed the sense of the Senate that the United States and the People's Republic of China should work together to reduce or eliminate tariff and nontariff barriers to trade in clean energy and environmental goods and services by various means, including "through the Asia Pacific Economic Cooperation and the World Trade Organization."

During the 110th Congress, only one proposed bill specifically mentioned APEC—the United States-China Diplomatic Expansion Act of 2007 (H.R. 3272) [53]. Introduced by Representative Mark Kirk, and cosponsored by Representatives Rick Larsen, Steve Israel, Susan Davis, and Charles Boustany, H.R. 3272 would have authorize the appropriation in FY2008 of $65 million for the construction of a new consulate in China, $10 million for additional personnel for the U.S. diplomatic mission in China, $6 million for other State Department personnel, $10 million for various Chinese language programs, and $2 million for rule of law initiatives in China. The bill also would have authorized the appropriation of $3 million for a U.S. contribution to APEC.

Senate Actions

On April 29, 2008, the Senate confirmed Patricia M. Haslach as United States Senior Coordinator for The Asia-Pacific Economic Cooperation (APEC) Forum at the rank of Ambassador. Haslach continues to serve under the Obama Administration.

As previously mentioned, the U.S.-Australia Defense Trade Cooperation Treaty signed during the APEC meetings is subject to the approval of the Senate. On December 3, 2007, President submitted the treaty to the Senate; no action has been taken since its submission.

Financial Support

The most direct issue would be the level of U.S. financial support for APEC. Although the President does have the authority under current federal law to determine the level of APEC's funding without action by Congress, Congress may choose to take up this issue (see above). For example, Congress could consider setting funding levels, directly or indirectly, for APEC's trade facilitation programs independently from the amounts previously appropriated.

In addition, Congress may consider expressing its preferences regarding the agenda and content of the 2011 APEC meetings to be held in the United States, possibly via appropriation legislation that provides funding for those meetings. The 110th Congress has already appropriated $2.3 million for the 2011 meetings, but additional funding is likely to be needed.

APEC as Vehicle for Promoting a FTAAP

Past Congresses have recognized the potential of APEC as a vehicle for promoting free trade. In addition, to the issue of a possible Free Trade Area of the Asia-Pacific, negotiations over regional trade integration under APEC would likely raise issues related to labor rights and environment protection, and whether the United States would be able to respond to foreign country violations of labor or environmental standards with economic sanctions or monetary fines (as stipulated in the U.S.-Singapore/Chile FTAs).

In addition, the announcement made late in the Bush Administration that the United States was entering into negotiations with the Trans-Pacific Strategic and Economic Partnership (TPP) has brought into question U.S. commitment to APEC and its role in fostering a FTAAP. According to Ambassador Haslach, U.S. interest in joining the TPP is consistent with APEC's objective of forming a FTAAP, as TPP membership may be an achievable a short-term objective and the APEC-based FTAAP constitutes a long-term goal. Some observers, however, are concerned that the possible negotiations with the existing TPP members – Brunei, Chile, New Zealand and Singapore – will divert the attention of the State Department and the USTR away from APEC, delaying progress on the FTAAP.

Progress on the Doha Round

Successful completion of the Doha Round was a major trade priority for the Bush Administration. It is yet to be determined if the issue will be a high priority for the Obama Administration.

Focus on Human Security Issues

In addition to the various economic and trade issues, Congress may also consider issues pertaining to human security as a result of the U.S. involvement with APEC. For example, U.S. recognition of the APEC Business Travel Card could raise domestic security concerns to the expedited visa and entry privileges extended to card bearers. Similarly, concerns about a potential influenza pandemic may engender interest in providing more support to APEC's Health Working Group.

Competition for Regional Influence

From a geopolitical perspective, APEC is a leading forum through which the United States can broadly engage the Asia-Pacific region. The United States is not included in the other regional multilateral associations, such as ASEAN and the East Asian Summit (EAS), and no other forum includes such a wide range of Asian economies. From a strategic perspective, many experts believe APEC could play a useful role in advancing U.S. interests in Asia.

Over the last few years, the United States' position as the leader in the region has been challenged by China. China's accession to the WTO, its recent efforts to negotiate BTAs across Asia (including the Comprehensive Economic Partnership Agreements with Hong Kong and Macau), and its unilateral liberalization of its trade regime, has arguably placed China as a competitor to the United States.

Many argue that the United States should re-energize its involvement in Asian trade discussion and elevate the importance of APEC to reassert U.S. leadership. They advocate both increased financial assistance to APEC, though the annual contribution and specific assistance programs, and alteration in U.S. laws and policies on key issues. Others say that APEC should reformulate its mission by focusing more narrowly on trade facilitation and economic integration, abandoning many of the working groups that are not central to the core goals, and strengthening the Secretariat. The annual Leaders' Meeting continues to provide prestige and offer an opportunity for heads of state, particularly those of smaller countries, to interact with top U.S. officials. APEC offers the additional benefit of including Taiwan and Hong Kong as member economies, unlike the EAS.

APPENDIX. ANNOTATED CHRONOLOGY OF PAST APEC MEETINGS

Year and Location	Key Outcomes
1989 - Canberra, Australia	Concept of forming APEC is discussed at an informal Ministerial-level dialogue group with 12 members.
1993 - Blake Island, U.S.A.	First formal APEC Leaders' Meeting includes representatives from 14 members: Australia, Brunei Darussalam, Canada, China, Hong Kong, Indonesia, Japan, New Zealand, Philippines, Singapore, South Korea, Thailand, and United States.
1994 - Bogor, Indonesia	APEC sets the Bogor Goals of "free and open trade and investment in the Asia-Pacific by [a] 2010 for developed economies and 2020 for developing economies."
1995 - Osaka, Japan	APEC adopts the Osaka Action Agenda (OAA) which provides a framework for meeting the [b] Bogor Goals.
1996 - Manila, the Philippines	The Manila Action Plan is adopted, which outlines the trade and investment liberalization and [c] facilitation measures to be taken by APEC members to reach the Bogor Goals. The APEC economies submit their first "Individual Action Plans," or IAPs, indicating how they intended to move toward fulfillment of the Bogor goals. Moreover, APEC Leaders called for conclusion of the Information Technology Agreement in the WTO, which acted as a decisive catalyst toward successful completion of this agreement in 1997.
1997 - Vancouver, Canada	Several APEC members are coping with a severe recession caused by the Asian Financial [d] Crisis. APEC ministers reject a Japanese-backed proposal to establish a separate Asian fund to provide financial support for countries coping with financial difficulties.

Appendix. (Continued)

Year and Location	Key Outcomes
1997 - Vancouver, Canada	However, APEC does endorse a proposal for Early Voluntary Sectoral Liberalization (EVSL) in 15 sectors, and decides that Individual Action Plans should be updated annually.
1998 - Kuala Lumpur, Malaysia	President Clinton does not attend because of the imminent bombing of Iraq. Economic recession continues for several APEC members, with varying levels of hardship. Malaysian Prime Minister Mahathir Mohamad, host of the APEC meetings, continues criticism of trade and investment liberalization, which he blames for causing the Asian Financial Crisis and his country's deep recession. APEC agrees on the first nine sectors for EVSL and seeks an EVSL agreement with non-APEC members at the World Trade Organization.
1999 - Auckland, New Zealand	APEC meetings occur earlier than usual because the World Trade Organization's Ministerial Conference is to be held in Seattle on November 30-December 3, 1999. The APEC leaders endorsed the launching of a new WTO round of multilateral trade negotiations and agreed that the new round of trade negotiations to be concluded within three years. The APEC Meetings occurs at a time of increasing violence in East Timor; APEC leaders put pressure on Indonesia to allow international peacekeepers into East Timor. APEC commits to paperless trading by 2005 in developed economies and 2010 in developing economies. APEC Business Travel Card scheme is approved.
2000 - Bandar Seri Begawan, Brunei Darussalam	APEC establishes an electronic Individual Action Plan (e-IAP) system, providing IAPs online. APEC also states that China should be accepted into the WTO soon, foll sometime later by Russia and Vietnam. Following a bilateral meeting, the United States and e Singapore announce that they would begin negotiations on a bilateral free trade agreement.
2001 - Shanghai, China	Meeting is held five weeks after the attacks on the World Trade Center and Pentagon. APEC adopts the Shanghai Accord, which focuses on Broadening the APEC Vision, Clarifying the Roadmap to Bogor and Strengthening the Implementation Mechanism. The e-APEC Strategy n hen market structu facilitate infrastructure investment and technology for on-line transactions and promoteentrepreneurship and human capacity building. A leaders' statement on counterterrorism is the first issued by APEC dealing explicitly with a non-economic topic. In the statement, the leaders condemned the attacks on the United States, committed themselves to preventing and suppressing all forms of terrorists acts in the future, to enhance counterterrorism cooperation, and take appropriate financial measures to prevent the flow of funds to terrorists.
2002 - Los Cabos, Mexico	APEC adopts a Trade Facilitation Action Plan, agreeing to reduce transaction costs in international trade by 5% by 2006. Policies on Trade and the Digital Economy and Transparency Standards are adopted. The leaders also declare support for the Doha negotiations (including the abolition of agricultural

Appendix. (Continued)

Year and Location	Key Outcomes
2002 - Los Cabos, Mexico	export subsidies) and call for their conclusion by January 1, 2005. In conjunction with the Mexico APEC Meetings, the United States announced the Enterprise for ASEAN Initiative, a new trade initiative with the Association of Southeast Asian Nations. APEC's second Counter-Terrorism Statement is delivered, along with the adoption of the Secure Trade in the APEC Region (STAR) Initiative.
2003 - Bangkok, Thailand	APEC issues first separate statement on Doha negotiations. The APEC ministers in attendance call for the reopening of the negotiation process based on the text of the unsuccessful proposal made during the WTO talks in Cancun, Mexico. APEC pledges to take specific actions to dismantle terrorist groups, eliminate the danger of weapons of mass destruction and confront other security threats. Members sign up to the APEC Action Plan on SARS and the Health Security Initiative to further protect personal security. The Leaders' statement calls for more six-party talks and for North Korea to demonstrate "verifiable" progress in dismantling its nuclear weapons program.
2004 - Santiago, Chile	APEC issues second statement on Doha Round, setting December 2005 as target date for completion of negotiations. APEC adopts "Best Practices" guidelines to ensure that FTAs and RTAs fully comply with or exceed WTO guidelines. APEC establishes an Anticorruption and Transparency (ACT) program to aid members in fighting corruption and increasing transparency; the United States is among the seven member economies funding the program.
2005 - Busan, South Korea	APEC adopts the "Busan Roadmap," which include deadlines for reducing transaction costs and developing a plan for structural reform to make member economies more business-friendly. The 21 leaders issue a special statement regarding the Doha negotiations encouraging member economies to exercise "the necessary flexibility" to resolve "the current impasse in agricultural negotiations, in particular in market access."
	The United States, Canada, and Australia push for the statement to single out the European Union for their protectionist measures, but other APEC members demur. Special attention is given to the threat of a pandemic influenza stemming from the incidences of avian flu in both birds a humans.
2006 - Hanoi, Vietnam	APEC initiates a study of regional economic integration to include consideration of U.S.-proposed Free Trade Area of the Asia-Pacific. The APEC Leaders issue a se on the Doha Round talks, calling for deeper reductions in trade-distorting farm subsidies and increasing market access for goods and services. The United States announces it will start recognizing the APEC Business Travel Card in 2007.

Appendix. (Continued)

Year and Location	Key Outcomes
2007 – Sydney, Australia	The main topics of discussion during the September 2007 two-day Leaders' Meeting and the two-day Ministerial Meeting were climate change and regional economic integration. The Leaders issued a separate joint declaration on climate change, which included "aspirational" commitments to reduce energy intensity by at least 25% by 2030 and to increase regional forest cover by at least 20 million hectares by 2020. APEC's consensus position on the latter topic entitled "Strengthening Regional Economic Integration," was endorsed by the Leaders. [d] the rece

[a.] The complete text of the Bogor Goals is available on APEC's web page at http://www.apec.org/apec/ leaders__declarations/1994.html.

[b.] The complete text of the 1995 Leaders' declaration and a link to the Osaka Action Agenda is available on APEC's web page at http://www.apec.org/apec/leaders__declarations/1995.html.

[c.] The complete text of the 1996 Leaders' declaration, including the Manila Action Plan is available on APEC's web page at http://www.apec.org/apec/leaders__declarations/1996.html#Manila.

[d.] See CRS Report RL30272, Global Financial Turmoil, the IMF, and the New Financial Architecture, by Dick K.Nanto.

[e.] See CRS Report RL31789, The U.S.-Singapore Free Trade Agreement, by Dick K. Nanto.

The table provides a brief summary of the past APEC Meetings. For more details about each meeting, see the official APEC web page, http://www.apec.org/.

REFERENCES

[1] APEC currently consists of 21 "member economies"—Australia, Brunei Darussalam, Canada, Chile, Chinese Taipei (Taiwan), Hong Kong (China), Indonesia, Japan, Malaysia, Mexico, New Zealand, Papua New Guinea, the People's Republic of China, Peru, the Republic of Korea, the Republic of the Philippines, the Russian Federation, Singapore, Thailand, the United States, and Vietnam. The members of APEC are referred to as economies or members—not nations or countries—due to the concurrent membership of Hong Kong, the People's Republic of China, and Taiwan.

[2] P.L. 109-163, section 1234(b).

[3] P.L. 109-163, section 1234(c)(4).

[4] "Press Briefing on the President's Trip to Australia and the APEC Summit by Senior Administration Officials," U.S. Department of State, August 30, 2007.

[5] ASEAN members include Brunei Darussalam, Burma (Myanmar), Cambodia, Indonesia, Laos, Malaysia, the Philippines, Singapore, Thailand, and Vietnam.

[6] The complete text of the Bogor Goals is available on APEC's web page at http://www.apec.org/apec/ leaders__ declarations/1994.html.

[7] For a more detailed discussion of APEC and the concept of "open regionalism," see Christopher M. Dent, *New Free Trade Agreements in the Asia-Pacific*, Palgrave MacMillan, 2006.

[8] See http://www.apec.org/apec/leaders__declarations/1994.html.

[9] The complete text of the 1995 Leaders' declaration and a link to the Osaka Action Agenda is available on APEC's web page at http://www.apec.org/apec/leaders__ declarations/1995.html.
[10] In 2006, the United States seconded Scott Smith to work with the APEC Secretariat.
[11] The Leaders' Meetings are technically not summits because of the presence of Hong Kong and Taiwan, whose leaders are not officially heads of state.
[12] In the past when it was still a British colony, Hong Kong also sent a special representative.
[13] A summary of the major achievements of the past Leaders' Meetings is provided in an appendix to this report.
[14] U.S. representatives to ABAC are Deborah Henretta, group president for Asia at the Procter & Gamble Company, Nick Reilly, president of General Motors Asia Pacific and Peter Scher, executive vice president for global government relations and public policy at JPMorgan Chase.
[15] The United States does not consider the ABTC as a substitute for a visa. Cardholders from non-Visa Waiver Program countries still need to present valid passports and obtain U.S. visas.
[16] G20 refers to the Group of 20, which includes 19 countries—Argentina, Australia, Brazil, Canada, China, France, Germany, India, Indonesia, Italy, Japan, Mexico, Russia, Saudi Arabia, South Africa, South Korea, Turkey, the United Kingdom, and the United States—and the European Union.
[17] "A New Commitment to Asia-Pacific Development," Economic Leaders' statement from the 16th APEC Economic Leaders' Meeting, Lima, Peru, November 23, 2008.
[18] The full text of the joint statement is available via APEC's home page at http://www.apec.org/apec/ministerial_statements/annual_ministerial/2008_20th_apec_ministerial.html
[19] In 2007, President Bush left the APEC Leaders' Meeting after the first day, a decision for which he was widely criticized by other APEC members. For more details, see CRS Report RL31038, *Asia Pacific Economic Cooperation (APEC) and the 2007 Meetings in Sydney, Australia*, by Michael F. Martin.
[20] "Lima APEC Leaders' Statement on the Global Economy," Lima, Peru, November 22, 2008, http://www.apec.org/apec/leaders__declarations/2008/aelm_globaleconomy.html.
[21] "A New Commitment to the Asia-Pacific Development," joint statement of the 16th APEC Economic Leaders' Meeting, Lima, Peru, November 23, 2008, http://www.apec.org/apec/leaders__declarations/2008.html.
[22] The 15 completed model measures cover the following chapters: Competition Policy; Cooperation; Customs Administration and Trade Facilitation; Dispute Settlement; Electronic Commerce; Environment; Government Procurement; Rule of Origin and Origin Procedures; Safeguards; Sanitary and Phytosanitary Measures; Technical Barriers to Trade; Temporary Entry for Business Persons; Trade in Goods; Trade Facilitation; and Transparency.
[23] For more information about the Georgia conflict and its implications for U.S. relations with Russia, see CRS Report RL34618, *Russia-Georgia Conflict in August 2008: Context and Implications for U.S. Interests*, by Jim Nichol.
[24] "Bush Blames Trade 'Backlash' for SKorea Pact Stall," *Agence France-Presse*, November 22, 2008.

[25] Ibid.
[26] For more on the evolution of relations between China and Taiwan, see CRS Report RL34683, *Taiwan-U.S. Relations: Recent Developments and Their Policy Implications*, by Kerry Dumbaugh.
[27] The four agreements, signed on November 4, 2008, covered direct shipping and flights, postal services and food safety.
[28] There has not been an official statement by all the APEC members as to whether they are "industrialized" or "developing" members. Australia, Canada, Chile, Hong Kong, Japan, New Zealand, Singapore, and the United States consider themselves as "industrialized" economies. Other possible members of this group—such as South Korea—have not made clear their status with respect to the Bogor Goals
[29] Full text of the IMF report is available online at http://www.imf.org/external/np/g20/pdf/031909a.pdf.
[30] "Singapore to Launch Tougher Public Order Law," *Reuters*, March 24, 2009.
[31] For more information on the impact of the Asian financial crisis on world trade, see CRS Report RL30517, *Asian Financial Crisis and Recovery: Status and Implications for U.S. Interests*, by Richard P. Cronin and CRS Report 98- 434, *The Asian (Global?) Financial Crisis, the IMF, and Japan: Economic Issues*, by Dick K. Nanto; for more information about the impact of the attacks on the World Trade Center and the Pentagon on world trade, see CRS Report RL31617, *The Economic Effects of 9/11: A Retrospective Assessment*, by Gail E. Makinen.
[32] For more on recent trends in global supply chains, see CRS Report R40167, *Globalized Supply Chains and U.S. Policy*, by Dick K. Nanto.
[33] For more on this subject, see CRS Report RL34524, *International Trade: Rules of Origin*, by Vivian C. Jones and Michael F. Martin.
[34] For a description of the recent growth of BTAs in Asia, see CRS Report RL33653, *East Asian Regional Architecture: New Economic and Security Arrangements and U.S. Policy*, by Dick K. Nanto.
[35] "APEC and Free Trade Agreements in the Asia Pacific," by Prof. Jane Kelsey. Paper presented at Asia-Pacific Research Network Policy Conference on Trade, July 11-13, 2005, Hong Kong. Paper available online at http://www.bilaterals.org/article-print.php3?id_article=2346.
[36] Kelsey, *op. cit.*
[37] "FTAs and the Prospects for Regional Integration in Asia,' by Razeen Sally. ECIPE Working Paper, No. 1, 2006.
[38] "A Complex Curse: East Asia Exposes the Limits of the Regional," by Alan Beattie, *Financial Times*, Nov. 13, 2006.
[39] "Put Effort into Doha Ahead of Proliferating Bilateral Deals," by Dr. Christopher M. Dent. *Financial Times*, Nov. 21, 2006, p. 12.
[40] Sally, op. cit.
[41] An example of this view is C. Fred Bergsten's speech, "The Free Trade Area of the Asia-Pacific Is the Next Step Forward for APEC (and for the World Trading System)," presented to APEC's CEO Summit on Nov. 18, 2006 in Hanoi, Vietnam
[42] Kelsey, *op. cit.*
[43] The ASEAN Regional Forum usually meets after the ASEAN Ministerial Conference and, in addition to the 10 members of ASEAN, includes the Australia, Canada, China,

the European Union, Japan, New Zealand, Russia, South Korea, and United States. For more information about the 1995 discussions, see Moosa, Eugene. *Regional Security Remains a Taboo at APEC*. Reuters Newswire Service. Nov. 19, 1995

[44] For more details about the CTTF, see http://www.apec.org/apec/apec_groups/som_special_task_groups/counter _terrorism.html.

[45] Copies of each member's CTAP are available online at http://www.apec.org/apec/apec_groups/som_special_task_groups/counter_terrorism/counter_terrorism_actionjlans.html.

[46] For more information about the STAR Initiative, see http://www.apec.org/apec/apec_groups/som_special_task_groups/counter_terrorism/secure_trade_in_the.html.

[47] For a study on the economic effects of SARS, see "Globalization and Disease: The Case of SARS," by Jong-Wha Lee and Warwick J. McKibbin, Brookings Discussion Papers in International Economics, February 2004. Available online at http://www.brookings.org/views/papers/mckibbin/20040203.pdf.

[48] H.R. 1674, Section 3(2).

[49] Department of State, Congressional Budget Justification, Fiscal Year 2009. In addition, an indeterminate amount of funds are utilized for APEC-related activities within various State Department funds (such as the Bureau of East Asian and Pacific Affairs, International Criminal Justice, Representation Allowances, Emergencies in the Diplomatic and Consular Service, and the East-West Center).

[50] Language now codified into U.S. Law under Title 10, Subtitle A, Part IV, Chapter 148, Subchapter VI, section 2540.

[51] Language now codified into U.S. Law under Title 7, Chapter 41, Subchapter IV, section 1736r.

[52] Language now codified into U.S. Law under Title 31, Chapter, Subtitle IV, Chapter 53, Subchapter II, section 770.

[53] The House and Senate passed separate resolutions—H.Res. 422 and S.Res. 203—that mention APEC in passing, "... its seat as a permanent member of the United Nations Security Council and on the Asia-Pacific Economic Cooperation, China is an emerging power...."

In: Political and Economic Developments in Asia
Editor: Felix Chin

ISBN: 978-1-61209-783-1
©2011 Nova Science Publishers, Inc.

Chapter 2

THE PROPOSED U.S.-SOUTH KOREA FREE TRADE AGREEMENT (KORUS FTA): PROVISIONS AND IMPLICATIONS[*]

William H. Cooper, Mark E. Manyin, Remy Jurenas and Michaela D. Platzer

ABSTRACT

On June 30, 2007, U.S. and South Korean trade officials signed the proposed U.S.-South Korean Free Trade Agreement (KORUS FTA) for their respective countries. If approved, the KORUS FTA would be the largest FTA that South Korea has signed to date and would be the second largest (next to North American Free Trade Agreement, NAFTA) in which the United States participates. South Korea is the seventh-largest trading partner of the United States and the United States is South Korea's third largest trading partner. Various studies conclude that the agreement would increase bilateral trade and investment flows. The final text of the proposed KORUS FTA covers a wide range of trade and investment issues and, therefore, could have substantial economic implications for both the United States and South Korea.

The agreement will not enter into force unless Congress approves implementation legislation. The negotiations were conducted under the trade promotion authority (TPA), also called fast-track trade authority, that the Congress granted the President under the Bipartisan Trade Promotion Act of 2002 (P.L. 107-2 10). The authority allows the President to enter into trade agreements that receive expedited congressional consideration (no amendments and limited debate). The Bush Administration did not send draft implementing legislation to Congress.

The Obama Administration has not indicated if and when it will send the draft implementing bill to Congress The Administration has stated that it is developing "benchmarks for progress" on resolving "concerns" it has with the KORUS FTA, particularly over market access for U.S. car exports. While U.S. Trade Representative Ron Kirk has called attention to the economic opportunities the KORUS FTA presents,

---

[*] This is an edited, reformatted and augmented version of CRS Report RL34330, dated March 24, 2009.

he also has said that if the Administration's concerns are not resolved, "we'll be prepared to step away....".

In South Korea, however, the politics of the KORUS FTA likely will make it difficult for the government of President Lee Myung-bak to appear to accede to new U.S. demands. This is particularly due to memories of events in 2008, when Lee reached an agreement with the United States to fully lift South Korea's ban on U.S. beef imports, triggering massive anti-government protests that forced the two governments to renegotiate the beef agreement. Lee lifted the ban to make it easier for the George W. Bush Administration to submit the KORUS FTA to Congress. The South Korean National Assembly has yet to vote on the KORUS FTA, and is debating whether or not to do so before the U.S. Congress acts. It is expected that the Assembly would pass the agreement, at least in its current version.

While a broad swath of the U.S. business community supports the agreement, the KORUS FTA faces opposition from some groups, including some auto and steel manufacturers and labor unions. Agricultural groups and some Members of Congress are monitoring the flow of U.S. beef to South Korea to judge whether and to what extent to support the agreement. Some U.S. supporters view passage of the KORUS FTA as important to secure new opportunities in the South Korean market, while opponents claim that the KORUS FTA does not go far enough. Other observers have suggested the outcome of the KORUS FTA could have implications for the U.S.- South Korean alliance as a whole, as well as on U.S. trade policy and Asia policy. This report will be updated as events warrant.

On June 30, 2007, United States Trade Representative Susan Schwab and South Korean Foreign Trade Minister Kim Hyung-chong signed the proposed U.S.-South Korean Free Trade Agreement (KORUS FTA) for their respective countries [1]. If approved, the KORUS FTA would be the largest FTA South Korea has signed to date and would be the second largest (next to the North American Free Trade Agreement) in which the United States currently participates. South Korea is the seventh-largest trading partner of the United States and the KORUS FTA, if enacted, is expected to expand bilateral trade and investment flows according to some studies.

The final text of the proposed free trade agreement (FTA) covers a wide range of trade and investment issues and, therefore, could have wide economic implications for both the United States and South Korea. The subjects include ones on which the two countries achieved early agreement, such as the elimination on tariffs on trade in most manufactured goods and the liberalization in services trade. But the text also includes a number of very sensitive issues on which agreement was reached only during the final hours of negotiations—autos, agriculture, and trade remedies, among others.

Congress will have to approve implementation legislation for the KORUS FTA before it can enter into force. The negotiations were conducted under the trade promotion authority (TPA), also called fast-track trade authority, that the Congress granted the President under the Bipartisan Trade Promotion Act of 2002 (the act) (P.L. 107-2 10). The authority allows the President to enter into trade agreements that receive expedited congressional consideration (no amendments and limited debate). The TPA sets no deadline for the President to do this.

The Obama Administration has not indicated if and when it will send the draft implementing bill to Congress. The Administration has stated that it is developing "benchmarks for progress" on resolving "concerns" it has with the KORUS FTA [2]. During the presidential campaign, then- Senator Obama opposed the agreement because he believed that it does not adequately address problems of market access in South Korea for U.S. exports of cars, among other issues. During his Senate Finance Committee confirmation hearing, USTR Ron Kirk stated that the KORUS FTA "presents one of the biggest economic opportunities we have of all of the bilateral agreements out there." He added that "the president has said—and I agree—that agreement as it is just simply isn't fair. And if we don't get that right, we'll be prepared to step away...."

In South Korea, there is an ongoing debate over whether or not to have the National Assembly vote on the KORUS FTA before the agreement is submitted to Congress. South Korea's President, Lee Myung-bak, has said he hopes to have the South Korean National Assembly and pass the agreement soon. Lee's Grand National Party controls a majority in the National Assembly, and most observers believe the agreement has the votes to pass. However, an uproar in South Korea over the April 2008 beef agreement appears to have made many politicians in Seoul wary of trying to pass the agreement before the U.S. Congress votes. In February 2009, the judiciary subcommittee of the National Assembly's Foreign Affairs, Trade and Unification Committee favorably reported the KORUS FTA ratification bill to the parent committee.

The United States and South Korea entered into the KORUS FTA as a means to further solidify an already strong economic relationship by reducing barriers to trade and investment between them and to resolve long festering economic issues. The United States specifically sought increased access to South Korean markets for agricultural products, services, and foreign investment. Of importance to South Korea was a change in U.S. trade remedy procedures which it considers to be discriminatory and U.S. recognition of products made in an industrial park in North Korea as eligible for preferential treatment under the KORUS FTA.

Supporters of the FTA argue that failure to approve the KORUS FTA would allow those opportunities to slip away, particularly if Seoul's strategy of negotiating a web of FTAs, with South Korea at the center, is successful. As of March 2009, South Korea and the European Union (EU) were in the final stages of FTA negotiations. However, some opponents of the KORUS FTA have argued that the agreement failed to go far enough in addressing South Korean trade barriers and would be a lost opportunity if approved in its current form. A congressionally mandated study by the United States International Trade Commission (USITC) concluded that investment and trade between the United States and South Korea would increase modestly as a result of the KORUS FTA [3]. This result is in line with other similar studies. In general and in the short-to-medium term, the KORUS FTA's largest commercial effects are expected to be microeconomic in nature. The U.S. services and agriculture industries, for instance, are expected to reap significant benefits if the agreement is implemented.

Many observers have argued that in addition to its economic implications, the KORUS FTA would have diplomatic and security implications. For example, they have suggested that it would help to deepen the U.S.-South Korean alliance. The United States and South Korea have been allies since the United States intervened on the Korean Peninsula in 1950 and fought to repel a North Korean takeover of South Korea. Over 33,000 U.S. troops were killed and over 100,000 were wounded during the three-year conflict [4]. South Korea subsequently has assisted U.S. deployments in other conflicts, most recently by deploying over 3,000 troops to play a noncombat role in Iraq. However, some counter this by positing that the KORUS FTA need not be seen as a necessary, let alone sufficient, condition for enhancing the U.S.-ROK alliance. Mutual interests on critical issues pertaining to North Korea and the rest of the region will continue to require close cooperation between the two countries in the national security sphere. Indeed, in many respects, the KORUS FTA's fate may have more profound implications for U.S. trade policy and East Asia policy than for U.S.-South Korean relations. For instance, some have also suggested that a KORUS FTA would help to solidify the U.S. presence in East Asia to counterbalance the increasing influence of China while failure to pass it could harm the alliance.

This report is designed to assist Members of the 111th Congress as they consider the costs and benefits of the KORUS FTA. It examines the provisions of the KORUS FTA in the context of the overall U.S.-South Korean economic relationship, U.S. objectives, and South Korean objectives. The report will be updated as events warrant.

THE KORUS FTA IN A NUTSHELL

The KORUS FTA was the product of much compromise. As negotiators from both countries stated, each country was able to accomplish some of its objectives, but neither side got everything it wanted. For example, South Korea made concessions in agriculture and services while the United States made concessions on rice and textiles. Yet, U.S. car manufacturers felt that South Korea did not go far enough in addressing barriers to auto imports and South Korea would have liked to have more U.S. concessions on trade remedies.

Some highlights of the results of the agreement are provided below. Background information and a more detailed examination of the agreement's provisions are provided in the main sections of this report.

Agriculture

Under the KORUS FTA's agricultural provisions, South Korea immediately would grant duty-free status to almost two-thirds of current U.S. agricultural exports. Tariffs and import quotas on most other agricultural goods would be phased out within 10 years, with the remaining commodities and products subject to provisions that phase out such protection by year 23. Exports of seven U.S. products (skim and whole milk powders, evaporated milk, in-season oranges, potatoes for table use, honey, and identity-preserved soybeans for food use) would be subject to Korean import quotas that slowly expand in perpetuity.

Much effort went into negotiating provisions covering three agricultural commodities of export interest to the United States. Under the KORUS FTA, South Korea agreed to eliminate its 40% tariff on beef muscle meats imported from the United States over a 15 year period. Also, South Korea would have the right to impose safeguard tariffs on a temporary basis in response to any potential surge in imports of U.S. beef meats above specified levels. However, negotiators did not reach a breakthrough by the end of the talks on the separate but parallel issue of how to resolve differences on the terms of access for all U.S. beef in a way that would address Korea's human health concerns arising from the 2003 discovery of mad cow disease in the U.S. cattle herd. Though sales of U.S. boneless beef from cattle aged less than 30 months did resume in April 2007 under the terms of a separate agreement reached in early 2006, sales of bone-in beef (e.g., ribs) only began in August 2008 after the conclusion of a difficult series of negotiations—prompted by widespread public protests in Korea—on a more comprehensive agreement. This agreement requires the removal of specified risk materials known to transmit mad cow disease during the processing of cattle less than 30 months old when slaughtered. Both countries view this "voluntary private-sector" arrangement as a transitional step intended to improve Korean consumer confidence in U.S. beef. (See Appendix A for additional information)

The KORUS FTA does not give U.S. rice and rice products any preferential access to South Korea's market. It only requires South Korea to continue to abide by its multilateral trade commitments to increase rice imports. Access for U.S. citrus products was not settled until just before the talks concluded. With South Korea protecting its orange sector by a 50% tariff, negotiators compromised on a multi-part solution. A small duty free quota was created for "in- season" U.S. navel oranges that would grow slowly in perpetuity. Sales during this September to February period in excess of this quota would continue to face the high 50% tariff. For "out-ofseason" oranges that pose less competition to South Korea's orange producing sector, the tariff would be phased out by year 7.

Automobiles

Trade in autos and autoparts proved to be among the most difficult issues tackled by U.S. and South Korean negotiators, pitting an increasingly competitive South Korean industry seeking to increase its market share in the United States and a U.S. industry that wants South Korea to eliminate policies and practices that seemingly discriminate against U.S. auto imports. The KORUS FTA would:

- *eliminate most South Korean tariffs on U.S.-made motor vehicles.* South Korea would immediately eliminate its 8% tariff on U.S.-built passenger cars and its 10% tariff on pickup trucks.
- *reduce discriminatory effects of engine displacement taxes.* South Korea would simplify its three-tier "Special Consumption Tax" and would also simplify its five-tier "Annual Vehicle Tax" both of which are based on engine displacement by making it a three-tier system.
- *harmonize standards and create an "Automotive Working Group."* The agreement provides for self-certification on safety and emissions standards for a limited number of U.S.-exported vehicles, and a commitment that South Korea will evaluate emissions using the methodology applied by the State of California. South Korea also agreed "not to adopt technical regulations that create unnecessary barriers to trade and to cooperate to harmonize standards."
- *eliminate U.S. tariffs and provide for "snapback" clause.* The United States would immediately eliminate its 2.5% duty on gasoline-fueled passenger vehicles with engine displacement up to 3000 cc, would phase out over three years the 2.5% duty on South Korean imports with larger engine capacity or that are diesel-powered , and would phase out over ten years the 25% duty on South Korean pickup trucks.

Other Key Provisions

The KORUS FTA would cover a broad range of other areas. According to the Office of the United States Trade Representative (USTR), most U.S.-South Korean trade in *consumer and industrial products* would become duty-free within three years after the agreement enters into force, and virtually all remaining tariffs would be lifted within 10 years. The two countries agreed to liberalize trade in *services* by opening up their markets beyond what they have committed to do in the World Trade Organization (WTO). About 60% of U.S.-South Korea trade in *textiles and apparel* would become duty-free immediately, and the KORUS FTA would provide a special safeguard mechanism to reduce the impact of *textile and apparel* import surges.

Trade remedies were a critical issue for South Korea and a sensitive issue for the United States. The FTA allows the United States to exempt imports from South Korea from a "global" escape clause (section 201) measure if they are not a major cause of serious injury or a threat of serious injury to the U.S. domestic industry. The FTA would also provide for a binational consultative committee to review trade remedy decisions involving one another [5].

In addition, South Korea and the United States agreed to establish an independent body to review recommendations and determinations regarding South Korean pricing and government reimbursement for *pharmaceuticals and medical devices* and to improve transparency in the process for making those determinations.

Furthermore, one year after the KORUS FTA enters into force, a binational committee would be formed to study the possibility of eventually including products from "Outward Processing Zones," such as the *Kaesong Industrial Complex*, that use North Korean labor.

ESTIMATES OF THE OVERALL ECONOMIC EFFECTS OF A KORUS FTA

Economists have released several studies estimating the potential effects of the KORUS FTA. As required by the TPA statute, the USITC conducted a study of the KORUS FTA at the request of the President [6]. The USITC study concludes that U.S. GDP would increase by $10.1 billion to $11.9 billion (approximately 0.1%) when the KORUS FTA is fully implemented, a negligible amount given the size of the U.S. economy. The USITC based this estimate primarily on the removal of tariffs and tariff-rate-quotas, that is, barriers that can be relatively easily quantified.

The study concludes that U.S. exports of goods would likely increase by $9.7 billion to $10.9 billion, primarily in agricultural products, machinery, electronics, transportation equipment, including passenger vehicles and parts. U.S. imports would increase $6.4 billion to $6.9 billion, primarily in textiles, apparel, leather products, footwear, machinery, electronics, and passenger vehicles and parts [7].

The range does not take into account the impact of the reduction of barriers to trade in services and to foreign investment flows and the impact of changes in regulations as a result of the KORUS FTA. The study notes that U.S. exports in services would increase as a result of South Korean commitments under the KORUS FTA, and that changes in the regulatory environment in both countries would also help to increase bilateral trade and investment flows.

The study estimates that changes in aggregate U.S. employment would be negligible given the much larger size of the U.S. economy compared to the South Korean economy. However, while some sectors, such as livestock producers, would experience increases in employment, others such as textile, wearing apparel, and electronic equipment manufacturers would be expected to experience declines in employment [8]

Other studies draw the same basic conclusions, although the magnitudes differ because they employ different models from the USITC study. For example, a University of Michigan analysis commissioned by the Korea Economic Institute estimates that U.S. GDP would increase by $25.12 billion (0.14% of U.S. GDP). This is larger than the USITC estimate, but in part this is because its authors quantified the effects of liberalization in services trade [9] The authors also analyzed the impact of a KORUS FTA before the final text had been released and assumed, among other things, that rice trade would be liberalized, which, in the end, was not the case.

In December 2005, the Korea Institute for International Economic Policy (KIEP) published a study measuring the potential economic impact of a U.S.-South Korean FTA on South Korea alone. The study estimated some of the dynamic, or long-run, economic effects in addition to the static, or one-time, effects of the FTA on South Korea. The KIEP study estimated that the FTA would eventually lead to a 0.42% to 0.59% increase in South Korea's GDP according to a static analysis, and 1.99% to 2.27% according to a dynamic analysis [10]

AN OVERVIEW OF THE U.S.-SOUTH KOREAN ECONOMIC RELATIONSHIP

Table 1. Annual U.S.-South Korea Merchandise Trade, Selected Years (Billions of U.S. Dollars)

Year	U.S. Exports	U.S. Imports	Trade balance	Total trade
1990	14.4	18.5	-4.1	32.9
1995	25.4	24.2	1.2	49.6
2000	26.3	39.8	-13.5	66.1
2003	22.5	36.9	-14.4	59.5
2004	25.0	45.1	-20.1	70.1
2005	26.2	43.2	-17.0	69.4
2006	30.8	44.7	-13.9	75.5
2007	33.0	45.4	-12.4	78.4
2008	33.1	46.7	-13.6	79.8
Major U.S. Export Items	Industrial machinery; chemicals; semiconductor circuits; corn & wheat; specialized instruments.			
Major U.S. Import Items	Cell phones; semiconductor circuits; cars & car parts; iron & steel.			

Sources: 1990 and 1995 data from Global Trade Information Services. 2000-2008 data from U.S. International Trade Commission.

South Korea is a major economic partner for the United States. In 2007, two-way trade between the two countries exceeded $78 billion, making South Korea the United States's seventh-largest trading partner. (See Table 1.) South Korea is among the United States's largest markets for agricultural products. Major U.S. exports to South Korea include semiconductors, machinery (particularly semiconductor production machinery), aircraft, and agricultural products.

South Korea is far more dependent economically on the United States than the United States is on South Korea. In 2007, the United States was South Korea's third-largest trading partner, second- largest export market, and the third-largest source of imports. It was among South Korea's largest suppliers of foreign direct investment (FDI). In 2003, China for the first time displaced the United States from its perennial place as South Korea's number one trading partner. In 2005 Japan overtook the United States to become South Korea's second-largest trade partner.

Increased economic interaction between the United States and South Korea has been accompanied by numerous disagreements over trade policies. In general, U.S. exporters and trade negotiators identify the lack of transparency of South Korea's trading and regulatory systems as the most significant barriers to trade with South Korea in almost every major product sector.

Table 2. Asymmetrical Economic Interdependence (2008)

	Total Trade	Export Market	Source of Imports	Source of FDI	
For the U.S., South Korea ranks	# 7	# 7	# 9	# 17	(2007)
For South Korea, the U.S. ranks	# 3	# 2	# 3	# 2	(2007)

Sources: U.S. Department of Commerce, U.S. Census Bureau and Bureau of Economic Analysis; Bank of Korea.

Many U.S. government officials also complain that Seoul continues to use government regulations and standard-setting powers to discriminate against foreign firms in politically sensitive industries, such as automobiles and telecommunications. Another major cross-sectoral complaint is that rigidities in the South Korean labor market, such as mandatory severance pay, raise the cost of investing and doing business. Finally, the United States and other countries have pressed South Korea to open further its agricultural market, which is considered one of the most closed among members of the Organization for Economic Co-operation and Development (OECD).11 Many of these issues arose during the KORUS FTA negotiations.

The intensity of these disputes has diminished considerably since the late 1980s and early 1990s, in part because South Korea enacted a set of sweeping market-oriented reforms as a quid pro quo for receiving a U.S.-led $58 billion package from the International Monetary Fund (IMF) following the near collapse of the South Korean economy in 1997. In particular, as a result of the reforms, South Korea opened its doors to foreign investors, ushering in billions of dollars of foreign portfolio and foreign direct investment (FDI). The result is that foreign companies, including U.S. firms, now are significant shareholders in many prominent industrial conglomerates (chaebol); at one point earlier in the decade, foreign firms owned about one-third of the South Korean banking industry and an estimated 40% of the value of the shares traded on South Korea's stock exchange. Since the 1997 crisis, FDI commitments by U.S. companies have totaled over $25 billion [12].

Additionally, the United States and South Korea appear to have become more adept at managing their trade disputes. This may be partly due to the quarterly, working-level "trade action agenda" trade meetings that were initiated in early 2001. Both sides credit the meetings, which appear to be unique to the U.S.-South Korean trade relationship, with creating a more constructive dialogue that helped pave the way for the two sides to feel sufficiently confident to launch FTA negotiations.

U.S. AND SOUTH KOREAN OBJECTIVES IN AN FTA

U.S. and South Korean policymakers shared certain goals in launching and completing the negotiations on the KORUS FTA. Both governments saw in the FTA a logical extension of an already important economic relationship that would provide a means by which the two trading partners could address and resolve fundamental issues and, thereby, raise the relationship to a higher level. For the United States these issues have included the high tariffs and other restrictions on agricultural imports. For South Korea, these difficult issues have included perceived U.S. discrimination toward South Korean imports in the application of trade remedies and treatment of products made at the Kaesong Industrial Complex in North Korea.

While sharing some broad objectives, U.S. and South Korean leaders also approached the KORUS FTA from different perspectives that were reflected in the conduct and outcome of the negotiations. A primary objective of the United States was to gain access to South Korean markets in agricultural products, pharmaceuticals and medical equipment, some other high-technology manufactured goods, and services, particularly financial and professional services— areas in which U.S. producers are internationally competitive but for which South Korean barriers seemed to be high.

For South Korea, gaining a large increase in market access was not as critical a priority since South Korean exporters already have a significant presence in areas in which they have proved to be competitive—consumer electronics and autos, for example, and in which they already face only low or zero U.S. tariffs. However, South Korea arguably did seek to preserve its share of the U.S. market in the face of growing competition from emerging East Asian producers from Thailand, Malaysia, Vietnam, and possibly China. South Korea likely also aimed to improve its competitive position in the U.S. market vis-a-vis Japan where the elimination of even low tariffs might give South Korean exporters some price advantage.

Launching the FTA negotiations was largely at the initiative of South Korea. Its main objective in securing an FTA with the United States was much broader than gaining reciprocal access to the U.S. market. Entering an FTA with the United States meshed with a number of former South Korean President Roh Moo-hyun's long term economic and strategic goals. Roh made an FTA the top economic priority for the remainder of his tenure, which expires in February 2008 [13]. Soon after his election in 2002, Roh committed himself to raising South Korea's per capita gross domestic product (GDP) to $20,000 by the end of the decade and to transforming South Korea into a major "economic hub" in Northeast Asia by expanding the economic reforms begun by his predecessor following the 1997 Asian financial crisis. Ongoing competitive pressure from Japanese firms, increased competition from

Chinese enterprises, and the rapid ageing of the South Korean workforce has heightened the sense of urgency about boosting national competitiveness. Continuing along this line of argument, ex-Prime Minister Han Duk-soo has said that a failure to adopt significant economic changes will mean that "Korea's long term growth potential is likely to deteriorate" [14]. Lee Myung-bak, who was elected President in December 2007, made the economy the centerpiece of his campaign and has supported the KORUS FTA as part of a larger program to promote South Korean economic growth.

During the negotiations, South Korean officials and other South Korean proponents of the KORUS FTA tended not to focus on the increased access to the U.S. market. Rather, they emphasized the medium and long-term gains that would stem from increased allocative efficiency of the South Korean economy, particularly in the services industries. This would presumably be brought about by an influx of U.S. investment and technology into South Korea and by the spur of increased competition with U.S. firms.15 The President and other senior officials in particular emphasized the need to boost the competitiveness of South Korean service industries. An FTA with the United States, they argued, will help address South Korea's increased economic polarization by spurring job creation in fields such as medical, legal, education, and accounting services in a free trade agreement [16]. Some, however, say an FTA will worsen South Korea's income gap [17]. Also, during the talks, there were continuous and often large scale anti-FTA protests, generally led by South Korean farmers and trade unionists.

The absence of mirror-image or reciprocal U.S. and South Korean objectives in the negotiations is reflected in the structure of the KORUS FTA. Except for some provisions dealing with issues specific to U.S.-South Korea economic relations, for example, South Korea taxation of autos and the *Kaesong* industrial complex, the structure of the KORUS FTA largely resembles the structure of other FTAs, such as Dominican Republic-Central American FTA (DR-CAFTA), that the United States has entered into.

This conclusion does not suggest that South Korea did not bring to the table its own specific demands, which it did (such as the exclusion of rice) and held to them firmly.

SECTOR-SPECIFIC ISSUES AND THE KORUS FTA

Under the KORUS FTA, U.S. and South Korean negotiators addressed a number of sector- specific issues. Some issues, such as elimination of tariffs on most manufactured goods, were not very controversial and were dealt with in early stages of the negotiations. Other issues, such as trade in agricultural products and in autos, were the most difficult and were not resolved until the final hours of the negotiations.

Agriculture and Sanitary and Phytosanitary Issues

Overview

Attaining comprehensive market access for U.S. agricultural products to South Korea's large market and finding a way to resolve Korea's continued restrictions on U.S. beef purchases (imposed to protect human health following the late 2003 discovery of mad cow disease in the U.S. cattle herd) were the two primary objectives pursued by U.S. agricultural negotiators. Though South Korea in 2007 was the 14th largest agricultural importer in the world, its farm sector is highly protected with high tariffs and quotas [18]. This reflects its farmers' longstanding political influence (particularly that of rice producers) and its urban population's deep ties to its rural roots.

In concluding the KORUS FTA, the United States secured nearly complete access for all U.S. agricultural commodities and food products into Korea's market. However, a breakthrough on the beef issue (technically not part of the FTA talks but nevertheless the subject of high-level discussions) did not occur until June 2008. This appears to reflected the newly elected Korean President's view that an agreement spelling out the rules that apply to beef imports from the United States had to be in place before President Bush could consider sending this agreement to Capitol Hill. Several Members of Congress had for months stated that South Korea must agree to fully reopen its market to U.S. beef under scientifically based international rules and in commercially significant quantities before Congress considers or approves the agreement. U.S. agricultural groups, well aware of this deal's potential benefits for producers, had also conditioned their support on the resumption of U.S. beef exports.

In 2008, South Korea was the 5th largest market for U.S. agriculture, as export sales totaled almost $5.6 billion. Under the KORUS FTA's agricultural provisions, South Korea immediately would grant duty-free status to almost two-thirds of current U.S. agricultural exports. Tariffs and tariff-rate quotas (TRQs) [19] on most other agricultural goods would be phased out within 10 years, with the remaining commodities and products subject to provisions that phase out such protection by year 23. Seven U.S. products (skim and whole milk powders, evaporated milk, in-season oranges, potatoes for table use, honey, and identity-preserved soybeans for food use) would be subject to Korean import quotas that slowly expand in perpetuity. However, the agreement does not give U.S. rice and rice products additional access to South Korea's market (see below) [20].

With the immediate elimination or phase out of most of South Korea's relatively high agricultural trade barriers under the KORUS FTA, the U.S. agricultural and food processing sectors would noticeably benefit from additional exports. The USITC estimates that the increase in U.S. exports of agricultural commodities and processed foods would account for up to one-third of the entire projected increase in total U.S. exports to South Korea's market once the KORUS FTA's provisions are fully implemented. Sale of agricultural products would be from $1.9 billion to $3.8 billion (44% to 89%) higher than exports under a no-agreement scenario. Almost half of this export increase would accrue to the U.S. beef sector, based on the USITC's assumption that U.S. beef exports recover to the level before South Korea imposed its restrictions import in late 2003. (For information on bilateral efforts that led to a mid-2008 agreement on new Korean rules that will apply to U.S. beef imports, see Appendix A.) About 20% of the export increase would benefit U.S. producers and exporters of pork, poultry and other meat products [21]. In another analysis, the American Farm Bureau Federation (AFBF) projects that U.S. agricultural exports by the end of the transition period (2027) would be more than $1.5 billion (45%) higher under the KORUS FTA than would be the case otherwise. Sales of beef, poultry, and pork would account for $644 million (or 42%) of this increase [22]

Because South Korean agricultural exports to the United States are small ($249 million in 2008) and largely complementary, there was no controversy in negotiating access to the U.S. market. The United States agreed to phase out tariffs and quotas on all agricultural imports from South Korea under seven phase-out periods ranging up to 15 years. One 10-year TRQ would apply to imports of fluid milk and cream, among other specified dairy products. The USITC projects that imports of agricultural products (primarily processed food products) from South Korea under the KORUS FTA would be from $52 million to $78 million (12% to 18%) higher than such imports under a no-agreement scenario.

Beef

Under the KORUS FTA, South Korea agreed to eliminate its 40% tariff on beef muscle meats imported from the United States over a 15 year period. Also, South Korea would have the right to impose safeguard tariffs on a temporary basis in response to any potential surge in imports of U.S. beef meats above specified levels. The trigger for this additional tariff would be 270,000 metric tons (MT) in year 1, which would increase 2% annually; in year 15, the trigger would be 354,000 MT [23]. In year 16, this protective mechanism would no longer apply. The 18% tariff on imports of beef offals (tongues, livers, tails and feet), and tariffs ranging from 22.5% to 72% on other beef products, would also be eliminated in 15 years.

Assuming that South Korea fully lifts its restrictions on U.S. beef and bilateral beef trade returns to normal, the USITC estimates that the phase out of South Korea's beef tariff and safeguard could increase U.S. beef exports from about $600 million to almost $1.8 billion (58% to 165%) above what would be the case otherwise. Under the KORUS FTA, the AFBF projects that U.S. beef sales would be $265 million higher as the United States recaptures its historic share of the South Korean market. However, its analysis notes that the market share of U.S. beef likely will not increase over time. That is because South Korean tastes have developed a preference for grass-fed Australian beef, which will continue to be competitive in price against U.S. beef even with the current 40% tariff removed.

On June 21, 2008, U.S. and South Korean negotiators reached agreement on the requirements that will apply to Korean imports of U.S. beef and beef products. Imports of boneless and in-bone beef, and other beef products, from cattle less than 30 months of age are allowed entry, but are subject to various conditions that U.S. beef exporters and the U.S. government must meet. This agreement occurred against the backdrop of mounting public protests in Korea against an earlier agreement, calls by opposition parties that the initial terms be renegotiated, and the Korean President's apologies for how his government mishandled this matter.

The Korean government secured these additional changes in order to allay public concerns about the safety of U.S. beef. Since mid-July 2008, U.S. beef sales have resumed, but have fluctuated for various reasons. The pace of future U.S. beef exports now will depend on how quickly Korean consumers resume purchases, in light of the controversy that swirled around this issue and of reduced purchasing power caused by the country's economic crisis. (See Appendix A for additional details.)

Rice

South Korean negotiators succeeded in excluding the entry of U.S. rice on preferential terms—its prime objective in negotiating agriculture in the KORUS FTA. This reflects Korea's efforts to maintain its stated policy of self sufficiency in rice production, the national sentiment that preserving rice production is inseparable from the country's identity, and the political reality that rice farming preserves the basis for economic activity in the countryside. That rice was a makeor-break issue for Seoul is seen in the comment made by a top U.S. trade official, Deputy United States Trade Representative Karan Bhatia, the day after the talks concluded: "Ultimately, the question that confronted us was whether to accept a very, very good albeit less perfect agreement or to lose the entire agreement because South Korea refused to move on rice." [24]. On rice, the KORUS FTA would only require South Korea to continue to abide by its multilateral trade commitments to increase rice imports.

At present, U.S. rice exporters have access to the South Korean market under (1) a 24% share (50,076 MT) of the rice import quota established under that country's multilateral World Trade Organization (WTO) commitments in 1995, and (2) a separate quota available to all countries [25]. Rice entering under both quotas faces a 5% tariff. Entries above each quota are prohibited—a unique concession that South Korea received in the last round of multilateral trade negotiations. U.S. rice exports against both quotas have fluctuated, but since 2005 have risen to reach $76 million (107,905 MT) in 2008. Future U.S. sales are expected to grow slowly in line with the expansion of the most recently established rice quota.

Though the U.S. rice industry expressed disappointment with the rice exclusion, the United States will have other opportunities in the future to negotiate access for additional U.S. rice in Korea's market. This could occur in the process of concluding a multilateral agreement (possibly by 2010) to further liberalize agricultural trade in the WTO's Doha Development Round, and might require South Korea to further open its rice market. Also, the United States and other rice exporting countries could press for additional access when Korea's current multilateral rice access provisions expire in 2014.

Oranges

Differences on how quickly to liberalize trade in fresh oranges were not resolved until just before the negotiations concluded. The United States sought the complete elimination of Korea's border protection on all citrus products, while South Korea wanted to retain its quotas and tariffs, primarily because of the importance of the citrus industry to the economy of Cheju Island. At present, South Korea imposes a 50% tariff on all imports of oranges, irrespective of whether they enter within or outside an existing TRQ.

In reaching a compromise, negotiators agreed to a multi-part solution. First, a small duty-free quota would be created for "in-season" U.S. navel oranges (a variety that is not produced in Korea) that would enter between September 1 and the end of February—a period that coincides with the Island's unshu (mandarin) orange harvest season. The initial 2,500 MT TRQ would increase at a compound 3% annual rate in perpetuity. Shipments in excess of this amount during this six-month period would continue to be subject to the 50% tariff. Second, in the first year, this high tariff would be reduced to 30% for "out-of-season" oranges that enter between March 1 and August 31, and then be completely phased out in stages by year 7. Third, South Korea's 144% tariff on mandarin oranges would be phased out over 15 years.

The cost of selling to what already is a leading U.S. export market for fresh oranges would be significantly reduced as Korea's high 50% tariff is phased out. In 2008, South Korea ranked second (after Canada), with U.S. sales totaling $90 million (100,883 MT). USDA estimates that the value of the in-season 2,500 MT quota and tariff reductions on all orange exports in the first year the agreement is in effect would be almost $18 million. Over seven years, USDA estimates the cumulative value of savings associated with these orange access provisions at $208 million [26].

Sanitary and Phytosanitary Provisions

As found in most other U.S. FTAs, the KORUS FTA establishes a bilateral standing committee to address food safety and animal/plant life or health issues that frequently emerge in agricultural trade. However, there are no commodity-specific sanitary and phytosanitary (SPS) provisions to address outstanding issues, such as Korea's import health requirements on U.S. beef imports or Korean standards that have prevented sales of some U.S. horticultural products to that market. The Committee on SPS Matters would serve as a forum to implement the WTO's Agreement on the Application of SPS Measures, enhance mutual understanding of each country's SPS rules, resolve future bilateral SPS disputes that arise, coordinate technical assistance programs, and consult on issues and positions in the WTO and other international bodies where SPS issues are considered. The text of the SPS chapter specifically states that neither the United States nor South Korea has recourse to pursue dispute settlement to address any SPS issue that arises. Instead, any matter would be resolved using the formal process established under the WTO's SPS Agreement.

U.S. beef producers had argued until the 2008 bilateral agreement was reached that Korea's stance on U.S. beef imports must be scientifically based upon internationally recognized guidelines issued by the World Organization for Animal Health, also known as OIE by its French acronym [27]. Other agricultural groups also have raised concerns about Korea's implementation of SPS measures on food additives and those that have restricted U.S. fruit and vegetable exports. This new standing committee potentially could be used as the venue to attempt to resolve future SPS disputes, taking into account latest available scientific findings and knowledge.

Autos

The export orientation of the South Korean motor industry, combined with the relatively low U.S. tariff of 2.5% on all imported motor vehicles except pickup trucks, has made the United States a good market of opportunity for South Korean exports. (For a discussion of the South Korean auto industry, see Appendix B.) Total Korean motor vehicle exports to the United States peaked at 860,000 units in 2004, according to U.S. Commerce Department data. It subsequently fell to 730,000 units in 2005, 695,000 units in 2006, and 675,000 units in 2007. There was a further decline of 8.7% in U.S. car and light truck imports from Korea, to 616,000 units in 2008 [28]. Hyundai has established a major U.S. assembly plant, thus substituting for some imports. Kia is also building a U.S. assembly plant expected to open in 2009 [29]. Falling imports from Korea probably were affected by a general softening of the U.S. market. U.S. exporters, including South Korean and other foreign-owned manufacturers, shipped a total of 13,654 vehicles to South Korea in 2008.

In terms of overall market share Hyundai and Kia have become more significant in recent years.

The total value of South Korean automotive exports to the United States, including parts, was $11.4 billion in 2008, compared to U.S. exports of similar products to South Korea of $791 million. That meant a U.S. bilateral deficit in autos of $10.6 billion, a little less than in 2007, but growing over the long term from a deficit of $5.5 billion in 2000, and $1.5 billion in 1990 [30]. Sang-yirl Nam, in an academic analysis of the effects of the proposed FTA, found in simulation models of projected market changes, Korea would always gain relative to the United States from bilateral liberalization, "because Korea has a comparative advantage over the United States in the automobile sector; in other words, Korea has been much more successful in accessing the U.S. market than the United States has been in accessing the Korean market." [31]

But Tom Walsh, writing in the Detroit Free Press, presents data to show that while the net U.S. bilateral automotive deficit will probably not decline substantially, the trends are favorable to the United States since 2004. Data attached to his article show that while the total value of U.S. imports from Korea rose by less than 1% from 2004 to 2007, the total value of U.S. exports in the other direction nearly doubled (up 87%) [32].

Through aggressive and successful marketing, Hyundai and Kia together have significantly increased U.S. market share during recessionary conditions in early 2009. Both brands saw small increases (for Hyundai, of both domestic and imported vehicles) in January-February 2009, even while the overall market declined by almost 40% compared to the same period in 2008. Their share of the U.S. market jumped from 4.3% in early 2008 to 7.3% in 2009.

By comparison, sales of Chevrolet's Aveo model, which is imported from Korea, fell by more than 50% during the period [33]. Part of Hyundai's success is attributed to the "Assurance" program, by which the company contracts to take back vehicles that it has sold to purchasers who subsequently lose their jobs in 2009. Both companies have also maintained sales by heavy use of incentives; Kia, in particular, doubled its incentives to more than $5,000 per model, second only to Chrysler among all brands in the U.S. market [34].

South Korean policies that allegedly restrict imports of foreign-made motor vehicles have been a major target of U.S. trade policy.

In 1995 and 1998, the USTR negotiated memoranda of understanding (MOUs) with South Korea, aimed at reducing formal and informal South Korean policies that were said to discriminate against imports of U.S.-made vehicles, and other foreign imports. U.S. policy primarily focused on motor vehicle taxation policies and South Korean motor vehicle standards, which supposedly did not conform to international standards, or those widely used in major markets [35].

The import share of the domestic market in South Korea has increased since the MOUs were signed—according to data calculated by CRS from standard industry sources cited above, total imports grew from a low of less than 1% of the market (5,000 units) in 2000 to a 3% market share by 2005.36 But such a rate of progress has evidently been too slow for both the U.S. government and the domestically owned motor vehicle industry.

Automotive Trade Provisions in KORUS FTA

The Office of the USTR states that KORUS FTA, "Includes a broad and unprecedented range of focused provisions designed to open up Korea's auto market to U.S. cars and ensure that U.S. automakers have a fair opportunity to compete in Korea." [37] These provisions may be summarized as follows:

- *Elimination of most South Korean tariffs on U.S.-made motor vehicles.* "Korea would immediately eliminate its 8% tariff on U.S.-built passenger cars and its 10% tariff on pickup trucks,"38 Tariffs would be immediately reduced to zero in each country for autoparts imported from the other [39]

- *Reduction of alleged discriminatory effects of engine displacement taxes.* A major U.S. complaint has been that South Korea has a steeply ascending vehicle tax schedule, with very high rates on vehicles with larger engine capacities, such as might be exported by U.S. producers. Moreover, the tax system has a "cascade" effect, so that subsequent taxation rates incorporate, for example, the 8% duty paid on an imported vehicle. According to the U.S. International Trade Commission (USITC) report on the agreement, 76% of the South Korean market is in vehicles with engine displacement less than 2000 cc, with 54% in the range 1601-2000 cc [40]. Currently, the consumer pays a "Special Consumption Tax" on purchase of a vehicle: cars below 800 cc are exempt, cars in the next range up to 2000 cc pay 5%, anything larger is charged 10%. After an interim reduction period of three years, South Korea under the FTA would simplify this to a two-tier system: under 1000 cc tax-free, anything larger would be taxed at 5%. Besides this purchase tax, owners must pay an "Annual Vehicle Tax," also based on engine displacement. Currently, there are five different ranges in this system, and the owner of a vehicle with an engine larger than the 1600-2000 cc market "sweet spot" pays an extra 10% per cc ownership tax. South Korea has agreed to simplify the ranges to three: 80 won/cc below 1000 cc engine capacity, 140 won/cc up to 1600 cc, and 200 won/cc for anything larger [41]. Both of these changes would include the majority of domestically produced cars, as well as imports, in the highest tax bracket.
- *Standards harmonization and creation of an "Automotive Working Group."* U.S. manufacturers have complained that South Korea sets safety regulations and automotive product standards in a manner that is closed to outsiders and not transparent, and that consequently results in standards idiosyncratic to Korea. South Korean-based producers, who hold the lion's share of the domestic market, can afford to operate one line for domestic production, and another for export. Foreign companies have difficulty affording the high unit cost of customizing a small number of vehicles for the South Korean market [42]. This problem is addressed in the KORUS FTA (Chapter 9—"Technical Barriers to Trade") and in an exchange of "confirmation letters" of June 30, 2007 between USTR Susan Schwab and South Korean Trade Minister Hyun Chung Kim. Essentially, the agreement provides for self-certification on safety and emissions standards for a limited number of U.S.-exported vehicles, and a commitment that South Korea will evaluate emissions using "the methodology applied by the State of California ..." [43] South Korea also agreed "not to adopt technical regulations that create unnecessary barriers to trade and to cooperate to harmonize standards."44 Under terms of Annex 9-B, the two parties agree to create an "Automotive Working Group," which will meet at least annually, and will review and resolve "issues with respect to developing, implementing and enforcing relevant standards, technical regulations and conformity assessment procedures." [45]
- *Elimination of U.S. tariffs and "snapback" clause.* The major commitment on the U.S. side with respect to automotive trade issues is the elimination of all tariffs on South Korean-produced motor vehicles. The United States would immediately eliminate its 2.5% duty on gasoline-fueled passenger vehicles with engine displacement up to 3000 cc. It would also phase out the same rate of duty on South Korean imports with larger engine capacity or that are diesel-powered over three

years. The 25% duty on pickup trucks, a residual rate dating from an earlier trade dispute with Europe, would be phased out on South Korean products over ten years [46]. However, the FTA, in Annex 22-A, also establishes a special bilateral dispute settlement panel, designed to resolve automotive issues within six months. "If panel finds a violation of an auto-related commitment or the nullification/impairment of expected benefits, the complaining Party may suspend its tariff concessions on passenger cars and assess duties at the prevailing MFN rate (i.e., 'snap-back' any tariff reductions provided by the FTA)." [47]. The USITC notes in its report that, "The dispute settlement provisions restrict the [U.S.] snapback penalty on light trucks ... to the rate for passenger cars, 2.5%," while South Korea could snap back to 8% [48].

Expected Impact and Industry Reaction

The USITC simulation model of the KORUS FTA estimates that while U.S. automotive exports to Korea would increase by a range of 45% to 59%, this would only amount to about $300-400 million because of the low current baseline [49]. It states that tariff elimination "would likely have a positive effect on U.S. exports ... further, the overall tax burden on the South Korean consumer who purchases an imported vehicle would be reduced, more or less equalizing the total taxes paid on imported and domestic vehicles." [50].

It particularly emphasizes the potential gain for U.S.- exported hybrid vehicles to Korea, though failing to note that most hybrids in the U.S. market today are imported from Japan [51]. However, as the Detroit-based U.S. manufacturers have plans to increase their hybrid fleets and there are no South Korean-produced hybrid vehicles at present, the U.S. manufacturers could have a head start on these products (assuming Japanese-owned companies in the United States do not also export hybrids from their incipient U.S. production to the South Korean market).

With respect to automotive imports from South Korea into the United States, the USITC simulation estimates an "increase by $1.3- 1.7 billion (9-12%)." However, it also finds that "approximately 55-57% [would be] represented by diverted imports from other trade partners" [52]. Jeffery Schott states that South Korea gave a "priority to eliminating the small U.S. tariff" primarily because of Japanese competition. Since 2001, the won has strengthened against the U.S. dollar, while the Japanese yen has weakened, creating a disadvantage in the U.S. market for Hyundai, whose vehicles must compete against Japanese companies' vehicles on price. One result has been reported significant declines in Hyundai earnings [53]. The USITC also notes plans by Hyundai to begin producing vehicles based on hybrid technology, indications that Hyundai and Kia were studying the development of pickup trucks, and actual exports of a small number of pickups to third markets by Ssangyong, a smaller producer [54]. Hyundai and Kia do already produce small pickup-type vehicles in Korea, but they would not appear to be suitable in design or style for the United States [55]

U.S. industrial interests' views on KORUS FTA may be described as follows:

- The Detroit "Big Three" are split. Ford and Chrysler are opposed, while General Motors (GM) is neutral.
- Automotive parts suppliers were reported to support the FTA.
- Broader-based industry organizations are favorable, despite the opposition of two major motor manufacturers and some other sectoral groups.

These views were reflected in the April 2007 report of the Industry Trade Advisory Committee on Automotive and Capital Goods (ITAC 2) to USTR of April 2007. The chair noted that,

> "Generally, the manufacturers of capital goods see [the FTA] as an important milestone in providing market access to a country and region historically protectionist.... However, in terms of U.S. automotive equipment manufacturers, the outcome is mixed." [56]

Both the U.S. motor vehicle industry representatives and the whole of ITAC 2 initially recommended an "unconventional" approach on automotive issues in the negotiations. It would have "precondion[ed] the phase-out of U.S. automotive tariffs on the demonstration of South Korean market openness in terms of improved import penetration that is on par with that of other OECD countries."

Fifteen Members of Congress, including Representative Charles Rangel, chair of the House Ways and Means Committee, wrote President Bush on March 2, 2007, with a proposal along the lines of the "performance metric" approach suggested by ITAC 2. Their proposal would have delayed full elimination of the U.S. import tariff cut for at least 15 years, while U.S. representatives assessed South Korea's performance in opening its market to U.S. exports. A formula would be used each year to determine the number of South Korean-produced vehicles that would receive duty-free treatment in return. They also proposed a "snapback" safeguard provision on the U.S. tariff should South Korean imports in the U.S. market be judged to increase too rapidly. The 25% U.S. tariff on pickup trucks would remain in place, subject to a multilateral agreement on automotive trade at the World Trade Organization [57].

Despite the fact that the final agreement did "not include a performance metric approach," most ITAC 2 members supported KORUS FTA anyway [58] The Ford Motor Company disagreed. In its statement appended to the report, Ford accepted that "some progress was achieved with respect to existing non-tariff barriers (NTBs)." But it noted that many of the exemptions for U.S.-made vehicles with respect to NTBs were very limited in volume or were temporary, that South Korea could continue to use a mix of U.S. and European standards, and that taxation rates were still exceptionally high for the types of product foreign companies would most likely export to South Korea. On the other hand, the immediate lifting of the U.S. 2.5% tariff on most South Korean imports would be a "lopsided benefit" that in effect "will reward South Korean manufacturers for 20 years of unfair trade practices by the South Korean Government" [59]. Similarly, a representative of Chrysler testified before Congress that, because of the "imbalance in U.S.-Korea auto trade ... we simply cannot support the U.S.-Korea Free Trade Agreement in its current form" [60].

By contrast, a GM statement appended to the ITAC-2 report concluded that the proposed FTA "has addressed the auto industry's concerns." But "given the current imbalance in trade between the two countries," GM foresaw that in the "near term" South Korea would be the greater beneficiary, and therefore GM would be neutral on the agreement. It noted that tax policy changes promised by the South Korean government would reduce the overall burden on the automotive sector and that there were no caps on U.S.-exported vehicles meeting compliance with California emission standards, because South Korea committed to establish emission requirements on the same basis. GM also commented that the sector-specific "snapback" rule on tariff reductions was a unique and positive addition to U.S. FTAs [61]. It should be added that GM's position is probably influenced by the fact that it has become a major investor in the South Korean motor industry through its acquisition of Daewoo. Since the acquisition, GM has increased Daewoo production from 310,000 in 2003 to 1.3 million in 2007 [62]. GM in 2007 sold 67,000 Chevrolet Aveos in the United States that were imported from its South Korean affiliate [63].

The United Auto Workers (UAW) union is strongly opposed to the FTA, and its literature on the subject includes a joint statement of opposition issued together with the South Korean Metal Workers' Union (KMWU) [64]. In testimony before the House Ways and Means Committee's Trade Subcommittee, UAW Legislative Director Alan Reuther endorsed the negotiating strategy proposed by Members of Congress, described above [65]. He stated that the final agreement as contemplated instead "would exacerbate the totally one-sided auto trade imbalance between South Korea and the U.S. and jeopardize the jobs of tens of thousands of American workers" [66]. Reuther further criticized the labor rights record of South Korea as "very problematic." He noted "numerous areas of worker rights violations in South Korea," cited in the U.S. Department of State's 2005 Country Reports on Human Rights Practices and the arrest of the KMWU president in 2006 in a protest against government efforts to change South Korean labor laws in a manner unfavorable to the union movement there. 67 In a February 2008 speech in Washington, UAW President Ron Gettelfinger criticized the proposed FTA in these terms: "That's not free trade and that's not fair trade. That is the theft of American jobs" [68] President Gettelfinger reiterated these views in testimony before Congress in September 2008 [69].

Both the management side and the labor side of the domestically owned U.S. automotive industry have used the word "unbalanced" to describe the benefits that may flow from the implementation of KORUS FTA. This may seem odd, given that the agreement has many provisions in various chapters dealing with specific South Korean policies and practices, and virtually none on the U.S. side, beyond the elimination of tariffs. This could be because the global competitive problems currently affecting the unionized, domestically owned sector of the U.S. motor vehicle industry go well beyond the scope of this FTA to solve [70]. Indeed, given major differences in the profiles of the U.S. and South Korean motor vehicle markets, it would appear unlikely that the Detroit Big Three, which tend to specialize domestically in the production of larger vehicles, could ever gain more than a fractional position there through exports from the United States. Thus, the UAW, Ford, and Chrysler oppose KORUS FTA as potentially only adding to the severe competitive pressure their side of the domestic U.S. industry is facing. GM has secured a solid investment position in South Korea that it is integrating into its global strategy. But possibly it may not want to antagonize its unionized U.S. employees, and has taken a neutral position.

Textiles and Apparel

Textiles and apparel are a small and dwindling portion of U.S. imports from South Korea. In 2007, textiles accounted for 2.2% of total U.S. imports from South Korea and apparel accounted for 1.5%. In 2007, the United States imported $0.7 billion in apparel and $1.0 billion in textiles from South Korea. South Korea's shares of the U.S. market for textiles and apparel has shrunk in relative and absolute terms over the years. In 1991, for example, South Korea was the fourth largest source of U.S. imports of apparel with an 8.0% share, but by

2007, it had dropped to the 27th largest source with a 0.8% share. This decrease came largely as the result of the surge in China's share of U.S. apparel imports, which grew from 15.1% in 1991, to 33.8% in 2007. South Korea's share of U.S. imports of textiles has held relatively steady. In 1991, South Korea was the 3rd largest source of U.S. textile imports with 8.4% but had dropped to the 4th largest source with 7.5% by 2007 [71]. The United States exports small volumes of textiles and apparel to South Korea—$74.9 million of apparel and $279.2 million of textiles in 2007 [72].

KORUS FTA would eliminate U.S. tariffs immediately on 52% (in terms of value) U.S. imports of South Korean textiles and apparel, and would phase out U.S. tariffs on 21% over five years and on the remaining 27% over 10 years [73]. Currently, the average U.S. MFN tariff on textiles is 7.9% with a maximum applied tariff of 34.0% and with 16.1% of textiles categories already entering the United States duty free. The average applied U.S. MFN tariff on apparel imports is 11.5% with a maximum tariff of 32%, and 3.3% of the tariff lines entering duty free [74].

The average South Korean applied tariff on textiles is 9.2% with a maximum of 13% and 0.3% of tariff lines entering duty free. The average South Korean tariff on apparel is 12.6% with none entering duty free and with a maximum tariff of 1 3% [75]. The KORUS FTA, would eliminate South Korean tariffs immediately on 77% (by value) of U.S. exports of textiles and apparel and would phase out tariffs on 13% over three years and the remaining 10% over five years [76].

The KORUS FTA, with some exceptions, would use the yarn-forward rule of origin for apparel imports; that is, apparel made from yarn or fabric originating in either the United States or South Korea would be eligible for duty-free treatment under the FTA. The FTA also includes a special safeguard provision whereby, if imports of textiles or wearing apparel to one KORUS FTA partner country from the other increases at such a rate as to cause or threaten to cause serious injury to the domestic industry of the importing country, the importing country can suspend further reduction of tariffs, or it can increase the duty on the imported product to (the lesser of) the MFN rate applicable at the time the action was taken or the MFN duty that was in force when the FTA went into effect.

The safeguard action can be in place for two years with a possible extension of two years but no more than a total of four years. However, the importing country will have to compensate the exporting country by making additional trade liberalizing concessions equivalent in value to the additional duties expected to result from the safeguard action. The concessions would be limited to textiles and apparel unless the two countries agree otherwise.

The USITC has estimated that, if implemented, the KORUS FTA would over time lead to an increase in U.S. imports of South Korean textiles of $1.7 billion to $1.8 billion and of apparel of $1.0 billion to $1.2 billion, with the major portion of the increase being diverted from other countries. The USITC also has estimated that KORUS FTA would lead to an increase in U.S. exports of textiles of $130 million to $140 million and of apparel of $39 million to $45 million to South Korea [77]. The KORUS FTA would allow some fibers, yarns, and fabrics originating outside of the United States and South Korea to become eligible for preferential treatment if the product is not available domestically in commercial quantities in either country. The agreement also provides for the establishment of a Committee on Textile and Apparel Trade Matters to raise concerns under the FTA regarding mutual trade in these products. The textile and apparel industry appears split on their views of the KORUS FTA according to the Industry Trade Advisory Committee on Textiles and Clothing (ITAC-

13) [78]. Some representatives of the textile producers support the yarn-forward rule as benefitting their industry and also conforming to provisions in other U.S. FTAs but also argue that it should be broader by including sewing thread, narrow fabrics and pocketing fabrics, which are excluded from the rule. Others, including some textile representatives and representatives from the apparel industry with supply chains in other countries, have criticized the yarn-forward rule as being restrictive and limiting trade opportunities. Members of the industry are also divided on the lack of cumulation provisions in the FTA, that is provisions which allow preferential treatment for limited amounts of apparel woven from components outside the FTA area. Textile producers supported the lack of cumulation provisions while apparel producers would have wanted them included. They also split on the phase-out periods for tariffs with textile producers arguing that some sensitive products were given immediate duty-free treatment. Apparel producers argued that all apparel and textiles should have been given immediate duty-free treatment. Footwear and travel goods are also covered under the FTA. Producers of both categories strongly support the FTA and how their products would be treated [79].

Other Manufactured Goods

The provisions of KORUS FTA affect a wide range of other industries beyond the automotive sector and textiles and apparel. Cross-sectoral trade associations that represent broad ranges of U.S. manufacturers have indicated their support for the agreement, not only because of the general elimination of South Korean tariffs on U.S. exports, but also because of such provisions as those promising to increase cooperation in the reduction of technical barriers to trade and the improvement in South Korea of the protection of U.S. companies' intellectual property rights [80]. Similarly, most sectoral trade associations expressed support, although some noted reservations with specific provisions [81]. The steel industry in particular was a notable dissenter.

Capital Goods Machinery and Equipment
U.S. machinery exports could be the largest single sectoral gainer from the FTA with South Korea. According to the USITC's simulation analysis, the sector stands to gain nearly $3 billion in exports if the agreement is approved [82]. The tariffs on U.S. machinery and equipment imported into South Korea range from 3% to 13%, but U.S. products are already competitive in many cases, and already account for 15-20% of total South Korean imports. (A specific example is U.S.-made computer-numerically controlled machine tools.) Most machinery tariffs would be immediately eliminated; others would be phased out over three to ten years [83].

As noted in the previous section on autos, the capital goods machinery industry representatives in ITAC 2 split with the motor vehicle industry representatives and supported the agreement. The ITAC report specifically cited, "U.S. manufacturers of electrical equipment [who] will benefit substantially by South Korean tariff reductions and eliminations, where the sector has already returned to running a trade surplus with South Korea." [84]. The USITC report further noted the export potential of electrical-power generating equipment, for which South Korean duties range up to 8% currently. U.S. exporters are nonetheless already leading suppliers of turbines, generators and nuclear reactors to South Korea [85]. The National Electrical Manufacturers Association (NEA) stated that U.S. exports to South Korea had risen steadily, by a total of 62%, since 2002, and that there was a U.S. surplus in bilateral trade. It calls for:

> legislators in both countries to ratify the Agreement as soon as possible. While the U.S. electrical equipment industry still has concerns relating to non-tariff barriers and intellectual property protection in South Korea, the overall FTA package would improve conditions for selling there by featuring the elimination—most of it immediate—of remaining tariffs on goods in NEA's product scope [86]

Another major capital goods item in which the United States has a strong bilateral trade position is aircraft. Total 2006 aircraft and parts exports to South Korea were $2.4 billion. However, civilian aircraft imports are already duty-free in South Korea [87]

Electronic Products and Components

Both South Korean and U.S. tariffs on most electronics products, such as semiconductors, telecommunications equipment, and computers, are already zero, as they are included in the multilateral Information Technology Agreement eliminating tariffs among more than 50 countries. The United States already has a substantial surplus with South Korea in semiconductors: $4.3 billion in 2006 exports, versus $2.9 billion in imports. The United States has a small deficit in computer equipment, plus large imports of computer and office equipment parts and accessories ($2.1 billion) and communications equipment ($5.6 billion) [88]

Sectoral organizations representing these industries supported KORUS FTA. It was argued the FTA would extend tariff-free treatment to consumer electronics products and could guarantee improvements for U.S. products in South Korea with respect to intellectual property protection, technical barriers, government procurement and competition policy [89]

One information technology organization supportive of KORUS FTA, the Semiconductor Industry Association, did caution that the trade remedies chapter of KORUS FTA could undermine U.S. industry's use of antidumping and countervailing duty (AD-CVD.) laws (see below). In 2003, the USITC found that Micron Corporation, the last remaining U.S.-based producer of dynamic random access mode semiconductors (DRAMs, widely used as memory chips in computers) was materially injured by government-subsidized DRAM semiconductors produced by Hynix Corporation of Korea. The Commerce Department subsequently established a 44% penalty tariff on Hynix DRAMs imported into the United States [90]

Steel

The American steel industry registered a strongly negative position on KORUS FTA through its industry advisory body to USTR, ITAC 12 (Steel). Its report noted that the agreement "does not provide for changes in U.S. AD-CVD statutes" and that each party retains its full rights under World Trade Organization rules. However, ITAC 12 objected to "changes to the related legal processes" in the KORUS FTA chapter on trade remedies with respect to three "key areas:"

- By Article 10.7.3, parties are required to notify each other whenever an AD-CVD application is filed, and prior to initiation of a formal investigation. They must afford the other government an opportunity to consult on the application. The steel industry

objects to "improperly politicizing] the consideration of a trade remedy provision filed by a U.S. industry, in a process that is already transparent and open," particularly in antidumping cases.
- In Article 10.4, either party must afford to the other an adequate opportunity for, and due consideration of price undertakings by respondent companies, "which, if accepted may result in suspension of an investigation" without imposition of penalty duties. The steel industry is concerned that the provision "would encourage the use of suspension agreements and the injection of foreign governments into the trade law process."
- The steel industry opposes the provision to establish a bilateral Commission on Trade Remedies (Article 10.8) as "unprecedented, unnecessary and would provide yet more opportunities for South Korea to weaken U.S. trade law enforcement." [91]

The specific details of the trade remedies chapter are discussed elsewhere in this report. Beyond these specific issues ITAC 12 also made a number of other critical points. It argued that the rules of origin provisions did not follow earlier precedents and there were concerns with products eventually being produced in the Kaesong Industrial Complex of North Korea. (See the section on the Kaesong Industrial Complex.) It objected to the proposed KORUS FTA's ignoring currency manipulation issues. They also supported their U.S. automotive customers' view that the FTA failed to insure adequately access to the South Korean market for U.S.-made motor vehicles. On these grounds, "especially with regard to the proposed AD-CVD provisions, ITAC 12 cannot conclude at this time that the KORUS FTA promotes the economic interests of the United States and provides for equity and reciprocity within the steel sector" [92].

Pharmaceuticals and Medical Devices

While pharmaceuticals and medical devices (P&M) are a relatively small part of U.S.-South Korean trade, they are products in which U.S. producers compete well in the South Korean market and ones in which manufacturers see increasing export opportunities as the South Korean economy matures. For years, the U.S. industry and government have complained about a number of South Korea's pharmaceutical policies that allegedly are designed to protect South Korean industry, which predominately produces generic drugs.

South Korea is among the world's top 12 largest markets for pharmaceuticals, accounting for about $8 billion in sales annually [93]. The South Korean market for medical devices accounts for roughly $2.5 billion in sales annually and is expected to grow 10-15 % each year in the next several years, in part due to the rapid aging of the population [94]. While potentially lucrative, South Korea is a market in which U.S. P&M manufactures claim government regulations have limited their ability to penetrate that market.

In 2007, the United States exported $580 million in medical devices to South Korea, accounting for 2.3% of total U.S. exports of those products and 1.7% of total U.S. exports to South Korea. In 2007, the United States exported $373 million in pharmaceuticals to South Korea accounting for 1.0% of total U.S. exports of pharmaceuticals and 1.1% of total U.S. exports to South Korea. In the same year South Korea exported $245 million in medical devices and $128 million in pharmaceuticals to the United States [95]

Of major concern was the South Korean government's May 2006 change in how it determined reimbursement amounts. Prior to the change, it maintained a "negative list" system, under which products would be eligible for reimbursement unless they appeared on the list. With the change, the South Korean government has switched to a "positive list" requiring a product to be listed before it would be eligible making it potentially more difficult for a product to become eligible. Announcement of the policy came without prior notification to U.S. officials or affected U.S. manufacturers and occurred at an early point in the negotiations placing a cloud over them. Despite complaints from the United States, South Korea went ahead with implementing its positive list system.

P&M manufacturers also have cited the South Korean government's policies on reimbursements for pharmaceuticals and medical devices under its single-payer health insurance program. U.S. manufacturers have argued that the policies discriminate against innovative pharmaceuticals because they establish relatively low reimbursement amounts for medicines thus not taking into account the costs that producers of leading-edge pharmaceuticals incur and that are reflected in higher prices. The manufacturers wanted the KORUS FTA to establish transparency as an important principal in South Korea's development and implementation of reimbursement policies, including an appeal process for decisions going against U.S. manufacturers.

In response, South Korea agreed in the KORUS FTA to allow U.S. pharmaceutical makers to apply for increased reimbursement levels based on safety and efficacy. South Korea also agreed to publish proposed laws, regulations, and procedures that apply to the pricing, reimbursement, and regulation of pharmaceuticals and medical devices in a nationally available publication and to allow time for comment. In addition, South Korea agreed to establish a process for U.S. manufacturers to comment on proposed changes in laws and regulations and for them to obtain a review of administrative determinations that adversely affect them.

Intellectual property rights protection in South Korea has been a critical issue for U.S. pharmaceutical manufacturers. Specifically, the failure of the South Korean government to protect from competitors proprietary data that manufacturers must submit for market approval. In addition, the South Korean government has, in some cases, approved marketing of some pharmaceuticals before it has determined that the applicant is the rightful owner of the patent and trademark [96]. In part for these reasons, the USTR has continued to place South Korea on the special 301 "Watch List" [97].

In response, under the KORUS FTA's data exclusivity provisions, South Korea would not allow a third company, such as a generic drug manufacturer, from marketing a new pharmaceutical using the safety and efficacy data, supplied by an original U.S. manufacturer as part of the market approval process, without the permission of the original U.S. maker for five years from the date of marketing approval for the original product. In addition, if a third party submits safety or efficacy information for a product that an FTA partner government had already approved, the government is to notify the original patent holder of the identity of the third party and is to prevent the marketing of the third party's product on its territory if permission had not been granted by the original patent holder. In a side letter, the United States and South Korea agreed to not invoke the data exclusivity provision until the FTA has been in effect 18 months. Furthermore, South Korea agreed of a patent-linkage system; that is, neither government is to approve the marketing to a generic drug while the original patent is still in effect. Another provision, known as patent-term extension, would require each FTA government to adjust the length of the effective period for patents on pharmaceuticals to take into account delays incurred in receiving patent approval and marketing approval. The KORUS FTA states that no provision would prevent either government from taking measures to protect the public health of its residents from HIV/AID, tuberculosis, malaria, and other epidemics, by ensuring access to medicines. The FTA would reaffirm each country's commitment to the WTO TRIPS/heath Declaration.

Reactions within the pharmaceutical and medical devices industries were somewhat split on the KORUS FTA. Makers of innovative products supported the provisions that are designed to preserve the rights of patent holders and provisions that are designed to make the South Korean regulatory, pricing, and reimbursement process more transparent and open to comments and procedural reviews. At the same time, industry representatives remain critical of South Korea's new reimbursement procedures and argue that the new system does not take into account the benefits of innovative drugs that cause drug prices to be higher. Generic drug manufacturers argue that the KORUS FTA does not contain provisions guaranteeing the availability of affordable drugs [98]

Financial and Other Services

South Korea was the seventh largest U.S. market for cross-border trade in services in 2007 [99]. U.S. service providers exported $13.6 billion in services to South Korea. Among them were South Korea travel to the United States ($2.5 billion) other transportation, such as freight services ($3.1 billion); royalties and license fees ($2.5 billion); and other private services, such as professional services, business services, banking, insurance, and other financial services ($4.5 billion) [100]. However, this amount probably undervalues the total volume of U.S. sales of services to South Korea as services are also sold through three other modes of delivery: by U.S. companies with a long-term presence in South Korea, by U.S. providers to South Korean residents located temporarily in the United States; and by U.S. providers temporarily located in South Korea.

In 2007, the United States imported $8.9 billion in services, including other transportation ($3.2 billion), U.S. travel to South Korea ($1.1 billion), expenditures by U.S. military ($2.3 billion), and other travel ($1.1 billion) [101]. This figure does not include services sold to U.S. residents by South Korean firms through the other modes of delivery.

U.S.-South Korean trade in services cuts across several chapters of the KORUS FTA—Chapter 12 (cross-border trade in services); chapter 13 (financial services); and Chapter 15 (telecommunications); chapter 11 (foreign investment); among others. A major U.S. objective in the KORUS FTA negotiations was to obtain South Korean commitments to reduce barriers to trade and investment in its services sector, especially in professional, financial, and telecommunications services.

In general the two countries would commit to:

- provide national treatment and most-favored-nation treatment to the services imports from each other;
- promote transparency in the development and implementation of regulations in services providing timely notice of decisions on government permission to sell services;

- prohibit limits on market access, such as a caps on the number of service providers, on the total value of services provided, on the total quantity of services provided, and on the total number of persons that can be employed by services providers;
- prohibit foreign direct investment requirements, such as export and local content requirements and employment mandates; and
- prohibit restrictions on the type of business entity through which a service provider could provide a service.

U.S. and South Korean negotiators agreed to several concepts under the KORUS FTA that could apply the agreements provisions to a broad scope of services. The two countries agreed to the "negative list" approach in making commitments in services. That is, the KORUS FTA is to apply to all types of services unless identified as an exception in the relevant annexes. In addition, the commitments are ratcheted—when new services emerge in the U.S. or South Korean economies, those services are automatically covered by the FTA unless identified as an exception; if either country unilaterally liberalizes a measure that it had listed as an exemption, it is automatically covered under the FTA. Furthermore, if one KORUS FTA partner extends preferential treatment to service providers from a third country under another FTA, it is to extend the preferential treatment to its KORUS FTA partner.

The United States sought greater reciprocity in the treatment of professional services and thereby gain increased access to the South Korean market for U.S. providers. The United States and South Korea agreed to form a professional services working group to develop methods to recognize mutual standards and criteria for the licensing of professional service providers. Under the KORUS FTA, South Korea would allow U.S. law firms to establish representative offices in South Korea no later than two years after the KORUS FTA entered into force. South Korea would also permit U.S. legal representative offices to establish cooperative operations with a South Korean firm to handle matters pertaining to domestic and foreign legal matters, and, no later than five years after the agreement's entry into force, would allow U.S. law firms to establish joint ventures with South Korean firms. However, South Korea would still reserve the right to restrict the activities of foreign lawyers.

Regarding financial services, under the KORUS FTA, if a domestic provider in one partner country develops and sells a new financial service in its home market, providers from the FTA partner country would be able to sell a like service in that market. The agreement would allow an FTA partner government to impose restrictions on the sale of financial services by providers from the other partner country for prudential reasons, for example, to protect investors, depositors, policy holders, or persons to whom a fiduciary duty is owed. The FTA would also permit either partner government to restrict monetary transfers in order to ensure the soundness of financial institutions.

The South Korean insurance market is the seventh largest in the world. The USITC estimates, therefore, that U.S. insurers would be poised to obtain sizeable gains in a liberalized South Korean services market [102]. U.S. insurance companies have been concerned that the state-owned Korea Post and the cooperative insurance providers—the National Agricultural Cooperative Federation and the National Federation of Fisheries Cooperative—are not regulated by the Korean Financial Supervisory Commission or by the Financial Supervisory Service, while both private-sector foreign and domestic providers are so regulated [103]. Under the KORUS FTA, South Korea agreed that those entities would be subject to an independent state regulator as opposed to being self-regulated [104]. In addition,

Korea Post would not be allowed to offer new insurance products. The two countries would allow a partner country financial services provider to transfer electronically information from its territory as necessary in the course of doing business [105]. This is a provision that the U.S. industry highlighted as being particularly important.

In telecommunications services, South Korea would reduce government restrictions on foreign ownership of South Korean telecommunications companies. Two years after the KORUS FTA enters into force, U.S. companies would be able to own up to 100% of voting shares in domestic South Korean telecommunications companies, and those companies would be able to own up to 100% of a facilities-based licensee [106]. These provisions do not apply to KT Corporation nor to SL Telecom Co for which a 49% foreign ownership limit would remain. In addition, each KORUS FTA partner would ensure that telecommunications providers from the other would have access to and use of its public telecommunications network for purposes of interconnection under nondiscriminatory conditions and would guarantee dialing portability among other conditions [107].

Those who represent U.S. services providers have been enthusiastic about the KORUS FTA and have urged its approval. In a statement, Robert Vastine, President of the Coalition of Services Industries claimed:

> We commend Ambassador Schwab and the team of negotiators who secured significant benefits for U.S. services providers in this agreement.... Korea is a key market for U.S. service companies, and this is a very high-quality agreement that merits swift passage by the Congress because it creates new commercial opportunities that will support new jobs [108]

Visas

For years, a priority for South Korea has been to convince the United States to ease restrictions on the issuance of visas for South Korean business representatives. The visa issue—along with South Korea's request to be added to the Visa Waiver program (VWP), which allows visa free travel for short-term visitors—was addressed in discussions outside of the KORUS FTA negotiations. On October 17, 2008, President Bush announced that South Korea was one of seven countries that would be admitted into the program in 4-6 weeks [109]. With this step, the VWP is likely to no longer be an issue in bilateral relations. South Korea is one of the United States' largest sources of foreign visitors. In FY2007 there were 811,251 short term visitors for business or pleasure from South Korea [110]

GENERAL PROVISIONS

The KORUS FTA text contains a number of provisions that cut across in many sectors in bilateral trade. Many of these provisions have become standard fare and have become part of the template for FTAs in which the United States participates.

Trade Remedies [111]

Trade remedies, laws and actions designed to provide relief to domestic industries that have been injured or threatened with injury by imports, are regarded by many in Congress as an important trade policy tool to mitigate the adverse effects of lower priced imports on U.S. industries and workers.

The three most commonly used trade remedies are antidumping (AD), countervailing duty (CVD), and safeguard actions. Antidumping (19 U.S.C. § 1673 et seq.) actions provide relief from the adverse impact of imports sold at prices shown to be less than fair market value, and countervailing duty (19 U.S.C. § 1671 et seq.) actions provide similar relief from goods that have been subsidized by a foreign government or other public entity. Safeguard actions (19 U.S.C. § 2251 et seq.) are designed to give domestic industries an opportunity to adjust to new competition and are triggered by import surges of fairly traded goods. The relief provided in a safeguard case is a temporary import duty, temporary import quota, or a combination of both, while the relief in an antidumping or countervailing duty action is an additional duty placed on the dumped or subsidized imports. These actions are authorized by the WTO as long as they are consistent with the rights and obligations of Article XIX of the General Agreement on Tariffs and Trade (GATT) 1994, the WTO Agreement on Safeguards and Countervailing Measures (Subsidies Agreement), and the WTO Agreement on Implementation of Article VI of the GATT 1994 (Antidumping Agreement) [112].

Many Members of Congress have expressed support for maintaining and strengthening U.S. trade remedy laws in the face of growing import competition. As a result, the preservation of U.S. authority to "enforce rigorously its trade laws" was a principal negotiating objective included in presidential Trade Promotion Authority (TPA) in the 107th Congress [113]

According to news reports, the "single most important South Korean demand" in the bilateral talks was changes to U.S. antidumping rules [114]. This may be due, in part, to the significant number of U.S. trade remedy cases brought by U.S. industries on South Korean goods. As of September 10, 2008, antidumping duties were being collected on 15 South Korean imports (mostly on stainless steel specialty products such wire rod and pipe fittings), and countervailing duties were being assessed on 5 South Korean products, while South Korea had 2 antidumping measures in place against U.S. products [115]. The U.S. global safeguard cases imposed on steel in February 2000 (line pipe) and March 2002 (many steel products) also significantly reduced South Korean steel imports to the United States [116]. Of the 13 WTO dispute resolution complainant cases South Korea has brought to date, seven have been disputes against U.S. trade remedy actions [117]. South Korea is also a member "Friends of Antidumping" group in the WTO Doha Round that insists on implementing changes to the Antidumping and Subsidies Agreements in any new multilateral agreement.

In the bilateral negotiations between the United States and South Korea, talks broke down in early December 2006 when South Korea presented the United States with a list of specific changes to U.S. antidumping laws on a "basically" take-it-or-leave-it basis, [118] but in mid-January 2007, South Korean officials softened their stance after accepting the assurances of U.S. negotiators that Trade Promotion Authority had granted the Bush Administration only limited flexibility to make concessions on trade remedy issues [119].

The KORUS FTA, just as in earlier FTAs the United States has entered into, proposes that each party to the agreement would retain all rights and obligations under the WTO agreements—meaning that the trading partners would be permitted to include each other in global safeguard actions (although, as in other FTAs, it does extend a possible exemption from global safeguard measures to either party if its imports are not a substantial cause of serious injury) and to implement AD and CVD actions against each other. Additionally, as in earlier FTAs, the trade remedies article would also authorize either party to the agreement to apply a transitional safeguard measure against imports of the other party if, as the result of the reduction or elimination of a duty mandated by the agreement, a product is being imported in increased quantities as to be a substantial cause of serious injury to a domestic industry that produces a like or directly competitive good [120]

In the case of a safeguard, the party imposing it must provide a mutually agreed-upon amount of compensation. If the parties do not agree, the other party may suspend concessions on imports of the other party in an amount that has trade effects substantially equivalent to the safeguard measure [121].

As such, the agreement does not seem to require any changes to U.S. AD, CVD, or global safeguard laws, or substantially change administrative procedures required to implement these actions [122]. However, in an apparent departure from previous FTAs, the KORUS FTA seems to require a few additional administrative steps prior to initiation of a trade remedy investigation involving goods from the other party. First, each party would have to notify the other if an antidumping petition is received regarding the other party's imports, as well as provide an opportunity for a meeting between the parties before an investigation is initiated [123]. Additionally, the party initiating an AD or CVD investigation would be required to provide written information regarding its procedures for negotiating a price or quantity undertaking (known in U.S. law as a suspension agreement [124]), and, after a preliminary affirmative determination is reached, "provide due consideration and adequate opportunity for consultations regarding proposed price undertakings" which could result in suspension of the investigation without imposition of duties provided a mutually agreeable undertaking is reached. [125]

The KORUS FTA would also establish a Committee on Trade Remedies (which would meet at least once a year) made up of representatives from each party who have responsibility for trade remedies matters. Committee functions would include enhancing knowledge of the parties' trade remedy laws and practices, overseeing the implementation of the trade remedies chapter of the agreement, improving cooperation between the parties, developing educational programs on trade remedy laws, and providing a forum for exchange of information on trade remedies and other topics of mutual interest [126].

As discussed earlier, the Industry Trade Advisory Committee on Steel (ITAC 12) believes that the procedural concessions made on trade remedies could politicize trade remedy actions, thus possibly weakening U.S. trade laws. In particular, the ITAC 12 stated that the U.S. AD-CVD investigative process is already transparent and that the pre-initiation notification and consultation requirements would delay and politicize the process [127]. It also objected to the "undertakings" provisions, saying that these provisions would encourage the use of suspension agreements and introduce actions of foreign governments into trade remedy procedures [128]. (For more information on the steel industry's reaction, see discussion in section on "Other Manufactured Goods.")

The ITAC 12 also opposes the establishment of a Committee on Trade Remedies, saying that it such a forum would give South Korea an opportunity to attempt to further try to weaken U.S. trade remedy laws [129]. Speaking in April 2007, Assistant U.S. Trade Representative for Korea, Japan, and APEC Wendy Cutler, the chief U.S. negotiator, implied that the consultative committee would focus on information sharing and "will not provide a forum to discuss specific cases." [130]. She also mentioned that the committee could be a benefit to the United States by providing a platform for discussing certain industrial subsidies that the South Korean government may be supplying to manufacturing firms, and that negotiators worked out an "accommodation" that was beneficial to both sides' needs on a very contentious part of the negotiations [131]

Kaesong Industrial Complex [132]

A consistent and significant goal for South Korea in the FTA talks was securing preferential treatment for products made in the Kaesong Industrial Complex (KIC) in North Korea, a position the United States adamantly throughout most of the negotiations. Located near the North Korean city of Kaesong (also spelled "Gaesong"), 40 miles north of Seoul, the KIC is designed for South Korean companies to employ North Korean workers. The factories of 15 South Korean manufacturing firms began operating when the site opened in 2004. As of November 2007, this number had increased to 52 firms, which employed about 20,000 North Korean workers. There are plans to expand the zone dramatically. The South Korean Unification Ministry expects that by the end of 2010, about 450 South Korean manufacturers and 100,000 North Korean workers will be in the KIC [133]. The KIC arguably has become the centerpiece for South Korea's "sunshine policy" of engaging North Korea.

In the final KORUS FTA agreement, the two sides reached a compromise on the KIC. One year after the KORUS FTA enters into force, a binational committee will be formed to study the possibility of eventually including products from "Outward Processing Zones" (OPZs) using North Korean labor sometime in the future [134]. The agreement identifies three general categories for which the committee is to develop more detailed criteria: progress in the denuclearization of North Korea, developments in intra-Korean relations; and wages, the environment, and labor standards. For the third category of issues, the committee is to consider relevant international norms as well as the "situation prevailing elsewhere on the Peninsula." After the committee has developed criteria, the OPZ provisions in the FTA lay out a three step process by which products made in the KIC could be incorporated into the FTA. First, the committee must deem that an outward processing zone meets the criteria it has established. Second, the two governments must agree that the FTA should be amended accordingly. Third, each government must seek "legislative approval for any amendments to the Agreement with respect to outward processing zones." The agreement does not lay out the size or composition of the committee, or how committee members will be chosen, or the procedures by which the committee is to arrive at decisions [135]

In the KORUS FTA negotiations, the United States backed away from the principle of its initial position of not ever expanding the KORUS FTA to North Korea-made products, a significant achievement for South Korea. At the same time, the United States appeared to give up little in substance in the near-to-middle term. The United States apparently would be able to control the decision to and pace of any move to grant preferential treatment to North Korea-made products. Any perceptions of foot-dragging by the United States, however, may come at a diplomatic price if future South Korean governments push for more rapid integration of North Korean industrial zones into the FTA.

Two important issues for the United States in considering South Korea's demand were the conditions for North Korean workers and the income the KIC provides for the North Korean government. Some U.S. labor and human rights advocates have argued that North Korean workers in Kaesong are being exploited. South Korean officials, as well as other analysts, counter by saying that conditions at Kaesong are far better than those in the rest of North Korea. Additionally, the North Korean government derives hard currency from several sources in the KIC project, including leasing fees and surcharges levied on North Korean workers' wages, which are paid to an arm of the North Korean government agency before being passed on to employees (in the form of North Korean won). To date, these revenue streams are likely to be relatively small, though not insignificant, given the small size of the North Korean economy and its shortage of hard currency. If the most ambitious goals for the Kaesong project are realized, by the middle of the next decade the North Korean government would likely derive tens if not hundreds of millions of dollars annually from tax revenues and its slice of North Korean workers' wages, assuming the KIC's current tax and wage structures remain in place [136]. Some South Koreans caution that the uncertainties over the future course of the KIC project make such projections highly speculative.

Foreign Investment

Foreign investment is becoming an increasingly significant element in the U.S.-South Korean bilateral economic relationship. Over the past 11 years, the stock of U.S.-South Korean foreign direct investment (FDI), valued on an historical cost basis, has increased substantially, due in no small part to the market-oriented reforms South Korea undertook after its 1997 financial crisis. In 1997, the value of stock of U.S. FDI in South Korea was $6.5 billion and had increased to $27.2 billion by the end of 2007. In 2007, 40% of U.S. FDI in South Korea was in manufacturing, especially in computers and electronic products, chemicals, and other manufacturing facilities. The remainder of the FDI was in services, with U.S. FDI in banking and other financial services accounting for much of this investment. South Korean FDI in the United States has also increased substantially in the last 11 years, albeit from a much lower base. In 1997, the stock of South Korean FDI in the United States was valued at $0.6 billion and had increased to $13.4 billion by the end of 2007. $9.4 billion, or 72% of this investment was in wholesale trade, perhaps reflecting the sharp retail facilities to sell South Korean-made vehicles in the United States [137]

Foreign investment has been a sensitive issue in U.S.-South Korean relations for many years as U.S. investors have tried to make inroads into the South Korean economy. U.S. investors' criticisms have included restrictions on foreign investment in key sectors, such as communications, and the lack of adequate protection for intellectual property. (See section on IPR provisions of the KORUS FTA.) Efforts to establish bilateral rules have failed in the past. In the 1990s, the two countries tried to negotiate a bilateral investment treaty (BIT), that would commit each party to provide national treatment to the investments from the other party and abstain from performance requirements for foreign investments from the other party. But the negotiations collapsed largely over U.S. opposition to South Korea's so-called screen quota on domestic films and the latter's resistance to lifting or reducing it. (The South Korean government reduced the screen quotas by half just before the KORUS FTA negotiations were launched in February 2006.) The KORUS FTA chapter on investment essentially contains the commitments that would otherwise have been in a BIT.

The FTA sets down general principals for the treatment by South Korea and the United States of investors and investments from one partner in the territory of the other [138]. The principle of national treatment—that one party to the agreement will treat covered investments and investors from the other party no-less favorably than it treats domestic investors and investments—is paramount. The FTA allows each party to make exceptions to the national treatment principle, but those exceptions must be specified in the relevant annexes to the agreement [139]. A second fundamental principal is most-favored-nation treatment (MFN)—the two parties agree to treat investors and investments from the other no less favorably than it treats investors and investments from third, non-party countries. A third principle is minimum standard of treatment, that is, each party shall accord to all covered investments treatment in accordance with customary international law, including fair and equitable treatment and full protection and security.

The KORUS FTA would set limits on government expropriation of covered investments—that they be only for public purpose and carried out in a non-discriminatory manner, and affected investors would be provided with prompt and adequate compensation (fair market value). It also would require each KORUS FTA partner-country government allow for the free transfer of financial capital pertaining to covered investments both into and out of the country with exceptions, such as cases related to criminal offenses. The KORUS FTA would prohibit the U.S. and South Korean governments from imposing performance requirements (domestic content requirements, export-ratios, import limits, etc.) on the investments from the other. It would allow exceptions for measures intended to accomplish social objectives, such as to increase employment in certain regions of the country, promote training of workforce, and protect the environment. The agreement would also prohibit a requirement that senior managers be of a particular nationality but would allow a requirement that the majority of board of directors be of a particular nationality.

Similar to other U.S. FTAs, the KORUS FTA would establish procedures for the settlement of investor-state disputes involving investments covered under the agreement where the investor from one partner-country alleges that the government of the other partner-country is violating his rights under the FTA. The FTA stipulates that the two parties should try to first resolve the dispute through consultations and negotiations. But, if that does not work, the agreement would provide for arbitration procedures and the establishment of tribunals as provided under the "Convention on the Settlement of Investment Disputes Between States and Nationals of Other States."

The USITC concluded that U.S. investors, especially investors in financial services, would likely gain from the KORUS FTA [140]. (See section on financial and other services.) The United States has been the predominate partner in terms of foreign investment and stands to gain the most from the protections provided by the KORUS FTA. However, South Korean investments in the United States are increasing, and therefore, South Korea could benefit as well.

Intellectual Property Rights

In addition to those sections addressing pharmaceutical manufacturing (see discussion above), the KORUS FTA contains other provisions on intellectual property rights (IPR) protection in U.S.- South Korean trade. Under the FTA the United States and South Korea would reaffirm their commitments under the WTO Trade-Related Aspects of Intellectual Property Rights (TRIPS) agreement and other international agreements and conventions on intellectual property. But the two countries would make IPR commitments beyond those agreements with provisions that would:

- require each government to extend national treatment to IPR holders from the other country; [141]
- require transparency through the publication of regulations and laws regarding intellectual property rights;
- facilitate the registration of and protection of trademarks and established limitations on the use of geographical indications;
- ensure the right of authors, performers, producers of recordings to determine use of copyrighted products;
- require copyright protection for no less than 70 years; thus, South Korea agrees to extend its copyright protection term, an objective of U.S. copyright holders;
- protect copyrighted material against piracy and provide penalties for those who abet piracy including the seizure and destruction of pirated and counterfeit products;
- protect copyrighted performances on the internet; and
- protect encrypted programming over satellites and cable signals.

Labor Rights and Conditions

On May 10, 2007, a bipartisan group of congressional leaders and the Bush Administration released a statement that provided language to be included in pending and future FTAs, including KORUS FTA. Among other things, the statement, or framework, called "The New Trade Policy for America," requires U.S. FTA partners to commit to enforcing the five basic international labor standards and would require that the commitment be enforceable under the FTA [142]. Neither country is to waive or otherwise derogate from its labor statutes that reflect the five labor rights in a manner that affects trade or investment between the two FTA countries. Each country is to ensure that those affected by their respective labor laws have access to tribunals that enforce their rights under those laws. During his nomination process, USTR Ron Kirk stated the Obama Administration's position that the KORUS FTA appropriately incorporates the May 10th agreement [143].

Under the KORUS FTA the two countries are to form a Labor Council made up of officials responsible for labor matters in each country, that will meet within the first year after the agreement enters into force. At least one session of the Council will be devoted to meeting with the public in each country to discuss matters related to the enforcement of the labor provisions of the FTA. Disputes regarding labor matters under the FTA are to be resolved first by consultations, but if those fail, the parties in dispute may take the matter to the Labor Council and eventually to a dispute settlement panel if these mechanisms fail to resolve the dispute. The KORUS FTA also calls for the establishment of a Labor Cooperation Mechanism whereby the two countries would develop and work in areas pertaining to labor rights in each country.

To many outside observers, South Korea's labor rights regime is generally considered to be strong for regular workers. South Korea ranks in the top third of the OECD's thirty members in terms of employment protection for regular workers [144]. Indeed, for years, a major complaint of U.S. multinationals is that restrictions in the South Korean labor market, such as mandatory severance pay, significantly raise the cost of investing and doing business in Korea. In contrast, U.S. union representatives argue that recent changes to make South Korean labor markets more flexible are reducing the rights of South Korean workers [145]. Korea's unions have earned a reputation for activism; the number of working days lost to strikes is regularly among the highest in the OECD. Hyundai Motors, for instance, has experienced a strike every year since 1994. Moreover, strikes in South Korea are notable in that they are sometimes accompanied by violence and the occupation of workplaces and public spaces (such as highways), to which the government often responds with police action. In its comments on the KORUS FTA, the Labor Advisory Committee for Trade Negotiations and Trade Policy (LAC), criticized South Korea for the imprisonment of around 200 unionists who were "exercising basic labor rights" and for mobilizing riot police against union activity [146]

Korea's labor pool is divided into two segments: (1) South Korean "salarymen" (salaried workers, overwhelmingly men, in large corporations) comprise less than one-third of the workforce. Over half of this segment of the workforce is represented by powerful unions. (2) The remainder of the workforce is comprised of employees in small-scale firms plus the country's temporary and day laborers. Few of these workers are unionized. The proportion of temporary workers has grown markedly, to nearly one-third of the workforce, one of the highest rates in the industrialized world [147]. These workers tend to receive low wages and receive limited coverage by the social safety net, points highlighted by the LAC. Labor markets are notoriously rigid.

Government Procurement

A great deal of business is conducted by governments through the purchase of goods and services for their own use. Most governments, including the United States have laws (The Buy American Act) which require such goods and services to be of domestic origin. However, the General Agreement on Tariffs and Trade (GATT) and now the WTO have some provisions, the WTO Government Procurement Agreement (GPA), under which the countries agree to open up some of their government procurement business, to foreign companies as a way to promote trade. This agreement is plurilateral, that is it only applies to those WTO members that have signed it. The United States and South Korea are among the 39 signatories to the GPA. The GPA established rules for governments to publish information about contract tenders, including technical specification, about qualification for suppliers, the awarding of contracts, with a specific emphasis on nondiscrimination and transparency in the conduct of government procurement.

The KORUS FTA reaffirms the GPA as a baseline for government procurement but would expand the criteria to include more contracts. The GPA applies to contracts valued at around $193,000 and above. The KORUS FTA would apply agreement to contracts valued at $100,000 and above, potentially increasing the value of bilateral government-procurement trade. The GPA applies only to contracts tendered by 79 U.S. Federal government agencies and by 42 South Korean central and subcentral agencies listed in the annex. Under the KORUS FTA, South Korea would add nine more agencies to be covered.

Environment Protection

In keeping with the May 2007 agreement on labor and the environment between the Bush Administration and congressional leaders, under the KORUS FTA, the United States and South Korea would commit to enforce a list of seven multilateral environmental agreements to which both are parties and to add to the list when other agreements enter into force. (See the Labor Rights and Conditions section above.) [148]. In addition, the FTA would prevent the two countries from easing environmental standards in order to allow firms on their territory from gaining a competitive trade advantage. Furthermore, violations of the environmental provisions are to handled in the same manner as commercial provisions through the dispute settlement mechanism of the KORUS FTA and subject to trade sanctions, unprecedented for U.S. FTAs. As mentioned earlier, the Obama Administration has indicated that the May 2007 agreement is incorporated into the KORUS FTA [149]

Transparency

Making information publically available is a fundamental principle imbedded in international trade rules and in each of the FTAs that the United States has entered into. For years U.S. exporters and trade negotiators identified the lack of transparency of South Korea's trading and regulatory systems as one of the most significant barriers to trade with South Korea, in almost every major product sector. Under KORUS FTA, the United States and South Korea would commit to publish relevant regulations and administrative decisions as well as proposed regulations; to allow persons from the other party to make comments and to ask questions regarding proposed regulations; to notify such persons of administrative proceedings and to allow them make presentations before final administrative action is taken; and to allow such persons to request review and appeal of administrative decisions.

Institutional Provisions and Dispute Settlement

The KORUS FTA would provide several options for the United States and South Korea to resolve disputes arising under the agreement, in addition to the special dispute settlement provisions under the foreign investment chapter and other chapters. KORUS FTA would require the two countries to establish a joint committee chaired by the USTR and the Minister of Foreign Trade or their designees to supervise the implementation of the agreement. The committee would establish a panel to adjudicate disputes between the two countries under the agreement, if consultations do not lead to a resolution of the dispute. Annex 22A of the KORUS FTA contains provisions for the settlement of disputes regarding motor vehicles, specifically the snap-back provision. (See discussion in section on auto trade.) Annex 22-B provides for eventual discussion of the inclusion of products made in outward processing zones in North Korea. (For more information, see discussion in Kaesong Industrial Park section.)

Other Technical Provisions

The KORUS FTA includes other sets of provisions intended to facilitate market access. *Technical barriers to trade* are standards and regulations that are intended ostensibly to protect the health and safety of consumers and for other legitimate non-trade purposes but may through design and implementation discriminate against imports. The KORUS FTA would commit both countries to uphold their obligations under the WTO Agreement on Technical Barriers to Trade (TBT). In addition, South Korea and the United States would promote transparency, by allowing persons from the other party to participate in the development of standards, technical regulations, and conformity assessment procedures.

Regarding *customs administration and trade facilitation*, the KORUS FTA would promote joint cooperation to ensure compliance with each other's customs laws and regulations. For example, it would require the two countries to adopt procedures and regulations to facilitate express delivery shipments.

Rules of origin define what are goods that originate in the FTA region and therefore are eligible for preferential treatment. (Textiles and apparel have separate rules of origin). The KORUS FTA would require that goods must be wholly obtained or produced in the territory of both countries or country. The FTA would set a regional value threshold to be met to be considered originating in the FTA territory and provides formulas for determining the regional values.

National *competition laws and regulations* are intended to ensure that one firm does not so dominate a sector of the economy as to inhibit market entry and stifle competition. Among other things, the KORUS FTA would require that the United States and South Korea inform persons, who are subject to administrative actions, of hearings and provide them the opportunity to make their case. The two countries would cooperate in enforcing competition laws through the exchange of information and consultation. In addition, designated monopolies and state- enterprises would have to operate in conformance with the agreement and in accordance with commercial considerations.

The KORUS FTA includes provisions to facilitate trade via electronic commerce (e-commerce). They would prohibit discrimination against digital products and imposing customs duties on these products. They would also require the recognition of electronic authentication and electronic signatures and would promote consumer access to the Internet.

NEXT STEPS, IMPLICATIONS, AND THE EMERGING DEBATE

The United States concluded and entered into (signed) the KORUS FTA within the parameters of the Trade Promotion Authority (TPA) under the Bipartisan Trade Promotion Act of 2002. (P.L. 107-210). Therefore, any implementing legislation would be subjected to expedited procedures, that is mandatory congressional consideration, limited debate, no amendments, and an up-ordown vote. TPA does not impose a deadline on the President to submit the draft implementing bill. It is generally assumed that the President would do so only when he expects to have sufficient support in Congress to pass it, although he could submit the bill without that assurance and risk the bill's failure. The June 2008 bilateral beef agreement allowing for the resumption of U.S. beef sales to South Korea removed the last impediment to sending the KORUS FTA to Congress, according to Bush Administration officials. However, differences over the implications of the KORUS FTA between the Bush Administration and the Democratic leadership prevented the implementing legislation from being introduced in the 110th Congress.

During the presidential campaign, then-Senator Obama opposed the agreement because he believed that it does not adequately address problems of market access in South Korea for U.S. exports of cars, among other issues. In February 2009, the Obama Administration stated it would establish "benchmarks" for resolving these concerns. USTR Ron Kirk said that if they were not resolved, the Administration would walk away from the KORUS FTA. During her trip to Seoul in February 2009, Secretary of State Hillary Rodham Clinton made little mention of the agreement.

Implications for South Korea and the U.S.-ROK Alliance

In South Korea, the KORUS FTA must be approved by a majority vote in the unicameral National Assembly to take effect. The Assembly is controlled by President Lee Myung Bak's Grand National Party, which officially supports the agreement. Unlike in the United States, trade agreements are not subject to any fast-track time lines. President Lee Myung Bak, who was elected in December 2007, has made passage of the KORUS FTA a priority for his government. Most opinion polls genially have shown a majority of South Koreans in favor of the agreement, though opposition has been intense from the opposition parties and rural interests, among others. Furthermore, most polls of South Korean legislators show broad support for the agreement within the National Assembly, which is controlled by President Lee's Grand National Party. The KORUS FTA was not a significant issue in either the 2007 presidential election campaign, despite the fact that one of the major candidates opposed the agreement, or the April 2008 parliamentary elections.

For South Korea, entering an FTA with the United States meshes with a number of Lee's economic and strategic goals. Ongoing competitive pressure from Japanese firms, increased competition from Chinese enterprises, and the rapid aging of the South Korean workforce has heightened the sense of urgency to boost national long-term competitiveness, particularly in the services industries, where South Korean productivity typically lags compared to other industrialized countries. Indeed, former President Roh and other South Korean officials have argued that the KORUS FTA is essential for South Korea's economic survival [150]. Similarly, if less grandiosely, President Lee has argued that passage of the KORUS FTA will help revitalize South Korea's economy. To accelerate Korea's reform efforts—and also to avoid being left out from other FTAs being created globally and in Asia—Presidents Roh and Lee have pursued an aggressive effort to negotiate FTAs. South Korea has entered into FTAs with Chile, Singapore, the European Free Trade Association (EFTA), the Association of Southeast Asian Nations (ASEAN), and is negotiating with other countries, including the European Union , India, and Australia [151].

The United States and South Korea negotiated the KORUS FTA in part as a means to restore the health of a critical foreign policy and national security alliance [152]. While the talks were ongoing, the KORUS FTA sometimes was discussed as a possible counterweight to the bilateral friction that was occurring over issues such as how to manage relations with North Korea and the repositioning of U.S. troops in South Korea. These tensions decreased markedly in 2007, following the Bush Administration's decision to place greater emphasis on engagement and negotiations with North Korea. The election of Lee, who has stressed the importance of rebuilding U.S.-South Korean ties, is expected to further improve relations. Thus, with the alliance apparently on firmer ground, the KORUS FTA no longer appears as an exceptional area of bilateral cooperation.

Although the FTA's utility as an acute salve for the alliance has been reduced, over the medium and longer term, some argue it could help to boost the alliance by deepening bilateral economic and political ties. The tensions over North Korea policy, which may resurface, have revealed the extent to which the two countries view North Korea differently. Most South Koreans' sense of threat from North Korea has declined over the past decade, even as Americans' threat perceptions have risen. With the central rationale for the alliance—deterring a North Korean attack—now open to question in South Korea, and with many South Koreans opposed to allowing U.S. troops in South Korea to deploy to other parts of Asia (such as the Taiwan Strait) in the event of a crisis, the future utility and form of the alliance is being debated. Entering into an FTA, some argue, is a way to help reorient the alliance to adapt to the changes on the Korean Peninsula and in East Asia. However, in concrete terms, it is difficult to see how the KORUS FTA would make a significant difference in the strategic relationship, as it is unlikely to alter either country's fundamental interests on the Peninsula or in Northeast Asia.

In contrast, while the passage of the KORUS FTA is unlikely to have a major substantive impact on the strategic relationship, a collapse of the KORUS FTA would probably have a profound symbolic effect, particularly upon the way South Koreans view the alliance. If the KORUS FTA is rejected or subjected to a prolonged delay by the United States, it would be a psychological blow to many South Korean policymakers, many of whom would likely see it as a betrayal. This would be particularly true since, in their eyes, they made politically costly concessions on autos, beef, labor, and the environment to help ensure the agreement would be more favorably received in the U.S. Congress. The KORUS FTA's failure in the United States, according to some Korean politicians and policymakers, would lend credence to arguments in South Korea that the U.S. commitment to Korea and Northeast Asia is declining. If these perceptions take hold, it would increase the political costs of South Korean leaders' taking unpopular decisions on behalf of the alliance, such as increasing South Korean payments for relocating U.S. troops on the Peninsula. If the KORUS FTA is rejected or delayed in the United States, U.S. policymakers could attempt to somewhat ameliorate the negative symbolic effects in South Korea by taking high profile steps to expand U.S.-ROK strategic, rather than economic, relations.

Implications for U.S. Trade Policy and U.S. Asia Policy

The fate of the KORUS FTA could affect U.S. efforts to institutionalize its economic presence in East Asia, a goal the Bush Administration has been pursuing in part through FTAs. In addition to the KORUS FTA, the United States has an FTA with Singapore. It has been negotiating with Malaysia and Thailand, but these negotiations have been slow or dormant. In September 2008, the United States announced it would launch negotiations to join the Trans-Pacific Strategic Economic Partnership Agreement (also called the "P-4" agreement), a trade liberalization arrangement among Brunei, Chile, New Zealand, and Singapore. The U.S. use of FTAs in Asia also has been a response to the plethora of bilateral and multilateral FTAs that are being negotiated in the region. None of the actual or proposed multilateral agreements include the United States. Failure of the KORUS FTA could be viewed as a serious blow to the U.S. "competitive liberalization" strategy. With FTAs throughout East Asia proliferating, a failure of the KORUS FTA to be implemented would also likely mean that the United States would be shut out of regional economic groupings in East Asia. In contrast, the implementation of the KORUS FTA could spark interest of other East Asian countries, such as Japan, to negotiate FTAs with the United States in order not to lose their share of the huge U.S. market to South Korea. Thus, if the proponents of the "competitive liberalization" argument are correct, the fate of the KORUS FTA could play an important role in accelerating or decelerating the move to open market regionalism in East Asia.

Similarly, the fate of the KORUS FTA is likely to be seen as a bellwether for broader U.S. trade policy, which is now in a period of re-evaluation. In addition to the KORUS FTA, U.S. FTAs with Colombia and Panama are pending and may be acted on during the 111th Congress. The Doha Development Agenda round in the WTO is, for all intent and purposes, on life support, if not dead. This raises questions in the minds of U.S. policymakers and other experts, regarding the future role of the WTO and multilateral negotiations in shaping the international trading framework. The KORUS FTA will likely play a role in this reassessment. For better or worse, its rejection or indefinite delay might call into question the viability of FTAs as a serious U.S. tool to strengthen economic ties with major trading partners.

APPENDIX A. SOUTH KOREA'S RULES ON IMPORTS OF U.S.

Beef

On April 18, 2008, U.S. and South Korean negotiators reached agreement on the sanitary rules that Korea will apply to beef imports from the United States. It allows for imports of all cuts of U.S. boneless and bone-in beef and other beef products from cattle, irrespective of age, as long as specified risk materials known to transmit mad cow disease are removed and other conditions are met. However, to address subsequent Korean concerns, both sides revised this deal on June 21, 2008, to limit sales of U.S. beef from cattle less than 30 months old.

Within a few days, South Korea published rules to put this agreement into effect, and quickly began to inspect U.S. beef shipments. The U.S. Department of Agriculture similarly began to implement a new program to verify that the beef sold is processed from cattle under 30 months old. U.S. beef exporters are now working to recapture a key overseas market. In 2003, South Korea was the third-largest market for U.S. beef exports, prior to the ban imposed after the first U.S. cow infected with mad cow disease, or BSE (bovine spongiform encephalopathy), was discovered. Korea's commercial significance is reflected in the position taken by several Members of Congress, who state that congressional consideration of, and support for, the Korea - U.S. Free Trade Agreement (KORUS FTA), depends upon South Korea fully opening its market to U.S. beef.

While the U.S. beef industry and U.S. policymakers welcomed the initial April deal, Korean TV coverage of the issue and Internet-spread rumors that questioned the safety of

U.S. beef resulted in escalating protests and calls for the beef agreement to be renegotiated or scrapped. U.S. officials countered that measures already in place to prevent the introduction of BSE in U.S. cattle herds meet international scientific standards. To address mounting public pressure, the Korean government twice pursued talks with the United States to find ways to defuse public concerns without "renegotiating" the beef agreement. In late June 2008, both governments confirmed a "voluntary private sector" arrangement that will allow Korean firms to import U.S. beef produced only from cattle less than 30 months old. Both view this as a transitional step until Korean consumers regain confidence in the safety of U.S. beef.

Exports of U.S. beef (including bone-in cuts such as ribs) resumed in mid-July 2008, and by year-end reached almost $300 million – slightly more than one-third of the record 2003 sales level. Though Australia is the main competitor in Korea's beef market, U.S. beef exporters did gain noticeable market share in the first few months. Sensing a change in consumer sentiment, three large Korean department stores (the major sales outlets for beef) began selling U.S. beef in late November. Reported sales of U.S. beef in these major sales outlets were strong in December, largely due to discount pricing intended to draw down accumulated inventories. Export shipments of U.S. beef rebounded in January 2009 in part to meet Lunar Year demand, but have since declined. Future sales will depend largely on three factors. These include the price competitiveness of U.S. beef compared to Australian beef; [153] the impact of Korea's economic crisis on household meat purchasing decisions; and the timing of when other major retailers might decide to stock U.S. beef on their shelves.

The anti-beef agreement protests in South Korea have subsided. However, because they eroded the Korean President's political standing, there may be lingering effects on his government's willingness and ability to accept the changes the Obama Administration has said would be necessary before the White House will consider submitting the KORUS FTA to Congress.

For more information, see CRS Report RL34528, *U.S.-South Korea Beef Dispute: Agreement and Status,* by Remy Jurenas and Mark E. Manyin.

APPENDIX B. SOUTH KOREAN MOTOR VEHICLE MANUFACTURING

South Korea came late to the table of major motor vehicle manufacturing nations. The 1980 edition of the Automotive News Market Data Book, an authoritative industry source, listed no South Korean production in its world table covering the period 1946-78, and no South Korean company among the top 50 global producers. By 1988, according to the same publication's 1990 edition, total South Korean car and truck production exceeded one million units. In the 2007 edition, total South Korean production of cars and trucks in 2006 is given as more than 3.8 million units, which ranks South Korea as the global number five national producer, behind, in order, Japan, the United States, China and Germany. Yet South Korea remains only a mid-level consumer of motor vehicles. Its national sales of 1.2 million ranked its market not only well behind the top three leading producers, but also behind each of the five largest western European nations, plus Russia, Brazil, India, and Canada, and just ahead of Mexico. Exports account for about 70% of Korea's motor vehicle production volume, a figure that is matched by no other major motor vehicle producing country.

South Korea has aggressively developed and protected a nationally owned automotive manufacturing base. Motor vehicle imports were prohibited in South Korea until 1987, and imports from Japan were banned until 1999 [154]. Originally the South Korean government promoted the development of a fleet of domestically owned producers, but this strategy failed. In the shakeout after Korea's economic crisis of 1997-98, only one major South Korean-owned company was left, Hyundai, which also took control of the number-two producer by volume, Kia. Others were marginalized, out of the business altogether, or controlled by foreign companies. Korea's third producer, and their only other major manufacturer left in the business, Daewoo, is now controlled by General Motors [155]. The lone major South Korean-owned producer, the Hyundai-Kia combination, in 2006 produced 3.8 million vehicles worldwide, ranking it number six globally. Of this output, 2.7 million vehicles were manufactured in South Korea, 72% of the country's total output of cars and light trucks, and more than double the total sales of all vehicles in South Korea [156].

While Hyundai is a world-class global competitor, with current and planned assembly operations in the United States and other countries, it is questionable whether Hyundai, or any other South Korean-owned firm, could maintain an independently operated market base in South Korea without continued formal and informal protection from the national government. Comparative analysis of motor vehicle import and sales data by CRS from the Automotive News Global Market Data Book and Ward's Motor Vehicle Facts & Figures indicates that import penetration in the South Korean market in 2005 was equal to 3% of sales, even lower than the 5% level in Japan.

By comparison, the U.S. level was 39% (20% if imports from Canada and Mexico are excluded), and in major European producer countries, Canada, and Mexico, the shares of imports were 50% or higher. The British authors Maxton and Wormald believe that the South Korean industry may be fated to become a "networked" producer in the long run, i.e., surviving only by linkages to other major market producers [157].

Jeffery Schott of the Peterson Institute for International Economics has presented an analysis of South Korean automotive production and shipments in 2005, based on Korean official statistics, which illustrates that large shares of South Korean vehicles of all types are exported. Among passenger cars, however, the significance of exports tends to decline with the size of the vehicle. The export share of South Korean-produced vehicles officially described as "light" was 69%, and of "small" vehicles was 82%. For "medium" cars, the export share dropped to 62%, and for "large" cars, the share was 53%. Schott noted that Ford and Chrysler representatives "argue that South Korean tariff and nontariff barriers have restricted the supply of imported large vehicles— which traditionally have higher profit margins—to reserve a large share of the market for domestic producers ... a surprisingly high percentage of South Korean production of larger cars is sold in the domestic market rather than exported, and these are cars that most directly compete with imports." [158]

REFERENCES

[1] For more specific information, you may contact the following CRS analysts: William Cooper, x7-7749 (general questions on the KORUS FTA); Stephen Cooney, x7-4887 (autos and other industrial goods); Remy Jurenas, x7-7281 (agricultural trade); and

[2] United States Trade Representative's Office, *2009 Trade Policy Agenda and 2008 Annual Report of the President of the United States on the Trade Agreements Program*, February 2009; United States Senate Committee on Finance, "Finance Committee Questions For The Record. Hearing on Confirmation of Mr. Ronald Kirk to be United States Trade Representative," March 9, 2009.

[3] United States International Trade Commission (USITC). *U.S.-Korea Free Trade Agreement: Potential Economy-wide and Selected Sectoral Effects.* Investigation No. TA-2104-24. USITC Publication 3949. September 2007.

[4] For more on the U.S.-South Korean alliance, see CRS Report RL33567, *Korea-U.S. Relations: Issues for Congress*, by Larry A. Niksch.

[5] Trade Remedy Piece of Korea FTA Ignores Korean ADF Demands. *Inside U.S. Trade.* April 13, 2007.

[6] Section 2104(f) Trade of 2002. P.L. 107-210. United States International Trade Commission (USITC). *U.S.-Korea Free Trade Agreement: Potential Economy-wide and Selected Sectoral Effects.* Investigation No. TA-2104-24. USITC Publication 3949. September 2007.

[7] USITC. p. xvii-xviii.

[8] USITC. p. xix.

[9] Kiyota, Kozo and Robert M. Stern. *Economic Effects of a Korea-U.S. Free Trade Agreement.* Korea Economic Institute, Special Studies 4. 2007.

[10] Lee, Junyu and Hongshik Lee. *Feasibility and Economic Effects of a Korea-U.S. FTA.* Korean Institute for International Economic Policy. December 2005. p. 86.

[11] OECD, *Economic Surveys - Korea*, 2007.

[12] Korea Economic Institute, "Current Economic Info, South Korean Economic Data," accessed at http://www.keia.org, on January 2, 2008.

[13] "ROK Editorial: Roh's 'Special Lecture'," *The Korea Times*, posted on the Open Source Center, KPP20060329042002, March 29, 2006

[14] Ministry of Finance and Economy Weekly Briefing, "Korea-US FTA Projected to Boost the Korean Economy," March 9, 2006.

[15] See, for instance, Junkyu Lee and Hongshik Lee, *Feasibility and Economic Effects of a Korea-U.S. FTA* (Seoul: Korea Institute for International Economic Policy, 2005), p. 116-117; Inbom Choi and Jeffrey Schott, *Free Trade between Korea and the United States?* (Washington, DC: Institute for International Economics, 2001), p. 79-82.

[16] "Roh's 'Special Lecture'," *The Korea Times*, March 26, 2006.

[17] Korea Broadcast System, March 31, 2006 Broadcast.

[18] South Korea's average applied agricultural tariff (2007) was 49%, compared to about 12% for the United States. WTO, Statistics Database, "Country Profile for Republic of Korea," at http://stat.wto.org/CountryProfiles/KR_e.htm; U.S. Department of Agriculture, Economic Research Service, *Profiles of Tariffs in Global Agricultural Markets*, AER-796, January 2001, p. 26.

[19] A TRQ is a two-part tool used by countries to protect their more sensitive agricultural and food products, often while transitioning over time to free trade. The quota component provides for duty-free access of a specified quantity of a commodity, which in an FTA usually expands over time. Imports above this quota are subject to a

prohibitive tariff that in an FTA frequently declines over time. At the end of a product's transition period to free trade under an FTA, both the quota and tariff no longer apply (with a few exceptions), allowing for its unrestricted access to the partner's market.

[20] A summary of commodity-specific market access provisions (tariff reduction schedules, transition periods, TRQ amounts and growth rates, and safeguards) is found in the USDA fact sheet "U.S. - Korea Free Trade Agreement Benefits for Agriculture," October 2008, available at http://www.fas.usda.gov/info/factsheets/korea.asp. Detailed fact sheets on the agreement's commodity provisions and prospective impacts for agriculture in selected states are available at http://www.fas.usda.gov/info/factsheets/Korea/us-koreaftafactsheets.asp.

[21] Derived from Table 2.2 in USITC, *U.S.-Korea Free Trade Agreement: Potential Economy-wide and Selected Sectoral Effects,* pp. 2-8 and 2-9.

[22] Derived from American Farm Bureau Federation's (AFBF) *Implications of a South Korea-U.S. Free Trade Agreement on U.S. Agriculture,* July 2007, p. 17. To be consistent with the agricultural and food product categories used to derive the USITC's estimate, AFBF's exports of fish products are not included in the estimated increase in agricultural exports and agriculture's share stated above.

[23] In 2003, U.S. exports of beef muscle meats to South Korea totaled 213,083 MT. The safeguard level in year 1 would allow for duty-free access for about 20% more U.S. beef than the average 2002-2003 level of U.S. beef exports to the South Korean market.

[24] *Inside U.S. Trade,* "USTR Says Beef Market Access Must Precede Signing of Korea FTA," April 6, 2007, p. 5.

[25] Following the 2004 renegotiation of South Korea's WTO agricultural commitments, the United States and most other rice exporting countries beginning in 2005 have been able to take advantage of this other rice quota. Expanding by 20,347 MT each year through 2014, market access is on a first-come, first served basis. By 2014, both rice import quotas (under country allocations made to four countries including the United States, and the quota available to any country) will total 408,700 MT. For background on Korea's market access and domestic policies for rice, see USDA, Economic Research Service, South Korea Briefing page titled "Policy," available at http://www.ers.usda.gov/Briefing/ SouthKorea/policy.htm#ricemarket.

[26] USDA, Foreign Agricultural Service, Fact Sheet "U.S.-Korea Free Trade Agreement— What's At Stake for Fresh Citrus and Orange Juice," September 2008.

[27] This stance is reflected in testimony by the National Cattlemen's Beef Association before the USITC on June 20, 2007.

[28] U.S. Dept. of Commerce. International Trade Administration. Office of Aerospace and Automotive Industries (Commerce Dept. OAAI). *U.S. Motor Vehicle Industry Domestic and International Trade Quick-Facts* (yearend 2008 data and earlier years).

[29] Federal Reserve Bank of Atlanta. *EconSouth,* "West Point Restarts Its Engines" (1st Qtr. 2008), pp. 3, 9.

[30] 2007 data from Commerce Dept. OAAI. Data for 1990 and 2000 quoted from CRS Report RL32883, *U.S. Automotive Industry: Recent History and Issues*, Appendix 5.

[31] Sang-yirl Nam, "Implications of Liberalizing Korea-U.S. Trade in the Automobile Sector: Potential Impact of the Korea-U.S. Free Trade Agreement," Korea Economic Institute *Academic Paper Series,* III:1 (February 2008), p. 10.

[32] Tom Walsh, "Time for an Honest Chat About Trade," *Detroit Free Press* (April 24, 2008).
[33] *Automotive News* data base, "U.S. Light-Vehicle Sales by Nameplate, February & 2 Months 2009."
[34] *Detroit Free Press*, "Chrysler, Kia Tops in Incentives" (March 4, 2009); *Automotive News*, "Hyundai Piles on Incentives" (March 9, 2009), p. 6.
[35] CRS Report RL32883, *U.S. Automotive Industry: Recent History and Issues*, p. 60.
[36] The USITC calculated a 2006 import market share of 4.2%, of which 60% was from Europe, 27% from Japan, and 7% from the United States. USITC. *U.S.-Korea Free Trade Agreement: Potential Economy-Wide and Selected Sectoral Effects*, Investigation no. TA-2104-24, USITC Publ. 3949 (September 2007), p. 3-74.
[37] Office of the USTR. "Free Trade with Korea: Summary of the KORUSFTA," *Trade Facts* (April 2007).
[38] USITC. *U.S.-Korea FTA*, p. 3-79 (Box 3.4).
[39] Office of USTR. *Report of Industry Trade Advisory Committee on Automotive and Capital Goods (ITAC 2)* (April 27, 2007), p. 2.
[40] Ibid., p. 3-76 (Table 3.16).
[41] Ibid., p. 3-78-8, incl. Box 3.4.
[42] Examples of how specific South Korean automotive standards discourage imports were provided by Stephen J. Collins, President of the Automotive Trade Policy Council, in testimony to the U.S. House. Committee on Ways and Means. Subcommittee on Trade (March 20, 2007), pp. 3-5. Dr. Thomas Becker of the German Verband der Automobilindustrie confirmed that European exporters confront the same problem in South Korea (CRS interview, March 12, 2007)
[43] Quoted from letter of South Korean Minister H.C. Kim to USTR Schwab (June 30, 2007), p. 1.
[44] USTR. "Summary," p. 2.
[45] USTR. *Text of U.S.-Korea Free Trade Agreement*, p. 9-9. The details of the FTA on automotive technical barriers are summarized in Office of the USTR. "Fact Sheet on Auto-Related Provisions in the U.S.-Korea free Trade Agreement," *Trade Facts* (April 3, 2007); and, USITC. *U.S.-Korea FTA*, p. 3-80 (Box 3.4).
[46] Ibid., Box 3.4.
[47] USTR, "Auto-Related Provisions," p. 1; USITC. *U.S.-Korea FTA*, p. 3-80 (Box 3-4).
[48] Ibid., p. 3-82 and Box 3.4.
[49] Ibid., Table 2.2.
[50] Ibid., p. 3-78.
[51] Ibid.
[52] Ibid., pp. 2-12 and 3-82, and Table 2.2. Dr. Nam's simulations from the paper cited above produce somewhat more modest results. He estimates a net Korean export gain of about $900 million, a U.S. gain of about $130 million, leading to an increase in the U.S. bilateral deficit of about $770 million. As with the ITC findings, he concludes, "bilateral tariff elimination between Korea and the United States ... will increase the two countries' exports and imports of automobiles and parts at the expense of other countries;" p. 10.
[53] Jeffrey J. Schott. *The Korea-US Free Trade Agreement: A Summary Assessment.* Peterson Institute Policy Brief No. PB07-7 (August 2007). p. 4.

[54] USITC. *U.S.-Korea FTA*, p. 3-83.
[55] According to *Ward's Automotive Yearbook*, in 2006, Hyundai produced 98,000 "Porters," and Kia produced 72,000 "Bongos," both described as pickups.
[56] ITAC 2 report, p. 1.
[57] Letter to President George W. Bush from Reps. Rangel, Levin, Dingell, Kildee, Kind, Tauscher, Upton, Knollenberg, Candice Miller, McCotter, and Ehlers, and Senators Levin, Voinovich, Bayh, and Stabenow (March 1, 2007).
[58] ITAC 2 report, p. 2.
[59] "Ford Motor Company Assessment of the Automotive Provisions of the US-Korea FTA," appended to ITAC 2 report.
[60] U.S. Senate. Committee on Commerce, Science and Transportation, Subcommittee on Interstate Commerce, Trade and Tourism. Hearing on the Imbalance in U.S.-Korea Auto Trade (September 24, 2008), Statement of John T. Bozzella, Chrysler LLC, p. 3.
[61] "General Motors Corporation Assessment of the Automotive Provisions of the US-Korea FTA," appended to ITAC 2 report.
[62] *Detroit News*, "Korea Becomes GM's Global Growth Engine" (May 9, 2008), http://www.detnews.com.
[63] Automotive News, 2007automotive sales data.
[64] "KMWU-UAW Joint Declaration in Opposition the Proposed Korea-U.S. Free Trade Agreement," issued at Seoul, Korea (May 1, 2007), available at UAW website.
[65] U.S. House of Representatives. Committee on Ways and Means. Subcommittee on Trade. Testimony of Alan Reuther (March 20, 2007), p. 3.
[66] Quoted from letter of Alan Reuther to all members of the House (April 18, 2007), p. 2. A similar letter was sent to all members of the Senate. It may be noted that, while all Detroit-based "Big Three" parts manufacturing and assembly plants are organized by the UAW or other unions, there are virtually no union-organized U.S. motor vehicle assembly plants operated by foreign-owned companies, including the Hyundai plant in Alabama; see CRS Report RL32883, *U.S. Automotive Industry: Recent History and Issues*, pp. 37-43.
[67] Reuther testimony, pp. 6-7. The Reuther letters to the House and Senate makes the same point more briefly.
[68] *Detroit Free Press*, "South Korea Called Threat: UAW Chief Says Market Steals U.S. Jobs," February 4, 2008.
[69] Senate Commerce Committee Hearing (September 24, 2008), Statement of Ron Gettelfinger.
[70] See especially Schott, pp. 5-6.
[71] Calculations by Global Trade Information Systems, Inc. based on U.S. Department of Commerce data.
[72] Ibid.
[73] United States International Trade Commission. *U.S.-Korea Free Trade Agreement: Potential Economy-Wide and Selected Sectoral Effects*. USITC Publication 3949. September 2007. p. 3-52.
[74] World Trade Organization. Tariff Profiles 2006. Located at http://www.wto.org.
[75] Ibid.
[76] USITC. p. 3-52.
[77] Ibid. p. 3-53.

[78] Report of the Industry Trade Advisory Committee on Textiles and Clothing (ITAC-13) on the South Korea/U.S. (KORUS) Free Trade Agreement. April 27, 2007.
[79] Ibid
[80] National Association of Manufacturers (NAM). "Support the U.S.-Korea Free Trade Agreement," ManuFacts(September 2007); U.S. Chamber of Commerce, "Chamber Welcomes Announcement of U.S.-Korea Free Trade Agreement" news release 07-57 (April 2, 2007), and "U.S. Chamber Welcomes Signing of U.S.-Korea Free Trade Agreement" news release 07-126 (June 30, 2007); Business Roundtable, "Business Roundtable Applauds Deal on U.S.-Korea Trade" (April 2, 2007).
[81] Thus, in its submission to the ITC, the NAM indicated, "the FTA is not perfect and noted concerns expressed by U.S. automakers about the FTA's tariff and nontariff provisions and the questions raised by the U.S. steel industry about trade rules and other barriers." USITC. *U.S.-Korea FTA*, p. 3-73.
[82] Ibid., Table 2.2.
[83] Ibid., pp. 3-68 and 3-71.
[84] ITAC 2, p. 1.
[85] USITC. *U.S.-Korea FTA*, p. 3-71.
[86] NEMA. "U.S.-South Korea Free Trade Agreement," *NEMA Issue Brief* (April 2007).
[87] USITC. *U.S.-Korea FTA*, p. 3-68 and Table 3.13.
[88] Ibid., Table 3.13.
[89] Ibid., pp. 3-68 through 3-73.
[90] USITC Investigation no. 701-TA-43 1. *Federal Register*, XVIII: 154 (August 11, 2003), pp. 47546-7, 47607.
[91] Office of the USTR. Industry Trade Advisory Committee on Steel (ITAC 12). *The U.S.-Korea Free Trade Agreement* (April 27, 2007). Main views are summarized in pp. 1-2.
[92] Ibid., p. 2.
[93] USITC. p. 3-64.
[94] Ibid. p. 3-91.
[95] USITC dataweb.
[96] Primosch, William. *Testimony of Senior Director, International Business Policy, National Association of Manufacturers on the Proposed United States-Korea Free Trade Agreement for the Trade Policy Staff Committee, Office of the U.S. Trade Representative.* March 14, 2006. p. 6.
[97] Office of the USTR. *Special 301 Report.* April 2007. "Special 301" refers to Section 182 of the Trade Act of 1974. Since the start of the Special 301 provision in 1989, the USTR has issued annually a three-tier list of countries judged to have inadequate regimes for IPR protection, or to deny access: (1) priority foreign countries are deemed to be the worst violators, and are subject to special investigations and possible trade sanctions; (2) priority watch list countries are considered to have major deficiencies in their IPR regime, but do not currently warrant a Section 301 investigation; and (3) watch list countries, which maintain IPR practices that are of particular concern, but do not yet warrant higher- level designations. See CRS Report RL34292, *Intellectual Property Rights and International Trade*, by Shayerah Ilias and Ian F. Fergusson.
[98] Report of the United States Industry Trade Advisory Committee for Chemicals, Pharmaceuticals, Health/Science Products, and Service (ITAC-3) on The United States-South Korea Trade Promotion Agreement. April 24, 2007.

[99] Ibid., 4-1.
[100] Data obtained from U.S. Department of Commerce. Bureau of Economic Analysis.
[101] Ibid.
[102] USITC. p. 4-8.
[103] Office of the United States Trade Representative. *2007 National Trade Estimates Report—Foreign Trade Barriers.* p. 366.
[104] The United States-Korea Free Trade Agreement (KORUS FTA). Report of the Industry Trade Advisory Committee on Services and Finance Industries (ITAC 10) April 2007.
[105] The Free Trade Agreement Between South Korea and the United States (KORUS FTA). Chapter 13 (Financial Services)—Confirming Letter.
[106] Annex -I (Korea).
[107] KORUS FTA Chapter 14 Telecommunications.
[108] Coalition of Service Industries. *Coalition of Service Industries Expresses Strong Support for U.S.-Korea FTA; Urges Swift Congressional Passage.* Press release. June 30, 2007.
[109] White House Office of the Press Secretary, "President Bush Discusses the Visa Waiver Program," October 17, 2008. South Korea's path to entry into the VWP was made possible by reforms of the VWP that were embodied in H.R. 1 (P.L. 110-53), the Implementing the 9/11 Commission Recommendations Act of 2007. For more on the U.S. Visa Waiver Program, see CRS Report RL32221, Visa Waiver Program, by Alison Siskin.
[110] Department of Homeland Security, Temporary Admissions in *Yearbook of Immigration Statistics: 2007* Table 28.
[111] This section on trade remedies was written by Vivian C. Jones, Specialist in International Trade and Finance, Foreign Affairs, Defense, and Trade Division, CRS.
[112] For more information, see CRS Report RL32371, *Trade Remedies: A Primer*, by Vivian C. Jones.
[113] P.L. 107-210, Trade Act of 2002, Section 2102(b)(14).
[114] "South Korea Retracts Key Demand in Anti-Dumping Rules: Leaked Government Report," Yonhap (South Korea), January 19, 2007.
[115] USITC. "Antidumping and Countervailing Duty Orders In Place As of September 10, 2008, by Country." Available at http://www.usitc.gov. Korea Trade Commission, TR Measures, available at http://www.ktc.go.kr/en/kboard_child/ list.jsp?bm=86&pg=1.
[116] Schott, Jeffrey J., Bradford, Scott C., and Moll, Thomas. *Negotiating the Korea - United States Free Trade Agreement*, Institute for International Economics, June 2006.
[117] World Trade Organization dispute settlement statistics, http://www.wto.org/english/ tratop_e/dispu_e/ dispu_by_country_e.htm. South Korea was one of the complainants in the WTO dispute brought against the U.S. safeguard measures on steel, as well as that against the Continued Dumping and Subsidy Offset Act ("Byrd Amendment").
[118] "Cutler says U.S.-Korea Talks Hit Snag in Three Negotiating Groups, *FDA Week*, December 8, 2006. Although the particulars of South Korean demands were not made public, according to news reports, one of Korea's demands was to be excluded from the cumulation of imports used to determine injury in a safeguards case, if its share of imports into the U.S. are below a certain threshold.
[119] "South Korea Retracts Key Demand on Anti-dumping Rules: Leaked Government Report." *Yonhap*, January 19, 2007.

[120] See Chapter 10, Section A, Article 10.1 Application of a Safeguard Measure and Article 10.5 Global Safeguard Actions.
[121] Article 10.4, Compensation.
[122] USITC. *U.S. Korea Free Trade Agreement: Potential Economy-wide and Selected Sectoral Effects.* Publication 3949, September 2007, p. 6-1.
[123] Chapter 10, Section B. Antidumping and Countervailing.
[124] CVD: 19 U.S.C. 1671c; AD: 19 U.S.C. 1673c. Under these statutes, a quantitative restriction or price offset suspension agreement must completely eliminate the injurious effect of the dumping or subsidy, must be in the public interest and must be able to be effectively monitored by U.S. authorities.
[125] Chapter 10, Section B. Antidumping and Countervailing Duties, Article 10.7, paragraphs 3 and 4.
[126] Chapter 10, Section C. Committee on Trade Remedies, Article 10.8, paragraph 2.
[127] ITAC (12) on Steel, Advisory Committee Report, April 27, 2007, p. 7.
[128] Ib id, p. 4.
[129] Ibid.
[130] "Trade Remedy Piece of Korea FTA Ignores Korean AD Demands," *Inside U.S. Trade*, April 13, 2007.
[131] Ibid.
[132] For more, see CRS Report RL34093, *The Kaesong North-South Korean Industrial Complex*, by Dick K. Nanto and Mark E. Manyin.
[133] Ministry of Unification, "Current Status of Operation in the Gaeseong Industrial Complex," November 23, 2007.
[134] Chapter 22, Annex B, Committee on Outward Processing Zones on the Korean Peninsula.
[135] April 2007 interviews with U.S. and Korean officials; remarks by Assistant U.S. Trade Representative for Japan, Korea and APEC Affairs Wendy Cutler at an April 5, 2007 Korea Economic Institute forum; "Behind the Korea FTA Negotiations," *Washington Trade Daily*, April 12, 2007.
[136] Moon Ihlwan, "Bridging the Korean Economic Divide," *Business Week*, March 8, 2006.
[137] CRS calculations based on data from U.S. Department of Commerce. Bureau of Economic Analysis. http://www.bea.gov.
[138] A range of factors determine the climate for foreign investment—government regulations, skills of local labor, general economic conditions, intellectual property rights protection, among others. Therefore, U.S.-South Korean investment ties could be affected by not only the provisions of the investment chapter of the agreement, but other chapters as well.
[139] The USITC report on the KORUS FTA points out that South Korea's list these "nonconforming measures" in the KORUS FTA is longer than in previous FTAs that the United States has signed; however, industry representatives generally believe that the KORUS FTA would still render significant opportunities for U.S. investors. USITC. p. 6-5.
[140] USITC. p. 6-5.
[141] A national treatment exception is made with respect to the secondary uses of recordings by means of analog communications, including over-the-air broadcasts, whereby a

Party can limit the rights of performers and producers of sound recordings from the other Party on its own territory. This exception was a disappointment to U.S. industry, which otherwise praise the agreement. *Korea-U.S. Free Trade Agreement: Benefits to America's Entertainment Industries.* Testimony Before the U.S. International Trade Commission by Greg Frazier, Executive Vice-President Worldwide Government Policy Motion Picture Association of America. June 6, 2007. p.7.

[142] The FTA would require each Party to adopt and maintain five internationally-accepted labor rights that are contained in the ILO Declaration on Fundamental Principles and Rights at Work and Its Follow-Up (1998) (ILO Declaration) Article 19:2 specifies these rights as the freedom of association, the effective recognition of the right to collective bargaining, the elimination of all forms of compulsory or forced labor, the effective abolition of child labor and the elimination of discrimination in respect of employment and occupation. The framework also requires FTAs to adhere to seven major multilateral environmental agreements and for this commitment to be enforceable under the FTA. "The Trade Policy for America" was completed after President Bush notified the Congress on April 1, 2007 of his intention to sign the KORUS FTA but prior to the signing on June 30. At first, South Korean officials balked at opening negotiations to add the language but eventually agreed to do so. After, the two sides held negotiations, they included the language in the final text that was signed on June 30, 2007.

[143] In Questions for the Record posed by members of the Senate Finance Committee, USTR Kirk was asked "Do you think that the labor and environment provisions of the U.S.-Korea FTA are appropriate?" He responded that "the U.S.- Korea FTA incorporates the May 10th Agreement, which established a strong foundation for bipartisan progress on trade." United States Senate Committee on Finance, "Finance Committee Questions For The Record. Hearing on Confirmation of Mr. Ronald Kirk to be United States Trade Representative," March 9, 2009.

[144] OECD, *Economic Survey—Korea 2007*, p. 138.

[145] Report of the Labor Advisory Committee for Trade Negotiations and Trade Policy (LAC) on the KORUS FTA, April 27, 2007, p. 9.

[146] *Ibid.*

[147] OECD, *Economic Survey—Korea 2007*, p. 128-40.

[148] The seven agreements are: the Convention on International Trade in Endangered Species; the Montreal Protocol on Ozone Depleting Substances; the Convention on Marine Pollution; the Inter-American Tropical Tuna Convention; the Ramsar Convention on the Wetlands; the International Convention for the Regulation of Whaling; and the Convention on Conservation of Antarctic Marine Living Resources.

[149] United States Senate Committee on Finance, "Finance Committee Questions For The Record. Hearing on Confirmation of Mr. Ronald Kirk to be United States Trade Representative," March 9, 2009.

[150] Korea Broadcast System, March 31, 2006 Broadcast in Korean, summarized by the Open Source Center, "ROK TV Carries Economic Minister's Comments on ROK-US FTA," April 10, 2006, FEA20060410021900. (Han was Finance Minister when he made these remarks.) South Korean Blue House, "Address to the Nation," April 2, 2007.

[151] EFTA is comprised of Iceland, Norway, Switzerland, and Liechtenstein. ASEAN consists of Brunei, Cambodia, Indonesia, Laos, Malaysia, Myanmar, Philippines, Singapore, Thailand, and Vietnam.

[152] For more, see CRS Report RL33567, *Korea-U.S. Relations: Issues for Congress*, by Larry A. Niksch.

[153] Between February 2008 and January 2009, the U.S. dollar strengthened by nearly 50% against the Korean won. As the dollar:won rate strengthened, U.S. beef became more expensive. At the same time, the Australian dollar has weakened against the U.S. dollar, giving Australian beef a price advantage in the Korean market.

[154] USITC. *Industry and Trade Summary: Motor Vehicles* (USITC Publication 3545, September 2002), p. 60.

[155] Ibid., pp. 60-61; Graeme P. Maxton and John Wormald, *Time for a Model Change: Re-Engineering the Global Automotive Industry.* Cambridge, U.K.: Cambridge University Press, 2004. p. 10 1-2; CRS Report RL32883, *U.S. Automotive Industry: Recent History and Issues*, p. 75-76.

[156] *Automotive News 2007 Global Market Data Book*, p. 29.

[157] Maxton and Wormald, pp. 10 1-2.

[158] Schott (August 2007), table 2 and p. 4. It may be argued that Hyundai's U.S. sales of its Sonata sedan, which may be considered a "medium" or "large" vehicle in Korea, were sourced out of its Alabama assembly plant starting in 2005, thus reducing the export share of that product. However, according to *Ward's Automotive Yearbook*, only 91,000 Hyundai vehicles were produced in the U.S. in the startup year of 2005.

In: Political and Economic Developments in Asia
Editor: Felix Chin
ISBN: 978-1-61209-783-1
©2011 Nova Science Publishers, Inc.

Chapter 3

NORTH KOREA'S NUCLEAR WEAPONS DEVELOPMENT AND DIPLOMACY[*]

Larry A. Niksch

ABSTRACT

Since August 2003, negotiations over North Korea's nuclear weapons programs have involved six governments: the United States, North Korea, China, South Korea, Japan, and Russia. Since the talks began, North Korea has operated nuclear facilities at Yongbyon and apparently has produced weapons-grade plutonium. Various estimates place North Korea's plutonium production at between 30 and 50 kilograms, enough for five to eight atomic weapons.

After North Korea tested a nuclear device in October 2006, the six party talks served as a framework for bilateral negotiations between the Bush Administration and North Korea, with significant Chinese influence on these bilateral talks. The Bush Administration negotiated four agreements with North Korea between February 2007 and October 2008; two were issued as six party accords. The agreements produced the initiation of a disablement of North Korean nuclear installations at Yongbyon, including a nuclear reactor and plutonium reprocessing plant; Bush Administration lifting of Trading With the Enemy Act sanctions against North Korea and removal of North Korea from the U.S. list of state sponsors of terrorism; a North Korean declaration of nuclear programs limited to known nuclear installations at Yongbyon and reportedly a plutonium stockpile of 31 kilograms; and a commitment by the five non-North Korean governments in the six party talks to provide North Korea with one million tons of heavy fuel oil or equivalent forms of energy assistance. The fourth of these agreements, negotiated in October 2008, established a system of verification and inspections but limited to the declared facilities at Yongbyon and not including the taking of samples by inspectors. The Bush Administration and North Korea disputed the contents of this agreement, especially over sampling.

As of early 2009, full implementation of the agreements requires a completion of deliveries of one million tons of heavy fuel oil to North Korea and North Korean completion of the disablement of the Yongbyon facilities. Oil deliveries are about 200,000 tons short, and the Yongbyon facilities are about 80% disabled. The Bush

---

[*] This is an edited, reformatted and augmented version of CRS Report RL33590, dated March 30, 2009.

Administration took the position that full implementation also would require North Korean Korean acceptance of inspection sampling at Yongbyon.

Completing the implementation of the agreement is one challenge facing the Obama Administration. A second challenge will be to develop a negotiating strategy for the next phase of nuclear negotiations, including decisions on how to respond to tough negotiating positions, which North Korea set forth at the start of 2009, which include a call for normalization of U.S.-North Korean relations prior to a final agreement to denuclearize the Korean peninsula and a demand that a final agreement include elimination of the "U.S. nuclear threat" to North Korea.

These agreements did not cover important components of North Korea's nuclear programs: the apparent production of a few atomic bombs; a highly enriched uranium program known to the United States since the late 1990s; and alleged nuclear collaboration with Iran and Syria. According to U.S. officials, collaboration with Syria involved the construction of a nuclear reactor, which Israel bombed in September 2007. Collaboration with Iran reportedly involves development of high enriched uranium, development of a nuclear warhead that could be mounted on a jointly developed intermediate range ballistic missile (North Korean Nodong, Iranian Shahab missile), collaboration in developing long-range missiles, and North Korean assistance in constructing deep underground installations to house part of Iran's nuclear program.

This report will be updated periodically.

U.S.-NORTH KOREA NUCLEAR AGREEMENT

The Bush Administration negotiated four agreements with North Korea between February 2007 and October 2008; two were issued as agreements of the parties to six party talks over North Korea's nuclear programs (United States, North Korea, China, South Korea, Japan, and Russia). The main aim of the Bush Administration in these agreements was to secure the disablement of North Korea's plutonium installations at Yongbyon. The agreements, however, were not implemented fully when the Bush Administration left office. This was due partly to the failure of the Bush Administration and North Korea to resolve this dispute over a verification system, especially the right of inspectors to take samples [1].

On June 26, 2008, the North Korean government and the Bush Administration took measures to implement the nuclear agreements that they had negotiated in 2007 into 2008. The details of the agreement were finalized in April 2008 at a meeting of the chief U.S. and North Korean negotiators in Singapore [2]. The agreements, if fully implemented, would complete the second phase of an accord reached by the six party conference on North Korean nuclear issues in February 2007 and detailed more fully in a six party statement of October 2007. Both of the six party accords had been negotiated bilaterally between the Bush Administration and North Korea; China had influenced the U.S.-North Korean negotiations.

The agreements created two obligations each for North Korea and the Bush Administration to fulfill. North Korea is to allow a process of disablement of its plutonium nuclear facilities at Yongbyon, a site 60 miles from the capital of Pyongyang. The shutting down of Yongbyon was a key provision of the 1994 Agreed Framework negotiated by the Clinton Administration and North Korea. Yongbyon ceased to operate between 1994 and the end of 2002. In late 2002, the Bush Administration suspended U.S. obligations under the Agreed Framework because of U.S. intelligence estimates that North Korea was operating a secret nuclear weapons program based on highly enriched uranium. North Korea responded by re-starting the Yongbyon facilities. Between early 2003 and the summer of 2007, the Yongbyon reactor and the plutonium reprocessing plant produced enough weapons grade plutonium for the production of several atomic bombs. North Korea tested an atomic device in October 2006.

The disablement process began in October 2007. The Bush Administration said in June 2008 that eight of eleven components of the disablement process have been completed [3]. A major uncompleted task is the removal of spent plutonium fuel rods from the five megawatt reactor. As of February 2009, about 6,100 of 8,000 spent fuel rods reportedly have been removed [4]. Bush Administration officials have stated that a completed disablement of the Yongbyon installations would be extensive enough so that it would take North Korea about a year to re-start them, [5] but subsequent developments indicated that North Korea could restart the plutonium reprocessing plant within three to four months.

North Korea's second obligation was to provide the United States and other members of the six party talks with a "complete and correct" declaration of nuclear programs. The declaration negotiated and reportedly finalized in Singapore and delivered to China on June 26, 2008, contains a declaration of the amount of plutonium that North Korea claims to possess. Reports asserted that North Korea declared 30.8 kilograms of plutonium [6]. U.S. intelligence estimates reportedly conclude that North Korea has accumulated 50 to 60 kilograms of plutonium [7]. However, other components of North Korea's nuclear programs reportedly are omitted from the declaration, apparently based on concessions the Bush Administration made to North Korea in the Singapore agreement. These include the number of atomic bombs North Korea possesses, information about the facilities where North Korea produces and tests atomic bombs, and the locations where North Korea stores plutonium and atomic bombs. The declaration also reportedly contains no information about North Korea's reported highly enriched uranium program or North Korea's reported nuclear collaboration activities with Iran and Syria. According to Bush Administration officials, the uranium enrichment and Syria issues are addressed in a "confidential minute" [8]. (They said nothing about Iran.) However, in the confidential minute, North Korea reportedly does not admit to uranium enrichment or proliferation activities with Syria. It merely "acknowledges" U.S. concerns that North Korea has engaged in these activities in the past [9].

The United States' two obligations under the agreements were to remove North Korea from the U.S. Trading with the Enemy Act and from the U.S. list of state sponsors of terrorism. Removal from the Trading with the Enemy Act allows U.S. companies to import North Korean goods and sell non-strategic goods to North Korea. It opens up possibilities for U.S. companies to invest in North Korea. However, given North Korea's communist economic system and its suspicions of foreign intrusions, there appears to be little likelihood of any meaningful trade or investment relations developing between the United States and North Korea.10 Removal from the Trading with the Enemy Act could give North Korea in the future access to $31.7 million in North Korean assets in the United States that have been frozen since the Korean War [11]

Removal from the U.S. list of state sponsors of terrorism will end the requirement that U.S. presidents oppose financial aid to North Korea from international financial agencies like the World Bank and the International Monetary Fund. In likely nuclear negotiations in 2009 under the Obama Administration, it is probable that North Korea will demand that the incoming Obama Administration "complete" North Korea's removal from the terrorism support with an "affirmative act" of initiating proposals for North Korea to receive financial aid from the World Bank and the International Monetary Fund.

North Korea may have three additional motives for its pressure on the Bush Administration to remove it from the list of state sponsors of terrorism. One is to reduce U.S. support for Japan on the issue of Japanese citizens kidnapped by North Korea. The Clinton and Bush administrations previously had cited a resolution of the Japanese kidnapping issue as linked to removal of North Korea from the terrorism support list. A second motive apparently is to improve the prospects for normalization of diplomatic relations with the United States, which North Korea says it wants [12]. A possible third motive may be to remove any U.S. incentive to examine the issue of North Korea's activities in the Middle East and deny to the United States a potential negotiating lever over North Korea's activities in the Middle East. Numerous reports indicate that North Korea's activities include providing training and weapons to Hezbollah and cooperation with the Iranian Revolutionary Guards in the development of both missiles and nuclear weapons. (See subsequent section on "Nuclear Collaboration with Iran and Syria." See also CRS Report RL30613, *North Korea: Terrorism List Removal?*)

THE IMPLEMENTATION PROCESS

On June 26, 2008, North Korea submitted its declaration of nuclear programs to China, the chairman of the six party talks. Simultaneously, President Bush announced that he had removed North Korea from the Trading with the Enemy Act. The President has full authority to renew annually Trading with the Enemy Act sanctions on North Korea or to lift those sanctions from North Korea.

President Bush also announced that he had sent to Congress notification of his intent to remove North Korea from the list of state sponsors of terrorism after 45 calendar days, on August 11, 2008. Under U.S. law, the President is required to notify Congress 45 days before removing a country from the list. The White House said that North Korea would be removed on August 11, 2008, unless Congress acted legislatively to block removal [13]. However, the White House also said on June 26, 2008, that removal of North Korea was conditioned on North Korean acceptance of provisions for U.S. verification of the North Korean declaration of nuclear programs.

Verification Issue

However, the Bush Administration did not remove North Korea from the list of state sponsors of terrorism on August 11, 2008. In July, the Bush Administration presented North Korea with a draft protocol on verification of North Korea's nuclear programs. The draft protocol would have given U.S. and other six party inspectors the right to conduct inspections at sites throughout North Korea [14] North Korea rejected the U.S. proposal, arguing that inspections should cover only those facilities at Yongbyon that it had listed in its declaration of June 26, 2008. North Korea retaliated by halting the disablement process at Yongbyon and announcing that it would restart the plutonium reprocessing plant at Yongbyon [15].

Neither the February 2007 nor the October 2007 six party nuclear agreements mentioned a system of verifying the implementation of the agreements. There is no evidence that the Singapore agreement of April 2008 detailed any system of verification. However, following the U.S.-North Korean meeting at Singapore, the Bush Administration began to seek supplemental agreements with North Korea regarding the establishment of verification mechanisms to examine North Korea's declaration of its plutonium stockpile. In early May 2008, the Bush Administration and North Korea negotiated an accord for North Korea to turn over to the United States over 18,000 documents related to its plutonium program, dating back to 1986. U.S. experts are examining these documents and have disclosed no revealing information from them. The White House announcement of June 26, 2008, stated that removal of North Korea from the terrorism support list after 45 days would be carried out "only after the six parties reach agreement on acceptable verification principles and an acceptable verification protocol; the six parties have established an acceptable monitoring mechanism; and verification activities have begun."

A six party meeting of July 10-12, 2008, reached agreement on verification principles, including inspection of Yongbyon facilities, review of documents, and interviews of North Korean nuclear scientists and technicians. Verification would be carried out by experts of the six parties. The International Atomic Energy Agency would have only an advisory role.

The Bush Administration reacted to North Korea's announcement of a restarting of the plutonium reprocessing by scaling back the scope of its verification proposals. Assistant Secretary of State Christopher Hill went to Pyongyang in early October and negotiated a verification deal, which would concentrate inspections only on Yongbyon [16]. North Korea agreed and announced a resumption of disablement. The Bush Administration followed on October 11, 2008, by the announcement of Secretary of State Condoleezza Rice that North Korea was removed from the U.S. list of state sponsors of terrorism.

The State Department's description of the verification agreement included the following points. Inspectors would have access only to the sites at Yongbyon in North Korea's June 16, 2008 declaration. Access to non-declared sites would be by "mutual consent." The inspection organization would be composed of the five non-North Korean members of the six party talks— the United States, China, South Korea, Japan, and Russia. The organization would make decisions on the basis of unanimous consent. The terms of the verification agreement were contained in a U.S.-North Korean document and in "certain other understandings" [17].

The Bush Administration and the State Department give few details on two other aspects of Hill's talks in Pyongyang and the verification agreement. One was the issue of inspectors being able to take samples of nuclear materials at the Yongbyon installations for laboratory analysis. A North Korean Foreign Ministry statement of November 11, 2008, and subsequent statements asserted that the written verification agreement said nothing about sampling and that North Korea only had to abide by the written agreement and nothing else. The State Department then acknowledged that Hill's discussion with North Koreans about sampling was only a verbal understanding [18]. This issue was not resolved in the December 2008 six party meeting.

The second aspect of Hill's talks was his meeting with North Korean Lt. General Lee Chan-bok. This was the first time that a North Korean military leader had participated in the nuclear talks. General Lee reportedly called for bilateral U.S.-North Korean military talks and may have linked U.S. acceptance of bilateral military talks to further progress on the nuclear issue [19]. Hill and the State Department have been silent on the content of this meeting, including whether or not Hill committed the United States to bilateral military talks in the near future.

Issues Facing the Obama Administration

If the nuclear agreements negotiated by the Bush Administration are fully implemented, the key accomplishment from the U.S. perspective would be the shutting down of Yongbyon through disablement. The Obama Administration named former Ambassador Stephen Bosworth, Dean of Tufts University, as its special envoy in dealing with North Korea. North Korea insisted as the Bush Administration left office that it would complete the disablement only when it receives the remainder of the one million tons of energy assistance (mainly heavy oil). An initial decision for the Obama Administration likely will be whether to proceed with this arrangement or whether to block the remainder of the energy assistance until North Korea agrees to a verification- inspections system, including sampling, that the Bush Administration claimed Christopher Hill negotiated with the North Korea in October 2008. If the Obama Administration should decide to set aside the verification issue, it would face the problem of arranging for the provision of the remaining energy assistance to North Korea. The remainder is composed principally of 200,000 tons that Japan was to provide; however, Japan has refused due to the lack of progress with North Korea over the issue of kidnapped Japanese. There has been discussion among U.S. experts that China, the chairman of the six party talks, could step into the void left by Japan and provide the remaining 200,000 tons [20]. Otherwise, the United States and several other nations would have to share the burden.

Even if implementation of the Bush Administration-North Korea agreements is completed, the Obama Administration undoubtedly will face significant difficulties in the next round of nuclear negotiations. If North Korea proceeds with its announced launch of a satellite in April 2009, based on long-range missile technology, the Obama Administration would confront a decision over whether to seek United Nations sanctions against North Korea and whether to enter into near term nuclear negotiations with Pyongyang.

Since January 1, 2009, the North Korean government has issued a number of statements outlining demanding positions it will take in any new round of nuclear talks with the Obama Administration. These have been official statements by the North Korean Foreign Ministry and, in a new development, statements by the North Korean military. They also came in statements that North Korean officials, including military officials, made to Selig Harrison of the Center for International Policy, who visited Pyongyang in mid-January 2009. Harrison had visited North Korea on numerous occasions since the early 1990s and had met with high-ranking North Korean officials.

The negotiating positions taken by North Korea can be summarized as follows:

- North Korea will not give up its nuclear weapons in return for normalization of relations with the United States and economic aid from the United States. Normalization of relations must come before denuclearization as a step toward denuclearization [21]. North Korean officials rejected Selig Harrison's proposal that North Korea turn over its plutonium stockpile to the International Atomic Energy Agency in return for U.S. diplomatic recognition and U.S. economic aid and trade

credits. They asserted to Harrison that North Korea wanted U.S. recognition of its status as a nuclear weapons state [22].
- North Korea no longer has a plutonium stockpile of 31 kilograms that it declared in June 2008 because North Korea has "weaponized" all of its plutonium. This implies a North Korea position that future negotiations on final denuclearization must deal only with North Korea's plutonium atomic weapons [23].
- Denuclearization must include the entire Korean peninsula and must include the elimination of the "U.S. nuclear threat" to North Korea [24]. Pyongyang's apparent position that a final denuclearization negotiation must deal only with its atomic weapons appears to aim at giving North Korea more negotiating leverage to press its demand that the United States must agree to measures to eliminate the U.S. "nuclear threat." North Korea repeatedly has defined the "U.S. nuclear threat" to include the composition and major operations of U.S. military forces in South Korea and around the Korean peninsula and the U.S. "nuclear umbrella" over South Korea embodied in the U.S.-South Korean Mutual Defense Treaty. North Korean strategy seems aimed at proposing that a final denuclearization agreement with the United States constitute the document that regulates the future U.S. military presence in and around the Korean peninsula, thus superseding the U.S.-South Korean Mutual Defense Treaty.
- Any system of verification and inspections must include inspections inside South Korea, including U.S. bases in South Korea. If North Korea holds to that position, negotiating an agreement on verification that would include sampling would pose additional difficulties and likely delays.

These negotiating positions, plus earlier positions laid out by Pyongyang, suggest that North Korea likely will assert that the next round of nuclear talks beyond completion of the Bush Administration-North Korean nuclear agreements should focus on only an agreement for the complete dismantlement of the Yongbyon installations—in short, moving from disablement to physical dismantlement [25]. Pyongyang likely will assert that negotiations over its nuclear weapons should be postponed until a later phase of the six party talks or that the issue be negotiated in separate U.S.-North Korean bilateral military-to-military negotiations. Pyongyang also may take the position that verification procedures, especially inspections and sampling, must be dealt with in this later, denuclearization phase of negotiations.

North Korea's negotiating positions also suggest the demands and conditions that Pyongyang likely would lay out for an agreement of dismantlement. North Korea appears ready to call on the United States to agree to diplomatic relations in a dismantlement agreement. North Korea also is certain to demand that the United States and the other six party governments begin a second project to construct light water nuclear reactors inside North Korea; [26] the 1994 Agreed Framework initiated the first light water reactor project, which was halted in 2002. North Korea also can be expected to insist that the actual physical dismantlement of Yongbyon would take place only when the construction of light water reactors is completed (a process that would take ten years or more, according to estimates by nuclear experts on the time required to construct a light water reactor). Another North Korean condition likely would be a continuation of heavy oil shipments until light water reactors are completed.

North Korea also may raise another condition related to the Bush Administration's removal of Pyongyang from the U.S. list of state sponsors of terrorism. North Korean negotiators may assert that the Obama Administration must "complete" North Korea's removal through a second step of proposing and supporting financial aid to North Korea from the World Bank and/or the International Monetary Fund. The Bush Administration's removal of North Korea lifted the requirement in U.S. law that the President must oppose aid to North Korea from international financial agencies because of its inclusion on the terrorism-support list [27].

North Korea's negotiating agenda presents the Obama Administration with important decisions regarding any future round of nuclear talks. The Administration would have to decide whether to accept Pyongyang's assertion that the next round of talks focus exclusively on the dismantlement of Yongbyon (a position China could be expected to support) or whether the Administration would counter-propose that the issues of North Korea's atomic weapons, plutonium stockpile, and verification be included in the talks. In negotiating over the dismantlement of Yongbyon, two of North Korea's likely demands would appear to present particular problems for the Obama Administration. North Korea's likely call for diplomatic relations in a dismantlement agreement runs counter to the longstanding U.S. position, reiterated by Secretary of State Clinton during her trip to East Asia, that the United States would normalize relations with North Korea only when North Korea's nuclear programs and weapons are eliminated [28]. North Korea's repeated demand for light water nuclear reactors also would force the Obama Administration to choose whether to go back into another light water reactor project that likely would take ten years or longer, or, alternatively, propose a package of incentives to North Korea, including energy incentives, that would not include light water reactors.

The Obama Administration would face a more fundamental decision if it sought early negotiations over North Korea's atomic weapons. North Korea has made clear that it will not accept a linkage between giving up its nuclear weapons and normalization of relations with the United States. Its heightened emphasis that the real linkage is with elimination of the "U.S. nuclear threat" would present the Obama Administration with the issue of whether it would be willing to negotiate major military concessions to North Korea regarding the composition and operations of U.S. forces in South Korea and around the Korean peninsula. Past U.S. administrations have refused to negotiate with North Korea over U.S. troops. South Korea's role in any U.S.-North Korean negotiations over U.S. forces also would be an important consideration.

Two other issues might be addressed by the Obama Administration in developing its negotiating strategy toward North Korea. One would be whether, in the next round of nuclear talks, to attempt to restore as negotiating issues North Korea's alleged highly enriched uranium program and its proliferation activities with Iran and Syria. The Bush Administration-North Korean agreements in effect removed these issues from the negotiating agenda. In its declaration of nuclear programs of June 26, 2008, North Korea did not admit to any uranium enrichment program or nuclear proliferation programs with Iran and Syria [29]. Restoring these issues in the negotiations would be difficult. North Korea could be expected to insist that the United States accepted its denials of these programs in 2008. China successfully urged the Bush Administration to remove these issues from the U.S. negotiating agenda with North Korea and concentrate on the plutonium program [30].

A second possible issue is whether the United States should continue to give close to 100% priority to the nuclear issue in its North Korean policy or whether it should begin to bring other issues into its North Korea policy. Selig Harrison testified that North Korean officials indicated to him that Pyongyang might be willing to negotiate with the Obama Administration over North Korea's missile programs. Another potential issue would be whether to follow through on U.S. and South Korean offers of late 2007 that once the six party agreements of February and October 2007 were implemented, including disablement of Yongbyon, the United States and South Korea would be willing to begin a separate negotiation with North Korea over a Korean peace treaty to replace the 1953 armistice agreement.

NORTH KOREA'S NUCLEAR PROGRAMS

Plutonium Program

Most of North Korea's plutonium-based nuclear installations are located at Yongbyon, 60 miles from the North Korean capital of Pyongyang. They are the facilities covered by the 1994 U.S.- North Korean Agreed Framework and by the freeze and disablement provisions in Phases One and Two of the February 2007 Six Party Nuclear Agreement. The key installations are as follows: [31]

- An atomic reactor, with a capacity of about 5 electrical megawatts that began operating by 1987. It is capable of expending enough reactor fuel to produce about 6 kilograms of plutonium annually—enough for the manufacture of a single atomic bomb annually. North Korea in 1989 shut down the reactor for about 70 days; U.S. intelligence agencies believe that North Korea removed fuel rods from the reactor at that time for reprocessing into plutonium suitable for nuclear weapons. In May 1994, North Korea shut down the reactor and removed about 8,000 fuel rods, which could be reprocessed into enough plutonium (25-30 kilograms) for 4-6 nuclear weapons. North Korea started operating the reactor again in February 2003, shut it down in April 2005, and said it had removed another 8,000 fuel rods. Under the February 2007 six party agreement, North Korea shut down the reactor in July 2007. As of early 2008, North Korea had completed about 80% of the disablement of the reactor.
- Two larger (estimated 50 megawatts and 200 electrical megawatts) reactors under construction at Yongbyon and Taechon since 1984. According to U.S. Ambassador Robert Gallucci, these plants, if completed, would be capable of producing enough spent fuel annually for 200 kilograms of plutonium, sufficient to manufacture nearly 30 atomic bombs per year. However, when North Korea re-opened the plutonium program in early 2003, reports indicate that construction on the larger reactors was not resumed.
- A plutonium reprocessing plant about 600 feet long and several stories high. The plant would separate weapons grade plutonium-239 from spent nuclear fuel rods for insertion into the structure of atomic bombs or warheads. U.S. intelligence agencies reportedly detected North Korean preparations to restart the plutonium reprocessing plant in February and March 2003. According to press reports, the CIA estimated in

late 2003 that North Korea had reprocessed some of the 8,000 fuel rods. In January 2004, North Korean officials showed a U.S. nuclear expert, Dr. Sigfried Hecker, samples of what they claimed were plutonium oxalate powder and plutonium metal. Dr. Hecker later said in testimony before the Senate Foreign Relations Committee (January 21, 2004) that, without testing, he could not confirm whether the sample was metallic plutonium "but all observations I was able to make are consistent with the sample being plutonium metal." IAEA monitors in July 2007 stated that the reprocessing plant was not in operation, and it remained shut down into early 2009.

Satellite photographs reportedly also show that the five megawatt reactor has no attached power lines, which it would have if used for electric power generation.

Persons interviewed for this study believe that North Korea developed the five megawatt reactor and the reprocessing plant with its own resources and technology. It is believed that Kim Jong-il, the son and successor of President Kim Il-sung who died in July 1994, directs the program, and that the military and the Ministry of Public Security implement it. North Korea reportedly has about 3,000 scientists and research personnel devoted to the Yongbyon program. Many have studied nuclear technology (though not necessarily nuclear weapons production) in the Soviet Union and China and reportedly Pakistan.

Highly Enriched Uranium (HEU) Program

North Korea's secret highly enriched uranium (HEU) program appears to date from at least 1996. Hwang Jang-yop, a Communist Party secretary who defected in 1997, has stated that North Korea and Pakistan agreed in the summer of 1996 to trade North Korean long-range missile technology for Pakistani HEU technology [32]. Other information dates North Korea-Pakistan cooperation to 1993. The Clinton Administration reportedly learned of it in 1998 or 1999, and a Department of Energy report of 1999 cited evidence of the program. In March 2000, President Clinton notified Congress that he was waiving certification that "North Korea is not seeking to develop or acquire the capability to enrich uranium." The Japanese newspaper Sankei Shimbun reported on June 9, 2000, the contents of a "detailed report" from Chinese government sources on a secret North Korean uranium enrichment facility inside North Korea's Mount Chonma. Reportedly, according to a CIA report to Congress, North Korea attempted in late 2001 to acquire "centrifuge-related materials in large quantities to support a uranium enrichment program" [33].

The CIA estimated publicly in November 2002 that North Korea could produce two atomic bombs annually through HEU beginning in 2005; [34] other intelligence estimates reportedly project a bomb producing capability between 2005 and 2007. Ambassador Robert Gallucci, who negotiated the 1994 U.S.-North Korean Agreed Framework, and Mitchell Reiss, head of the State Department's Policy Planning Bureau until 2004, have stated that a functioning North Korean HEU infrastructure could produce enough HEU for "two or more nuclear weapons per year." The Washington Post of April 28, 2004, quoted an U.S. intelligence official saying that a North Korean HEU infrastructure could produce as many as six atomic bombs annually. Administration officials have stated that they do not know the locations of North Korea's uranium enrichment program or whether North Korea has assembled the infrastructure to produce uranium-based atomic bombs [35]

International Assistance

Knowledgeable individuals believe that the Soviet Union did not assist directly in the development of Yongbyon in the 1980s. The U.S.S.R. provided North Korea with a small research reactor in the 1960s, which also is at Yongbyon. However, North Korean nuclear scientists continued to receive training in the U.S.S.R. up to the demise of the Soviet Union in December 1991. East German and Russian nuclear and missile scientists reportedly were in North Korea throughout the 1990s. Since 1999, reports have appeared that U.S. intelligence agencies had information that Chinese enterprises were supplying important components and raw materials for North Korea's missile program [36]

Nuclear Collaboration with Iran and Syria

In April 2008, the Bush Administration disclosed that a facility at Al Kibar in northeast Syria bombed by Israel on September 6, 2007, was a plutonium nuclear reactor under construction with the apparent aim of producing nuclear fuel rods that could be converted into nuclear weapons- grade plutonium. For months after the Israeli bombing, press reports had cited information and evidence that the facility was a nuclear reactor and that North Korea was assisting Syria in its construction. This nuclear collaboration reportedly was ongoing since 1997.37 U.S. intelligence officials on April 24, 2008, privately briefed Members of Congress on North Korea's role, and they provided a background news briefing to the media [38] (See CRS Report RL33487, *Syria: Background and U.S. Relations.*)

U.S. officials presented several forms of evidence for North Korean involvement in the Syrian reactor. A U.S. photograph showed a top North Korean nuclear official visiting Syrian nuclear experts. U.S. intelligence officials released photographs of the outside and inside of the reactor showing marked similarities with the North Korean nuclear reactor at Yongbyon. The photos of the interior of the reactor reportedly showed North Koreans inside the reactor [39]. A leading South Korean newspaper had reported that U.S. intelligence agencies had obtained a list of North Korean officials involved in the Syrian reactor project and that chief U.S. negotiator, Christopher Hill, had confronted North Korean nuclear negotiators with the list [40]

At the time of the Bush Administration's disclosures, South Korean intelligence officials stated that they had information that the Israeli bombing had killed ten North Koreans [41]

U.S. officials said that the Al Kibar reactor was nearly operational at the time of the Israeli bombing. However, non-government nuclear experts questioned that assertion, asserting that there was no evidence of a plutonium reprocessing plant and a facility to produce nuclear fuel for the reactor in Syria [42]

One potential answer to the question of the absence of other reactor-related plutonium facilities in Syria came in reports later in 2008 that Iran also was involved in the Syrian reactor with North Korea and that a plutonium reprocessing plant was in Iran. The online service of the German news publication *Der Spiegel* cited "*intelligence reports seen by Der Spiegel*" that North Korean and Iranian scientists were working together at the reactor site at the time of the Israeli bombing. Some of the plutonium fuel rod production from the reactor was to have gone to Iran, which viewed the reactor as a "reserve site" to produce weapons-grade plutonium as a supplement to Iran's own highly enriched uranium program [43]. A similar description of North Korean-Iranian cooperation in the Syrian reactor came in two reports from Washington in the Japanese newspaper Sankei Shimbun. The newspaper reported in September 2008 information from *"a source familiar with the Syrian nuclear issue"* that *"a secret Iranian Revolutionary Guards base"* in Iran housed a plutonium reprocessing facility designed to reprocess nuclear fuel rods from the Syrian reactor [44]. Sankei Shimbun reported from Washington in July 2008 several visits of Iranian officials to the Syrian reactor in 2005 and 2006 [45].

Additional information pointing to North Korean-Iranian collaboration in plutonium nuclear development came from European and Israeli defense officials in early 2007. They stated that North Korea and Iran had concluded a new agreement for North Korea to share data from its October 2006 nuclear test with Iran [46].

These reports describe a direct collaborative relationship between North Korea and Iran in developing nuclear weapons. Additionally, since the early 1990s, a body of reports has accumulated pointing to a significant collaborative North Korean-Iranian nuclear relationship inside Iran, with North Korea's principal interlocutor being the Iranian Revolutionary Guards (IRGC). Some of these reports cite the Central Intelligence Agency or Western intelligence sources as sources of information. Other reports seem to be based, at least in part, on Israeli intelligence sources. Specific events or factors in the alleged North Korean-Iranian nuclear collaboration are described in multiple reports.

Numerous reports have asserted that the IRGC occupies a leadership role in Iran's nuclear program. A State Department's 2007 Fact Sheet asserted that *"the IRGC attempted, as recently as 2006, to procure sophisticated and costly equipment that could be used to support Iran's ballistic missile and nuclear program"* [47].

Nuclear collaboration reportedly began at the same time North Korea negotiated with the IRGC for cooperation in developing and manufacturing Nodong missiles. The first reports, in 1993 and 1994, said that North Korea and Iran had signed an initial agreement for nuclear cooperation. An Economist Foreign Report cited "CIA sources" that Iran was helping to finance North Korea's nuclear program and that North Korea would supply Iran with nuclear technology and equipment [48]. A report of the U.S. House of Representatives Republican Research Committee claimed that Iran would provide $500 million to North Korea for the joint development of nuclear weapons [49]. The "CIA sources" cited by the *Economist Foreign Report* mentioned the development of enriched uranium as a goal of the new North Korean-Iranian agreements.

The next reported stage in nuclear collaboration, in 2003 and afterwards, appears to have been connected to the reported joint advancement of the program to produce a model of North Korea's Nodong intermediate ballistic missile in Iran. Production of the Nodong in Iran was a main element of the reported North Korean-Iranian agreements of 1993. By 1997, North Korean missile experts were working in Iran with the IRGC to produce the Shahab 3 and Shahab 4 missiles, the Iranian name for the Nodong [50]. Success in developing and testing the Shahab missile reportedly led to a North Korean-Iranian agreement, probably in 2003, to either initiate or accelerate work to develop nuclear warheads that could be fitted on the Shahab missile. Iran was reported to have offered shipments of oil and natural gas to North Korea to secure this joint development of nuclear warheads [51]. North Koreans reportedly were seen at Iranian nuclear facilities in 2003. By this time, a large number of North Korean nuclear and missile specialists reportedly were in Iran.52 Der Spiegel quoted "western intelligence service circles" as describing Iran in 2005 as offering North Korea economic aid if Pyongyang "continues to cooperate actively in developing nuclear missiles for Tehran" [53].

In 2006 and 2008, U.S. intelligence officials, the International Atomic Energy Agency, and other diplomatic sources disclosed that Iran was trying to modify the Shahab missile, especially the nose cone, so that it could carry a nuclear warhead. U.S. intelligence officials described this work as part of an Iranian Project 11 1—"a nuclear research effort that includes work on missile development" [54].

In March 2006, Reuters reported "an intelligence report given to Reuters by a non-U.S. diplomat" that described Iran's plans to develop nuclear warheads for the Shahab 3 missile [55]. Two years later, the International Atomic Energy Agency confronted Iran at several 2008 meetings with documents and photographs showing Iranian work in redesigning the nose cone of the Shahab-3 missile in order for it to carry a nuclear warhead [56].

The National Council of Resistance of Iran is an exiled opposition group that in 2002 had revealed correctly the existence of secret Iranian nuclear facilities at Natanz and Irak. It issued a report in February 2008 that gave reputed details of North Korean-Iranian collaboration in nuclear warhead development. It alleged that the Iranian Defense Ministry has a secret facility at Khojir on the edge of Tehran, code-named B 1 -Nori-8500, that is engaged in the development of nuclear warheads for intermediate range ballistic missiles. North Korean specialists are at this facility, according to the National Council [57]. The Japanese newspaper Sankei Shimbun reported on March 2, 2009, that North Korean missiles experts had worked with Iranian counterparts in Iran's launch of a satellite on February 2, 2009.

Iran's Safir 2 missile, reportedly based on the North Korean Taepodong missile, was launch vehicle for the February 2 satellite [58]

Another form of North Korean-Iranian nuclear collaboration reportedly involved a huge Iranian project to develop underground bunkers and tunnels for elements of Iran's nuclear program. The project, estimated to have cost hundreds of millions of dollars, included the construction of 10,000 meters of underground halls for nuclear equipment connected by tunnels measuring hundreds of meters branching off from each hall. Specifications reportedly called for reinforced concrete tunnel ceilings, walls, and doors resistant to explosions and penetrating munitions [59].

The IRGC implemented the project. North Korea reportedly participated in the design and construction of the bunkers and tunnels. In early 2005, Myong Lyu-do, a leading North Korean expert on underground facilities, traveled to Tehran to run the program of North Korean assistance [60]. North Korea is believed to have extensive underground military installations inside North Korea. Its collaboration with the IRGC reportedly has involved extensive aid to Hezbollah in constructing underground military installations in Lebanon. (See CRS Report RL30613, *North Korea: Terrorism List Removal?*)

The Japanese newspaper, Sankei Shimbun, reported two visits of high level Iranian officials to North Korea in February and May 2008. The Iranian delegation included officials of Iran's Atomic Energy Organization and National Security Council. The apparent purpose of these visits, according to the reports, was to ensure that North Korea would maintain secrecy about its nuclear collaboration with Iran in its negotiations with U.S. Assistant Secretary of State Christopher Hill [61]

North Korea's Delivery Systems

North Korea's missile launchings of July 4, 2006, re-focused U.S. attention on North Korea's missile program and Pyongyang's apparent attempts to develop long-range missiles that could strike U.S. territories. North Korea succeeded by 1998 in developing a "Nodong" missile with a range estimated at up to 900 miles, capable of covering South Korea and most of Japan. North Korea reportedly deployed nearly 100 Nodong missiles by 2003 and also had jointly developed with Iran the Shahab version of the Nodong. On August 31, 1998, North Korea test fired a three-stage rocket, apparently the prototype of the Taepodong I missile; the third stage apparently was an attempt to launch a satellite. U.S. intelligence estimates reportedly concluded that such a missile would have the range to reach Alaska, Guam, and the Northern Marianas Commonwealth. Media reports in early 2000 cited U.S. intelligence findings that North Korea aimed to deploy an intercontinental ballistic missile that would be capable of striking Alaska, Hawaii, and the U.S. west coast. U.S. officials claimed in September 2003 that North Korea had developed a more accurate, longer-range intermediate ballistic missile that could reach Okinawa and Guam (site of major U.S. military bases). Subsequent reports in February 2009 quoted South Korea's Defense Ministry that North Korea had deployed this missile with a range of at least 1,800 miles [62].

However, the apparent failure of the Taepodong missile launched July 4, 2006, indicated that North Korea had not succeeded in developing such a long-range missile. In March 2009, North Korea announced plans to launch a satellite between April 4 and 8, 2009. U.S., Japanese, and South Korean officials reacted that such a launch, in effect, would be a test of a long-range missile.

Evaluations of all seven of the missiles launched on July 4, 2006, by intelligence agencies of the United States and other governments reportedly have concluded that North Korea has increased the accuracy of its Scud and Nodong missiles and that the launches displayed the ability of North Korea's command and control apparatus to coordinate multiple launchings of missiles at diverse targets [63]. (For additional information, see CRS Report RS21473, *North Korean Ballistic Missile Threat to the United States*, by Steven A. Hildreth.)

The Clinton Administration pressed North Korea for new talks over North Korea's missile program. In talks held in 1999 and 2000, North Korea demanded $1 billion annually in exchange for a promise not to export missiles. U.S. negotiators rejected North Korea's demand for $1 billion but offered a lifting of U.S. economic sanctions. This laid the ground for the Berlin agreement of September 1999, in which North Korea agreed to defer further missile tests in return for the lifting of major U.S. economic sanctions. President Clinton formalized the lifting of key economic sanctions against North Korea in June 2000. North Korea continued the moratorium, but it appears to have used Pakistan and Iran as surrogates in testing intermediate-range missiles based on North Korean technology [64]

State of Nuclear Weapons Development

A CIA statement of August 18, 2003, reportedly estimated that North Korea had produced one or two simple fission-type nuclear weapons and had validated the designs without conducting yield-producing nuclear tests [65]. The initial estimate of one or two nuclear weapons is derived primarily from North Korea's approximately 70-day shutdown of the five megawatt reactor in 1989, which would have given it the opportunity to remove nuclear fuel rods, from which plutonium is reprocessed. The U.S. Central Intelligence Agency (CIA) and the Defense Intelligence Agency (DIA) reportedly estimated in 1993 that North Korea extracted enough fuel rods for about 12 kilograms of plutonium—sufficient for one or two atomic bombs. The CIA and DIA apparently based their estimate on the 1989 shutdown of the five megawatt reactor [66]

South Korean and Japanese intelligence estimates reportedly were higher: 16-24 kilograms (Japan) and 7-22 kilograms (South Korea). These estimates reportedly are based on the view that North Korea could have acquired a higher volume of plutonium from the 1989 reactor shutdown and the view of a higher possibility that North Korea removed fuel rods during the 1990 and 1991 reactor slowdowns. Russian Defense Ministry analyses in late 1993 reportedly came to a similar estimate of about 20 kilograms of plutonium, enough for two or three atomic bombs. General Leon LaPorte, former U.S. Commander in Korea, stated in an interview in April 2006 that North Korea possessed three to six nuclear weapons before the 1994 U.S.-North Korean Agreed Framework [67].

Russian intelligence agencies also reportedly have learned of significant technological advances by North Korea toward nuclear weapons production. On March 10, 1992, the Russian newspaper Argumenty I Fakty (Arguments and Facts) published the text of a 1990 Soviet KGB report to the Soviet Central Committee on North Korea's nuclear program. It was published again by Izvestiya on June 24, 1994. The KGB report asserted that "According to available data, development of the first nuclear device has been completed at the DPRK nuclear research center in Yongbyon." The North Korean government, the report stated, had decided not to test the device in order to avoid international detection.

Additionally, a number of reports and evidence point to at least a middle-range likelihood that North Korea may have smuggled plutonium from Russia. In June 1994, the head of Russia's Counterintelligence Service (successor to the KGB) said at a press conference that North Korea's attempts to smuggle "components of nuclear arms production" from Russia caused his agency "special anxiety." U.S. executive branch officials have expressed concern in background briefings over the possibility that North Korea has smuggled plutonium from Russia. One U.S. official, quoted in the Washington Times, July 5, 1994, asserted that "There is the possibility that things having gotten over the [Russia-North Korea] border without anybody being aware of it." The most specific claim came in the German news magazine Stern in March 1993, which cited Russian Counterintelligence Service reports that North Korea had smuggled 56 kilograms of plutonium (enough for 7-9 atomic bombs) from Russia.

If, as it claims, North Korea reprocessed the 8,000 nuclear fuel rods in 2003 that it had moved from storage at the beginning of that year, North Korea gained an additional 25-3 0 kilograms of plutonium, according to Dr. Sigfried Hecker in his testimony before the Senate Foreign Relations Committee on January 21, 2004. Dr. Hecker, former director of the Los Alamos Laboratories, had visited North Korea's Yongbyon nuclear complex in January 2004. U.S. officials and nuclear experts have stated that this amount of plutonium would give North Korea the potential to produce between four to eight atomic bombs [68]. Nuclear expert David Albright estimated in February 2007 that North Korea had a stockpile of reprocessed plutonium of 28-5 0 kilograms, enough for between 5 and 12 nuclear weapons [69]. These estimates appear to be based on projections that a country like North Korea would need 6-8 kilograms of plutonium to produce one atomic bomb. The IAEA has had a standard that a non-nuclear state would need about eight kilograms of plutonium to produce an atomic bomb.

The question of whether North Korea produced additional nuclear weapons with the plutonium that it apparently acquired after 2003 may depend on the degree of success/failure of North Korea's nuclear test of October 2006 and whether North Korea is able to develop a nuclear warhead that could be fitted onto its missiles. Experts believe that any atomic bombs developed likely are similar to the plutonium bomb dropped by the United States on Nagasaki in August 1945. However, North Korea has few delivery systems that could deliver such a bomb to a U.S. or Japanese target. Thus, Pyongyang probably would not produce additional Nagasaki-type bombs but would retain its weapons-grade plutonium until it could use it to produce a nuclear warhead. Statements by U.S. officials reflect an apparent uncertainty over whether North Korea has achieved a warheading capability, [70] and they have not addressed publicly the reports of North Korean-Iranian collaboration in nuclear warhead development.

According to press reports in late 2002, the CIA concluded that North Korea accelerated its uranium enrichment program in the 1999, 2000, and 2001. According to U.S. News and World Report, September 1, 2003, the CIA estimated that North Korea could produce a uranium-based atomic weapon by the second half of 2004. Another report, in the Washington Post, April 28, 2004, stated that U.S. intelligence officials had "broadly concluded" that a North Korean uranium enrichment program would be operational by 2007, producing enough material for as many as six atomic bombs [71]. However, U.S. officials have stated that they know less about the secret uranium enrichment program (HEU) than they know about the plutonium program. North Korea received designs for uranium enrichment centrifuges from Pakistan nuclear "czar," A.Q. Khan, and has attempted to purchase overseas key components for uranium enrichment centrifuges; but some of these purchases have been blocked [72]. Assistant Secretary of State Christopher Hill stated on September 28, 2005, that "where there is not a consensus is how far they [North Korea] have gone with this [the HEU program]" [73] (See also CRS Report RL34256, *North Korea's Nuclear Weapons*, by Mary Beth Nikitin.)

SELECT CHRONOLOGY

10/9/06—North Korea announced that it has carried out an underground nuclear test.

2/13/07—The six party governments negotiating over North Korea's nuclear programs announced an agreement for a freeze and disablement of North Korea's nuclear facilities accompanied by energy and diplomatic benefits to North Korea.

6/25/07—A diplomatic deadlock involving $24 million in frozen North Korean funds in a Macau bank, Banco Delta Asia, was ended when U.S.-initiated measures to unfreeze the money and transfer it to North Korea.

7/18/07—The International Atomic Energy Agency announced that nuclear facilities at Yongbyon are shut down in accordance with the freeze provisions of the February 2007 six party nuclear agreement.

1 0/3/07—The six parties issued a statement to implement the second phase of the February 2007 nuclear agreement, focusing on the disablement of Yongbyon, a North Korean declaration of its nuclear programs, and a U.S. promise to lift economic sanctions on North Korea and remove North Korea from the U.S. list of state sponsors of terrorism.

4/8/08—Assistant Secretary of State Christopher Hill and North Korea's Kim Kye-gwan negotiated an agreement reportedly limiting the information that North Korea would have to provide in a declaration of nuclear programs.

6/26/08—North Korea transmitted a declaration of nuclear programs to China, the chairman of the six party talks. President Bush announced a lifting of economic sanctions on North Korea and an intention to remove North Korea from the U.S. list of state sponsors of terrorism by August 11, 2008.

8/11/08—The Bush Administration announced that it would not remove North Korea from the list of state sponsors of terrorism because Pyongyang rejected U.S. proposals for a verification system of inspections inside North Korea.

10/3/08—Assistant Secretary of State Hill and North Korean officials negotiate an agreement in Pyongyang for a verification system.

FOR ADDITIONAL READING

CRS Report RL31555, *China and Proliferation of Weapons of Mass Destruction and Missiles: Policy Issues*, by Shirley A. Kan.

CRS Report RL31785, *Foreign Assistance to North Korea*, by Mark E. Manyin.

CRS Report RL33567, *Korea-U.S. Relations: Issues for Congress*, by Larry A. Niksch. CRS Report RL3 1696, *North Korea: Economic Sanctions*, by Dianne E. Rennack.

CRS Report RS21473, *North Korean Ballistic Missile Threat to the United States*, by Steven A. Hildreth.

CRS Report RL33324, *North Korean Counterfeiting of U.S. Currency*, by Dick K. Nanto.

CRS Report RL33709, *North Korea's Nuclear Test: Motivations, Implications, and U.S. Options*, by Emma Chanlett-Avery and Sharon Squassoni.

CRS Report RL34256, *North Korea's Nuclear Weapons*, by Mary Beth Nikitin.

REFERENCES

[1] Glenn Kessler, "N. Korea doesn't agree to written nuclear pact," *Washington Post*, December 12, 2008.

[2] "Bush OKs Singapore Agreement: WH [White House]," Yonhap News Agency (Seoul), April 14, 2008. Melanie Lee and Daryl Loo, "Nuclear talks with N. Korea make progress, US says," Reuters, April 8, 2008.

[3] White House Press Spokesman, Press Fact Sheet: Presidential Action on State Sponsor of Terrorism (SST) and the Trading with the Enemy Act (TWEA), June 26, 2008.

[4] Cited inCRS Report RL34256, *North Korea's Nuclear Weapons*, by Mary Beth Nikitin.

[5] "Restoring disabled N. Korea nukes would need year—US," *Reuters,* November 22, 2007.

[6] "North Korea tells China 30.8 kg of plutonium extracted," *Agence France Presse,* October 24, 2008.

[7] Glenn Kessler, "U.S. increases estimate of N.Korean plutonium," *Washington Post*, May 14, 2008.

[8] Anne Gearan, "U.S. official: North Korea has agreed to intensive US verification of its plutonium production," Associated Press, June 26, 2008. Helene Cooper, "Past deals by N.Korea may face less study," *New York Times*, April 18, 2008. p. A5.
[9] Anne Gearan, "U.S. official: North Korea has agreed to intensive US verification of its plutonium production," *Associated Press*, June 26, 2008.
[10] Missy Ryan, "Slim trade impact seen in US move on N.Korea sanctions," *Reuters*, June 26, 2008.
[11] U.S. Treasury Department, *Calendar Year 2006 Fifteenth Annual Report to the Congress on Assets in the United States of Terrorist Countries and International Terrorism Program Designees*, September 2007.
[12] "N Korea wants normalized relations with the US," *Dong-A Ilbo* (Seoul, internet), June 6, 2008.
[13] White House Press Spokesman, Fact Sheet: Presidential Action on State Sponsor of Terrorism (SST) and the Trading with the Enemy Act (TWEA), June 26, 2008.
[14] Glenn Kessler, Far reaching U.S. plan impaired N. Korea deal; demands began to undo nuclear accord, *Washington Post*, September 26, 2008, p. A20.
[15] Glenn Kessler, "Far-reaching U.S. plan impaired N.Korea deal; demands began to undo nuclear accord," *Washington Post*, September 26, 2008, p. A20.
[16] Special briefing by State Department spokesman, Sean McCormack, M2 Presswire, October 11, 2008.
[17] Ibid.
[18] "N. Korea rejects contentions it is delaying denuclearization," *Kyodo News*, November 12, 2008. "NKorea will not let nuclear samples out of country," *Reuters*, November 12, 2008.
[19] "N. Korea proposes military talks with U.S.," *Kyodo News*, October 5, 2008. "Jin Dae-woong: N.K. delivered U.S. Ultimatum on Nuke Dispute," *Korea Herald* (internet), October 7, 2008.
[20] Woodrow Wilson International Center for Scholars, Selig S. Harrison reports on his trip to Pyongyang, February 4, 2009.
[21] DPRK Foreign Ministry's spokesman dismisses U.S. wrong assertion, Korean Central News Agency (KCNA), January 17, 2009. DPRK Foreign Ministry spokesman's press statement on denuclearization of Korean peninsula, KCNA, February 5, 2009.
[22] Woodrow Wilson International Center for Scholars, Selig S. Harrison reports on his trip to Pyongyang, February 4, 2009.
[23] Choe Sang-hun, Tensions rise on Korean peninsula, *New York Times* (internet), January 19, 2009.
[24] DPRK's principled stand on denuclearization of Korean peninsula, KCNA, February 2, 2009. Statement by the General Staff of the Korean People's Army, KCNA, February 2, 2009. DPRK Foreign Ministry's spokesman dismisses U.S. wrong assertion, January 16, 2009.
[25] Selig A. Harrison, Living with a nuclear North Korea, Washington Post, February 17, 2009, p. A13. According to Harrison, North Korean officials in Pyongyang went into detail with him over future negotiations over a dismantlement of Yongbyon.
[26] Ibid.
[27] For a hint of this North Korean position, see the January 2, 2009, article in Choson Sinbo, a North Korean newspaper in Japan. Choson Sinbo noted that "there was no

immediate change in the conditions of [North Korean] international economic activities" after the removal from the U.S. terrorism support list and that the removal constituted "a first step toward a [U.S.] policy shift."

[28] Clinton reaffirms pledge for N. Korea's nuclear dismantlement, *Asia Pulse,* February 18, 2009
[29] Helene Cooper, Past deals by N.Korea may face less study, New York Times, April 18, 2008, p. A5. Anne Gearan, U.S. official: North Korea has agreed to intensive US verification of its plutonium production, *Associated Press*, June 26, 2008.
[30] Nicholas Kralev, U.S. urges monitoring flow of nuclear materials, *Washington Times*, February 26, 2008, p. A1.
[31] Albright, David and O'Neill, Kevin. *Solving the North Korean nuclear puzzle.* Washington, DC, Institute for Science and International Security Press, 2000. pp. 57-82.
[32] Kim Min-cheol. "Hwang tells of secret nuke program." *Choson Ilbo* (Seoul, internet version), July 5, 2003.
[33] Pincus, Walter. "N. Korea's nuclear plans were no secret." *Washington Post*, February 1, 2003. p. A1.
[34] CIA unclassified point paper distributed to Congress, November 19, 2002.
[35] Kessler, Glenn. "New doubts on nuclear efforts by North Korea." *Washington Post*, March 1, 2007. p. A1.
[36] "ROK source views CIA report on DPRK production of plutonium." *Chungang Ilbo* (internet version), February 25, 2001. Gertz, Bill. "Pyongyang's launch met by indifference." *Washington Times*, May 16, 1999. p. C1.
[37] Sara A. Carter and Bill Gertz, "Intelligence on Syria delayed to avoid fight," *Washington Times*, April 25, 2008, p. A1.
[38] David E. Sanger, "Bush Administration released images to bolster its claims about Syrian reactor," *New York Times*, April 25, 2008, p. A1.
[39] Robin Wright, "N. Koreans taped at Syrian reactor," *Washington Post*, April 24, 2008, p. A. 1.
[40] "U.S. called N. Korea's bluff over Syria," *Chosun Ilbo* (internet), April 1, 2008.
[41] "N.Koreans killed in Syria during Israeli raid," *Chosun Ilbo* (internet), April 29, 2008. "N. Koreans may have died in Israel raid in Syria—NHK," Reuters, April 28, 2008.
[42] Nicholas Kralev and Sara A. Carter, "Syria's nuke facility was nearly finished," *Washington Times*, April 24, 2008, p. A1. Robin Wright, "N. Koreans taped at Syrian reactor," *Washington Post*, April 24, 2008, p. A1.
[43] "Asad's risky nuclear game," *Spiegel Online*, June 23, 2008.
[44] Takashi Arimoto, "Reprocessing facility of bombed nuclear base in Iran; intimate ties between Syria and North Korea," *Sankei Shimbun* (internet), September 12, 2008.
[45] Takashi Arimoto, "Iran involved in nuclear program: trilateral cooperation of Syria, Iran, North Korea," *Sankei Shimbun* (internet), July 12, 2008.
[46] Jin Dae-woong, "Concerns grow over missile links between N. Korea, Iran," *Korea Herald* (internet), January 28, 2007. "UK press: North Korea aids Iran in nuclear testing," *Dow Jones International News*, January 24, 2007. "Israel PM to charge NKorea link with Iran, Syria," Agence France Presse, February 26, 2008.
[47] U.S. Department of State, Fact Sheet: Designation of Iranian Entities and Individuals for Proliferation Activities and Support for Terrorism, October 25, 2007.

[48] "An Israeli lesson for North Korea?" *Economist Foreign Report*, April 22, 1993, p. 2. See also: "DPRK reportedly aids Iranian nuclear project," Yonhap News Agency, January 26, 1993. "DPRK military delegation's Iran visit reported," Seoul KBS-1 Radio Network, February 24, 1994.

[49] "U.S. report on DPRK-Iran missile deal cited," Yonhap News Agency, July 16, 1993. The $500 million figure also was cited in: "Iran funds North Korea's drive to build nuclear bombs," *U.S. News and World Report*, March 29, 1993, p. 18.

[50] Con Coughlin, "China, N. Korea send experts to hone Iran's long-range missiles," *London Daily Telegraph*, November 23, 1997, p. A5. Bill Gertz, "North Korea send missile parts technology to Iran," *Washington Times*, April 18, 2001, p. A3.

[51] Douglas Frantz, "Iran closes in on ability to build a nuclear bomb; Tehran's reactor program masks strides toward a weapons capability, a Times investigation finds," *Los Angeles Times*, August 4, 2003, p. A1. "Military source: DPRK, Iran planning joint development of nuclear warheads," *Sankei Shimbun* (internet version), August 6, 2003.

[52] "Iranian nuke experts visited N. Korea this year," Kyodo World Service, June 10, 2003. Douglas Frantz, "Iran closes in on ability to build a nuclear bomb," *Los Angeles Times*, August 4, 2003, p. A1. "Military source: DPRK, Iran planning joint development of nuclear warheads," *Sankei Shimbun* (internet), August 6, 2003.

[53] "Mullahs helping Stalinists," *Der Spiegel* (internet), November 28, 2005.

[54] Dafna Linzer, "Strong leads and dead ends in nuclear case against Iran," *Washington Post*, February 8, 2006, p. AO1.

[55] Louis Charbonneau, "Iran said to step up plans for Shahab missiles," *Reuters*, March 6, 2006.

[56] David E. Sanger, "Nuclear agency says Iran has used new technology," *New York Times*, February 23, 2008, p. A3. Mark Heinrich, "IAEA shows photos alleging Iran nuclear missile work," *Reuters*, September 16, 2008.

[57] "Iran still developing nuclear warheads: exiled opposition group," Agence France Presse, February 20, 2008. Marc Champion, "Iran arms claim is lodged—Tehran is developing nuclear warheads, exile group tells U.N.," *Wall Street Journal Asia*, February 21, 2008, p. 9. Koki Mirua, "Anti-Iranian government organ points to 'DPRK's cooperation in Iran's nuclear development,'" *Tokyo Shimbun* (internet), September 24, 2008.

[58] Takashi Arimoto, North Korea cooperates in Iran's satellite launch, secretly linked to development of long-range ballistic missiles, Sankei Shimbun Online, March 2, 2009.

[59] "Nukes too deep to hit." *Newsweek*, November 3, 2008, p. 8, 10.

[60] Robin Hughes, "Tehran takes steps to protect nuclear facilities," *Jane's Defence Weekly*, January 25, 2006, p. 4-5.

[61] Takashi Arimoto, "Iranian delegation makes top secret visit to North Korea in late February; for discussions on nuclear issue?" *Sankei Shimbun* (internet), March 20, 2008. "Iran involved in nuclear program: trilateral cooperation of Syria, Iran, North Korea," *Sankei Shimbun* (internet), July 12, 2008.

[62] Jae-soon Chang, SKorea: NKorea has deployed new ballistic missile, *Associated Press*, February 23, 2009.

[63] "An expert is amazed by the targeting accuracy: an exclusive report based on complete data on the landing points of North Korean missiles," *Yomiuri Weekly* (Tokyo) in Japanese, August 6, 2006. p. 22-23.

[64] Gertz, Bill. "Pakistan's missile program aided by North Korea." *Washington Times*, September 14, 1998. p. A1. Alon, Ben-David. "Iran successfully tests Shahab 3," *Janes Defence Weekly* (internet version), July 9, 2003. Coughlin, Con. "China, N. Korea send experts to hone Iran's long-range missiles, *New York Times*, November 23, 1997. p. A5.

[65] Sanger, David E. "North Korea's bomb: untested but ready, C.I.A. concludes," *New York Times*, November 9, 2003. p. 4.

[66] Edith M. Lederer, "Fuel for speculation; reactor shutdown seen as N. Korean nuke source," *Washington Times*, January 10, 1994, p. 1. David Albright, "North Korean Plutonium Production." ISIS Paper, 1994, p. 10-13.

[67] Kang Chan-ho. "Former USFK commander: transfer of wartime control should not be carried out overnight," *Joong Ang Ilbo* (Seoul), April 3, 2006. p. 13.

[68] Kessler, Glenn. "N. Korea nuclear estimate to rise," *Washington Post*, April 28, 2004. p. A1. "U.S. Expert says N. Korea has plutonium to make 8 bombs," *Yonhap News Agency*, January 2, 2006.

[69] David Albright and Paul Brannan, "The North Korean Plutonium Stock," Institute for Science and International Security, February 20, 2007.

[70] Cloud, David S. and Sanger, David E. "U.S. aide sees arms advance by North Korea," *New York Times*, April 29, 2005. p. A1. Morgan, David. "U.S. not certain North Korea has nuclear weapons," *Reuters*, February 28, 2005.

[71] Kessler, "N. Korea nuclear estimate to rise," *Washington Post*, April 28, 2004. p. A1.

[72] Albright and Hinderstein, *Dismantling the DPRK's nuclear weapons program*, pp. 35-36.

[73] "Parties concur N.K. has HEU material, but disagree on program's progress: Hill," *Yonhap News Agency*, September 29, 2005.

In: Political and Economic Developments in Asia
Editor: Felix Chin

ISBN: 978-1-61209-783-1
©2011 Nova Science Publishers, Inc.

Chapter 4

BURMA AND TRANSNATIONAL CRIME[*]

Liana Sun Wyler

ABSTRACT

Transnational organized crime groups in Burma (Myanmar) operate a multi-billion dollar criminal industry that stretches across Southeast Asia. Trafficked drugs, humans, wildlife, gems, timber, and other contraband flow through Burma, supporting the illicit demands of the region and beyond. Widespread collusion between traffickers and Burma's ruling military junta, the State Peace and Development Council (SPDC), allows organized crime groups to function with impunity. Transnational crime in Burma bears upon U.S. interests as it threatens regional security in Southeast Asia and bolsters a regime that fosters a culture of corruption and disrespect for the rule of law and human rights.

Congress has been active in U.S. policy toward Burma for a variety of reasons, including combating Burma's transnational crime situation. At times, it has imposed sanctions on Burmese imports, suspended foreign assistance and loans, and ensured that U.S. funds remain out of the regime's reach. Most recently, the 110th Congress passed P.L. 110-286, the Tom Lantos Block Burmese JADE Act of 2008 (signed by the President on July 29, 2008), which imposes further sanctions on SPDC officials and prohibits the indirect importation of Burmese gems, among other actions. On the same day, the President directed the U.S. Department of Treasury to impose financial sanctions against 10 Burmese companies, including companies involved in the gem- mining industry, pursuant to Executive Order 13464 of April 30, 2008. The 111th Congress may choose to conduct oversight of U.S. policy toward Burma, including the country's role in criminal activity.

This report analyzes the primary actors driving transnational crime in Burma, the forms of transnational crime occurring, and current U.S. policy in combating these crimes. This report will be updated as events warrant. For further analysis of U.S. policy to Burma, see CRS Report RL33479, *Burma-U.S. Relations*, by Larry A. Niksch.

---

[*] This is an edited, reformatted and augmented version of CRS Report RL34225, dated April 27, 2009.

SCOPE OF THE PROBLEM

Transnational organized crime groups flourish in Burma, trafficking contraband that includes drugs, humans, guns, wildlife, gems, and timber. Transnational crime is highly profitable, reportedly generating roughly several billion dollars each year. The country's extra-legal economy, both black market and illicit border trade, is reportedly so large that an accurate assessment of the size and structure of the country's economy is unavailable. Contraband trafficking also remains a low-risk enterprise, as corruption among officials in Burma's ruling military junta, the State Peace and Development Council (SPDC), appears to facilitate trafficking and effectively provide the criminal underground immunity from law enforcement and judicial action [1] Synergistic links connect various forms of contraband trafficking; smugglers use the same routes for many forms of trafficking, following paths of least resistance, where corruption and lax law enforcement prevail.

The continued presence of transnational crime in Burma and the illicit trafficking routes across Burma's borders share many features of so-called "ungoverned spaces"—regions of the world where governments have difficulty establishing control or are complicit in the corruption of the rule of law [2]. Among the commonalities that Burma's border regions share with other ungoverned spaces is physical terrain that is difficult to control. Burma's long borders, through which much smuggled contraband passes, stretch across vast trackless hills and mountains that are poorly patrolled. In addition, continuing ethnic tensions with some ethnic armed rebel groups hamper government control in some regions of the country, which is another common feature of ungoverned spaces. Recent cease-fire agreements in other border regions have not markedly improved the situation; instead, these cease-fires have provided groups known for their activity in transnational crime with near autonomy, essentially placing these areas beyond the reach of Burmese law.

Congress has long been active in U.S. policy toward Burma for a variety of reasons, including on issues related to transnational crime. Because the State Department lists Burma as a major drug- producing state, the country is barred access from U.S. foreign assistance under several longstanding legislative provisions [3]. Congress also authorizes sanctions against countries that the State Department deems in non-compliance with the minimum standards for the elimination of trafficking in persons, which includes Burma [4].

Most recently, the 110th Congress has sought to strengthen unilateral sanctions against Burma. In response to the Burmese government's forced suppression of anti-regime protests in August and September of 2007, as well as its internationally criticized humanitarian response to destruction resulting from tropical cyclone Nargis in May 2008, Congress passed P.L. 110-286, the Tom Lantos Block Burmese JADE Act of 2008 (signed by the President on July 29, 2008). This law imposes further sanctions on SPDC officials and prohibits the indirect import of Burmese gems, among other actions. H.Rept. 110-418, which accompanies H.R. 3890, also cites "Burma's rampant drug trade" and "its role as a source for international trafficking in persons and illicit goods" as additional reasons for these new sanctions. The 111th Congress may choose to continue its interest in oversight of U.S. policy toward Burma, including the country's role in criminal activity.

PRIMARY ACTORS AND MOTIVES

Organized Crime, Ethnic Gangs, and Insurgent Groups

The United Wa State Army (UWSA), Shan State Army-South (SSA-S), Shan State Army-North (SSA-N), Democratic Karen Buddhist Army (DBKA), ethnic Chinese criminal groups (including the Triads), and other armed groups have criminal networks that stretch from India to Malaysia and up into China. Many of the transnational criminal elements along Burma's border are linked to past or ongoing ethnic insurgencies. While not necessarily a threat to SPDC control, they continue to constitute a transnational security threat for Burma and the region. The State Department states that the UWSA is the largest of the organized criminal groups in the region and operates freely along the China and Thailand borders, controlling much of the Shan State with a militia estimated to have 16,000 to 20,000 members [5]. Other criminal groups, including the 14K Triad, reportedly operate in the north of the country and in major population centers [6]. According to the Economist Intelligence Unit (EIU), these criminal organizations remain nearly immune from SPDC interference, because of widespread collusion with junta military, police, and political officials [7]. Many analysts agree that much of this apparent collusion is part of concerted SPDC efforts to coopt ethnic groups and avoid hostilities with them. One possible consequence of this policy is that the influence of organized crime in Burma and the region could remain virtually impossible to reduce.

Official Corruption

The U.S. State Department and other observers indicate that corruption is common among the bureaucracy and military in Burma. Burmese officials, especially army and police personnel in the border areas, are widely believed to be involved in the smuggling of goods and drugs, money laundering, and corruption [8]. Burma has no laws on record specifically related to corruption and has signed but not ratified the UN Convention against Corruption. The 2006 EIU country report on Burma states that "corruption and cronyism" are widespread "throughout all levels of the government, the military, the bureaucracy and business communities." Burma ties with Somalia as the most corrupt country in the world according to Transparency International's 2007 Corruption Perceptions Index; this is a worsening from its 2006 position as the second-most corrupt country in the world [9]. In addition, the State Department states that Burma's weak implementation of anti-money laundering controls remains at the root of the continued use by narcotics traffickers and other criminal elements of Burmese financial institutions [10]. Burma has signed, but not ratified, the United Nations Convention against Corruption, which entered into force in December 2005.

Although there is little direct evidence of top-level regime members' involvement in trafficking- related corruption, there is evidence that high-level officials and Burmese military officers have benefitted financially from the earnings of transnational crime organizations. In the case of the drug trade, reports indicate Burmese military officials at various levels have several means to gain substantial shares of narcotics trafficking earnings. Some reports indicate that the Burmese armed forces, or Tatmadaw, may be directly involved in opium poppy cultivation in Burma's Shan state. Some local Tatmadaw units and their families reportedly work the poppy fields and collect high taxes from the traffickers, as well as fees for military protection and transportation assistance [11]. According to the State Department, Burma has not indicted any military official above the rank of colonel for drug-related corruption [12].

The SPDC also reportedly allows and encourages traffickers to invest in an array of domestic businesses, including infrastructure and transportation enterprises, receiving start-up fees and taxes from these enterprises in the process. The traffickers usually deposit the earnings from these enterprises into banks controlled by the military, and military officers reportedly deposit much of their crime-related money in foreign bank accounts in places like Bangkok and Singapore [13].

In 2003, the Secretary of the Treasury reported that some Burmese financial institutions were controlled by, or used to facilitate money laundering for, organized drug trafficking organizations [14]. In the same report, the Secretary of the Treasury also stated that Burmese government officials were suspected of being involved in the counterfeiting of U.S. currency.

Possible links between drug trafficking operations and official corruption have been raised recently in the context of SPDC reconstruction contracts in the aftermath of cyclone Nargis. Specifically, some reports have pointed to SPDC's reconstruction contract with Asia World Company Ltd., a firm managed by Steven Law (Tun Myint Naing), as a possible indication of continued links between drug traffickers and official corruption [15].

Steven Law, against whom the U.S. government has maintained financial sanctions since February 2008, allegedly provides material support to the Burmese junta, receives business concessions from the junta, facilitates the movement of illicit narcotics, and launders drug profits through his firms, including Asia World Company Ltd [16]

Regional Demand

The most frequent destinations for much of Burmese contraband—opium, methamphetamine, illegal timber, endangered wildlife, and trafficked humans—are China and Thailand [17]. Other destinations include India, Laos, Bangladesh, Vietnam, Indonesia, Malaysia, Brunei Darussalam, South Korea, and Cambodia. Demand for Burma's contraband reaches beyond the region, including the United States.

The U.S. Drug Enforcement Administration (DEA), for example, reports that Burmese-trafficked methamphetamine pills have been confiscated within the United States [18]. The United States is also reputed to be among the world's largest importers of illegal wildlife; [19] no concrete data exist, however, to link such transnational ties with Burma.

Peasants and Urban Poor

Ready recruits for organized crime activities can be found in both urban ghettos and impoverished rural areas [20]. According to the Asian Development Bank, 27% of Burma's population live below the poverty line, making the country one of the poorest in Southeast Asia. Many analysts state that peasant farmers, rural hunters, and other poor often serve at the base of Burma's international crime network, growing opium poppy crops, poaching exotic and endangered species in Burma's lush forests, and serving as couriers and mules for contraband. In addition, the State Department and other observers have found that many victims of transnational crime in Burma are the poor, becoming commodities themselves as they are trafficked to be child soldiers for the junta or slaves for sexual exploitation [21]

ILLICIT ECONOMIES IN BURMA

Drugs

Burma is party to all three major United Nations international drug control treaties—the 1961 Single Convention on Narcotic Drugs, as amended; the 1971 Convention on Psychotropic Substances; and the 1988 Convention against the Illicit Traffic in Narcotic Drugs and Psychotropic Substances. Burma's official strategy to combat drugs aims to end all production and trafficking of illegal drugs by 2014, a goal that parallels the region's ambition to be drug free by 2015 [22]. Many analysts, however, consider the goal of achieving a drug-free Burma as unlikely. In September 2007, the Administration once again included Burma on the list of major drug transit or major illicit drug producing countries [23]. Located at the heart of the "Golden Triangle" of narcotics trafficking, Burma is among the world's top producers of opium, heroin, and methamphetamine [24]. Illicit narcotics reportedly generate between $1 billion and $2 billion annually in exports. In addition, Burma's drug trafficking activities appear to be linked to the recent spread of HIV and AIDS in the region, as drug users along Burma's trafficking routes share contaminated drug injection needles.

Some analysts warn that clashes between the government of Burma, rebel groups in the border areas of Burma, and neighboring countries could be possible. For example, should the SPDC begin to combat the drug trade more vigorously, current ceasefire groups may choose to break their agreements with the SPDC in order to protect their drug trade territories. Several ceasefire groups, including the UWSA, have chosen not to heed calls by the SPDC to disarm and reportedly use illicit drug proceeds to equip and maintain their paramilitary forces [25]. Further, some suggest that the continued flow of illicit drugs from Burma to Thailand may be a source of tension between the two countries—especially in the face of Thailand's renewed war on drugs. The most recent campaign to combat illegal drugs, which began in April 2009, is a reprise of a 2003 campaign. Though media reports indicate that the current Thai war on drugs appears to be more restrained than the 2003 version, which resulted in the deaths of several thousand people over a three-month period, human rights activists remain on alert [26]

Heroin and Opium

Burma is the world's second-largest producer of illicit opium, behind Afghanistan. Further, the DEA reports that Burma accounts for 80% of all heroin produced in Southeast Asia and is a source of heroin for the United States [27]. Although poppy cultivation has declined significantly in the past decade, prices have increased significantly in recent years, reflecting ongoing demand despite production declines since a decade ago (see Table 1). Much of the decline in recent years has been attributed to UWSA's 2005 public commitment to stop its activity in the opium and heroin markets, after prolonged international pressure to do so. However, recent reports suggest that the UWSA's self-imposed ban may be short-lived. The UWSA has reportedly warned that alternative livelihood sources will be necessary in order to sustain its ban against opium poppy cultivation—a point with which many international observers agree [28]

Most analysts acknowledge that opium production in certain parts of Burma is one of the few viable means for small-scale peasant farmers to compensate for structural food security shortages. A 2008 United Nations Office on Drugs and Crime (UNODC) study supports this, finding that households in former poppy-growing villages were unable to find sufficient substitutes for their lost income from opium [29]. According to the same UNODC study, the average annual cash income of a household involved in opium poppy cultivation was approximately $501, while the annual income of a household not involved in opium poppy cultivation was approximately $445. In the meantime, reports indicate that opium poppy production is shifting to areas controlled by other ceasefire ethnic groups, and to areas apparently administered by Burma's armed forces, the Tatmadaw, who tax the farmers and traders for a portion of the farmgate value [30]. The UWSA may also be organizing Wa poppy farmers to seasonally migrate to nearby provinces, where the UWSA did not commit to a ban, in order to continue their cultivation [31]

Table 1. Opium Cultivation, Production, and Price Trends in Burma, 1997-2007

Year	Opium Poppy Cultivation (hectares)	Significant Opium Poppy Eradication Reported (hectares)	Potential Opium Production (metric tons)	Total Potential Farm Gate Value of Opium Produced (U.S. constant dollars)
1997	155,150	1,938	1,676	$590
1998	130,300	3,093	1,303	$454
1999	89,500	3,172	895	$145
2000	108,700	9,824	1,087	$308
2001	105,000	1,643	1,097	$291
2002	81,400	9,317	828	$147
2003	62,200	7,469	810	$121
2004	44,200	2,820	370	$98
2005	00	7	312	$63
2006	21,500	3,970	315	$72
2007	27,700	3,598	460	$120
2008	00	0	410	$123

Source: CRS calculations based on United Nations Office on Drugs and Crime (UNODC), *World Drug Report,* 2004-2008; U*NODC, Opium Poppy Cultivation in South East Asia,* December 2008; and UNODC, *Global Illicit Drug Trends, 2003-1999.*

Methamphetamine and Synthetic Drugs

In addition to producing heroin and opium, Burma is reportedly the largest producer of methamphetamine in the world and a significant producer of other synthetic drugs.32 Methamphetamine is produced in small, mobile labs in insurgent-controlled border areas, mainly in eastern Burma (for export mainly to Thailand) and sometimes co-located with heroin refineries.33 Burma's rise to prominence in the global synthetic drug trade is in part the consequence of UWSA's commitment to ban opium poppy cultivation.

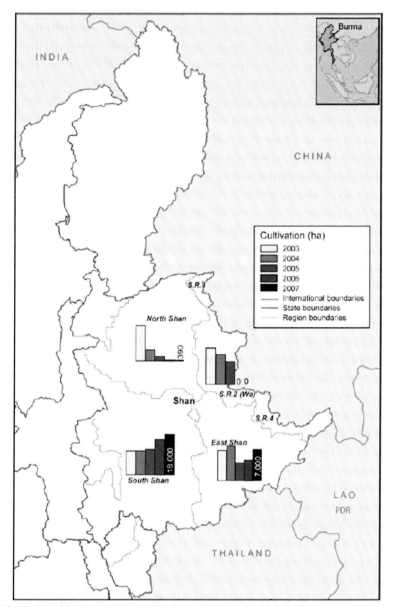

Sources: UNODC, World Drug Report, 2004-2007; UNODC, Global Illicit Drug Trends, 2003-1999. Graphics adapted by CRS.

Figure 1. Opium Poppy Cultivation in Burma's Shan State, 2003-2007.

According to some, UWSA leadership may be intentionally replacing opium cultivation with the manufacturing and trafficking of amphetamine-type stimulants.34 As a result, Burma has emerged as one of the world's largest producers of methamphetamine and other amphetamine-type stimulants. The State Department states that this sharp increase in methamphetamine trafficking is "threatening to turn the Golden Triangle into an '*Ice Triangle*.'" [35]

A July 2008 media report indicates that international assistance for relief from the cyclone Nargis may have been used as a cover to smuggle illegal drugs into Burma. According to the Irrawaddy, an independent Burmese newspaper, several customs officials were suspected of involvement in a scheme to smuggle ecstasy pills into Burma as part of shipments of relief aid from Burmese communities abroad [36].

Humans

Burma is a party to the United Nations Convention against Transnational Organized Crime and its protocol on migrant smuggling and trafficking in persons. However, Burma has been designated as a "Tier 3" state in every Trafficking in Persons (TIP) Report ever published by the State Department. Tier 3 is the worst designation in the TIP Report, indicating that the country does not comply with minimum standards for combating human trafficking under the Trafficking Victims Protection Act of 2000, as amended (Division A of P.L. 106-386, 22 U.S.C. 7101, et seq.). As the TIP reports explain, laws to criminally prohibit sex and labor trafficking, as well as military recruitment of children, exist in Burma—and the penalties prescribed by these laws for those convicted of breaking these laws are "sufficiently stringent." Nevertheless, the State Department continues to report that these laws are arbitrarily enforced by the SPDC and that cases involving high-level officials or well-connected individuals are not fully investigated.

Victims are trafficked internally and regionally, and junta officials are directly involved in trafficking for forced labor and the unlawful conscription of child soldiers, according to several reports [37]. Women and girls, especially those of ethnic minorities groups and those among the thousands of refugees along Burma's borders, are reportedly trafficked for sexual exploitation.

Victims are reportedly trafficked from rural villages to urban centers and commerce nodes, such as truck stops, border towns, and mining and military camps [38]. One incident in early 2008 revealed the risks associated with migrant smuggling from Burma to Thailand, when 54 Burmese migrants were found dead in the back of a seafood truck headed to Thailand after the truck's air conditioning failed. Based on media accounts, 67 migrants survived, including at least 14 minors [39].

Natural Resources Timber and Wildlife

Burma is rich in natural resources, including extensive forests, high biodiversity, and deposits of minerals and gemstones. Illegal trafficking of these resources is reportedly flowing to the same destination states and along the same trafficking routes as other forms of trafficking. Global Witness, a London-based non-governmental organization, estimates that 98% of Burma's timber exports to China, from 2001 to 2004, were illegally logged, amounting to an average of $200 million worth of illegal exports each year [40]. Many analysts also claim that the region's illegal timber trade is characterized by complex patronage and corruption systems [41]

Wild Asiatic black bears, clouded leopards, Asian elephants, and a plethora of reptiles, turtles, and other unusual animals reportedly are sold in various forms—whole or in parts, stuffed, ground, or, sometimes, alive—in open-air markets in lawless border towns [42]. Growing demand in countries such as China and Thailand has increased regional prices for exotic wildlife; for example, a tiger's skin can be worth up to $20,000, according to media reports [43]. One report suggests that valuable wildlife is used as currency in exchange for drugs and in the laundering of other contraband proceeds [44].

Gems

Rubies, sapphires, jade, and other gems have also been used as non-cash currency equivalents for transborder smuggling. The legal sale of Burmese gems is among the country's most significant foreign currency earners—$297 million during the 2006-2007 fiscal year, according to Burma's customs department; more may be traded through illicit channels [45]. Some observers claim that the junta is heavily involved in both the legal and illegal trade of gemstones, as the regime controls most mining operations and the sale of gems through official auctions and private sales reportedly arranged by senior military officers [46]. Congress has also accused the Burmese regime of attempting to evade U.S. sanctions against the import of Burmese gemstones by concealing the gems' origin from potential buyers [47]. Congress estimates that while 90% of the world's rubies originate from Burma, only 3% of those entering the United States are claimed to have originated there.

Other Contraband

AK-47s, B-40 rocket launchers, and other small arms are reportedly smuggled into Burma along the Thai-Burmese border. These weapons reportedly go to the Karen guerrillas, who continue to fight a decades-long insurgency against the Burmese junta. Another report implicates the Shan State Army in trafficking in military hardware [48]. Although analysts say it is unlikely that the ruling junta benefits from the criminal profits of small arms trafficking, reports indicate that the government distributes such weapons to its cadre of child soldiers [49]. Other less high-profile markets for contraband reportedly exist, including trafficking in cigarettes, cars, CDs, pornography, antiques, religious items, fertilizer, and counterfeit documents—many of which are believed to involve at least the complicity of some Burmese government officials.

In April 2008, Japan's public broadcaster NHK reported that Burma has been importing multiple- launch rockets from North Korea, raising international concerns and speculation about why Burma would seek out such weapons in violation of U.N. sanctions imposed on North Korea after its nuclear test in October 2006 [50]. Some observers speculate that the Burmese military has been seeking to upgrade its artillery to improve the country's protection against potential external threats [51]. Burma and North Korea are thought to have been involved in conventional weapons trade in violation of U.N. sanctions since spring 2007, when North Korea and Burma resumed diplomatic relations with each other. Observers further claim that "Western intelligence officials have suspected for several years that the regime has had an interest in following the model of North Korea and achieving military autarky by developing ballistic missiles and nuclear weapons" [52].

Money Laundering

The State Department reports in 2008 that Burma is a money laundering risk because of its underdeveloped financial sector and large volume of informal trade. In 2001, the international Financial Action Task Force on Money Laundering (FATF) designated Burma as a Non- Cooperative Country or Territory (NCCT) for deficient anti-money laundering provisions and weak oversight of its banking sector [53]. A year later in 2002, the U.S. Department of Treasury's Financial Crimes Enforcement Network (FinCEN) issued an advisory to U.S. financial institutions to give enhanced scrutiny to any financial transaction related to Burma [54]. In 2003, two of Burma's largest private banks—Myanmar Mayflower Bank and Asia Wealth Bank—were implicated by FATF as involved in laundering illicit narcotics proceeds and counterfeiting. The Secretary of the Treasury in 2003 listed Burma as a "major money laundering country of primary concern" and in 2004 imposed additional countermeasures [55]. Burma has since revoked the operating licenses of the two banks implicated in 2003. However, the U.S. government and international bodies, such as FATF, continue to monitor the widespread use of informal money transfer networks, sometimes also referred to as "hundi" or "hawala." Monies sent through these informal systems are usually legitimate remittances from relatives abroad. The lack of transparency and regulation of these money transfers remain issues of concern for the United States. In other parts of the world, hawala or hawala-like techniques have been used, or are suspected of being used, to launder proceeds derived from narcotics trafficking, terrorism, alien smuggling, and other criminal activities [56]

U.S. POLICY

Sanctions and Special Measures

Burma is subject to a broad sanctions regime that addresses issues of U.S. interest, which include democracy, human rights, and international crime [57] Specifically in response to the extent of transnational crime occurring in Burma, the President has taken additional actions against the country under several different legislative authorities. Burma is listed as a major drug-producing state, and because of its insufficient effort to combat the narcotics trade, the country is barred access to some U.S. foreign assistance [58]. As an uncooperative, major drug-producing state, Burma is also subject to trade sanctions [59]. In 2005, the Department of Justice indicted eight Burmese individuals identified in 2003 by the U.S. Treasury's Office of Foreign Assets Control (OFAC) for their alleged role in drug trafficking and money laundering [60]. On November 13, 2008, OFAC named 26 individuals and 17 companies tied to Burma's Wei Hsueh Kang and the UWSA as Specially Designated Narcotics Traffickers pursuant to the Foreign Narcotics Kingpin Designation Act (21U.S.C. 1901-1908) [61].

Burma is characterized by the State Department's 2008 Trafficking in Persons report as a Tier 3 state engaged in the most severe forms of trafficking in persons; as such, Burma is subject to sanctions, barring the country from non-humanitarian, non-trade-related U.S. assistance and loss of U.S. support for loans from international financial institutions [62]. As a major money laundering country—defined by Section 481 (e)(7) of the Foreign Assistance Act of 1961, as amended, as one "whose financial institutions engage in currency transactions including significant amounts of proceeds from international narcotics trafficking"—Burma is subject to several "special measures" to regulate and monitor financial flows.

These include Department of Treasury advisories for enhanced scrutiny over financial transactions, as well as five special measures listed under 31 U.S.C. 531 8A [63]. The United States does not apply sanctions against Burma in specific response to its activity in other illicit trades, including wildlife [64]. The Block Burmese JADE (Junta's Anti-Democratic Efforts) Act of 2007 (H.R. 3890), however, would prohibit the importation of gems and hardwoods from Burma, among other restrictions [65]

After more than a decade of applying sanctions against Burma, however, many analysts have concluded that the sanctions have done little to change the situation. The effectiveness of U.S. sanctions is limited by several factors [66].

These include (1) unevenly applied sanctions against Burma by other countries and international organizations, including the European Union and Japan; (2) a booming natural gas production and export industry that provides the SPDC with significant revenue; (3) continued unwillingness of Burma's fellow members in the Association of Southeast Asian Nations (ASEAN) to impose economic sanctions against Burma; (4) Burma's historical isolation from the global economy; and (5) China's continued economic and military assistance to Burma. In addition, some analysts suggest that sanctions are, in part, culpable for the flourishing black markets in Burma, including trafficking in humans, gems, and drugs, because legal exports are barred [67]. Several analysts indicate that many Burmese women who lost their jobs in the textile industry as a result of Western sanctions are among the victims of trafficking for sexual exploitation [68]

Regional Border Control Assistance

The United States is assisting neighboring countries with stemming the flow of trafficked contraband from Burma into their territories. Although most U.S. assistance to combat transnational crime in Burma remains in suspension, the United States is working to train law enforcement and border control officials in neighboring countries through anti-crime assistance programs [69]. Currently, the bulk of funding to *Burma's neighbors* remains concentrated in counter- narcotics and anti-human trafficking projects; no funding is allocated to the State Department for combating "organized and gang-related crime" in the region. Overall funding to combat trafficking has been in decline for several years; the Administration's FY2008 appropriations request for Foreign Operations in the region represents a 24.2% decrease from FY2006 actual funding.

A New Approach?

Despite Burma's recent progress in reducing opium poppy cultivation, most experts believe U.S. policies have not yielded substantial leverage in combating transnational crime emanating from Burma. In light of the most recent displays of junta violence against political demonstrators in September 2007, however, there are indications of increasing political interest in re-evaluating U.S. policy toward Burma. Among the considerations that policy makers have recently raised are (1) whether the United States should increase the amount of humanitarian aid sent to Burma; (2) what role ASEAN and other multilateral vehicles for dialogue could play in increasing political pressure on the junta regime; (3) what role the United States sees India, as the world's largest democracy and Burma's neighbor, playing in ensuring that Burma does not become a source of regional instability; and (4) how the United States can further work with China and Thailand, as the largest destinations of trafficked goods from Burma, to address transnational crime along Burma's borders.

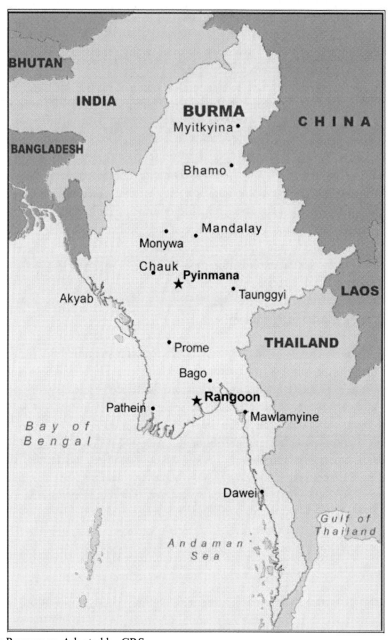

Source: Map Resources. Adapted by CRS.

Figure 2. Map of Burma.

REFERENCES

[1] See discussion on "Official Corruption."

[2] For example, the 2006 *National Security Strategy of the United States* (at http://www.whitehouse.gov/nsc/nss.html) identifies addressing ungoverned areas as among U.S. national security priorities because of concern that they could be used as safe havens for terrorists. See also Angel Rabasa et al., *Ungoverned Territories: Understanding and Reducing Terrorism Risks* (Santa Monica, CA: Rand Corporation, 2007).

[3] Laws under which drug-related sanctions are authorized include Section 489(a)(1) of the Foreign Assistance Act of 1961 (P.L. 87-195), as amended (22 U.S.C. 2291j(a)(1)); the Narcotics Control Trade Act (P.L. 99-570), as amended (19 U.S.C. 2491 et seq.); and Section 138 of Title I, Subtitle D, of the Customs and Trade Act of 1990 (P.L. 101-382).

[4] Pursuant to the Victims of Trafficking and Violence Protection Act of 2000 (P.L. 106-386), as amended.

[5] U.S. Department of State, *International Narcotics Control Strategy Report*, vol. 1 (2008).

[6] Jane's Sentinel Security Assessment: Southeast Asia, April 30, 2008; Antonio Nicaso and Lee Lamothe, *Angels, Mobsters, and Narco-Terrorists: The Rising Menace of Global Criminal Enterprises* (Ontario, Canada: John Wiley & Sons, 2005).

[7] Economist Intelligence Unit, *Myanmar (Burma) Country Profile* (2006).

[8] U.S. Department of State, *International Narcotics Control Strategy Report*, vols. 1 and 2 (2008); Jane's Sentinel Security Assessment: Southeast Asia, April 30, 2008, *op cit.*; Economist Intelligence Unit, op cit.; Transparency International, *Corruption Perceptions Index* (2007). According to some analysts, corruption among police and border patrol officials in Burma's neighboring countries also eases the flow of trafficked goods out of Burma. See also Nora Boustany, "Burmese Activist Urges Stronger U.S. Sanctions," *The Washington Post*, November 2, 2007. In this news article, Maung Maung, secretary general of the National Council of the Union of Burma, stated that "the country's revenue from gas, rubies, teak, timber, rice, gas, uranium, and diamonds is being pilfered for the personal enrichment of junta members or their families."

[9] Transparency International, *op cit.*; Transparency International, *Corruption Perceptions Index* (2006).

[10] 2008 *International Narcotics Control Strategy Report*, vol. 1, *op cit.*

[11] Michael Black and Anthony Davis, "Wa and Peace: The UWSA and Tensions in Myanmar," *Jane's Intelligence Review*, March 2008.

[12] 2008 *International Narcotics Control Strategy Report*, vol. 1, op *cit.*

[13] See CRS Report RL33479, Burma-U.S. Relations, by Larry A. Niksch; Christopher S. Wren, "Road to Riches Starts in the Golden Triangle," *New York Times*, May 5, 1998; Robert S. Gelbard, "Slorc's Drug Links," *Far Eastern Economic Review*, November 21, 1996; Anthony Davis, "The Wa Challenge Regional Stability in Southeast Asia," *Jane's Intelligence Review*, January 2003.

[14] "Imposition of Special Measures against Burma as a Jurisdiction of Primary Money Laundering Concern," *Federal Register*, Vol. 68, No. 227, November 25, 2003.

[15] See for example Colin Freeman, "Burmese Drug Lord Lands Lucrative Reconstruction Contracts," *Edmonton Journal* (Alberta), May 25, 2008.
[16] U.S. Department of the Treasury, "Treasury Sanctions Additional Financial Operatives of the Burmese Regime," Press Release, February 25, 2008; U.S. Department of the Treasury, "Steven Law Financial Network," Report, February 2008; and "Key Financial Operatives of the Burmese Regime Designated by OFAC," World-Check, March 3, 2008.
[17] See United Nations Office on Drugs and Crime (UNODC), *World Drug Report* (2008); 2008 *International Narcotics Control Strategy Report, op cit.*; Global Witness, *A Choice for China: Ending the Destruction of Burma's Northern Frontier Forests* (2005); Jolene Lin, "Tackling Southeast Asia's Illegal Wildlife Trade," *Singapore Year Book of International Law*, vol. 9 (2005); and U.S. Department of State, *Trafficking in Persons Report* (2007).
[18] U.S. Drug Enforcement Administration, "Methamphetamine: The Current Threat in East Asia and the Pacific Rim," *Drug Intelligence Brief*, September 2003.
[19] U.S. Fish and Wildlife Service, Annual Report FY2006, August 2007; "Wildlife Smuggling Boom Plaguing L.A., Authorities Say," *National Geographic News*, July 26, 2007.
[20] Michael Lyman, *Organized Crime* (Upper Saddle River, NJ: Prentice Hall, 2007).
[21] 2007 *Trafficking in Persons Report, op cit.*
[22] Association of Southeast Asian Nations (ASEAN), "Cooperation on Drugs and Narcotics: Overview," at http://www.aseansec.org/5682.htm; 2008 *International Narcotics Control Strategy Report*, vol. 1, *op cit.*
[23] This annual list is required by section 706(1) of the Foreign Relations Authorization Act, Fiscal Year 2003 (P.L. 107- 228).
[24] The "Golden Triangle" refers to an area of approximately 135,000 square miles of mountains that surround the Burma-Laos-Thailand border region. In the 1980s and 1990s, the Golden Triangle reigned as the world's largest producer of opium poppy.
[25] Jane's Sentinel Security Assessment: Southeast Asia, April 30, 2008, op cit. Note, however, that not all ceasefire groups are involved in the illegal drug trade.
[26] See for example, "Thai PM Launches New 'War on Drugs,'" *Agence France Presse*, March 19, 2008; Brian McCartan, "Despite Strong Rhetoric, Thailand's Latest Drug War a Restrained Campaign," World Politics Review, May 2008; Daniel Ten Kate, "Thailand to Restart War on Drugs," *Asia Sentinel*, March 2008.
[27] U.S. Drug Enforcement Administration, *Drugs of Abuse*, 2005, available at http://www.usdoj.gov/dea/pubs/abuse/ doa-p.pdf.
[28] Tor Norling, "Haven or Hell," *The Irrawaddy*, July 11, 2008.
[29] UNODC, *World Drug Report* (2008), *op cit.*; see also: Jane's Sentinel Security Assessment: Southeast Asia, April 30, 2008, *op cit.*
[30] Black and Davis, *op cit.* See also: Central Intelligence Agency, *World Factbook* (2007); 2008 *International Narcotics Control Strategy Report*, vol. 1, *op cit.*
[31] Ibid.
[32] U.S. Department of State, 2008 *International Narcotics Control Strategy Report*, vol. 1, *op cit.*; Jane's Sentinel Security Assessment: Southeast Asia, April 30, 2008, *op cit.*; and David Johnson, Assistant Secretary of State for International Narcotics and Law Enforcement Affairs, News Briefing, February 29, 2008.

[33] Jane's Sentinel Security Assessment: Southeast Asia, April 30, 2008, *op cit.*
[34] U.S. Department of State, 2008 *International Narcotics Control Strategy Report*, vol. 1, *op cit.*
[35] Ibid.
[36] "Intelligence: Drug Scam Suspected," *The Irrawaddy*, July 2008.
[37] 2008 *Trafficking in Persons Report*; Sold to Be Soldiers: Human Rights Watch, *The Recruitment and Use of Child Soldiers in Burma*, October 2007. See also "Burma/Myanmar: After the Crackdown," *International Crisis Group*, Asia Report No. 144, January 31, 2008.
[38] 2007 *Trafficking in Persons Report*, *op cit.*, p. 71.
[39] Kocha Olarn, "Myanmar Migrant Survivors Fined and Deported," *CNN*, April 12, 2008.
[40] Global Witness (2005), *op cit.*
[41] See, for example, Vaudine England, "The Mekong Connection in Illegal Log Trade," *Sunday Morning Post* (Hong Kong), March 23, 2008.
[42] Christopher Shepherd and Vincent Nijman, "An Assessment of Wildlife Trade at Mong La Market on the Myanmar-China Border," *TRAFFIC Bulletin*, vol. 21, no. 2 (2007).
[43] "Factbox: Why Are Asia's Endangered Animals So Sought After?" *Reuters News*, September 3, 2007.
[44] Lin, *op cit.*
[45] "Myanmar Rubies, Sapphires for Sale at Gems Fairs," *Reuters News*, October 19, 2006.
[46] See "Burma: Gem Trade Bolsters Military Regime, Fuels Atrocities," *Human Rights Watch*, November 12, 2007; "Burma and Blood Gems," Leber Jeweler, Inc., available at http://www.leberjeweler.com/stones/ burma_bloodgems.php3.
[47] See P.L. 108-61; U.S. House of Representatives, Block Burmese JADE (Junta's Anti-Democratic Efforts) Act of 2007, H.Rept. 110-418, Part 1, October 31, 2007.
[48] Eric Tagliacozzo, "Border Permeability and the State in Southeast Asia: Contraband and Regional Security," *Contemporary Southeast Asia*, vol. 23, no. 2 (2001).
[49] Human Rights Watch, *Small Arms and Human Rights: The Need for Global Action; A Human Rights Watch Briefing Paper for the U.N. Biennial Meeting on Small Arms* (2003).
[50] "N. Korea Exporting Multiple-Launch Rockets to Myanmar—Report," *CNBC*, April 2, 2008; "North Korea Sells Rocket Launchers to Myanmar—Report," *Reuters News*, April 3, 2008; and U.N. Security Council Resolution 1718 (2006).
[51] See for example "Oslo-Based Website: Burma's Purchase of North Korean Arms Threatens Stability," *BBC Monitoring Asia Pacific*, April 6, 2008; "Thai-Based Website: U.S. Concerned over Reports of North Korean Weapons to Burma," *BBC Monitoring Asia Pacific*, April 6, 2008.
[52] Michael Green and Derek Mitchell, "Asia's Forgotten Crisis: A New Approach to Burma," *Foreign Affairs*, November/December 2007, Vol. 86, Issue 6.
[53] Created in 1989, the Financial Action Task Force (FATF) is an inter-governmental body whose purpose is the development and promotion of national and international policies to combat money laundering and terrorist financing.
[54] See 31 CFR Part 103, *Department of the Treasury, Financial Crimes Enforcement Network, Imposition of Special Measures against Burma*.

[55] Pursuant to 31 U.S.C. 5318A, as added by Section 311 of the USA PATRIOT Act (P.L. 107-56), these countermeasures prohibited U.S. banks from establishing or maintaining correspondent or payable-through accounts in the United States for or on behalf of Myanmar Mayflower and Asia Wealth Bank and, with narrow exceptions, for all other Burmese banks. See 2007 *International Narcotics Control Strategy Report*, vol. 2, *op cit.*

[56] Patrick M. Jost and Harjit S. Sandhu, *The Hawala Alternative Remittance System and its Role in Money Laundering* (Lyon, France: Interpol General Secretariat, 2000).

[57] Notable sanctions among those not specifically related to international crime include the Burmese Freedom and Democracy Act of 2003 (P.L. 108-61, extended by P.L. 108-272 and P.L. 109-39); Executive Order 13047, issued May 20, 1997, under Section 570 of the Foreign Appropriations Act, 1997 (P.L. 104-208); and Executive Order 13310, issued July 28, 2003, to implement P.L. 108-61 (the President announced additional modifications September 25 and 27, 2007). See also CRS Report RS22737, *Burma: Economic Sanctions*, by Larry A. Niksch and Martin A. Weiss.

[58] Pursuant to Section 489(a)(1) of the Foreign Assistance Act of 1961, as amended.

[59] Trade sanctions are pursuant to the Narcotics Control Trade Act (19 U.S.C. 249 1-2495) and the Customs and Trade Act of 1990 (P.L. 101-382).

[60] The indictments were made using the Foreign Narcotics Kingpin Designation Act (21 U.S.C. 1901-1908). The indicted Burmese have yet to be arrested or brought to trial in the United States.

[61] U.S. Department of State, International Narcotics Control Strategy Report, Vol. 2, March 2009. Kang was designated by the President as a Foreign Narcotics Kingpin on June 1, 2000, and the UWSA on June 2, 2003.

[62] Sanctions are pursuant to the Victims of Trafficking and Violence Protection Act of 2000 (P.L. 106-386). The decision to apply sanctions under P.L. 106-3 86 is left to presidential discretion.

[63] These include (1) record-keeping and reporting of certain financial transactions, (2) collection of information relating to beneficial ownership, (3) collection of information relating to certain payable-through accounts, (4) collection of information relating to certain correspondent accounts, and (5) prohibition or conditions on the opening or maintaining of correspondent or payable-through accounts for a foreign financial institution. See Douglas N. Greenburg, John Roth, and Katherine A. Sawyer, "Special Measures under Section 311 of the USA PATRIOT Act," *The Review of Banking and Financial Services*, vol. 23, no. 6, June 2007.

[64] Notably, President Bill Clinton in 1994 used the 1971 Pelly Amendment to the Fishermen's Protective Act of 1967, as amended (22 U.S.C. 1978), as a means by which to impose sanctions against Taiwan for its alleged insufficient progress toward eliminating the country's illegal trade in rhino and tiger parts and products. The sanction temporarily banned the importation of certain fish and wildlife products from Taiwan.

[65] Last major action to H.R. 3890: passed Senate with an amendment and an amendment to the Title on December 19, 2007.

[66] See CRS Report RL33479, *Burma-U.S. Relations*, *op cit.*

[67] Fareed Zakaria, "Sleepwalking to Sanctions, Again," *Newsweek,* October 15, 2007.

[68] See, for example, "U.S. Sanctions 'Hit Burma Hard,'" BBC News, October 3, 2003.

[69] Under authorities granted in Section 2291 of the Foreign Assistance Act of 1961, as amended, the State Department is responsible for coordinating foreign assistance and law enforcement training for counter-narcotics and anti-crime programming. According to the Administration's FY2008 Foreign Operations Budget Justification, such programs exist in four of Burma's neighbors: Thailand, Laos, India, and Bangladesh.

Chapter 5

CHINA'S CURRENCY: A SUMMARY OF THE ECONOMIC ISSUES[*]

Wayne M. Morrison and Marc Labonte

ABSTRACT

Many Members of Congress charge that China's policy of accumulating foreign reserves (especially U.S. dollars) to influence the value of its currency constitutes a form of currency manipulation intended to make its exports cheaper and imports into China more expensive than they would be under free market conditions. They further contend that this policy has caused a surge in the U.S. trade deficit with China in recent years and has been a major factor in the loss of U.S. manufacturing jobs. Although China made modest reforms to its currency policy in 2005, resulting in a gradual appreciation of its currency (about 19% through June 3, 2009), many Members contend the reforms have not gone far enough and have warned of potential punitive legislative action. Although an undervalued Chinese currency has likely hurt some sectors of the U.S. economy, it has benefited others. For example, U.S. consumers have gained from the supply of low-cost Chinese goods (which helps to control inflation), as have U.S. firms using Chinese- made parts and materials (which helps such firms become more globally competitive). In addition, China has used its abundant foreign exchange reserves to buy U.S. securities, including U.S. Treasury securities, which are used to help fund the Federal budget deficit. Such purchases help keep U.S. interest rates relatively low. For China, an undervalued valued currency has boosted exports and attracted foreign investment, but has lead to unbalanced economic growth and suppressed Chinese living standards.

The current global economic crisis has further complicated the currency issue for both the United States and China. Although China is under pressure from the United States to appreciate its currency, it is reluctant to do so because that could cause further damage to export sector and lead to more layoffs. China has halted its gradual appreciation of its currency, the renminbi (RMB) or yuan to the dollar in 2009, keeping it relatively constant at about 6.83 yuan per dollar. The federal budget deficit has increased rapidly since FY2008, causing a sharp increase in the amount of Treasury securities that must be sold. The Obama Administration has encouraged

---

[*] This is an edited, reformatted and augmented version of CRS Report RS21625, dated June 17, 2009.

China to continue purchasing U.S. debt. However, if China were induced to further appreciate its currency against the dollar, it could slow its accumulation of foreign exchange reserves, thus reducing the need to invest in dollar assets, such as Treasury securities. Legislation has been introduced in the 111th Congress to address China's currency policy.

China's currency policy appears to have created a policy dilemma for the Chinese government. A strong and stable U.S. economy is in China's national interest since the United States is China's largest export market. Thus, some analysts contend that China will feel compelled to keep funding the growing U.S. debt. However, Chinese officials have expressed concern that the growing U.S. debt will eventually spark inflation in the United States and a depreciation of the dollar, which would negatively impact the value of China's holdings of U.S. securities. But if China stopped buying U.S. debt or tried to sell off a large portion of those holdings, it could also cause the dollar to depreciate and thus reduce the value of its remaining holdings, and such a move could further destabilize the U.S. economy. Chinese concerns over its large dollar holdings appear to have been reflected in a paper issued by the governor of the People's Bank of China, Zhou Xiaochuan on March 24, 2009, which called for replacing the U.S. dollar as the international reserve currency with a new global system controlled by the International Monetary Fund. China has also signed currency swap agreements with six of its trading partners, which would allow those partners to settle accounts with China using the yuan rather than the dollar. This report will be updated as events warrant.

INTRODUCTION

From 1994 until July 2005, China maintained a policy of pegging its currency, the renminbi (RMB) or yuan, to the U.S. dollar at an exchange rate of roughly 8.28 yuan to the dollar [1]. The Chinese central bank maintained this peg by buying (or selling) as many dollar-denominated assets in exchange for newly printed yuan as needed to eliminate excess demand (supply) for the yuan. As a result, the exchange rate between the yuan and the dollar basically stayed the same, despite changing economic factors which could have otherwise caused the yuan to either appreciate or depreciate relative to the dollar. Under a floating exchange rate system, the relative demand for the two countries' goods and assets would determine the exchange rate of the yuan to the dollar. Many economists contend that for the first several years of the peg, the fixed value was likely close to the market value. But in the past few years, economic conditions have changed such that the yuan would likely have appreciated if it had been floating. The sharp increase in China's foreign exchange reserves (which grew from $403 billion in 2003 to $1.95 trillion as of March 2009) and China's large trade surplus with the world ($297 billion in 2008) are often viewed by critics of China's currency policy as proof that the yuan is significantly undervalued.

CHINA REFORMS THE PEG

The Chinese government modified its currency policy on July 21, 2005. It announced that the yuan's exchange rate would become "adjustable, based on market supply and demand with reference to exchange rate movements of currencies in a basket" (it was later announced that the composition of the basket includes the dollar, the yen, the euro, and a few other currencies) and that the exchange rate of the U.S. dollar against the yuan was adjusted from 8.28 to 8.11, an appreciation of 2.1%. Unlike a true floating exchange rate, the yuan would be allowed to fluctuate by up to 0.3% (later changed to 0.5%) on a daily basis against the basket.

Since July 2005, China has allowed the yuan to appreciate steadily, but very slowly. It has continued to accumulate foreign reserves at a rapid pace, which suggests that if the yuan were allowed to freely float it would appreciate much more rapidly. The current situation might be best described as a "managed float"—market forces are determining the general direction of the yuan's movement, but the government is retarding its rate of appreciation through market intervention. From July 21, 2005 to April 13, 2009, the dollar-yuan exchange rate went from 8.11 to 6.83, an appreciation of 18.7%. The effects of the yuan's appreciation are unclear. The price index for U.S. imports from China in 2008, rose by 3.0% (compared to a 0.9% rise in import prices for total U.S. imports of non-petroleum products) [2]. In 2008, U.S. imports from China rose by 5.1% over the previous year, compared to import growth of 11.7% in 2007; however, U.S. exports over this period were up 9.5% compared with an 18.1% rise in 2007. The current global economic slowdown appears to have sharply reduced bilateral trade. During the first three months of 2009, U.S. exports to, and imports from, China were down by 20% and 11%, respectively.

U.S. CONCERNS OVER CHINA'S CURRENCY POLICY

Many U.S. policymakers and business and labor representatives have charged that China's currency is significantly undervalued vis-à-vis the U.S. dollar (even after the recent revaluation), making Chinese exports to the United States cheaper, and U.S. exports to China more expensive, than they would be if exchange rates were determined by market forces. They further argue that the undervalued currency has contributed to the burgeoning U.S. trade deficit with China (which was $266 billion in 2008) and has hurt U.S. production and employment in several U.S. manufacturing sectors that are forced to compete domestically and internationally against "artificially" low-cost goods from China. Furthermore, some analysts contend that China's currency policy induces other East Asian countries to intervene in currency markets in order to keep their currencies weak against the dollar in order to compete with Chinese goods. Critics contend that, while it may have been appropriate for China during the early stages of its economic development to maintain a pegged currency, it should let the yuan freely float today, given the size of the Chinese economy and the impact its policies have on the world economy.

CHINA'S CONCERNS OVER MODIFYING ITS CURRENCY POLICY

Chinese officials argue that its currency policy is not meant to favor exports over imports, but instead to foster economic stability through currency stability, as many other countries do. They have expressed concern that floating its currency could spark an economic crisis in China and would especially be damaging to its export industries at a time when painful economic reforms (such as closing down inefficient state-owned enterprises) are being implemented. They further contend that the Chinese banking system is too underdeveloped and burdened with heavy debt to be able to deal effectively with possible speculative pressures that could occur with a fully convertible currency. The global financial crisis has had a significant impact on China's trade and foreign direct investment (FDI) flows. China's trade (exports and imports) and inflows of FDI declined each month from November 2008 to April 2009 on a year-on-year basis. In February 2009, China's exports and imports were down 25.7% and 24.1%, respectively (year-on-year basis), the biggest monthly decline recorded since reforms began in 2009 [3] Thousands of export- oriented factories have reportedly been shut down. The Chinese government has estimated that 20 million migrant workers lost their jobs because of the global financial crisis in 2008. Chinese officials view economic stability as critical to sustaining political stability; they fear an appreciated currency could cause even more employment disruptions and thus could cause worker unrest. However, Chinese officials have indicated that their long-term goal is to adopt a more flexible exchange rate system and to seek more balanced economic growth through increased domestic consumption and the development of rural areas, but they claim they want to proceed at a gradual pace.

IMPLICATIONS OF CHINA'S CURRENCY POLICY FOR ITS ECONOMY

If the yuan is undervalued vis-à-vis the dollar (estimates rage from 15% to 40% or higher), then Chinese exports to the United States are likely cheaper than they would be if the currency were freely traded, providing a boost to China's export industries (and, to some degree, an indirect subsidy). Eliminating exchange rate risk through a managed peg also increases the attractiveness of China as a destination for foreign investment in export-oriented production facilities. However, an undervalued currency makes imports more expensive, hurting Chinese consumers and Chinese firms that import parts, machinery, and raw materials. Such a policy, in effect, benefits Chinese exporting firms (many of which are owned by foreign multinational corporations) at the expense of non-exporting Chinese firms, especially those that rely on imported goods. This may impede the most efficient allocation of resources in the Chinese economy. Another major problem is that the Chinese government must expand the money supply in order to keep purchasing dollars, which has promoted the banks to adopt easy credit policies [4]. In addition, in the past, "hot money" has poured into China from investors speculating that China will continue to appreciate the yuan. At some point, these factors could help fuel inflation, overinvestment in various sectors, and expansion of nonperforming loans by the banks—each of which could threaten future economic growth.

IMPLICATIONS OF CHINA'S CURRENCY POLICY FOR THE U.S. ECONOMY

Effect on Exporters and Import-Competitors

When exchange rate policy causes the yuan to be less expensive than it would be if it were determined by supply and demand, it causes Chinese exports to be relatively inexpensive and U.S. exports to China to be relatively expensive. As a result, U.S. exports and the production of U.S. goods and services that compete with Chinese imports fall, in the short run [5]. Many of the affected firms are in the manufacturing sector [6].

This causes the trade deficit to rise and reduces aggregate demand in the short run, all else equal [7] Some analysts contend that China's currency policy constitutes a de facto or indirect export subsidy and should be subject to U.S. countervailing laws.

Effect on U.S. Consumers and Certain Producers

A society's economic well-being is usually measured not by how much it can produce, but how much it can consume. An undervalued yuan that lowers the price of imports from China allows the United States to increase its consumption through an improvement in the terms-of-trade. Since changes in aggregate spending are only temporary, from a long-term perspective the lasting effect of an undervalued yuan is to increase the purchasing power of U.S. consumers.

Imports from China are not limited to consumption goods. U.S. producers also import capital equipment and inputs to final products from China. An undervalued yuan lowers the price of these U.S. products, increasing their output.

Effect on U.S. Borrowers

An undervalued yuan also has an effect on U.S. borrowers. When the U.S. runs a current account deficit with China, an equivalent amount of capital flows from China to the United States, as can be seen in the U.S. balance of payments accounts. This occurs because the Chinese central bank or private Chinese citizens are investing in U.S. assets, which allows more U.S. capital investment in plant and equipment to take place than would otherwise occur. Capital investment increases because the greater demand for U.S. assets puts downward pressure on U.S. interest rates, and firms are now willing to make investments that were previously unprofitable. This increases aggregate spending in the short run, all else equal, and also increases the size of the economy in the long run by increasing the capital stock.

Private firms are not the only beneficiaries of the lower interest rates caused by the capital inflow (trade deficit) from China. Interest-sensitive household spending, on goods such as consumer durables and housing, is also higher than it would be if capital from China did not flow into the United States. In addition, a large proportion of the U.S. assets bought by the Chinese, particularly by the central bank, are U.S. Treasury securities, which fund U.S. federal budget deficits. According to the U.S. Treasury Department, China held $$764 billion in U.S. Treasury securities as of April 2009, making it the largest foreign holder of such securities. If the U.S. trade deficit with China were eliminated, Chinese capital would no longer flow into this country on net, and the government would have to find other buyers of U.S. Treasuries. This could increase the government's interest payments.

Net Effect on the U.S. Economy

In the medium run, an undervalued yuan neither increases nor decreases aggregate demand in the United States. Rather, it leads to a compositional shift in U.S. production, away from U.S. exporters and import-competing firms toward the firms that benefit from Chinese capital flows. Thus, it is expected to have no medium or long run effect on aggregate U.S. employment or unemployment. As evidence, one can consider that the U.S. had a historically large and growing trade deficit throughout the 1990s at a time when unemployment reached a three-decade low. However, the gains and losses in employment and production caused by the trade deficit will not be dispersed evenly across regions and sectors of the economy: on balance, some areas will gain while others will lose. And by shifting the composition of U.S. output to a higher capital base, the size of the economy would be larger in the long run as a result of the capital inflow/trade deficit.

Although the compositional shift in output has no negative effect on aggregate U.S. output and employment in the long run, there may be adverse short-run consequences. If output in the trade sector falls more quickly than the output of U.S. recipients of Chinese capital rises, aggregate spending and employment could temporarily fall. This is more likely to be a concern if the economy is already sluggish than if it is at full employment. Otherwise, it is likely that government macroeconomic policy adjustment and market forces can quickly compensate for any decline of output in the trade sector by expanding other elements of aggregate demand. The deficit with China has not prevented the U.S. economy from registering high rates of growth.

The U.S.-China Trade Deficit in the Context of the Overall U.S. Trade Deficit

While China is a large trading partner, it accounted for only 16.1% of U.S. merchandise imports in 2008 and 33% of the sum of all U.S. bilateral trade deficits [8]. Over a span of several years, a country with a floating exchange rate can consistently run an overall trade deficit for only one reason: a domestic imbalance between saving and investment. Over the past two decades, U.S. saving as a share of gross domestic product (GDP) has been in gradual decline. On the one hand, the U.S. has high rates of productivity growth and strong economic fundamentals that are conducive to high rates of capital investment. On the other hand, it has a chronically low household saving rate, and recently a negative government saving rate as a result of the budget deficit. As long as Americans save little, foreigners will use their saving to finance profitable investment opportunities in the United States; the trade deficit is the result [9]. The returns to foreign-owned capital will flow to foreigners instead of Americans, but the returns to U.S. labor utilizing foreign-owned capital will flow to U.S. labor.

More than half of China's exports to the world are produced by foreign-invested firms in China, many of which have shifted production to China in order to gain access to low-cost labor. (The returns to capital of U.S. owned firms in China flow to Americans.) Such firms import raw materials and components (much of which come from East Asia) for assembly in China. As a result, China tends to run trade deficits with East Asian countries (such as Taiwan, South Korea, and Japan) and trade surpluses with countries with high consumer demand, such as the United States. These factors imply that much of the increase in U.S.

imports (and hence, the rising trade deficit with China) is largely the result of China becoming a production platform for many foreign companies, rather than unfair Chinese trade policies.

THE GLOBAL FINANCIAL CRISIS AND CHINA'S CURRENCY

The impact of the global financial crisis has raised concerns in the United States over the future course of China's currency policy. Prior to the crisis, there were high expectations among many analysts that China would continue to appreciate its currency and implement financial reforms to pave the way towards eventually adopting a floating currency. However, China's economy has slowed significantly in recent months, due largely to a fall in global demand for Chinese products. The Chinese government appears to have halted the yuan's appreciation over the past few months. The rate of exchange between the yuan and the dollar on January 1, 2009 and June 3, 2009 stayed relatively constant 6.83 yuan per dollar, indicating that the Chinese government has, at least temporarily, halted its policy of allowing the yuan to gradually appreciate.

It is not known the extent to which the government is intervening to maintain the current exchange rate, and whether the government is buying dollars to limit appreciation, or selling dollars, to limit further devaluation. Either way, a stable exchange rate with the dollar benefits China in a number of ways:

- *Exports and Foreign Direct Investment.* Keeping the exchange rate with the dollar stable may help to stem further declines in exports and FDI and thus halt further factory closings and layoffs in such sectors.
- *China as a "Responsible Stakeholder."* Over the past several years, Chinese leaders have sought to portray China as a responsible stakeholder (and increasingly a leader) on global economic issues. Chinese officials contend that during the 1997-98 Asian crisis, when several other nations sharply devalued their currencies, China "held the line" by not devaluing its currency, which might have prompted a new round of destructive devaluations across Asia. This policy was highly praised at the time by U.S. officials, including President Clinton. Although devaluing the RMB against the dollar could help China's trade sector, it could cause other economies in the Asia to devalue their currencies, which could further undermine economic stability in the region and negatively affect China's relations with its neighbors.
- *Avoiding Trade Tensions.* Chinese officials appear to be deeply concerned over "growing protectionism" in the United States. They are keenly aware that numerous congressional proposals have been introduced in the past which would take tough action against China's currency policy.
- *Protecting the Value of China's Investments.* China is believed to hold more than $1 trillion in U.S. securities. A major concern for Chinese officials as it has gradually appreciated the currency (until recently) has been the decline in value of these assets brought about by that appreciation. Thus, halting the appreciation of the yuan halts further losses from U.S.-held assets.

There may be a number of reasons why holding the exchange rate constant may not beneficial to China:

- *Continued Reliance on Exports and Fixed Investment.* Numerous economists contend that China needs to rebalance its economy by lessening its dependence on exports and fixed investment, which have been largely driven by China's currency policy, and do more to promote domestic consumption, improve the social safety net, and boost living standards among the poor. Such analysts contend that an appreciation of the yuan to "market levels" is a key factor to attaining a more balanced economy (by eliminating economic distortions caused by an undervalued currency).
- *Holding the Line May Not be Enough to Stop Congressional Action.* Although China allowed its currency to appreciate somewhat after 2005, it did not stem the tide of congressional criticism over its exchange rate policy. China has constantly argued that it has increasingly making its exchange rate system more flexible. Halting appreciation of the yuan may be viewed by some Members as an abandonment of China's commitments to reform the currency. Keeping the exchange rate with the dollar roughly the same could lessen the chance that such bills would be acted upon (see "Legislation," below).
- *The View That China Could Do More to Promote Global Recovery.* Chinese officials have stated that their biggest contribution to a global economic recovery is to maintain its rapid economic growth. To that end, the government is in the process of implementing a $586 billion stimulus plan (announced in November 2008), a large share of which will go into infrastructure projects. It is not clear to what extent the stimulus package will promote imports. Some analysts have contended that if China combined domestic spending with more market opening measures, including adopting a more flexible exchange rate policy, it would greatly boost China's imports. This would help stimulate economic recoveries in other countries, and also improve living standards in China [10]

The Obama Administration has encouraged China to continue purchasing U.S. debt. Secretary of State Hillary Clinton was reportedly quoted as saying,

> Well, I certainly do think that the Chinese government and the central bank here in China is making a very smart decision by continuing to invest in treasury bonds for two reasons.... (Second,) the Chinese know that, in order to start exporting again to its biggest market, namely, the United States, the United States has to take some very drastic measures with this stimulus package, which means we have to incur more debt. It would not be in China's interest if we were unable to get our economy moving again. So, by continuing to support American Treasury instruments, the Chinese are recognizing our interconnection [11].

China's currency policy appears to have created a policy dilemma for the Chinese government. A strong and stable U.S. economy is in China's national interest since the United States is China's largest export market. Thus, some analysts contend that China will feel compelled to keep funding the growing U.S. debt. However, Chinese officials have expressed concern that the growing U.S. debt will eventually spark inflation in the United States and a depreciation of the dollar, which would negatively impact the value of China's holdings of

U.S. securities. But if China stopped buying U.S. debt or tried to sell off a large portion of those holdings, it could also cause the dollar to depreciate and thus reduce the value of its remaining holdings, and such a move could further destabilize the U.S. economy. Chinese concerns over its large dollar holdings appear to have been reflected in a paper issued by the governor of the People's Bank of China,

Zhou Xiaochuan on March 24, 2009, which called for replacing the U.S. dollar as the international reserve currency with a new global system controlled by the International Monetary Fund [12]. China has also signed currency swap agreements totaling 650 billion yuan (or about $95 billion) with Hong Kong, Argentina, Indonesia, South Korea, Malaysia, and Belarus, which would allow those partners to settle accounts with China using the yuan rather than the dollar in order to facilitate bilateral trade and investment [13]. It is not clear if such a move signifies a gradual effort on the part of the Chinese government to eventually make the yuan an internationally traded currency.

Chinese data indicate that its accumulation of foreign exchange reserves has slowed sharply in 2009. From the end of December 2008 to the end of March 2009, those reserves grew by only $7.7 billion, reflecting sharp decreases in China's net exports, foreign direct investment, and hot money inflows (see Figure 1).

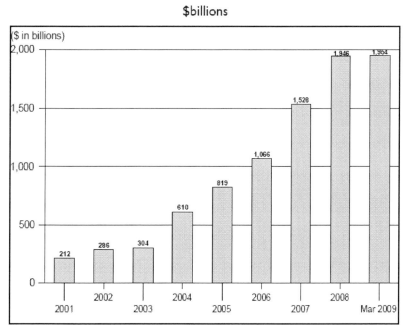

Source: Chinese State Administration of Foreign Exchange.
Note: End-year or end-month data.

Figure 1. China's Accumulation of Foreign Exchange Reserves: 2001-March 2009.

If this trends continues, it will lessen China's need to intervene to keep the value of yuan against the dollar within its targeted range. However, it could also slow China's purchases of U.S. securities [14]. In fact, China's holdings of U.S. Treasury Securities fell by $4.4 billion in April 2009 over March 2009 holdings.

LEGISLATION

Numerous bills have been introduced over the past few years that seek to induce China to reform its currency. Bills in the 111th Congress include the following.

- H.R. 2378 (Tim Ryan) and S. 1027 (Stabenow) would make fundamental exchange-rate misalignment by any foreign nation actionable under U.S. countervailing laws (dealing with government subsidies and antidumping (dealing with products sold at fair market value).
- S. 1254 (Schumer) would require the Treasury Department to identify currencies that are fundamentally misaligned and to designate currencies for "priority action" under certain circumstances. Such action would include factoring currency undervaluation in U.S. anti-dumping cases, banning federal procurement of products or services from the designated country, and filing a case against that country in the WTO.

REFERENCES

[1] The official name of China's currency is the renminbi (RMB), which is denominated in yuan units. Both RMB and yuan are used to describe China's currency.

[2] Bureau of Labor Statistics, *Import/Export Price Indexes*, Press Release, January 14, 2009.

[3] See CRS Report RS22984, *China and the Global Financial Crisis: Implications for the United States*, by Wayne M. Morrison.

[4] Prior to the current global economic slowdown, easy monetary policies were contributing to inflationary pressures in China.

[5] Many such firms contend that China's currency policy constitutes one of several unfair trade advantages enjoyed by Chinese firms, including low wages, lack of enforcement of safety and environmental standards, selling below cost (dumping) and direct assistance from the Chinese government.

[6] U.S. production has moved away from manufacturing and toward the service sector over the past several years. U.S. employment in manufacturing as a share of total nonagricultural employment fell from 31.8% in 1960, to 22.4% in 1980, to 10.2% in 2007. This trend is much larger than the Chinese currency issue and is caused by numerous other factors.

[7] Putting exchange rate issues aside, most economists maintain that trade is a win-win situation for the economy as a whole, but produces losers within the economy. Economists generally argue that free trade should be pursued because the gains from trade are large enough that the losers from trade can be compensated by the winners, and the winners will still be better off.

[8] This figure is somewhat misleading because the United States run trade deficits with some countries and surpluses with others. A different approach would be to sum up the balances of those countries in which the United States ran a trade deficit with. In 2008, the United States ran trade deficits with 91 countries in 2008, totaling $951.9 billion; the U.S. trade deficit with China was equal to 27.9% of this amount.

[9] Most economists believe that the United States runs a trade deficit because it fails to save enough to meet its investment needs and must obtain savings from other countries with high savings rates. China has one of the world's largest savings rate.

[10] Many Chinese have become increasing critical of China's currency policy because the large levels of foreign exchange reserves generated by that policy are invested in overseas assets with relatively low (and sometimes negative) returns.

[11] Secretary Clinton, Interview With Yang Lan of Dragon TV, Beijing, China, February 22, 2009.

[12] For copy of the proposal, see the Chinese People's Bank of China website at http://www.pbc.gov.cn/english/detail.asp?col=6500&id=178.

[13] Under a currency swap arrangement, two parties exchange currencies for a certain length of time and agree to reverse the transaction at a later date. See, the Federal Reserve Bank of New York, *the Basics of Foreign Trade and Exchange,* available at http://www.ny.frb.org/
education/fx/foreign.html.

[14] See, CRS Report RL34314, *China's Holdings of U.S. Securities: Implications for the U.S. Economy*, by Wayne M. Morrison and Marc Labonte.

In: Political and Economic Developments in Asia
Editor: Felix Chin

ISBN: 978-1-61209-783-1
©2011 Nova Science Publishers, Inc.

Chapter 6

CHINA-U.S. TRADE ISSUES[*]

Wayne M. Morrison

ABSTRACT

U.S.-China economic ties have expanded substantially over the past three decades. Total U.S. - China trade has risen from $5 billion in 1980 to $409 billion in 2008. In 2008, China was the second largest U.S. trading partner, its third largest export market, and its biggest source of imports. About 12% of total U.S. global trade is now with China. According to U.S. data, U.S. firms have invested around $28 billion in China (through 2007), some of which is aimed at the Chinese domestic market, while other investment has gone into export-oriented manufacturing facilities.

With a huge population and a rapidly expanding economy, China is a potentially huge market for U.S. exporters. However, bilateral economic relations have become strained over a number of issues, including large and growing U.S. trade deficits with China ($266 billion in 2008), China's failure to fully implement its World Trade Organization (WTO) commitments (especially in regards to protection of intellectual property rights), its refusal to adopt a floating currency system, its use of industrial policies (such as subsidies) and other practices deemed unfair and/or harmful to various U.S. economic sectors, and its failure in some cases to ensure that its exported products meet U.S. health and safety standards.

Further complicating the bilateral economic relationship is China's large holdings of U.S. debt, such as Treasury securities. In September 2008, China overtook Japan to become the largest foreign holder of such securities. Some analysts welcome China's purchases of U.S. debt securities, which help fund U.S. budget deficits, while others have expressed concerns that growing Chinese holdings of U.S. debt may increase its leverage over the United States.

The current global economic crisis could further challenge China-U.S. economic ties. Many analysts have expressed concern that the Chinese government may, in an effort to help its sagging export industries, implement new trade barriers, boost industrial subsidies, and/or depreciate its currency, which could harm some U.S. firms and workers. Many U.S. policymakers have urged China to lessen its reliance on exports for its economic growth and instead implement policies to promote domestic consumption.

---

[*] This is an edited, reformatted and augmented version of CRS Report RL33536, dated June 23, 2009.

Central to this position is the belief that China should appreciate its currency and eventually adopt a floating exchange rate system, which would boost its imports.

Several Members of Congress have urged the Obama Administration to take a more assertive approach in dealing with Chinese economic practices, including increasing the use of U.S. antidumping, countervailing, and safeguard provisions; bringing more dispute resolution cases against China to the WTO; and continuing pressure on China to appreciate its currency. Others have warned against using "protectionist" measures to block imports of Chinese goods and have advocated using high-level bilateral talks (such as the Strategic Economic Dialogue that began during the Bush Administration in 2006) to resolve major trade disputes.

Economic and trade reforms (begun in 1979) have helped transform China into one of the world's fastest growing economies. China's economic growth and trade liberalization, including comprehensive trade commitments made upon entering the World Trade Organization (WTO) in 2001, have led to a sharp expansion in U.S.-China commercial. Yet, bilateral trade relations have grown increasingly strained in recent years over a number of issues, including a large and growing U.S. trade deficit with China, the refusal by China to adopt a floating currency, its failure to fully implement many of its WTO obligations, especially in regards to protection of intellectual property rights (IPR), and problems relating to the health and safety of Chinese-made products. Several Members of Congress have called on the Obama Administration to take a tougher stance against China to induce it to eliminate economic policies deemed harmful to U.S. economic interests and/or are inconsistent with WTO rules.

This report provides an overview of U.S.-China economic relations, surveys major trade disputes, and lists bills introduced in the 111th Congress that would impact bilateral commercial ties.

U.S. TRADE WITH CHINA [1]

U.S.-China trade rose rapidly after the two nations re-established diplomatic relations (in January 1979), signed a bilateral trade agreement (July 1979), and provided mutual most-favored-nation (MFN) treatment beginning in 1980 [2]. In 1978 (before China's reforms began), total U.S.-China trade (exports plus imports) was $1 billion; China ranked as the 32nd largest export market and the 57th largest source of U.S. imports. In 2008, bilateral trade hit $409 billion, making China the second largest U.S. trading partner (after Canada), the third largest U.S. export market, and the largest source of U.S. imports. In recent years, China has been one of the fastest growing U.S. export markets and the importance of this market is expected to grow even further as living standards continue to improve and a sizable Chinese middle class emerges.

The U.S. trade deficit with China has surged in recent years as imports from China have grown much faster than U.S. exports to China (although it grew by only $10 billion in 2008). That deficit rose from $34 billion in 1995 to $266 billion in 2008 (see Table 1 and Figure 1).

Table 1. U.S. Merchandise Trade with China: 1980-2008 and Projections for 2009*
($ in billions)

Year	U.S. Exports	U.S. Imports	U.S. Trade Balance
1980	3.8	1.1	2.7
1985	3.9	3.9	0.0
1990	4.8	15.2	-10.4
1995	11.7	45.6	-33.8
2000	16.3	100.1	-83.8
2001	19.2	102.3	-83.1
2002	22.1	125.2	-103.1
2003	28.4	152.4	-124.0
2004	34.7	196.7	-162.0
2005	41.8	243.5	-201.6
2006	55.2	287.8	-232.5
2007	65.2	321.5	-256.3
2008	71.5	337.8	-266.3
2009 projection*	59.2	296.9	-237.7

Source: USITC DataWeb.
* 2009 projections based on actual data for January-April 2009.

Table 2. U.S. Merchandise Trade Balances with Major Trading Partners: 2008
($ in billions)

Country or Trading Group	U.S. Trade Balance
World	-800.0
China	-266.3
Organization of Petroleum Exporting Countries (OPEC)	-175.6
European Union (EU27)	-93.4
Canada	-74.6
Japan	-72.7
Mexico	-64.4
Association of Southeast Asian Nations (ASEAN)	-50.6

Source: USITC DataWeb.

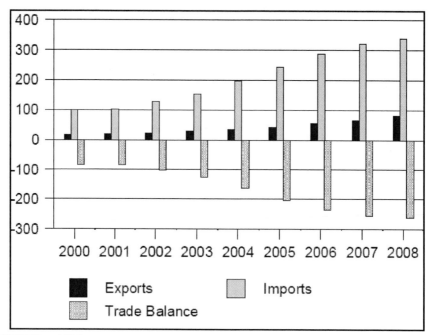

Source: USITC DataWeb.

Figure 1. U.S. Trade With China: 2000-2008 ($billions).

It was significantly larger than that with any other U.S. trading partner and several trading groups. For example, it was nearly equal to the combined U.S. deficits with the countries that make up the Organization of the Petroleum Export Countries (OPEC) and the 27 countries that make up the European Union (EU27), and it was more than three times larger than the trade deficit with Japan (see Table 2).

Some analysts view the huge U.S. trade deficit with China as an indicator that China's economic and trade policies are restrictive or unfair, while others contend that the growing deficit reflects a shift in export-oriented production from other countries (largely in Asia) to China.

The global financial crisis has had a significant impact on U.S.-China trade flows. During the first four months of 2009, U.S. exports to, and imports from, China were down 17.2% and 12.1%, respectively over the same period in 2008. At this rate, the U.S. trade deficit with China could decline to $238 billion in 2009.

Major U.S. Exports to China

U.S. merchandise exports to China in 2008 were $71.5 billion, up 9.5% (compared to an 18.1% rise in 2007) over the previous year [3]. In 2007, China overtook Japan to become the third largest U.S. export market and was third in 2008 (see Figure 2). U.S. exports to China in 2008 accounted for 5.5% of total U.S. exports (compared to 3.9% in 2003). The top five U.S. exports to China in 2008 were waste and scrap, semiconductors and electronic components, oilseeds and grain, aircraft and parts, and resins and synthetic rubber and fibers (see Table 3) [4]. China is a significant market for U.S. agricultural products. It was the fourth largest destination for U.S. agricultural exports in 2008 at $12.1 billion, up 46.5% over the previous year. Major U.S. agricultural exports to China include soybeans, meat products, and cotton [5].

Over the past few years, China has been one of the fastest growing U.S. export markets, as can be seen in Table 4. U.S. exports to China rose by nearly 240% from 2001 to 2008, which was higher than that of any other top 10 U.S. trading partner.

Many trade analysts argue that China could prove to be a much more significant market for U.S. exports in the future. China is one of the world's fastest-growing economies, and rapid economic growth is likely to continue in the near future, provided that economic reforms are continued.

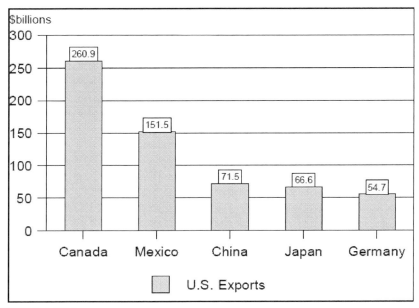

Source: USITC DataWeb.

Figure 2. Top Five U.S. Export Markets: 2008 ($billions).

Table 3. Major U.S. Exports to China: 2008 ($ in millions and percent change)

NAIC Number and Description	2004	2005	2006	2007	2008	Percent Change 2007 - 2008
	\multicolumn{5}{c}{$ millions}	
9100 Waste and scrap	2,508	3,670	6,071	7,331	7,562	3.1%
3344 Semiconductors and other electronic components	3,565	4,015	6,830	7,435	7,475	0.5%
1111 Oilseeds and grains	2,829	2,339	2,593	4,145	7,316	76.5%
3364 Aerospace products and parts	2,111	4,535	6,309	7,447	5,471	-26.5%
3252 Resin, synthetic rubber, and artificial & synthetic fibers &	1,631	2,127	2,548	3,290	3,524	7.1%

Source: USITC DataWeb.
Notes: North American Industry Classification system, 4-digit level.

Table 4. U.S. Merchandise Exports to Major Trading Partners in 2001 and 2008 ($ in billions and % change)

	2001	2008	% Change from 2007-2008	% Change from 2001-2008
Canada	163.7	260.9	5.0	59.4
Mexico	101.5	151.5	11.0	49.3
China	19.2	71.5	9.5	272.3
Japan	57.6	66.6	6.2	15.6
Germany	30.1	54.7	10.2	31.9
United Kingdom	40.8	53.8	6.9	31.9
Netherlands	19.5	40.2	21.9	106.2
South Korea	22.2	34.8	6.9	56.8
Brazil	15.9	32.9	33.6	106.9
France	19.9	29.2	6.5	46.7
World	731.0	1,300.1	11.8	77.9

Source: USITC DataWeb. Ranked by top 10 U.S. export markets in 2008.

China's goals of modernizing its infrastructure, upgrading its industries, and improving rural living standards could generate substantial demand for foreign goods and services. Finally, economic growth has substantially improved the purchasing power of Chinese citizens, especially those living in urban areas along the east coast of China. China's growing economy and large population make it a potentially enormous market. To illustrate:

- China currently has the world's largest mobile phone network and one of the fastest-growing markets, with an estimated 679 million mobile phone users (as of April 2009), compared to 87 million users in 2000.
- Boeing Corporation predicts that China will be the largest market for commercial air travel outside the U.S. for the next 20 years (2008-2027); during this period, China will buy 3,710 aircraft valued at $390 billion [6] On April 11, 2006, Boeing announced it had signed a general purchase agreement with China for 80 Boeing 737s. On September 6, 2007, China announced it would buy 55 Boeing aircraft valued at $3.8 billion.
- It is estimated that China in 2008 replaced the United States as the world's largest Internet user: 253 million users versus 221 million respectively (as of June 2008) [7] Yet, the percentage of the Chinese population using the Internet is small relative to the United States: 19% versus 73%, respectively.
- The Chinese government projects that by the year 2020, there will be 140 million cars in China (seven times the current level), and that the number of cars sold annually will rise from 7.2 million units (2006) to 20.7 million units in 2020 [8]

According to some estimates, China is now the world's second largest market for new cars. General Motors (GM) and Ford reportedly sold 1.09 million and 306 thousand vehicles, respectively, in China in 2008 [9].

Major U.S. Imports from China

China was the largest source of U.S. imports in 2008 at $338 billion, or 16.1% of total U.S. imports (up from 6.5% of total in 1996) [10] U.S. imports from China rose by 5.1% in 2008 over the previous year (compared with an 11.7% rise in 2007). The importance (ranking) of China as a source of U.S. imports has risen dramatically, from eighth largest in 1990, to fourth in 2000, to second in 2004-2006, to first in 2007-2008. The top five U.S. imports from China in 2008 were computers and parts, miscellaneous manufactured articles (such as toys, games, etc.), communications equipment, apparel, and audio and video equipment (see Table 5).

Throughout the 1 980s and 1 990s, nearly all of U.S. imports from China were low-value, labor- intensive products such as toys and games, consumer electronic products, footwear, and textiles and apparel. However, over the past few years, an increasing proportion of U.S. imports from China has comprised of more technologically advanced products, such as computers. According to the U.S. Census Bureau, in 2008, U.S. imports of advanced technology products from China totaled $91.4 billion (27.1% of total U.S. imports from China), compared with $29.3 billion in 2003 (19.2% of total U.S. imports from China). In addition, imports of advanced technology products from China accounted for 27.5% of total U.S. imports of such products in 2008, compared with 14.1% in 2003, indicating that U.S. dependency on China for advanced technology products is rapidly increasing. U.S. exports of advanced technology to China in 2008 were $18.7 billion; these accounted for 26.2% of total U.S. exports to China and 6.8% of total U.S. advanced technology exports [11].

Table 5. Major U.S. Imports From China: 2008
($ in millions and percent change)

NAIC Number and Description	2004	2005	2006	2007	2008	Percent Change 2007 - 2008
3341 computer equipment	29,486	35,467	40,046	44,462	45,820	3.1%
3399 Miscellaneous manufactured commodities	23,712	26,449	28,888	34,827	35,835	2.9%
3342 Communications equipment	9,015	14,121	17,977	23,192	26,618	14.8%
3152 Apparel	10,530	16,362	19,228	22,955	22,583	-1.6%
3343 Audio and video equipment	12,421	15,287	18,789	19,075	19,715	3.4%

Source: USITC DataWeb.
Notes: North American Industry Classification system, 4-digit level.

Many analysts contend that the sharp increase in U.S. imports from China (and hence the growing trade deficit) is largely the result of movement in production facilities from other (primarily) Asian countries to China [12]. That is, various products that used to be made in Japan, Taiwan, Hong Kong, etc., and then exported to the United States are now being made in China (in many cases, by foreign firms in China) and exported to the United States. An illustration of this shift can be seen in Table 6, which lists U.S. imports of computer equipment and parts from 2000-2008. For example, in 2000, Japan was the largest foreign supplier of U.S. computer equipment (with a 19.6% share of total shipments), while China ranked fourth (with a 12.1% share).

In just eight years, Japan's ranking fell to fourth, the value of its shipments dropped by over half, and its share of U.S. computer imports declined to 7.7% (2008). China was by far the largest foreign supplier of computer equipment in 2008 with a 53.6% share of total U.S. imports. While U.S. imports of computer equipment from China rose by 452% over the past eight years, the total value of U.S. computer imports from the world rose by only 25%. Many analysts contend that a large share of the increase in Chinese computer production has come from foreign computer companies that have moved manufacturing facilities China.

Table 6. Major Foreign Suppliers of U.S. Computer Equipment Imports: 2000-2008 ($ in billions and % change)

	2000	2002	2004	2006	2008	2000-2008 % change
Total	68.5	62.3	73.9	83.8	85.4	24.7
China	8.3	12.0	29.5	40.0	45.8	451.8
Malaysia	4.9	7.1	8.7	11.1	9.0	83.7
Japan	13.4	8.1	6.3	6.3	6.6	-50.7
Mexico	6.9	7.9	7.4	6.6	6.2	-10.1
Singapore	8.7	7.1	6.6	5.6	4.0	-54.0

Source: U.S. International Trade Commission Trade Data Web.
Note: Ranked according to top five suppliers in 2008.

China has become a major source of U.S. agricultural imports. It was the third largest supplier of such imports in 2008 (compared with 12th largest in 2000), at $4.7 billion. U.S. agricultural imports from China rose by 42.2% in 2008 and by 104.5% from 2004-2008. Major agricultural imports from China include seafood products, vegetables and fruit, and animal foods.

Investment Ties

Investment plays a major role in U.S.-China commercial ties [13] China's investments in U.S. assets can be broken down into two categories: holdings of U.S. securities and foreign direct investment (FDI). The Treasury Department defines foreign holdings of U.S. securities as "U.S. securities owned by foreign residents (including banks and other institutions) except where the owner has a direct investment relationship with the U.S. issuer of the securities."

These include long-term (LT) U.S. Treasury securities, LT U.S. government agency securities, [14] LT corporate securities (some of which are asset-backed), equities (such as stocks), and short-term debt [15]. The U.S. Bureau of Economic Analysis (BEA) defines FDI (in the United States) as "the ownership or control, directly or indirectly, by one foreign resident of 10 percent or more of the voting securities of an incorporated U.S. business enterprise or the equivalent interest in an unincorporated U.S. business enterprise." [16] BEA classifies FDI flows according to broad industrial sections, including mining; utilities; manufacturing (broken down into nine subsectors [17]); wholesale trade; information; depository institutions; finance (excluding depository institutions); professional, scientific, and technical services; nonbank holding companies; and other industries.

Table 7. China's Holdings of U.S. Securities: June 2002-June 2008 ($ billions and percent change)

2002	2003	2004	2005	2006	2007	2008	2002-2008 % change
188	255	341	527	699	922	1,205	566%

Source: U.S. Department of Treasury.
Notes: U.S. securities include short term and long-term debt, including Treasury securities, U.S. government agency securities, corporate securities, and equities.

Table 8. China's Holdings of U.S. Treasury Securities: 2002-2008 Year-End and April 2009 ($ billions and as a percent of total foreign holdings)

	2002	2003	2004	2005	2006	2007	2008	April 2009
China's Holdings ($billions)	118.4	159.0	222.9	310.0	396.9	477.6	727.4	763.5
Holdings As a Percent of Total Foreign Holdings	9.6%	10.4%	12.1%	15.2%	18.9%	20.3%	23.6%	23.4

Source: U.S. Treasury Department.
Notes: Data based on periodical surveys by the Treasury Department, which often revises estimates for the previous year but not for all years and thus should be interpreted with caution.

China's Holdings of U.S. Securities [18]

The Treasury Department performs annual surveys of foreign holders of U.S. securities, the latest of which was released in February 2009 (preliminary data) for holding as of June 2008 [19] China's total holdings of U.S. securities at the end of June 2008 were estimated at $1,205 billion, compared to $922 billion in June 2007 (an increase of 31%). From June 2002 to June 2008, China's holdings of U.S. securities as a share of total foreign holdings of U.S. securities rose from 3.9% to 11.7% and its ranking increased from fifth to second (after Japan at $1,250 billion).

China is likely became the largest holder in late 2008 or early 2009 (see Table 7). From June 2002 to June 2008, China's U.S. securities holdings grew by nearly $1.1 trillion (or 5 66%), which was by far the largest increase in U.S. securities holdings of any other country [20]. These holding are largely the result of China's currency policy (discussed below). The largest type of U.S. securities held by China are U.S. Treasury securities, which are used to finance U.S. budget deficits; data for foreign holdings of these type of securities are reported on a monthly basis. China's holdings of U.S. Treasury securities rose from $118 billion (or

9.6% of total foreign holdings) at the end of 2002 to $727.4 billion (23.6% of foreign holdings) in December 2008. China's holdings as of April 2009 were $764 billion or 23.5% of total foreign holdings (see Table 8) [21] Since September 2008, China has become the largest foreign holder of U.S. Treasuries. China's holdings in April 2009 were down by $4.4 billion over its March 2009 holdings.

Many U.S. policymakers have raised concern over China's large and growing holdings of U.S. securities, stating that while such purchases have helped the United States meet its investment needs and have helped fund the growing U.S. Federal budget deficit, they could give China increased leverage over the United States on major political and economic issues. On the other hand, Chinese officials have expressed concern over the "safety" of their large holdings of U.S. debt. Many analysts contend that China's economy is so dependent on a healthy and stable U.S. economy that China has no choice but to keep buying U.S. government debt. However, Chinese officials have expressed concern that growing U.S. government debt will spark inflation in the United States and a sharp depreciation of the dollar, which would diminish the value of China's dollar assets [22].

U.S. Holdings of Chinese Securities

The Treasury Department also does surveys on U.S. holdings of Chinese securities; these data are on a year-end basis. The last survey (issued in October 2008) estimated total U.S. holdings of Chinese securities at $97.2 billion in 2007 (98% of which were in equities), up from $13.7 billion in 2003. U.S. holdings of Chinese securities in 2007 were equal to about 1.3% of total U.S. holdings of foreign securities [23].

Bilateral FDI Flows

China's FDI in the United States is quite small relative to its holdings of U.S. securities: $1.1 billion (cumulative at the end of 2007) versus $922 billion (as of June 2007), respectively [24]. In 2007, China ranked as the 30th largest source for FDI in the United States [25]. On the other hand, total U.S. FDI in China in 2007 was $28.3 billion (nearly 26 times China's FDI in the United States), making China the 21st largest U.S. destination for FDI (see Table 9) [26].

Table 9. China's Cumulative FDI in the United States and U.S. FDI in China: 2002-2007($ in millions and percent change)

	2000	2002	2004	2006	2008	2000-2008 % change
Total	68.5	62.3	73.9	83.8	85.4	24.7
China	8.3	12.0	29.5	40.0	45.8	451.8
Malaysia	4.9	7.1	8.7	11.1	9.0	83.7
Japan	13.4	8.1	6.3	6.3	6.6	-50.7
Mexico	6.9	7.9	7.4	6.6	6.2	-10.1
Singapore	8.7	7.1	6.6	5.6	4.0	-54.0

Source: U.S. Bureau of Economic Analysis. Notes: Data on a historical-cost basis.

MAJOR U.S.-CHINA TRADE ISSUES

Although China's economic reforms and rapid economic growth have expanded U.S.-China commercial relations in recent years, tensions have arisen over a wide variety of issues, including the growth and size of the U.S. trade deficit with China (which many Members contend is an indicator that the trade relationship is unfair), concerns over unsafe Chinese food and consumer products, China's currency policy (which many Members blame for the size of the U.S. trade deficit with China and the loss of U.S. manufacturing jobs), China's mixed record on implementing its obligations in the WTO, including its, failure to provide adequate protection of U.S. intellectual property rights (IPR), and Chinese industrial policies used to promote and protect domestic industries.

Legislation has been introduced to respond to several of these issues (see "U.S.-China Trade Legislation in the 111th Congress").

Health and Safety Concerns over Certain Imports from China [27]

Reports throughout 2007 of tainted or unsafe food and consumer products (including seafood, pet food, toys, and tires) from China raised concerns in the United States over the health, safety, and quality of imports from China. Some analysts contend that China maintains a poor regulatory framework for enforcing its health and safety regulations and standards, and that this is proving to be a growing problem for U.S. consumers. Many U.S. policymakers have raised concern over how to press China to improve enforcement of its health and safety standards of its exports as well as the ability of U.S. regulatory agencies to ensure the health and safety of imports from China (and other countries).

In 2007 and 2008, there were numerous recalls, warnings, and safety concerns involving Chinese products, as the following instances illustrate.

The Food and Drug Administration (FDA) in March 2007 issued warnings and announced voluntary recalls on over 150 brands of pet foods (and products such as rice protein concentrate and wheat gluten used to manufacture pet food and animal feed) from China believed to have caused the sickness and deaths of numerous pets in the United States [28] In May 2007, the FDA issued warnings on certain toothpaste products (some of which were found to be counterfeit) found to originate in China that contained poisonous chemicals. In June 2007, the FDA announced import controls on all farm-raised catfish, basa, shrimp, dace (related to carp), and eel from China after antimicrobial agents, which are not approved in the United States for use in farm-raised aquatic animals, were found. The FDA ordered that such shipments will be detained until they are proven to be free of contaminants [29] On January 25, 2008, the FDA posted on its website a notice by Baxter Healthcare Corporation that it had temporarily halted the manufacture of its multiple-dose vials of heparin (a blood thinner) for injection because of recent reports of serious adverse events associated with the use of the drug, including 246 deaths from January 2007 to May 2008. Some analysts have speculated that an unlicensed drug company in China, which produces ingredients for the drug, may be the source of the problem [30]. On September 12, 2008, the FDA issued a health information advisory on infant formula in response to reports of contaminated milk-based infant formula manufactured and sold in China, and later issued a warning on other products containing milk imported from China. On November 12, 2008, the FDA issued a new alert stating that all products containing milk imported from China would be detained unless proven to be free of melamine. On December 2, 2008, the Chinese government reported that melamine-tainted formula had so far killed six children and sickened 294,000 others (51,900 of whom had to be hospitalized and 154 were in serious condition) [31]

The National Highway Traffic Safety Administration (NHTSA) in June 2007 was informed by Foreign Tire Sales, Inc., an importer of foreign tires, that it suspected that up to 450,000 tires (later reduced to 255,000 tires) made in China may have a major safety defect (i.e., missing or insufficient gum strip inside the tire). The company was ordered by the NHTSA to issue a recall. The Chinese government and the manufacturer have maintained that the tires in question meet or exceed U.S. standards.

The Consumer Product Safety Commission (CPSC) has issued alerts and announced voluntary recalls by U.S. companies on numerous products made in China. From January-December 2007, over four-fifths of CPSC recall notices involved Chinese products. Over this period, roughly 17.6 million toys were recalled because of excessive lead levels. Recalls were also issued on 9.5 million Chinese-made toys (because of the danger of loose magnets), 4.2 million "Aqua Dots" toys (because of beads that contained a chemical that can turn toxic if ingested) and 1 million toy ovens (due to potential finger entrapment and burn hazards) [32]. China is the dominant supplier of toys to the United States, accounting for 89% of total U.S. imports (2007). U.S. recalls of lead- tainted Chinese-made toys were sharply down in 2008, totaling about 2.5 million toy units [33]. During the first five months of 2009, recalls of lead-tainted Chinese toys totaled 1.1 million units.

China's Poor Regulatory System and Implications

China is believed to have a rather weak health and safety regime for manufactured goods and agricultural products. Problems include:

- weak consumer protection laws and poorly enforced regulations,
- lack of inspections and ineffective penalties for code violators,
- underfunded and understaffed regulatory agencies and poor interagency cooperation,
- the proliferation of fake goods,
- the existence of numerous unlicensed producers,
- falsified export documents,
- extensive pollution, [34]
- intense competition that often induces firms to cut corners,
- the relative absence of consumer protection advocacy groups,
- failure by Chinese companies to effectively monitor the quality of their suppliers' products,
- restrictions on the media, [35] and
- widespread government corruption and lack of accountability, especially at the local government level.

Although China has criticized the United States for its actions against unsafe Chinese products, [36] it has pledged to improve and strengthen food and drug safety supervision and standards, beef up inspections, require safety certificates before some products can be sold, and crack down on government corruption.

The United States and China reached a number of agreements in 2007 to address health and safety concerns:

- On September 11, 2007, the CPSC and its Chinese counterpart, the General Administration of Quality Supervision, Inspection and Quarantine (AQSIQ), signed a Joint Statement on enhancing consumer product safety. China pledged to implement a comprehensive plan to intensify efforts (such as increased inspections, efforts to educate Chinese manufacturers, bilateral technical personal exchanges and training, regular meetings to exchange information with U.S. officials, and the development of a product tracking system) to prevent exports of unsafe products to the United States, especially in regard to lead paint in toys.
- On September 12, 2007, the NHTSA signed a Memorandum of Cooperation with its Chinese counterpart on enhanced cooperation and communication on vehicles and automotive equipment safety.
- On December 11, 2007, the U.S. Department of Health and Human Services (HHS) announced that it had signed two Memoranda of Agreements (MOA) with its Chinese counterparts; the first covering specific food and feed items that have been of concern to the United States, and the second covering drugs and medical devices. Both MOAs would require Chinese firms that export such products to the United States to register with the Chinese government and to obtain certification before they can export. Such firms would also be subject to annual inspections to ensure they meet U.S. standards. The MOAs also establish mechanisms for greater information sharing, increase access of production facilities by U.S. officials, and create working groups in order to boost cooperation. In March 2008, the FDA announced that it would post eight FDA inspectors in China.

China's Currency Policy [37]

Unlike most advanced economies (such as the United States), China does not maintain a market- based floating exchange rate. Between 1994 and July 2005, China pegged its currency, the renminbi (RMB) or yuan, to the U.S. dollar at about 8.28 yuan to the dollar. In July 2005, China appreciated the RMB to the dollar by 2.1% and moved to a "managed float," based on a basket of major foreign currencies, including the U.S. dollar. In order to maintain a target rate of exchange with the dollar (and other currencies), the Chinese government has maintained restrictions and controls over capital transactions and has made large-scale purchases of U.S. dollars (and dollar assets). According to the Bank of China, from July 21, 2005, to June 23, 2009, the dollar-yuan exchange rate went from 8.11 to 6.83 yuan per dollar, an appreciation of 1 8.7% [38]. During 2009, China's has kept the exchange rate with the dollar at about 6.83 yuan per dollar, indicating that it has abandoned (at least for now) its policy of gradual appreciation.

Many U.S. policymakers and business representatives have charged that China's currency policy has made the RMB significantly undervalued vis-à-vis the U.S. dollar (with estimates ranging from 15% to 40%) and that this makes Chinese exports to the United States cheaper, and U.S. exports to China more expensive, than they would be if exchange rates were determined by market forces. They complain that this policy has particularly hurt several U.S. manufacturing sectors (such as textiles and apparel, furniture, plastics, machine tools, and steel), which are forced to compete against low-cost imports from China, and further contend that it has been a major factor in the size and growth of the U.S. trade deficit with China. Numerous bills have been introduced over the past few years to pressure China to either significantly appreciate its currency or to let it float freely in international markets.

Chinese officials have argued that its currency policy is not meant to favor exports over imports, but instead to foster domestic economic stability. They have expressed concern that abandoning its currency policy could cause an economic crisis in China and would especially hurt its export industries sectors at a time when painful economic reforms (such as closing down inefficient state-owned enterprises and restructuring the banking system) are being implemented. Chinese officials view economic stability as critical to sustaining political stability; they fear an appreciated currency could reduce jobs and lower wages in several sectors and thus cause worker unrest.

Section 3004 of the 1988 Omnibus Trade and Competitiveness Act (P.L. 100-418) requires the Secretary of Treasury to issue a report every six months on international economic policy (including exchange rate policy) and to determine if any country is manipulating its currency in order to prevent an effective balance of payments adjustment or to gain an unfair competitive advantage in international trade. After China reformed its currency in July 2005, the Bush Administration continued to press China to further reform its currency and its financial sector, but declined to cite China for currency manipulation. In April 2009, the Treasury Department under the Obama Administration issued its report on exchange rates, stating "China's continued large current account surplus and accumulation of foreign exchange reserves suggest the renminbi remains undervalued." [39] However, Treasury did not cite China as a currency manipulator.

Further complicating the issue of China's currency policy is its large holdings of U.S. debt (such as Treasury securities). The Chinese government has had to make large-scale purchases of U.S. dollars to meet its exchange rate targets. Rather than hold dollars (which earn no interest), China has sought to invest its dollars in U.S. assets, primarily U.S. government debt securities. On the one hand, some analysts welcome China's purchases of U.S. debt securities, especially during the current financial crisis in the United States where efforts to stimulate the economy will likely require the government to issue large amounts of new debt. They warn that threatening China over its currency policy could induce the Chinese government to slow its purchases, or even sell off current holdings, of U.S. Treasury Securities, which could contribute to higher U.S. interest rates. On the other hand, some policymakers have expressed concern that growing Chinese holdings of U.S. debt may increase its leverage over the United States on a number of economic and non-economic issues, and some contend that China's currency policy was a contributing factor to the current global economic crisis [40]

China and the World Trade Organization

Negotiations for China's accession to the General Agreement on Tariffs and Trade (GATT) and its successor organization, the WTO, began in 1986 and took over 15 years to complete. During the WTO negotiations, Chinese officials insisted that China was a developing country and should be allowed to enter under fairly lenient terms. The United States insisted that China could enter the WTO only if it substantially liberalized its trade regime. In the end, a compromise was reached that requires China to make immediate and extensive reductions in various trade and investment barriers, while allowing it to maintain some level of protection (or a transitional period of protection) for certain sensitive sectors. China's WTO membership was formally approved at the WTO Ministerial Conference in Doha, Qatar on November 10, 2001. Taiwan's WTO membership was approved the next day. On November 11, 2001, China notified the WTO that it had formally ratified the WTO agreements, and on December 11, 2001, it formally joined the WTO. Under the WTO accession agreement, China agreed to:

- Reduce the average tariff for industrial goods and agriculture products to 8.9% and 15%, respectively (with most cuts made by 2004 and all cuts completed by 2010).
- Limit subsidies for agricultural production to 8.5% of the value of farm output and eliminate export subsidies on agricultural exports.
- Within three years of accession, grant full trade and distribution rights to foreign enterprises (with some exceptions, such as for certain agricultural products, minerals, and fuels).
- Provide non-discriminatory treatment to all WTO members. Foreign firms in China will be treated no less favorably than Chinese firms for trade purposes. End discriminatory trade policies against foreign invested firms in China, such as domestic content rules and technology transfer requirements.
- Implement the WTO's Trade-Related Aspects of Intellectual Property Rights (TRIPS) Agreement upon accession. (That agreement establishes basic standards on IPR protection and rules for enforcement.)
- Accept a 12-year safeguard mechanism in cases where a surge in Chinese exports cause or threaten to cause market disruption to U.S. (or other WTO members) domestic producers, which allow temporary restrictions on those products. China also agreed that the United States (and other WTO members) could continue to apply a non-market economy methodology for measuring dumping in antidumping investigations of imports from China for 15 years.
- Fully open the banking system to foreign financial institutions within five years (by the end of 2006). Joint ventures in insurance and telecommunication will be permitted (with various degrees of foreign ownership allowed).

WTO Implementation Issues

China's record on implementing its WTO commitments has been mixed. China's average overall tariff has dropped from 15.6% in 2001 to 9.9% in 2009 (the tariff rate on industrial goods and agricultural products is 8.9 and 15.2, respectively) and a number of non-tariff measures have been eliminated. However, there have been several areas where China's implementation is considered to be incomplete. The USTR's seventh annual China WTO compliance report (issued in December 2008) identified several areas of concern, including failure by the Chinese government to maintain an effective IPR enforcement regime (discussed below), industrial policies and national standards that attempt to promote Chinese firms (while discriminating against foreign firms), restrictions on trading and distribution rights (especially in regards to IPR products, such as movies, books, and music), discriminatory and unpredictable health and safety rules on imports (especially agricultural products), burdensome regulations and restrictions on services (including excessive capital requirements), and failure to provide adequate transparency of trade laws and regulations [41].

The USTR's December 2008 China WTO report stated that China's failure to comply with key areas of its WTO commitments largely stemmed from its incomplete transition to a market based economy. A significant part of the economy, including the banking system and state owned enterprises (SOEs), are controlled by the central government—remnants of the old command economy that existed before reforms began in 1979. Although China agreed to make SOEs operate according to free market principles when it joined the WTO, U.S. officials contend that SOEs are still being subsidized, especially through the banking system. In addition, China is attempting to promote the development of several industries (such as autos, steel, telecommunications, and high technology products) deemed by the government as important to China's future economic development and has implemented policies to promote and protect them.

When China joined the WTO, it agreed to provide a full description of all its subsidy programs, but to date has failed to fully do so. In addition, China agreed to make its state-owned enterprises operate according to market principles; yet such firms continue to receive direction and subsidies. Some major issues of concern to the United States include the following.

- In November 2008, the government announced a $586 billion economic stimulus plan, which included policies that would be implemented to assist 10 pillar industries (including, autos, steel, shipbuilding, textiles, machinery, electronics and information, light industry, petrochemicals, non-ferrous metals, and logistics) to promote their long-term competitiveness. Government support policies for the 10 industries are expected to include tax cuts and incentives (including export tax rebates), industry subsidies and subsidies to consumers to purchase certain products (such as consumer goods and autos), fiscal support, directives to banks to provide financing, direct funds to support technology upgrades and the development of domestic brands, government procurement policies, the extension of export credits, and funding to help firms invest overseas [42]. Some analysts contend that these new subsidy programs could violate China's WTO commitments.
- In December 2006, the Chinese government designated seven industries (military equipment, power generation and distribution, oil, telecommunications, coal, civil aviation, and shipping) as critical to the nation's economic security and stated it must retain "absolute control" and limit foreign participation [43]

- On June 30, 2006, China announced a partial opening of its beef market, which had been completely closed to U.S. imports in 2003, due to concerns over mad cow disease. However, U.S. officials have expressed disappointment that China has failed to develop a science-based trading protocol for importing beef from the United States, which would enable the United States to resume beef trade with China [44]
- In July 2005, the Chinese government issued new guidelines on steel production, which reportedly include provisions for the preferential use of domestically produced steel-manufacturing equipment and domestic technologies; extensive government involvement in determining the number, size, location, and production quantities of steel producers in China; technology transfer requirements on foreign investment; and restrictions on foreign majority ownership. On June 14, 2006, Assistant U.S. Trade Representative for China Tim Stratford stated that China's steel guidelines were "troubling, because it attempts to dictate industry outcomes and involves the government in making decisions that should be left to the marketplace. " [45] The U.S. steel industry has expressed growing fears that Chinese government policies have led to overinvestment and overcapacity in China's domestic steel industry, which could lead it to flood world markets with cheap steel [46]. Such concerns led the USTR to begin a Steel Dialogue with China (which first met in March 2006) to discuss issues of concern to the U.S. steel industry.
- China's Automotive Industrial Policy, issued by the government in May 2004, includes provisions discouraging the importation of auto parts and encouraging the use of domestic technology, while requiring new automobile and automobile engine plants to include substantial investment in research and development facilities. New auto parts regulations that went into effect in April 2005 discriminate against imported auto parts by assessing an additional charge on imported parts if they are incorporated into a vehicle that does not meet minimum levels of domestic content, discussed below [47]

To date, the United States has initiated eight WTO dispute resolution cases against China, five of which have been resolved or ruled upon [48]. China has filed three cases against the United States. These cases are summarized below.

Pending U.S. Cases Against China

- On June 23, 2009, the United States and the EU filed a case against China's export restrictions (such as export quotas and taxes,) on raw materials (bauxite, coke, fluorspar, magnesium, manganese, silicon metal, silicon carbide, yellow phosphorus, and zinc). The United States charges that such policies are intended to lower prices for Chinese firms (steel, aluminum, and chemical sectors) in order to help them obtain an unfair competitive advantage.
- On December 19, 2008, the USTR filed a WTO case against China over its support for "Famous Chinese" brand programs, charging that such programs utilize various export subsidies (including cash grant rewards, preferential loans, research and development funding to develop new products, and payments to lower the cost of

export credit insurance) at the central and local government level to promote the recognition and sale of Chinese brand products overseas.
- On April 10, 2007, the USTR filed two IPR-related cases against China: the first case charges that China has failed to comply with the TRIPS agreement (namely in terms of its enforcement of IPR laws) and the second case charges that China has failed to provide sufficient market access to IPR-related products, namely in terms of trading rights and distribution services. On January 26, 2009, the WTO ruled that many of China's IPR enforcement policies failed to WTO obligations (see IPR section, below).
- Resolved U.S. Cases Against China
- On March 3, 2008, the USTR requested WTO dispute resolution consultations with China regarding its discriminatory treatment of U.S. suppliers of financial information services in China. On November 13, 2008, the USTR announced that China had agreed to eliminate discriminatory restrictions on how U.S. and other foreign suppliers of financial information services do business in China.
- On February 5, 2007, the USTR announced it had requested WTO dispute consultations with China over government regulations that give illegal (WTO inconsistent) import and export subsidies to various industries in China (such as steel, wood, and paper) that distort trade and discriminate against imports [49]. China's WTO accession agreement required it to immediately eliminate such subsidies. On November 29, 2007, China formally agreed to eliminate the subsidies in question by January 1, 2008.
- On March 30, 2006, the USTR initiated a WTO case against China for its use of discriminatory regulations applied to imported auto parts (which often applies the high tariff rate on finished autos to certain auto parts), stating that the purpose of these rules was to discourage domestic producers from using imported parts and encouraging foreign firms to move production to China. On February 13, 2008, a WTO panel ruled that China's discriminatory tariff policy was inconsistent with its WTO obligations (stating that the auto tariffs constituted an internal charge rather than ordinary customs duties, which violated WTO rules on national treatment). China appealed the decision, but a WTO Appellate Body largely upheld the WTO panels decision.
- On March 30, 2006, the USTR initiated a WTO case against China for its use of discriminatory regulations applied to imported auto parts (which often applies the high tariff rate on finished autos to certain auto parts), stating that the purpose of these rules was to discourage domestic producers from using imported parts and encouraging foreign firms to move production to China. On February 13, 2008, a WTO panel ruled that China's discriminatory tariff policy was inconsistent with its WTO obligations (stating that the auto tariffs constituted an internal charge rather than ordinary customs duties, which violated WTO rules on national treatment). China appealed the decision, but a WTO Appellate Body largely upheld the WTO panels decision.
- On March 18, 2004, the USTR announced it had filed a WTO dispute resolution case against China over its discriminatory tax treatment of imported semiconductors. The United States claimed that China applied a 17% VAT rate on semiconductor chips

that were designed and made outside China, but gave VAT rebates to domestic producers. Following consultations with the Chinese government, the USTR announced on July 8, 2004, that China agreed to end its preferential tax policy by April 2005. However, the USTR has expressed concern over new forms of financial assistance given by the Chinese government to its domestic semiconductor industry.

Chinese WTO Cases Against the United States

- On April 17, 2009, China brought a WTO case against the United States over a provision in the Omnibus Appropriations Act of 2009 that effectively prohibits the establishment or implementation of any measures that would allow poultry products to be imported from China.
- On 14 September 2007, China requested consultations with the United States on the preliminary anti-dumping and countervailing duty determinations on free sheet paper from China.
- On September 19, 2008, China initiated a WTO case against the United States in regards to its use of antidumping and countervailing measures against certain Chinese-made steel pipes, tires and laminated woven sacks.

Violations of U.S. Intellectual Property Rights

The United States has pressed China to improve its IPR protection regime since the late 1980s. In 1991, the United States (under a Section 301 case) threatened to impose $1.5 billion in trade sanctions against China if it failed to strengthen its IPR laws. Although China later implemented a number of new IPR laws, it often failed to enforce them, which led the United States to once again threaten China with trade sanctions. The two sides reached a trade agreement in 1995, which pledged China to take immediate steps to stem IPR piracy by cracking down on large-scale producers and distributors of pirated materials and prohibiting the export of pirated products, establishing mechanisms to ensure long-term enforcement of IPR laws and providing greater market access to U.S. IPR-related products.

Under the terms of its accession to the World Trade Organization (WTO) in 2001, China agreed to immediately bring its IPR laws in compliance with the WTO's Trade-Related Aspects of Intellectual Property Rights (TRIPS) agreement, which include a commitment to establish an effective IPR enforcement regime. The U.S. Trade Representative's (USTR) office has stated on a number of occasions that China has made great strides in improving its IPR protection regime, noting that it has passed several new IPR-related laws, closed or fined several assembly operations for illegal production lines, seized millions of illegal audio-visual products, curtailed exports of pirated products, expanded training of judges and law enforcement officials on IPR protection, and expanded legitimate licensing of film and music production in China. However, the USTR has indicated that much work needs to be done to improve China's IPR protection regime, especially in terms of deterrence.

Many business groups contend that poor IPR protection is one of the most significant obstacles for doing business in China. To illustrate:

- According to IPR industry groups, China has some of the highest piracy rates in the world: 95% for entertainment software, 90% for records and music, and 82% for business software. Piracy in China for business and entertainment software alone is estimated to cost U.S. firms $3.5 billion in lost trade annually, which were was than losses from any other foreign country [50].
- The U.S. Customs and Border Protection (CBP) reported that China accounted for 81% ($221 million domestic value) of pirated goods seized by the agency in FY2008 [51]

Piracy also has a number of negative effects on China's economy. For example:

- The Chinese government estimates that counterfeits constitute between 15% and 20% of all products made in China and are equivalent to about 8% of China's annual gross domestic product.
- A study by the Motion Picture Association of America estimated that China's domestic film industry lost about $1.5 billion in revenue to piracy in 2005 (and that the combined losses of both foreign and Chinese film makers totaled $2.7 billion) [52] It also found that about half of pirated films in China are Chinese movies.
- A Business Software Alliance study estimates that a 10 percentage point reduction in China's PC software piracy rates would raise its GDP by $20.5 billion and create an additional 355,179 jobs.

Opinions differ as to why the Chinese government has been unable (or unwilling) to make a significant reduction in the level of piracy in China. Some explanations put forward by various analysts include the following:

- China's transformation from a Soviet-style command economy (in which the government owned and controlled nearly every aspect of the economic life) to one that is becoming more market-based is a very recent occurrence. IPR is a relatively alien or unfamiliar concept for most people in China to grasp (as is the concept of private property rights) and thus it is difficult for the government to convince the public that piracy is wrong [53]
- Chinese leaders want to make China a major producer of capital-intensive and high-technology products, and thus, they are tolerant of IPR piracy if its helps Chinese firms become more technologically advanced [54]
- Although the central government may be fully committed to protect IPR, local government officials are often less enthusiastic to do so because production of pirated products generates jobs and tax revenue, and some officials may be obtaining bribes or other benefits which prompts them to tolerate piracy. The USTR's April 2009 report on IPR stated it was concerned by reports that government officials in China were urging more lenient enforcement of IPR laws because of the impact of the global financial crisis.
- As a developing country, China lacks the resources and a sophisticated legal system to go after and punish IPR violators, and establishing an effective enforcement regime will take time [55]

- As a practical matter, IPR enforcement in China will be problematic until Chinese-owned companies begin to put pressure on the government to protect their own brands and other IPR-related products. U.S. trade officials note that the Chinese government took aggressive action during the 2008 summer Olympics in Beijing to stop infringement activities.
- Chinese trade barriers and regulatory restrictions on IPR-related products and their distribution are so onerous that they prevent legitimate products from entering the market, or raise costs so high that they are unaffordable to the average individual, thus creating a huge demand for low-cost pirated products.

The U.S. WTO Cases Against China on IPR

On April 10, 2007, the USTR brought two IPR cases against China in the WTO involving a number of complaints: [56]

- The thresholds for criminal prosecutions of IPR violations in China are too high, meaning the government will only pursue cases it considers to be serious or excessively large, creating a safe harbor for smaller producers or violators. In addition, the thresholds for prosecuting IPR violations are based on the value of the pirated products rather than the value such legitimate products would fetch in the marketplace. Such thresholds make it very difficult to pursue cases against many commercial producers of illegal IPR-related products.
- China often allows seized imported pirated goods to re-enter the market rather than disposing of them.
- China's copyright laws fail to protect imported works (such as movies) that are under review by Chinese censorship authorities (and must be approved before the works can be distributed in China). As a result, pirated copies of the works can be widely distributed without violating copyright law and thus do not face prosecution.
- Chinese IPR laws do not appear to allow producers of pirated products to be prosecuted unless they also illegally distribute such products.
- China has not abided by its 2001 WTO accession agreement to liberalize its rules on trading rights and distribution services. As a result, U.S. IPR-related products face significant trade barriers in China, and such barriers are a major factor for causing the high rate of piracy in China.

On January 26, 2009, a WTO panel ruled on the case dealing with IPR enforcement issues, finding that China failed to protect IPR works under review by the government for content and in regards to the disposal of seized pirated products. However, the panel determined that it needed more evidence on the issue of thresholds for criminal prosecutions of IPR piracy before a determination could be made. The USTR, while admitting disappointment on the WTO findingson thresholds, noted that, right before it filed the WTO case on China's IPR enforcement, China lowered its threshold criminal copyright threshold from 1,000 to 500 infringing copies.

Applying U.S. Countervailing Laws to China [57]

Many critics of Chinese trade policies contend that the Chinese government provides a significant level of subsidies to many of its industries, such as preferential bank loans and grants, debt forgiveness, and tax breaks and rebates [58] In addition, some analysts charge that China's currency policy constitutes a form of government export subsidy [59]. Such critics contend that U.S. countervailing laws, which seek to address the negative impact foreign government subsides on exported products may have on U.S. producers in the United States, should be applied to nonmarket economies such as China [60]

Until very recently, the Commerce Department contended that U.S. countervailing laws could not be applied to a non-market economy because of the assumption that most production and prices in such an economy are determined by the government, and thus it would be impractical to determine the level of government subsidy that might be conveyed to various exported products. However, in November 2006, the Commerce Department decided to pursue a countervailing case against certain imported Chinese coated free sheet paper products. On March 30, 2007, the Commerce Department issued a preliminary ruling to impose countervailing duties (ranging from 11% to 20%) against the products in question. Commerce contends that, while China was still a non-market economy for the purposes of U.S. trade laws, economic reforms in China have made several sectors of the economy relatively market based, and therefore it is possible to identify the level of government subsidies given to the Chinese paper firms in question [61] Thirteen countervailing cases have been brought against a number of other Chinese products since 2006 [62]

Many Members of Congress have called on the Administration to expand its use of countervailing measures against Chinese products. Some have proposed codifying the use of countervailing laws against non-market economies, and others have sought to make China's undervalued currency a factor in determining the level of countervailing duties (see "U.S.-China Trade Legislation in the 111th Congress").

China Safeguard Provisions

As noted earlier, when China entered the WTO, it agreed to allow the United States to continue to treat it as a non-market economy for 12 years (codified in U.S. law under Sections 421-423 of the 1974 Trade Act, as amended) for the purpose of safeguards [63]. This provision enables the United States to impose restrictions (such as quotas and/or increased tariffs) on imported Chinese products that have increased in such quantities that they have caused, or threaten to cause, market disruption to U.S. domestic producers [64] The Bush Administration on six different occasions chose not to extend relief to various industries under the China-specific safeguard (even though in four cases, the USITC recommended relief). Some Members have called for limits on the President's discretion to prevent import relief. On June 18, 2009, the USITC announced that it had determined that U.S. imports of passenger vehicle and light truck tires cause or threaten to cause market disruption to U.S. domestic producers of like or directly competitive products. The USITC will determine potential remedies and send these recommendations to the President.

Textile and Apparel Products [65]

Various U.S. industry groups have called on the Administration to invoke special safeguard provisions (included in China's WTO accession package) that would enable the United States to restrict imports of certain Chinese products deemed harmful to U.S. industries. U.S. producers of textile and apparel products have been particularly vocal over the competitive pressures they face from China, especially since U.S. textile and apparel quotas on Chinese goods were eliminated in January 2005 [66] According to the U.S. Commerce Department, China is the largest foreign supplier of textiles and apparel to the United States at $32.7 billion, or 35.1% (2008); from 2002 to 2008, U.S. textile and apparel imports from China rose by 274%. [67]

The sharp rise in textile and apparel imports from China, and U.S. industry contention that these imports were disrupting U.S. markets, led the Bush Administration to seek an agreement with China to limit its exports to the United States. On November 8, 2005, China agreed to restrict various textile and apparel exports to the United States (according to specified quota levels) from January 2006 through the end of 2008.

The U.S.-China Strategic and Economic Dialogue

On September 29, 2006, President George Bush and Chinese President Hu Jintao agreed to establish a Strategic Economic Dialogue (SED) in order to have discussions on major economic issues at the "highest official level." According to a U.S. Treasury Department press release, the intent of the SED was to "discuss long-term strategic challenges, rather than seeking immediate solutions to the issues of the day," in order to provide a stronger foundation for pursuing concrete results through existing bilateral economic dialogues [68] The first meeting was held in December 2006. Four subsequent rounds of talks were held (the last was in December 2008).

While attending the G-20 summit in London on the global financial crisis on April 1, 2009, President Obama and Chinese President Hu agreed to continue the high-level forum, renaming it the U.S.-China Strategic and Economic Dialogue.

The new dialogue will be based on two tracks. The first (the "Strategic Track") will be headed up by the Secretary of State on the U.S. side and focus on political and strategic issues, while the second track (the "Economic Track") is headed up by the U.S.

Treasury Secretary on the U.S. side and will focus on financial and economic issues. Areas of discussion will include the economic and trade issues, counterterrorism, law enforcement, science and technology, education, culture, health, energy, the environment (including climate change), non-proliferation, and human rights. The first round of talks are scheduled to be held at the end of July 2009.

U.S.-CHINA TRADE LEGISLATION IN THE 111TH CONGRESS

Several bills have been introduced in the 111th Congress to address various concerns over China's economic policies:

- H.Res. 44 would condemn China for its "socially unacceptable business practices, including the manufacturing and exportation of unsafe products, casual disregard for the environment, and exploitative employment practices."
- H.R. 471 would limit the President's discretion to deny relief under the special China safeguard provision.
- H.R. 496 would ensure that the Commerce Department continued to apply U.S. countervailing laws to non-market countries (such as China), establish an alternative method for determining countervailing duties on Chinese products, and would limit the President's discretion to deny relief under the special China safeguard provision.
- H.R. 499 would codify the application of U.S. countervailing laws to non-market economies, establish an alternative method for determining countervailing duties on Chinese products, and would require congressional approval before China (and other non-market economies) could be treated as a market economy.
- H.R. 1105 (P.L. 111-8) contains a provision to continue a prohibition on the U.S. Department of Agriculture from rulemaking that would allow imports of cooked chicken from China.
- H.R. 2310 would attempt to boost U.S. exports China, especially by small-and-medium sized firms. It would provide grants to States to establish and operate offices to promote exports to China, establish 50 China market advocate positions in U.S. Export Assistance Centers, and provide assistance to U.S. small- and medium-sized businesses (such as for trade missions to China).
- H.R. 2312 would authorize the Secretary of Energy to make grants to encourage cooperation between the United States and China on joint research, development, or commercialization of carbon capture and sequestration technology, improved energy efficiency, or renewable energy sources.
- H.Amdt. 119 to H.R. 1728 would require the requires the Secretary of HUD to study the effects of the presence of Chinese dry wall on foreclosures and the availability of property insurance for residential structures where Chinese dry wall is present.
- S.Res. 76 would express the sense of the Senate that the United States and China should work together to reduce or eliminate tariff and nontariff barriers to trade in clean energy and environmental goods and services.
- S.Res. 77 would express the sense of the Senate that the United States and China should negotiate a bilateral agreement on clean energy cooperation.
- S.Res. 91 would call on the Consumer Product Safety Commission, the Secretary of the Treasury, and the Secretary of Housing and Urban Development to take action on Potential safety issues relating to drywall imported from China.
- S. 739 would require the Consumer Product Safety Commission to study drywall imported from China in 2004 through 2007 in regards to potential safety hazards and to ban future drywall imports from China.

- S. 1254 would require the Treasury Department to identify currencies that are fundamentally misaligned and to designate currencies for "priority action" under certain circumstances. Such action would include factoring currency undervaluation in U.S. anti-dumping cases, banning federal procurement of products or services from the designated country, and filing a case against that country in the WTO.
- S. 119 1would require the Secretary of Energy to prepare a report on climate change and energy policy in China and India.

REFERENCES

[1] For more information on China's economy, see CRS Report RL33534, *China's Economic Conditions*, by Wayne M. Morrison. For general information on U.S.-China ties, see CRS Report RL33877, *China-U.S. Relations in the 110th Congress: Issues and Implications for U.S. Policy*, by Kerry Dumbaugh.

[2] The United States suspended China's MFN status in 1951, which cut off most bilateral trade. China's MFN status was conditionally restored in 1980 under the provisions set forth under Title IV of the 1974 Trade Act, as amended (including the Jackson-Vanik freedom of emigration provisions). China's MFN status (which was re-designated under U.S. trade law as normal trade relations status, or NTR) was renewed on an annual basis through January 2002, when permanent NTR was extended to China (after it joined the WTO).

[3] The United States also exports a significant level of private services to China; these totaled $14.2 billion in 2007.

[4] Based on the North American industry Classification System, 4-digit level.

[5] Some U.S. analysts have expressed concern over the composition of U.S. exports to China, noting that much of it consists of scrap products, components, and food, as opposed to high-value assembled manufactured products (such as cars). Chinese official complain that U.S. export controls on high tech trade has a significant negative impact on the composition and size of U.S. exports to China.

[6] Boeing, Current Market Outlook, 2008-2027.

[7] New York Times, "China Surpasses U.S. in Number of Internet Users," July 26, 2008.

[8] *China Daily*, September 9, 2004.

[9] According to GM's website, it operates seven joint ventures and two wholly owned foreign enterprises and has more than 20,000 employees in China.

[10] U.S. imports from China as a share of total imports in 2007 was 16.5%.

[11] Note, these figures do not indicate the level of sophistication of these products. Many U.S. imports of advanced technology products are parts.

[12] Chinese data indicate that the share of China's exports produced by foreign-invested enterprises (FIEs) in China rose from 1.9% in 1986 to 55% in 2008.

[13] U.S. data on FDI flows to and from China differ sharply from Chinese data on FDI flows to and from the United States. This section uses U.S. data.

[14] Agency securities include both federal agencies and government-sponsored enterprises created by Congress (e.g., Fannie Mae and Freddie Mac) to provide credit to key sectors of the economy. Some of these securities are backed by assets (such as home mortgages).

[15] LT securities are those with no stated maturity date (such as equities) or with an original term to maturity date of more than one year. Short-term debt includes U.S. Treasury securities, agency securities, and corporate securities with a maturity date of less than one year.

[16] The 10% ownership share is the threshold considered to represent an effective voice or lasting influence in the management of an enterprise. See, BEA, International Economic Accounts, BEA Series Definitions, available at http://www.bea.gov/international.

[17] These sectors include food; chemicals; primary and fabricated metals; machinery; computers and electronic products; electrical equipment, appliances and components; transportation equipment, and other manufacturing.

[18] For additional information on this issue, see CRS Report RL34314, *China's Holdings of U.S. Securities: Implications for the U.S. Economy*, by Wayne M. Morrison and Marc Labonte.

[19] U.S. Treasury Department, Preliminary *Report on Foreign Portfolio Holdings of U.S. Securities as of June 30, 2008*, February 27, 2009. A final report expected in April 2009.

[20] U.S. Treasury Department, *Report on Foreign Portfolio Holdings of U.S. Securities,* various editions. Note, 2002 was the first year in which surveys listed data as of June. Prior to that, survey data were listed as of March or December.

[21] U.S. Treasury Department, *Major Foreign Holders of U.S. Treasury Securities*, June 15, 2009. Note, the Treasury Department often revises its estimates of foreign holdings for a given year, but not for previous years.

[22] See China View, "U.S. stimulus-related debt could hurt investors, China warns," February 18, 2009.

[23] U.S. Treasury Department, *Report on U.S. Portfolio Holdings of Foreign Securities as of December 31, 2007*, October 2008.

[24] All BEA data is on a historical-cost, or book value, basis.

[25] In comparison, total U.S. FDI in China in 2007 was $28.3 billion—nearly 26 times China's FDI in the United States –making China the 21st largest U.S. destination for FDI.

[26] Chinese FDI data differ significantly from U.S. data. China estimates that cumulative U.S. FDI in China through 2007 was $56.6 billion (7.4% of total FDI in China) and that its FDI in the United States was $1.9 billion (equal to 1.6% of total Chinese FDI).

[27] For additional information on this issue, see CRS Report RS22713, *Health and Safety Concerns Over U.S. Imports of Chinese Products: An Overview*, by Wayne M. Morrison.

[28] For a legal overview of FDA recalls, see CRS Report RL34 167, The *FDA's Authority to Recall Products*, by Vanessa K. Burrows.

[29] In addition, FDA has refused shipments of a variety of Chinese food and drug products. See CRS Report RL34080, *Food and Agricultural Imports from China*, by Geoffrey S. Becker.

[30] *New York Times*, "China Didn't Check Drug Supplier, Files Show," February 16, 2008.

[31] On October 15, 2008, the Chinese government issued an urgent notice to recall all dairy products made prior to September 14, 2008, so that they could be tested.

[32] For a list of company recalls of Chinese products, see the CPSC website at http://www.cpsc.gov/cpscpub/prerel/ prerel.html. In addition, several U.S. retailers have announced that they have halted sales of certain Chinese products, due to health and safety concerns, which do not appear on the CPSC website.

[33] Congressional concerns over product safety led to the enactment of the *Consumer Product Safety Improvement Act of 2008* (P.L. 110-314) in August 2008. The law tightened requirements on children products, including mandatory testing. See CRS Report RL34684, *Consumer Product Safety Improvement Act of 2008: P.L. 110-314*, by Margaret Mikyung Lee.

[34] For example, many fish farmers in China are believed to feed various drugs to the fish to help keep them alive in polluted waters. See *Washington Post*, "Farmed in China's Foul Waters, Imported Fish Treated with Drugs; Traditional Medicine, Banned Chemicals Both Used," July 6, 2007, p. A1.

[35] China's media often reports on health and safety problems, but rarely criticizes the central government for such problems.

[36] In June 2007, China impounded U.S. shipments of apricots and orange pulp, claiming that they contained excessive bacteria. In July 2007, China had suspended some frozen chicken and pork products imported from the U.S., citing various health concerns. In August 2007, China rejected a shipment of U.S. pacemakers, due to quality concerns. Some analysts contend these have been retaliatory moves over U.S. recalls and detentions of Chinese products.

[37] For additional information on this issue, see CRS Report RS21625, *China's Currency: A Summary of the Economic Issues*, by Wayne M. Morrison and Marc Labonte.

[38] Source: Calculated from Bank of China data using the official middle rate.

[39] Treasury Department, R*eport to Congress on International Economic and Exchange Rate Policies*, April 2009. Copies of the past 8 Treasury reports can be found at: http://www.treas.gov/offices/international-affairs/economicexchange-rates.

[40] For additional information on this issue, see CRS Report RL34314, *China's Holdings of U.S. Securities: Implications for the U.S. Economy*, by Wayne M. Morrison and Marc Labonte; and CRS Report RS22984, *China and the Global Financial Crisis: Implications for the United States*, by Wayne M. Morrison.

[41] USTR, *2008 Report to Congress on China's WTO Compliance*, December 23, 2008.

[42] On May 18, 2009, China's State Council, announced plans to create 3 million new jobs in light industry over the next three years by providing financial support to small and medium-sized light industry firms with "good development potential."

[43] *China Daily*, "Nation Lists Sectors Critical to National Economy," December 19, 2006.

[44] In 2009, China imposed restrictions on pork imports from certain U.S. states because of concerns relating to the outbreak of influenza A(H1N1), or swine flu.

[45] Statement of Timothy Stratford, Assistant U.S. Trade Representative for China Affairs, before the Congressional Steel Caucus, June 14, 2006.

[46] China is now the world's largest steel producer, accounting for 31% of the world's steel production. Its steel production levels rose by 25% over the previous year. According to U.S. officials, China's excess steel capacity in 2006 could be larger than total U.S. steel production.

[47] China applies higher tariffs on imported auto parts when a specific combination of parts is used to produce cars in China, or if the value of these parts amounts to 60% or more of the cost of a car made in China. This policy increases tariffs on some auto parts from about 10% to about 25% (which is the tariff China currently applies to imports of completed autos).

[48] For an overview of the WTO dispute resolution process, see CRS Report RS20088, *Dispute Settlement in the World Trade Organization (WTO): An Overview*, by Jeanne J. Grimmett.

[49] Some programs give tax preferences, tariff exemptions, discounted loans, or other benefits to firms that meet certain export performance requirements, while others give tax breaks for purchasing Chinese-made equipment and accessories over imports.

[50] Estimates made by the International Intellectual Property Rights Alliance for 2007.

[51] See CBP website at http://www.CBP.gov.

[52] *Reuters*, "China Piracy Costs Film Industry $2.7 Billion in 2005," June 19, 2006.

[53] Some Chinese officials have noted that some individuals who were arrested for IPR piracy violations expressed shock at their arrest because in their minds they were not harming anybody.

[54] On the other hand, IPR piracy may prevent foreign firms from investing in high-tech production in China.

[55] Some critics of this argument note that China seems to be very efficient at going after political dissenters and others deemed to be "threats" to social stability.

[56] See USTR April 9, 2007, Press Release and related documents at http://www.ustr.gov/index.html.

[57] For additional information on this issue, see CRS Report RL33550, *Trade Remedy Legislation: Applying Countervailing Action to Nonmarket Economy Countries*, by Vivian C. Jones.

[58] See USTR *2007 National Trade Estimates of Foreign Trade Barriers*, April 2, 2007.

[59] They charge that government intervention in currency markets to keep the value of the yuan low vis-a-vis the dollar, keeps the price of Chinese exports low.

[60] The relief comes in the form of additional duties that are imposed on the imported products in question after a determination is made that a foreign government subsidized export to the United States has harmed a U.S. producer. The additional duties are intended to offset the impact of the subsidy.

[61] Countervailing investigations have also been initiated of Chinese off-the-road tires (June 18, 2007) and Chinese steel pipe (June 14, 2007).

[62] *Inside U.S. Trade*, "China-Focused Trade Remedy Cases Expected To Increase," November 26, 2008.

[63] The U.S. International Trade Commission (USITC) is in charge of making market disruption determinations under the safeguard provisions for most products (with the exception of textiles and apparel, which are handled by the Committee for the Implementation of the Textile Agreements, an inter-agency committee chaired by the U.S. Commerce Department). Import relief is subject to presidential approval.

[64] Normally, safeguard provisions apply to all imported products. The China safeguard in U.S. trade law applies only to China.

[65] For additional information, see CRS Report RL34106, *U.S. Clothing and Textile Trade with China and the World: Trends Since the End of Quotas*, by Michael F. Martin.
[66] For additional information on U.S.-China textile issues, see CRS Report RL32168, *Safeguards on Textile and Apparel Imports from China*, by Vivian C. Jones.
[67] For more detailed data on U.S. imports of textile and apparel products from China, see Department of Commerce, Office of Textiles and Apparel Office website at http://www.otexa.ita.doc.gov/.
[68] U.S. Treasury Department press release, December 15, 2006.

In: Political and Economic Developments in Asia
Editor: Felix Chin

ISBN: 978-1-61209-783-1
©2011 Nova Science Publishers, Inc.

Chapter 7

ASSISTANCE TO NORTH KOREA[*]

Mark E. Manyin and Mary Beth Nikitin

ABSTRACT

Since 1995, the United States has provided North Korea with over $1.2 billion in assistance, about 60% of which has paid for food aid and about 40% for energy assistance. U.S. aid fell significantly in the mid-2000s, bottoming out at zero in 2006.

The Bush Administration resumed energy aid in the fall of 2007, after progress was made in the Six-Party Talks over North Korea's nuclear program. The Six-Party Talks involve North Korea, the United States, China, South Korea, Japan, and Russia. The United States and other countries began providing heavy fuel oil (HFO) in return for Pyongyang freezing and disabling its plutonium-based nuclear facilities in Yongbyon. By the second week of December 2008, the United States had provided all of the 200,000 MT of HFO it had promised under this "Phase Two" of the Six-Party Talks process. The talks themselves have been at a standstill since a December 2008 meeting failed to achieve agreement on verification procedures. Russia completed its promised shipments of energy aid in January 2009. China and South Korea appear to be calibrating their Six-Party-related assistance to progress in disabling Yongbyon, which was slowed by North Korea in early 2009. Plans for a "satellite launch" by North Korea, reportedly to take place in early April, further complicated progress in the Six Party Talks.

The United States also provides technical assistance to North Korea to help in the nuclear disablement process, a role that could be expanded should North Korea move to dismantle its nuclear facilities. In 2008, Congress took legislative steps to legally enable the President to give expanded assistance for this purpose.

For over a decade, North Korea has suffered from chronic, massive food deficits. Food aid – largely from China, the United States, and South Korea – has been essential in filling the gap. In 2008, United Nations officials issued calls for international donations of food to avert a "serious tragedy" in North Korea. In May 2008, the Bush Administration announced it would resume food assistance to North Korea by providing 500,000 metric tons (MT) of food, 80% of which was to be channeled through the United Nations World Food Programme (WFP). The rest was to be sent through a consortium of U.S. non-governmental organizations (NGOs).

---

[*] This is an edited, reformatted and augmented version of CRS Report R40095, dated April 2, 2009.

The United States has shipped nearly 170,000 MT of food under the program. In December 2008, U.S. shipments to the WFP were suspended due to differences between the U.S. and North Korean governments over implementing the agreement. Food shipments via the NGOs continued. In March 2009, however, North Korea shut down the NGO portion of the U.S. program.

Food aid to the DPRK has been scrutinized because Pyongyang has resisted making the economic reforms that many feel would help the country distribute food more equitably and pay for food imports to make up for its domestic shortfall. Additionally, the North Korean government restricts the ability of donors to operate in the country. In the past, various sources have asserted that some of the food assistance going to North Korea is routinely diverted for resale in private markets or other uses. Compounding the problem, China, North Korea's largest source of food aid, has little to no monitoring systems in place. The Bush Administration's May 2008 food aid pledge came after Pyongyang agreed to loosen its restrictions on access and monitoring.

Finally, in 2008, the Bush Administration began a new, $4 million program to provide assistance to several rural and provincial hospitals in North Korea.

This report will be updated periodically to track changes in U.S. provision of aid to North Korea.

INTRODUCTION

For four decades after the end of the Korean War in 1953, U.S. strategy toward the Democratic People's Republic of Korea (DPRK, commonly referred to as North Korea) was relatively simple: deter an attack on South Korea. This included a freeze on virtually all forms of economic contact between the United States and North Korea in an attempt to weaken and delegitimize the North Korean government. In the 1990s, two developments led the United States to rethink its relationship with the DPRK: North Korea's progress in its nuclear weapons and missile programs and massive, chronic food shortages there. In response, the United States in 1995 began providing the DPRK with foreign assistance, which has totaled over $1.2 billion. This aid has consisted of energy assistance, food aid, and a small amount of medical supplies. (See Table 1) [1]

U.S. aid fell significantly in the mid-2000s, bottoming out at zero in FY2006. The Bush Administration halted energy assistance in the fall of 2002, following North Korea's reported admission that it had secretly been developing a uranium-based nuclear program.

This energy assistance, which primarily took the form of heavy fuel oil, was channeled through the Korean Peninsula Energy Development Organization (KEDO). After a decade of being one of the largest providers of food aid to North Korea, the United States gave no food aid in FY2006 or 2007, in large part due to new restrictions that the North Korean government imposed upon humanitarian agencies.

The Bush Administration resumed assistance to North Korea in 2007. In July of that year, after initial progress in the Six-Party Talks over North Korea's nuclear programs, the United States and other countries began providing heavy fuel oil (HFO) in return for Pyongyang freezing and disabling its plutonium-based nuclear facilities in Yongbyon [2]. The United States also provides technical assistance to North Korea to help in the nuclear disabling processes, and is expected to continue to provide assistance for nuclear dismantlement should that be undertaken.

Table 1. U.S. Assistance to North Korea, 1995-2008

Calendar or Fiscal Year (FY)	Food Aid (per FY) Metric Tons	Food Aid (per FY) Commodity Value ($ million)	KEDO Assistance (per calendar yr; $ million)	6-Party Talks-Related Assistance (per FY; $ million) Fuel Oil	6-Party Talks-Related Assistance (per FY; $ million) Nuclear Disablement	Medical Supplies & Other (per FY; $ million)	Total ($ million)
1995	0	$0.00	$9.50	—	—	$0.20	$9.70
1996	19,500	$8.30	$22.00	—	—	$0.00	$30.30
1997	177,000	$52.40	$25.00	—	—	$5.00	$82.40
1998	200,000	$72.90	$50.00	—	—	$0.00	$122.90
1999	695,194	$222.10	$65.10	—	—	$0.00	$287.20
2000	265,000	$74.30	$64.40	—	—	$0.00	$138.70
2001	350,000	$58.07	$74.90	—	—	$0.00	$132.97
2002	207,000	$50.40	$90.50	—	—	$0.00	$140.90
2003	40,200	$25.48	$2.30	—	—	$0.00	$27.78
2004	110,000	$36.30	$0.00	—	—	$0.10	$36.40
2005	25,000	$5.70	—	—	—	—	$5.70
2006	0	$0.00	—	—	—	$0.00	$0.00
2007	0	$0.00	—	$25.00	$20.00	$0.10	$45.10
2008	148,270	$93.70[a]	—	$106.00	—	$0.00	$199.70
2009	21,000	$7.10[a]	—	$15.00	—	$4.00	$26.10
Total	2,258,164	$706.75	$403.70	$146.00	$20.00	$9.40	$1,285.85

Source: Compiled by CRS from USAID; US Department of Agriculture; State Department; KEDO (Korean Peninsula Energy Development Organization).
[a]Estimate.

In May 2008, the Bush Administration announced it would resume food assistance to North Korea by providing 500,000 metric tons (MT) of food, 80% to be sent through the World Food Program and 20% to be channeled through a consortium of U.S. non-governmental organizations (NGOs). Later in December 2008, U.S. shipments to the WFP were suspended due to differences between the U.S. and North Korean governments over implementing the agreement.

In March 2009, North Korea shut down the NGO portion of the U.S. program. Under the program, the United States shipped a total of 169,270 MT of food aid, at an estimated cost of $100 million.

Aid to North Korea has been controversial since its inception, and the controversy is intricately linked to the overall debate in the United States, South Korea, and other countries over the best strategy for dealing with the DPRK. North Korea is deemed a threat to U.S. interests because it possesses advanced nuclear and missile programs, has a history of proliferating missiles, may have exported its nuclear technology, is suspected of possessing chemical and biological weapons programs, and has large (albeit deteriorating) conventional forces on the border with South Korea, a key U.S. ally.

Instability inside North Korea could spill over into China, South Korea, and possibly Japan and/or Russia. Additionally, Pyongyang also is characterized as one of the world's worst violators of human rights and religious freedom, a record that some Members of

Congress and interest groups say should assume greater importance in the formation of U.S. priorities toward North Korea.

CONGRESS' ROLE IN U.S. ASSISTANCE TO NORTH KOREA

Congress and Energy Assistance

The provision of aid to North Korea has given Congress a vehicle to influence U.S. policy toward the DPRK. From 1998 until the United States halted funding for KEDO in FY2003, Congress included in each Foreign Operations Appropriation requirements that the President certify progress in nuclear and missile negotiations with North Korea before allocating money to KEDO operations [3]. To support the Six-Party Talks, Congress provided funds for energy assistance in the FY2008 Supplemental Appropriations Act (P.L. 110-252). Also in this bill, Congress gave authority to the executive branch to waive Arms Export Control Act sanctions on Pyongyang. Congress has also encouraged continued funding for the denuclearization of North Korea, for example in the FY2008 Defense Authorization Act (see "Denuclearization Assistance" section below). Although this waiver has not yet been issued by the President, potential inclusion of budget items for denuclearization in North Korea as part of a future Department of Energy budget proposal could be an indicator of the Obama Administration's intent to exercise this authority.

Congress and Food Assistance

With regard to food aid, some Members have supported continued donations on humanitarian grounds of helping the North Korean people, regardless of the actions of the North Korean regime. Other Members have voiced their outright opposition to food aid to the DPRK, or have called for food assistance to be conditioned upon North Korean cooperation on monitoring and access. The congressional debate over food assistance to North Korea also has been colored by the competing demands for other emergency situations that have stretched U.S. food aid funds and commodities. The North Korean Human Rights Act (P.L. 108-333) included non-binding language calling for "significant increases" above current levels of U.S. support for humanitarian assistance to be conditioned upon "substantial improvements" in transparency, monitoring, and access. The re-authorized act (P.L. 110-346) does not include this language, and drops the extensive discussion of humanitarian assistance that was included in P.L. 108-333. Both the original and the re-authorized act require annual reports to Congress on U.S. humanitarian assistance to North Korea [4].

Congress' ability to direct the amounts, manner, and recipients of food aid is relatively limited. The 500,000 MT of food that the U.S. pledged to North Korea in May 2008 is to come from the Bill Emerson Humanitarian Trust, a reserve of commodities and cash that is intended to provide food aid when other statutory sources of aid are unavailable. The Secretary of Agriculture has authority to release up to 500,000 metric tons of eligible commodities for urgent humanitarian relief. Historically, P.L. 480 has been the main vehicle for providing U.S. agricultural commodities as food aid overseas, and from FY2003-FY2005 was the program that funded nearly all of the U.S. food commitments to North Korea. When commodities or cash are released from the Emerson Trust, they are provided under the authority of P.L. 480 Title II. The Emerson Trust statute essentially authorizes the use of commodities or cash in the Trust to be used as a backup to Title II when there are unanticipated humanitarian needs. Congress directly appropriates P.L. 480 aid, and therefore could, although it rarely does, direct how the food should or should not be disbursed [5].

ENERGY ASSISTANCE

Korean Peninsula Energy Development Organization (KEDO)

From 1995 to 2002, the United States provided over $400 million in energy assistance to North Korea under the terms of the U.S.-North Korean 1994 Agreed Framework, in which the DPRK agreed to halt its existing plutonium-based nuclear program in exchange for energy aid from the United States and other countries [6]. After Washington and Pyongyang reached their agreement, the United States, Japan, and the Republic of Korea formed an international consortium, the Korean Peninsula Energy Development Organization (KEDO) to manage the assistance [7]. The planned aid consisted of the construction of two light-water nuclear reactors (LWRs) and the provision of 500,000 metric tons of heavy fuel oil annually while the reactors were being built. The two turnkey light-water reactors were to replace the DPRK's graphite-moderated reactors that were shut down under the agreement. The LWR plants would have had a generating capacity of approximately 1,000 MW(e) each and were to be constructed by 2003 [8]. The United States' contributions covered only heavy fuel oil shipments and KEDO administrative costs.

In October 2002, KEDO board members decided to halt fuel oil shipments following a dispute over North Korea's alleged clandestine uranium enrichment program. In December, North Korea expelled inspectors from its Yongbyon nuclear site, withdrew from the Nuclear Nonproliferation Treaty (NPT), and resumed operations at Yongbyon. The Bush Administration thereafter sought to permanently end the KEDO program [9]. In 2003 and 2004, KEDO's Executive Board (the United States, South Korea, Japan, and the European Union) decided to suspend construction on the LWRs for one-year periods. In the fall of 2005, the KEDO program was formally terminated. In January 2006, the last foreign KEDO workers left the LWR construction site at Kumho, North Korea.

Assistance Related to the Six-Party Talks

As with KEDO, the Bush Administration and other members of the Six-Party Talks – South Korea, Japan, China, and Russia – have promised energy assistance to North Korea as inducement to end its nuclear program. In January 2003, President Bush said that he would consider offering the DPRK a "bold initiative" including energy and agricultural development aid if the country first verifiably dismantled its nuclear program and satisfied other U.S. security concerns [10]. The Six-Party process began with talks in August 2003 [11]. In June 2004, the United States offered a proposal that envisioned a freeze of North Korea's weapons program, followed by a series of measures to ensure complete dismantlement and eventually a permanent security guarantee, negotiations to resolve North Korea's energy problems, and discussions on normalizing U.S.-North Korean relations that would include lifting the remaining U.S. sanctions and removing North Korea from the list of terrorist-supporting countries [12].

In September 2005, the six parties issued a joint statement agreeing to "promote economic cooperation in the fields of energy, trade and investment, bilaterally and/or multilaterally." The United States, China, South Korea, Japan, and Russia also stated their "willingness to provide energy assistance to the DPRK." The agreement said that the parties would discuss the provision of a light water nuclear power reactor to North Korea "at the appropriate time." This document serves as the foundation for subsequent agreements [13].

North Korea tested a nuclear device in October 2006, resulting in the swift passage of U.N. Security Council Resolution 1718, which imposed international sanctions banning trade of military goods, WMD and missile-related goods, and luxury items to North Korea [14]. In the Six- Party Talks held in December 2006, as well as in meetings held earlier that month with North Korean negotiators, U.S. officials reportedly spelled out a detailed package of humanitarian, economic, and energy aid that would be available to Pyongyang if it gave up nuclear weapons and technology [15].

The resulting Denuclearization Action Plan of February 2007 called for a first phase to include the shut-down of key nuclear facilities and initial provision of 50,000 metric tons of heavy fuel oil to North Korea. In the second-phase, the parties agreed to provide North Korea with "economic, energy and humanitarian assistance up to the equivalent of 1 million tons of heavy fuel oil, including the initial shipment of 50,000 tons of heavy oil." Concurrently, North Korea promised to provide a declaration of its nuclear programs and to disable its nuclear facilities at Yongbyon. A future Phase Three envisioned under the agreement would involve assistance for the permanent dismantlement of North Korea's nuclear facilities, the removal of spent fuel rods from the country, and eventual dismantlement of its weapons and weapon sites as part of 'denuclearization.'

Heavy Fuel Oil Shipments

The shipments of fuel oil or equivalent (i.e., steel products to renovate aging power plants) assistance were to happen on an "action for action" basis, as North Korea made progress on the second phase steps (nuclear disablement at Yongbyon and declaration of nuclear facilities and activities). An October 2007 joint statement on "Second-Phase Actions" confirmed these commitments [16]. The shipments of 1 million tons (MT) of heavy fuel oil or equivalent were to be divided equally by the five parties – i.e., 200,000 MT each.

As of March 2009, the DPRK had received 500,000 MT of heavy fuel oil and equipment and 190,000 MT of fuel equivalent assistance. South Korea provided the initial shipment of 50,000 metric tons of heavy fuel oil in July 2007 under Phase One of the February 2007 Six-Party agreement. The United States has contributed its promised share of 200,000 MT of heavy fuel oil. Russia shipped its last shipment in January 2009. China and South Korea have each contributed 50,000 MT of heavy fuel oil and 95,000 MT of heavy fuel oil equivalent. The remainder of China and South Korea's contribution is to be fuel oil equivalent.

Table 2. Six-Party Talks-Related Energy Assistance to North Korea July 2007-March 2009

Donor Country	Amount of HFO (MT) Delivered	Amount of HFO Equivalent (MT) Delivered	Amount left to be Delivered
China	50,000	95,000	55,000 HFO equivalent
Japan	0	0	200,000
Russia	200,000	0	0
South Korea	50,000	95,000	55,000 HFO equivalent
United States	200,000	0	0
Total	500,000	190,000	310,000

Source: Compiled by the Congressional Research Service.
Notes: Japan has stated it will not deliver energy assistance to North Korea until the issue of abductions of Japanese citizens by North Korea is resolved.

Japan has said it would not provide its share of energy assistance to Pyongyang until North Korea had satisfactorily resolved the issue of Japanese citizens abducted by North Korea [17]. However, press reports have said that the United States was arranging for other countries such as Australia, New Zealand and European states to provide the HFO aid in its stead. Australia and New Zealand have each reportedly agreed to donate $10 million, approximately equal to 30,000 metric tons of heavy fuel oil [18]. Japan may instead contribute the equivalent of 200,000 metric tons of HFO (approximately 16 billion yen or $164 million) as technical assistance related to North Korea's nuclear dismantlement. [19]

North Korea has said it would predicate its actions on disablement on the pace of energy assistance shipments. Pyongyang several times slowed down removal of the spent fuel rods at Yongbyon, saying, for example, in June 2008 that while 80% of the disablement steps had been completed, only 36% of energy aid had been delivered [20]. Responding to this, the five parties agreed in July to work out a binding agreement for the provision of their remaining share of nonHFO assistance by the end of October 2008, but this has been delayed [21]. North Korea again delayed disablement work in August, September, and October 2008, although those instances appear to be linked to disputes over when the U.S. would remove the DPRK from its State Sponsors of Terrorism List and negotiations over verification measures.

The United States had delayed its fuel shipments while these issues were being negotiated. After an informal agreement on verification had been reached bilaterally, the United States removed North Korea from the SST List and resumed HFO shipments [22]. However, Pyongyang in November 2008 denied having agreed to the verification measures the United States sought, and once again slowed disablement work, saying that energy shipments were not proceeding as planned [23]. The United States announced its fourth shipment of 50,000 metric tons HFO on November 12.

The six parties met on December 8 to discuss verification issues, and were also expected to finalize a schedule for future HFO shipments and disablement steps. Since no agreement was reached on verification measures at the December meeting, no HFO delivery schedule was set.

This schedule is still under discussion. However, some announcements followed on provision of energy assistance. As stated above, the United States and Russia completed their shipments in November and January, respectively. However, State Department spokespersons said in December 2008 that future HFO shipments from other countries would not be sent because North Korea had not agreed to verification measures [24]. This does not appear to have been coordinated or agreed to by the other parties. Russia and China, for example, appear to link the provision of energy assistance with progress on Yongbyon disablement, not with progress on verification. South Korea, on the other hand, said it would review its shipment of 3,000 tons of steel plate for delivery to North Korean power stations in December in light of lack of progress on disablement and other matters [25]. The North Korean negotiator responded by saying that disablement would be slowed if fuel shipments were not forthcoming [26]. In mid-March 2009, a South Korean official announced that North Korea had further slowed disablement [27]. South Korea, as chair of the Six- Party Energy and Economy Cooperation Working Group, is charged with coordinating the provision of energy assistance going forward. The planned missile test, or satellite launch as North Korea calls it, has further complicated progress on these issues as regional tensions rise.

Heavy fuel oil provided by the United States was paid for through the FY2008 Supplemental Appropriations Act (P.L. 110-252), passed in May 2008. The FY2008 supplemental allocated $53 million for energy assistance to North Korea in support of the Six-Party Talks, "after the Secretary of State determines and reports to the Committees on Appropriations that North Korea is continuing to fulfill its commitments under such agreements," and notwithstanding any other provision of law. The Supplemental also gives notwithstanding authority for an additional $15 million of energy-related assistance for North Korea, under the State Department's Economic Support Fund.

Denuclearization Assistance

As part of Phase Two under the Six-Party agreements, the Departments of State and Energy have been working to disable the nuclear facilities at the Yongbyon complex in North Korea [28]. This effort is funded through the State Department's Nonproliferation and Disarmament Fund (NDF). The State Department is paying the North Korean government for the labor costs of disablement activities, and also paying for related equipment and fuel.

Approximately $20 million in FY2007 and $25 million in FY2008 was approved for this purpose. NDF funds may be used "notwithstanding any other provision of law" and therefore may be used to pay North Korea. DOE's National Nuclear Security Administration (NNSA) has been contributing its personnel as technical advisors to the U.S. Six-Party delegation and as technical teams on the ground at Yongbyon overseeing disablement measures. NNSA has estimated it has spent approximately $15 million in support of Phase Two (Yongbyon disablement) implementation [29]

North Korea's nuclear test triggered sanctions under Section 102 (b) (the "Glenn Amendment" 22 U.S. C. 2 799aa-1) of the Arms Export Control Act, which prohibits assistance to a non-nuclear weapon state under the NPT that has detonated a nuclear explosive device.

Due to this restriction, DOE funds cannot be spent in North Korea without a waiver. Congress passed language in the FY2008 Supplemental Appropriations Act (P.L. 110-252) that would allow the President to waive the Glenn Amendment restrictions and that stipulates that funds may only be used for the purpose of eliminating North Korea's WMD and missile-related programs [30]. If the President does exercise the Glenn Amendment waiver authority, then DOE "will be able to procure, ship to North Korea, and use equipment required to support the full range of disablement, dismantlement, verification, and material packaging and removal activities that Phase Three will likely entail" [31].

NNSA has estimated that this could cost over $360 million in FY2009 if verification proceeds and North Korea agrees to the packaging and disposition of separated plutonium and spent fuel at Yongbyon. The Congressional Budget Office estimated that nuclear dismantlement in North Korea will cost approximately $575 million and take about four years to complete [32].

Department of Defense funds must be specifically appropriated for use in North Korea. Section 8045 of the FY2008 Defense Appropriations Act (P.L. 110-116) says that "none of the funds appropriated or otherwise made available in this act may be obligated or expended for assistance to the Democratic People's Republic of Korea unless specifically appropriated for that purpose." Section 8044 of the FY2009 Consolidated Security, Disaster Assistance, and Continuing Appropriations Act, 2009 (P.L. 110-329) also contains this language. However, authorization was given for Department of Defense's Cooperative Threat Reduction (CTR) funds to be used globally in the FY2008 Defense Authorization Act (P.L. 110-181, see Section 1305) and expressly encourages "activities relating to the denuclearization of the Democratic People's Republic of Korea" as a potential new initiative for CTR work.

Senator Richard Lugar has proposed that the CTR program be granted "notwithstanding authority" [33] for this work since the Defense Department's experience in the former Soviet Union, expertise and resources could make it well- positioned to conduct threat reduction work in North Korea and elsewhere. The United States has provided $1.8 million to the IAEA to support its monitoring activities at Yongbyon. Japan has provided the agency with $500,000 for this purpose [34]. The European Union contributed approximately $2.2 million (1.78 million euros) to the IAEA for Yongbyon shut-down monitoring.

FOOD ASSISTANCE

Since 1996, the United States has sent over 2.2 million metric tons (MT) of food assistance, worth nearly $800 million, to help North Korea alleviate chronic, massive food shortages that began in the early 1990s.

A severe famine in the mid-1990s killed an estimated 600,000 to three million North Koreans [35]. Over 90% of U.S. food assistance to Pyongyang has been channeled through the U.N. World Food Programme (WFP), which has sent over 4.2 million MT of food—an amount that includes U.S. contributions—to the DPRK since 1996. The United States has been by far the largest cumulative contributor to the WFP's North Korea appeals. The second largest donor of food aid to North Korea through WFP is South Korea.

As discussed below, North Korea's largest sources of food assistance have come from bilateral donations (i.e., those not channeled through the WFP) from China and South Korea.

U.S. Food Aid Policy

U.S. official policy in recent times has de-linked food and humanitarian aid from strategic interests, including the Six-Party talks. Since June 2002, the Bush Administration officially linked the level of U.S. food aid to three factors: the need in North Korea, competing needs on U.S. food assistance, and "verifiable progress" in North Korea allowing the humanitarian community improved access and monitoring [36]

In practice, some argue that the timing for U.S. pledges sometimes appears to be motivated also by a desire to influence talks over North Korea's nuclear program, and that the linkage between U.S. donations and improvements in North Korea's cooperation with the WFP occasionally has been tenuous [37].

Prior to 2008, there was conflicting evidence on this front. For instance, in February 2003, the Bush Administration announced it would provide 40,000 MT of food and would make an additional 60,000 MT contingent upon the DPRK allowing greater access and monitoring. In December 2003, the Administration announced that it would donate the additional 60,000 MT because of the continued poor humanitarian situation in North Korea and improvements in North Korea's cooperation with the WFP.

Those improvements, however, were widely thought to be marginal. Administration officials denied the decisions were motivated by a desire to influence the Six-Party Talks on North Korea's nuclear programs, which at the time had reached an impasse. On the other hand, in late 2005, despite another impasse in the Six-Party Talks, the United States halted its food aid shipments in response to North Korea's tightening of restrictions on the WFP's operations. The cessation included the second half of a 50,000 MT pledge that the United States had made in June 2005.

Events in 2008 and 2009, when the Bush Administration resumed food assistance, appear to indicate a weaker link between U.S. decisions on food aid and the nuclear talks. Instead, U.S. food aid decisions appeared to be more tightly linked to issues of access and monitoring of food shipments. In late 2008, when Bush Administration officials felt North Korea was violating its agreement with the WFP, they halted food shipments through the WFP but continued sending food through the consortium of NGOs that were handling one-fifth of the United States' 500,000 MT pledge.

WFP Assistance

As shown in Figure 1, after peaking at over 900,000 MT in 2001, assistance provided by the WFP fell dramatically. There were two primary reasons for the decline in WFP assistance. The first was "donor fatigue," as contributing nations objected to the North Korean government's continued development of its nuclear and missile programs as well as tightened restrictions on the ability of donor agencies to monitor food shipments to ensure that food is received by the neediest.

The emergence of other emergency food situations around the globe also has stretched the food aid resources of the United States and other donors. Whatever the causes, the WFP was unable to fill its goal of 150,000 MT for the 2006-2008 period.

During this time, increased bilateral assistance—outside the WFP's program—that China and South Korea shipped directly to North Korea, as well as improved harvests in North

Korea, appear to have made up much of the gap, which generally is estimated to be in the range of one million MT per year.

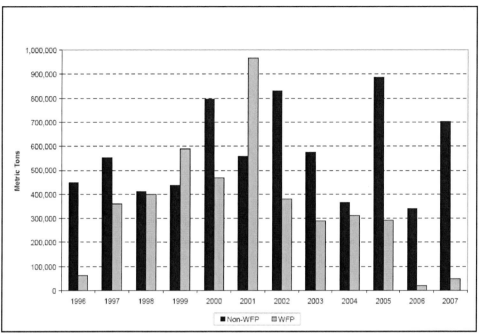

Source: Interfais database.

Figure 1. Food Aid to North Korea, WFP and Non-WFP.

Diversion, Triage, and North Korea's "Aid-Seeking" Behavior

Various sources assert that some—perhaps substantial amounts—of the food assistance going to North Korea is routinely diverted for resale in private markets or other uses [38]. Although there has been much public concern about diversion to the North Korean military, WFP officials and other experts have say they have seen little to no evidence that the military is systemically diverting U.N. food donations, and further, that the North Korean military has no need for WFP food, since it receives the first cut of North Korea's national harvest. Even if the military is not directly siphoning off food aid, however, such assistance is fungible; funds that otherwise would have been spent on food can be spent on other items, such as the military.

The North Korean government's desire to maintain control over the country is inextricably linked to the food crisis and its chronic reliance on food aid. Residency in North Korea is tightly controlled and highly politicized, with the elite permitted to live in or around Pyongyang, where food shortages are less acute than in the country's more remote areas, where politically less desirable families live. For this reason, the United States generally has shipped its food aid to the northern provinces. Additionally, North Korea is believed to expend little of its foreign currency to import food, relying instead upon the international community. Moreover, since 2007, the government has taken many steps to reimpose state controls over farmers and markets [39].

2006 Restrictions

In 2006 the WFP drastically scaled down its program after the North Korean government imposed new restrictions on the WFP, constraining the organization's size and ability to distribute and monitor its shipments. The WFP and Pyongyang then negotiated a new agreement that would feed 1.9 million people, less than a third of the 6.4 million people the WFP previously had targeted. North Korea's total population is approximately 22 million. In the deal, the WFP expatriate staff was cut by 75%, to 10 people, all of whom were based in Pyongyang. Before 2006, the WFP had over 40 expatriate staff and six offices around the country conducting thousands of monitoring trips every year [40]. The North Korean government did not allow any Korean speakers to serve on the WFP's in-country staff.

The Easing of Restrictions in the Summer of 2008

In 2008, the WFP warned that food shortages and hunger had worsened to levels not seen since the late 1990s. Not only was the country confronting the results of decades of poor agricultural planning and large-scale floods in 2007, but also shipments declined significantly from the two largest bilateral food providers, China and South Korea. According to the WFP, as of the end of June 2008, bilateral food imports and aid totaled 110,000 MT, compared to 738,000 MT for the same period in 2007 [41]. In April 2008, the WFP agency issued a call for more international donations and for the North Korean government to relax its restrictions on donor activities [42]. In December 2008, the WFP and U.N. Food and Agriculture Organization (FAO) issued a report summarizing a food security survey taken in October. The agencies estimated that the number of "hungry" has jumped from 6.2 million to 8.7 million, more than a third of North Korea's population [43].

The following month, the United States Agency for International Development announced that the United States would resume food assistance to North Korea by providing 500,000 MT for one year beginning in June 2008. Of this amount, 400,000 MT is to be channeled through the WFP. Approximately 100,000 tons would be funneled through non-governmental organizations (NGOs), including World Vision, Mercy Corps, Samaritan's Purse, Global Resource Services and Christian Friends of Korea. The announcement stated that the resumption was made possible by an agreement reached with Pyongyang that allowed for "substantial improvement in monitoring and access in order to allow for confirmation of receipt by the intended recipients" [44]. The U.S. move came not long after a breakthrough was reached in the Six-Party Talks. Bush Administration officials have repeatedly stated their policy that decisions on food assistance are unrelated to the nuclear negotiations.

On June 27, 2008, an agreement was signed with Pyongyang that stipulated terms for increased WFP personnel and access for monitoring the delivery of the food aid. It allowed WFP to expand its operations into 131 counties, versus an earlier 50, in regions at particular risk of famine [45]. NGOs have access to an additional 25 counties (see Table 3). In 2005, the WFP had access to 158 of 203 counties and districts, representing approximately 83% of the population [46]. The agreement allowed the WFP to issue a new emergency appeal for over 600,000 MT for 6.2 million North Koreans. The agreement also expanded the WFP's rights and ability to monitor the shipments of food aid, in order to better ensure that the food was not diverted from its target recipients.

The NGO portion of the distribution was in the two northwestern provinces of Chagang and North Pyongan. The NGO partnership, had a staff of 16 people based in North Korea, reached around 900,000 people [47].

Table 3. Comparing Past and Present WFP Food Aid Agreements with North Korea

	Tons of Food pledged/planned	Number of People Targeted	Counties Accessed	Permanent Staff	Korean Speakers Allowed
2005 WFP	504,000 MT	6.4 million	158	40	No
2006-08 WFP	150,000 MT	1.9 million	50	10	No
2008 Total	730,000 MT	7.1 million	156	75	Yes
- of which:					
- WFP	630,000 MT	6.2 million	131	59	Yes
- U.S. NGOs	100,000 MT	0.9 million	25	16	Yes

Sources: WFP and NGO press releases; CRS interviews with aid officials.

Cessation of the 2008-2009 Program

Since the late summer of 2008, operating conditions for the WFP appear to have worsened. The North Korean government reportedly has not allowed the U.N. agency to fully implement parts of its WFP agreement. In particular, the Bush Administration has had disagreements with Pyongyang over the number of Korean speakers and Americans allowed in the country. Due in part to these difficulties, the United States has not sent a shipment of food to the WFP 's North Korea appeal since August 2008. In remarks reported in the Washington Post that appeared to indicate a disagreement between the WFP and the Bush Administration, WFP Asia director Tony Banbury said that North Koreans "are fulfilling their obligations," but that the WFP 's North Korea program was running short of food [48].

As of early March 2009, WFP had received less than 5% of the donations needed to reach its targets for its 2008-2009 North Korea appeal. On March 5, the WFP announced it was scaling back its program to "a core minimum" that would allow the organization to rapidly expand its operations if it receives more donations in the future. The announcement stated that the WFP was feeding incomplete rations to only 2 million of the 6.2 million people it had originally targeted [49].

Meanwhile, according to U.S. officials and representatives of the NGO consortium, the NGO portion of the U.S. program continued to proceed smoothly, with marked improvements in cooperation between the aid providers and their North Korean counterparts. For this reason, throughout the winter of 2008-2009, the United States continued to send shipments via the consortium. However, in March 2009, North Korea asked the United States and the NGOs to shut down their portion of the U.S. program by the end of the month. The program had been scheduled to run until May 2009. Many speculated that North Korea had closed the program in part due to the overall deterioration in relations with the United States and South Korea. The consortium delivered 71,000 MT of food during its ten-month tenure, reaching more than 900,000 people [50].

Chinese and South Korean Bilateral Food Assistance

China is widely believed to be North Korea's single-largest cumulative provider of food (and energy). All Chinese food shipments are given bilaterally, that is, directly to the North

Korean government. It is believed that China does not have any systems for monitoring its food shipments to North Korea. As mentioned above, Chinese bilateral food shipments reportedly were down significantly in the first half of 2008.

For much of the past decade, South Korea's yearly shipments of food made it North Korea's largest or second-largest annual provider. Most of this was provided bilaterally, and South Korea had few monitoring systems in place. Seoul also provided 300,000 MT in fertilizer every year. However, in 2008, South Korea sent no food or fertilizer to North Korea. Earlier in the year, the newly inaugurated government of Lee Myung-bak indicated that it would provide humanitarian aid upon North Korea's request (the previous government had simply offered the assistance). The move coincided with the Lee government's announcement that new forms of North-South cooperation would be conditioned upon progress in denuclearizing North Korea. In response to the new policy from Seoul, North Korea has not requested humanitarian assistance from the South.

OTHER FORMS OF ASSISTANCE

In 2008, the Bush Administration allocated $4 million in assistance to U.S. NGOs to help several North Korean rural and provincial hospitals by improving their electrical supplies and by providing medical equipment and training. The four recipient NGOs are Mercy Corps, The Eugene Bell Foundation, Global Resource Services, and Samaritan's Purse [51].

During the Bush Administration, various officials, including the President, issued vague pledges of more extensive U.S. assistance that might be forthcoming if North Korea dismantled its nuclear programs and satisfied other U.S. security concerns dealing with missiles and the deployment of conventional forces [52]. The Administration reportedly was preparing to offer a version of this "bold initiative" to North Korea in the summer of 2002, but pulled it back after acquiring more details of Pyongyang's clandestine uranium nuclear weapons program [53]. Similarly, South Korean President Lee Myung-bak has adopted a "3000 Policy," whereby South Korea would help North Korea raise its per capita income to $3,000 over the next ten years by providing a massive aid package if North Korea dismantles its nuclear program.

With regard to U.S. development assistance programs, in the near term, the President has considerable flexibility to offer some forms of development assistance. The Foreign Assistance Act of 1961, for instance, allows the President annually to provide up to $50 million per country for any purpose [54]. Longer-term initiatives, however, would likely require changes in U.S. law and thereby require congressional action. For instance, the FY2005 Consolidated Appropriations Act specifically bans many forms of direct aid to North Korea, along with several other countries [55]. Many health and emergency disaster relief aid programs are exempt from such legislative restrictions because they have "notwithstanding" clauses in their enacting legislation. Additionally, if the Administration were to designate North Korea as a country involved in drug production and trafficking – as some have advocated – then by law North Korea would be ineligible for receiving most forms of U.S. development assistance [56].

REFERENCES

[1] From 1995-2002, the energy assistance was provided through the Korean Peninsula Energy Development Organization (KEDO), the multinational group established to provide energy aid to North Korea in exchange for Pyongyang's shutdown of its existing plutonium-based nuclear program.

[2] The Six–Party Talks involve North Korea, the United States, China, South Korea, Japan, and Russia.

[3] President Clinton was responding to Section 5 82(3) of P.L. 105-277, the Omnibus Consolidated and Emergency Supplemental Appropriations Act, 1999. In response, Section 1211 of the John Warner National Defense Authorization Act for Fiscal Year 2007 (P.L. 109-364; 120 Stat. 2420) required the Bush Administration to appoint a special envoy for North Korea. Christopher Hill, the Assistant Secretary for East Asian and Pacific Affairs, was named to the post.

[4] See CRS Report RS22973, *Congress and U.S. Policy on North Korean Human Rights and Refugees: Recent Legislation and Implementation*, by Emma Chanlett-Avery.

[5] P.L. 480 (originally P.L. 83-480) was reauthorized most recently by the 2008 farm bill (P.L. 110-246, 7 USC 1691).

[6] See "Total Financial Support by Country: March 1995 to December 2005," Table B, Appendix 1, KEDO 2005 Annual Report. http://www.kedo.org/pdfs/KEDO_AR_2005.pdf.

[7] Membership in KEDO expanded to include additional states and international organizations that contributed funds, goods or services: Argentina, Australia, Canada, Chile, the Czech Republic, the European Union (as an executive board member), Indonesia, New Zealand, Poland, and Uzbekistan. KEDO also received material and financial support from nineteen other non-member states. Details at http://www.kedo.org/au_history.asp

[8] Full text of the KEDO-DPRK supply agreement at http://www.kedo.org/pdfs/SupplyAgreement.pdf.

[9] State Department Daily Press Briefing by Adam Ereli, Deputy Spokesman, November 5, 2003.

[10] The Administration reportedly was preparing to offer this plan in 2002, but pulled it back after acquiring more details of Pyongyang's clandestine uranium nuclear weapons program. Testimony of Richard Armitage, State Department Deputy Secretary, before the Senate Foreign Relations Committee, February 4, 2003. http://www.nti.org/e_research/official_docs/dos/dos020403.pdf.

[11] See CRS Report RL33590, *North Korea's Nuclear Weapons Development and Diplomacy*, by Larry A. Niksch, and CRS Report RL34256, *North Korea's Nuclear Weapons*, by Mary Beth Nikitin.

[12] See CRS Report RL3 0613, North Korea: Terrorism List Removal?, by Larry A. Niksch.

[13] Joint Statement of the Fourth Round of the Six-Party Talks Beijing, September 19, 2005. http://www.state.gov/r/pa/prs/ps/2005/53490.htm

[14] http://www.un.org/News/Press/docs/2006/sc8853.doc.htm

[15] Helene Cooper and David Sanger, "U.S. Offers North Korea Aid for Dropping Nuclear Plans," *New York Times*, December 6, 2006.
[16] These commitments were reaffirmed in the October 3, 2007 Agreement on "Second-Phase Actions for the Implementation of the Joint Statement." http://www.state.gov/r/pa/prs/ps/2007/oct/93223.htm
[17] See CRS Report RS22845, *North Korea's Abduction of Japanese Citizens and the Six-Party Talks*, by Emma Chanlett-Avery.
[18] "Japan mulls funding N. Korea denuclearization, others to give oil aid," *Japan Economic Newswire*, October 21, 2008.
[19] "Japan may pay cash for North Korea's denuclearization, says report," *BBC Monitoring Asia Pacific*, October 22, 2008.
[20] Lee Chi-dong, "N Korea Complains About Slow Provision of Energy Aid," *Yonhap News*, June 5, 2008.
[21] Press Communique of the Heads of Delegation Meeting of the Sixth Round of the Six-Party Talks, Beijing, July 12, 2008. http://www.mofa.go.jp/region/asia-paci/n_korea/6party/press0807.html
[22] http://www.state.gov/r/pa/prs/ps/2008/oct/110922.htm
[23] "N. Korea slows nuclear disablement to snail's pace," *Japan Economic Newswire*, November 8, 2008.
[24] December 12 and 15, 2008 State Department Daily Press Briefings.
[25] "Six Party Confusion," *The Korea Herald,* December 18, 2008.
[26] "N. Korea envoy warns halt in aid would slow disablement work," *Japan Economic Newswire*, December 13, 2008.
[27] "N. Korea slows down nuke disarmament: Seoul official," *Agence France Presse*, March 18, 2009.
[28] Nuclear disablement should be distinguished from nuclear dismantlement, the former referring to a process that could be reversed.
[29] Statement of William H. Tobey, National Nuclear Security Administration, U.S. Department of Energy, to the Senate Committee on Armed Services, July 31, 2008.
[30] Similar language appeared in the Senate version of the FY2009 Duncan Hunter National Defense Authorization Act (P.L. 110-417), but was not included in the House version. The final act includes it under "legislative provisions not adopted" under Title XII, since the waiver authority was passed earlier in the FY2008 Supplemental. See joint explanatory note:http://armedservices.house.gov/pdfs/fy09ndaa/FY09conf/FY2009NDAAJointExplanatoryStatement.pdf.
[31] Tobey testimony, ibid.
[32] The CBO's cost estimate takes into account the dismantling of the reactor and three associated plants at Yongbyon as well as the transport and reprocessing of the spent fuel outside North Korea. Congressional Budget Office, "Cost Estimate: S. 3001 National Defense Authorization Act for Fiscal Year 2009," June 13, 2008. http://www.cbo.gov/ftpdocs/93xx/doc9390/s3001.pdf
[33] So that funds may be used "notwithstanding any other provision of law." Senator Richard Lugar, Remarks to National Defense University, October 2, 2008. http://lugar.senate.gov/record.cfm?id=304026&&

[34] Christopher R. Hill, Assistant Secretary for Bureau of East Asian and Pacific Affairs Testimony before House Committee on Foreign Affairs Subcommittee on Asia, the Pacific and the Global Environment and Subcommittee on Terrorism, Nonproliferation, and Trade Washington, DC, October 25, 2007.

[35] For a short review of the estimates of the famine's death toll, see Stephan Haggard and Marcus Noland, *Famine in North Korea. Markets, Aid, and Reform*, (New York: Columbia University Press, 2007), p. 73-76.

[36] USAID Press Release, June 7, 2002.

[37] Andrew S. Natsios, The Great North Korean Famine, United States Institute of Peace Press, Washington, DC, 2001, pp. 135, 143-148. Mark Noland, Avoiding the Apocalypse: The Future of the Two Koreas, Peterson Institute of International Economics, June 2000, pp. 159, 186, 189. Stephen Haggard, Marcus Noland, and Erik Weeks "Markets and Famine in North Korea," *Global Asia*, Vol. 3, No.2, August 2008.

[38] See, for instance, Stephan Haggard and Marcus Noland, Hunger and Human Rights: The Politics of Famine in North Korea (Washington, DC: U.S. Committee for Human Rights in North Korea, 2005), in which the authors argue that up to half of the WFP's aid deliveries did not reach their intended recipients.

[39] Stephen Haggard, Marcus Noland, and Erik Weeks "Markets and Famine in North Korea," *Global Asia*, Vol. 3, No.2, August 2008.

[40] WFP Press Release, "WFP Set to Resume Operations in North Korea," 11 May 2006; undated WFP document, Projected 2007 Needs for WFP Projects and Operations, Korea, DPR.

[41] World Food Programme, "Emergency Operation Democratic People's Republic of Korea: 10757.0- Emergency Assistance to Population Groups Affected by Floods and Rising Food and Fuel Prices," Undated Document.

[42] WFP Press Releases: "WFP Warns of Potential Humanitarian Food Crisis in DPRK Following Critically Low Harvest, April 16, 2008; "DPRK Survey Confirms Deepening Hunger for Millions, July 30, 2008.

[43] "8.7 Million North Koreans Need Food Assistance," *FAO/WFP News Release*, December 8, 2008.

[44] USAID Press Release, "Resumption of U.S. Food Assistance to the North Korean People," May 16, 2008.

[45] WFP, "Operational Priorities, September 2008, D.P.R. Korea," EMOP 10757.0 – Emergency Assistance to Population Groups Affected by Floods and Rising Food and Fuel Prices.

[46] USAID, *Report on U.S. Humanitarian Assistance to North Koreans*, April 25, 2005; March and April 2005 e-mail exchanges and phone conversations with WFP and USAID.

[47] "Aid Agencies Send Fourth U.S. Food Shipment to North Korea," Mercy Corps and World Vision press release, October 16, 2008.

[48] Blaine Harden and Glenn Kessler, "Dispute Stalls U.S. Food Aid To N. Korea," *Washington Post*, December 9, 2008.

[49] "WFP does what little it can for North Koreans," WFP Press Release, March 5, 2009.

[50] "Statement of NGO Partners on Cessation of Food Aid Program in the Democratic People's Republic Of Korea (DPRK)," Mercy Corps, Samaritan's Purse, World Vision, March 19, 2009.
[51] "U.S. Spends $4 Million On Medical Aid For N.Korea In 2008," *Korea Herald*, December 21, 2008; December 2008 communication with U.S. State Department.
[52] Testimony of Richard Armitage, State Department Deputy Secretary, before the Senate Foreign Relations Committee, February 4, 2003.
[53] Testimony of Richard Armitage, State Department Deputy Secretary, before the Senate Foreign Relations Committee, February 4, 2003.
[54] Section 614 of the Foreign Assistance Act of 1961, P.L. 87-195.
[55] Section 607 of P.L. 110-161, the FY2008 Consolidated Appropriations Act, which also bans direct aid to Cuba, Iran, and Syria.
[56] See CRS Report RL32167, *Drug Trafficking and North Korea: Issues for U.S. Policy*, by Raphael F. Perl.

In: Political and Economic Developments in Asia
Editor: Felix Chin
ISBN: 978-1-61209-783-1
©2011 Nova Science Publishers, Inc.

Chapter 8

TAIWAN-U.S. RELATIONS: DEVELOPMENTS AND POLICY IMPLICATIONS*

Kerry Dumbaugh

ABSTRACT

Policy toward and support for Taiwan are a key element in U.S.- relations with the People's Republic of China (PRC) and an important component of U.S. policy in Asia. Official U.S. relations with the Republic of China (ROC) government on Taiwan became a casualty of the U.S. decision to recognize the PRC government as China's sole legitimate government. Since then, unofficial U.S. relations with Taiwan have been built on the framework of the 1979 Taiwan Relations Act (TRA – P.L. 96-8) and shaped by three U.S.-PRC communiques. Under these, the United States maintains official relations with the PRC, but continues to have unique and critical interests in Taiwan, including significant commercial ties, objections to PRC threats to use force against Taiwan, arms sales and security assurances, and support for Taiwan's democratic development. U.S. policy today remains rooted in a general notion of maintaining the "status quo" between Taiwan and the PRC. But other factors have changed dramatically since 1979, including growing PRC power and importance, Taiwan's democratization, and the deepening of Taiwan-PRC economic and social linkages. These changes have led to periodic discussions about the efficacy of current U.S. policy and whether or not it should be reviewed or changed.

Taiwan's current president, Ma Ying-jeou, elected in March 2008, moved quickly to jump start Taiwan-PRC talks that had been stalled since 1998. The talks to date have yielded a number of agreements, including agreements to establish regular direct weekend charter flights, direct sea and air transportation, postal links, and food safety mechanisms. Taiwan also has lifted long-standing caps on Taiwan investment in the PRC and lowered the profile of its bids for participation in U.N. agencies. These and other initiatives are welcomed by many as having contributed to greater regional stability. More pessimistic observers see growing PRC-Taiwan ties eroding U.S. influence, strengthening PRC leverage and, particularly in the face of expanding economic links, jeopardizing Taiwan autonomy and economic security.

---

* This is an edited, reformatted and augmented version of CRS Report R40493, dated April 2, 2009.

The changing dynamic between Taiwan and the PRC poses increasingly difficult, competing policy challenges for the United States. Along with new policy challenges – such as what U.S. policy should be if Taiwan should continue to move closer to or even align with the PRC – the Obama Administration will be faced with other challenges familiar from past years, including decisions on new arms sales to Taiwan, which are anathema to the PRC; how to accommodate requests for visits to the United States by President Ma and other senior Taiwan officials; the overall nature of U.S. relations with the Ma government; whether to pursue closer economic ties with Taiwan; what role, if any, Washington should play in cross-strait relations; and more broadly, what form of defense assurances to offer Taiwan. In addition, the Taiwan government also is seeking to raise its international profile in other ways involving the United States. Taiwan is seeking to be removed from the U.S. Special 301 "Watch List" for intellectual property rights violations, and is seeking to qualify for the U.S. Visa Waiver Program (VWP), which eliminates some visa requirements for qualified countries. The Taiwan government also continues to ask for a U.S.-Taiwan Free Trade Agreement (FTA), which would broaden the current avenue for U.S.- Taiwan trade discussions, the 1994 Trade and Investment Framework (TIFA).

Legislation in the 111th Congress concerning Taiwan includes H.Con.Res. 18, urging that the United States resume diplomatic relations with Taiwan; and H.Con.Res. 55, expressing *U.S. support for and commitment to Taiwan. This report will be updated as events warrant.*

RECENT DEVELOPMENTS

March 27, 2009 – Taiwan's Council for Economic Planning and Development issued a report, Taiwan's Economic Situation and Outlook, that cited a 28.6% drop in exports from February 2008 to February 2009 and a serious slowdown for the economy beginning in the 4th quarter of 2008.

March 18, 2009 – U.S. American Institute in Taiwan (AIT) chairman Ray Burghardt said that the United States was "comfortable with what's happening" in Taiwan-PRC engagement. The same day, former Taiwan President Chen Shui-bian appeared at his final pre-trial hearing before going on trial for corruption, scheduled to begin March 26, 2009.

March 17, 2009 – The first luxury cruise ship (Ocean Mystery) to sail directly to Taiwan from the PRC (Shanghai) arrived at Keelung, reportedly carrying 1,600 PRC tourists.

March 16, 2009 – In its first quadrennial report (QDR), Taiwan's Ministry of Defense said that Taiwan would cut its military personnel from 275,000 to 215,000 over the next five years – part of a plan to create an all-volunteer force by December 2014.

March 14, 2009 – The Taiwan government urged the PRC to jettison its "anti-secession" law. The law, passed in March 2005, justifies the use of force to prevent Taiwan independence.

March 11, 2009 – The second session of the 11th National People's Congress began in Beijing. At the close of the three-day meeting, Premier Wen Jiabao said that the PRC would be "willing to have consultations" for Taiwan to participate in international organizations.

KEY U.S. POLICY QUESTIONS

U.S. policy on Taiwan, which is enshrined in the 1979 Taiwan Relations Act (the TRA, P.L. 96-8), remains rooted in a general notion of maintaining the "status quo" as it existed when the TRA was enacted. The United States has interpreted the "status quo" as the preservation of peace and stability in the Taiwan Strait until such time as the undecided issue of Taiwan's political status can be resolved peacefully by agreement between Taiwan and the PRC. Some in the United States also see the "status quo" as the maintenance of a relative military, economic, and diplomatic balance between the two sides [1]. Everything that has followed since then in U.S. policy toward Taiwan has been bound up within this delicate balance.

But while U.S. policy has remained static, the circumstances it was designed to address have changed dramatically. Complex political changes have occurred in both Taiwan and the PRC. The military balance is shifting inexorably in the PRC's favor, there have been dramatic improvements in the PRC's economic fortunes, and the two sides have increasingly connected economic interests. These changes have resulted in periodic speculation about whether the current U.S. policy framework remains appropriate or should be revised. Issues involving Taiwan's unresolved political status remain key features in other U.S. interactions with both Taiwan and the PRC. They include complex policy trade-offs and questions such as:

- how far the United States should go in trying to accommodate PRC sensitivities about Taiwan without compromising U.S. principles supporting Taiwan's democratic development;
- how much the United States should try to pressure either China or Taiwan or both to avoid provocative actions;
- whether the United States should change its policy of not arbitrating or facilitating negotiations between Taiwan and the PRC in favor of a more direct, interventionist approach; and
- whether the United States should conduct a reassessment of its Taiwan policy in light of changing circumstances, and what the extent of such a possible reassessment should be.

BRIEF BACKGROUND TO TAIWAN'S POLITICAL LANDSCAPE

Once a U.S. World War II ally, China's situation changed dramatically after the civil war victory of Mao Tse-tung in 1949. The reigning Chinese government, led by Chiang Kai-shek and his Kuomintang (KMT) party, fled mainland China and moved to Taiwan, an island off the southern Chinese coast. For the next thirty years, the United States continued officially to recognize the government on Taiwan while both regimes—the KMT government on Taiwan and the People's Republic of China (PRC) government on the mainland—claimed legitimacy as the sole legal government of the Chinese people.

With these competing claims of sovereignty, official U.S. relations with the government on Taiwan became a casualty of the 1979 decision to establish U.S. diplomatic relations with the PRC government as the sole government of all China. U.S. unofficial relations with Taiwan, meanwhile, have been shaped since then by three U.S.-China communiques and built on the framework of the 1979 Taiwan Relations Act (P.L. 96-8). Under these agreements, the United States maintains its official relations with the PRC while selling Taiwan military weapons and having extensive economic, political, and security interests there. Since then, absent formal diplomatic relations, the United States still has maintained substantial economic and security relationships with Taiwan, including the sale of defensive military weapons and services [2] But continuing political and economic transformations in both the PRC and Taiwan since 1979 mean that U.S. policymakers are facing a different set of complex policy choices with each passing year.

This report focuses on current developments in Taiwan, analyzing how those developments are affecting choices the United States makes about its policy toward Taiwan specifically and toward the PRC more broadly. Other CRS reports provide more details about the myriad historical complexities of Taiwan's current situation in U.S. policy, such as: historical background about how the ROC on Taiwan went from a U.S. ally to a government with no diplomatic U.S. relations, including the fundamentals governing U.S. policy toward Taiwan today (CRS Report RS22388, *Taiwan's Political Status: Historical Background and Ongoing Implications*); the increase in U.S.-Taiwan tensions under the former administration of President Chen Shui-bian (CRS Report RL33684, U*nderlying Strains in Taiwan-U.S. Political Relations*); the 2008 elections in Taiwan (CRS Report RS22853, *Taiwan's 2008 Presidential Election*, all by Kerry Dumbaugh; as well as the subtle permutations of the "one-China" policy over three decades and its role in U.S. policy (CRS Report RL3 034 1, *China/Taiwan: Evolution of the "One China" Policy—Key Statements from Washington*, Beijing, and Taipei) and U.S. arms sales to Taiwan (CRS Report RL30957, *Taiwan: Major U.S. Arms Sales Since 1990*), both by Shirley A. Kan.

Fundamentals of U.S. Policy

The fundamental framework of U.S. policy toward Taiwan was laid down decades ago, beginning with the Nixon opening to the People's Republic of China (PRC) in 1971 that resulted in the severing of official relations with the government on Taiwan in 1979. U.S. policy toward Taiwan since then has been defined by four primary documents: the Taiwan Relations Act (P.L. 9 6-8, enacted in 1979); and three U.S. communiques with the PRC:

- the Shanghai Communique (1972), in which the United States "acknowledge[d]" that both China and Taiwan maintain there is but one China, declared it did "not challenge that position," and reaffirmed its interest in a peaceful settlement of the Taiwan question.
- the Communique on Normalization of Relations with the PRC (1979), in which the United States recognized the PRC government as the sole legitimate government of all China and "acknowledge[d] the Chinese position that there is but one China and Taiwan is part of China", and

- the August 17 Communique on Arms Sales to Taiwan (1982), in which the United States stated it had no intention of pursuing a "two-China" policy; that it appreciated China's pledges to strive for a peaceful solution to the Taiwan question; and that it did not plan on a long-term policy of arms sales to Taiwan.

In addition, U.S. policy has been shaped during these decades by a combination of other factors. Among these are a set of six policy assurances the United States gave Taiwan in the 1980s; [3] the precedents set by a collection of sensitive "guidelines on Taiwan" that the executive branch has adopted to define and constrain its actions; a variety of statements by successive U.S. Administrations about the nature of U.S. policy toward Taiwan and the PRC; and periodic initiatives by Members of Congress intended to affect U.S. policy in some way.

The Taiwan Relations Act (P.L. 96-8)

In 1979, the Carter Administration announced the United States would sever official relations with Taiwan and recognize the PRC as the legitimate government of China. While Members of the 96th Congress clearly concurred with the strategic imperative of such a move, many Members were unhappy with what they saw as the Carter Administration's minimal proposals for continued dealings with the government on Taiwan. In particular, some were concerned that the package of legislation the White House submitted to Congress to govern future unofficial relations with Taiwan – the "Taiwan Enabling Act" – did not go far enough in protecting either Taiwan or U.S. interests. Congressional debate on the legislation in 1979 was extensive and complicated. The end result was passage of a much amended version of the Administration's proposal — the Taiwan Relations Act (TRA – P.L. 96-8) — which remains the domestic legal authority for conducting unofficial U.S. relations with Taiwan today [4]. Much of the TRA deals with the logistics of U.S.- Taiwan relations: the establishment of the American Institute in Taiwan (AIT) as the unofficial U.S. representative for diplomatic interactions with Taiwan, including details about its staffing, functions, and funding; and the continued application of existing U.S. laws and treaties affecting Taiwan after the severing of ties [5].

Although it is a common American misperception that the TRA mandates the United States to defend Taiwan in case of attack, nothing in the TRA specifically obligates the United States to do so or to resort to military conflict on Taiwan's behalf. In 1995-1996, precedent was set for potential U.S. involvement when the United States sent two carrier battle groups to the area after China conducted an unprecedented series of live-fire missile exercises in the Taiwan Strait. In light of the lack of a mandate in the TRA but the apparent U.S. willingness to act in the Taiwan Strait missile crisis, there remain questions about how the United States may react in a comparable situation now.

Of particular relevance for long-term U.S. policy are Section 2 (b) and Section 3 of the TRA, dealing with U.S. strategic interests in and arms sales commitments to Taiwan [6]. Section 2 of the TRA speaks in broad terms about U.S. interests for peaceful resolution to the Taiwan question, saying that any forceful resolution would be of "grave concern to the United States." It further states that U.S. policy is to "maintain the capacity of the United States to resist ... coercion" in addressing the Taiwan issue. Section 3 provides for the sale of U.S. defense articles and services to Taiwan, but is non-specific about the nature of these articles. It merely calls for "such defense articles and services ... as may be necessary to enable Taiwan to maintain a sufficient self-defense capability." It also gives Congress a role in determining what needs Taiwan may have. Much of the U.S. debate on Taiwan arms sales since the TRA was enacted has involved differing judgments — often between Congress and the White House — about what should be the capabilities and quantities of the "necessary" articles and services the United States provide to Taiwan under Section 3.

Changing Political Dynamics in Taiwan

Until the mid-1980s, Taiwan had a one-party system in which Chiang Kai-shek's authoritarian Nationalist Party (KMT) ruled under martial law [7]. The KMT permitted no political opposition and held no democratic elections. In 1986, the party began to liberalize, allowing the formation of opposition parties, including the Democratic Progressive Party (DPP), a party whose platform advocated Taiwan independence from China. The KMT government also ended martial law (in 1987), and for the first time opened government positions to native "Taiwanese"—the 85% of the island's population who predated the influx of the two million "mainlanders" fleeing civil war in China. In the ensuing years, members of the ROC legislature on Taiwan, elected on mainland China over 40 years earlier, were asked to retire, and a new, streamlined legislature was elected in 1992.

In 1996, Taiwan held its first direct presidential election, which was won by KMT leader Lee Teng-hui, himself a native Taiwanese. During his presidency, Lee increasingly distanced himself from his party's long-standing position that there was only "one China" and that Taiwan was part of it. Instead he began emphasizing Taiwan's distinct culture and identity apart from the PRC's. This posed complications for one of the fundamental tenets on which U.S. relations with the PRC were based—the statement that "The United States acknowledges that all Chinese on either side of the Taiwan Strait maintain that there is but one China and that Taiwan is a part of China." [8].

The uninterrupted KMT dynasty on Taiwan finally was broken on March 18, 2000, when DPP candidate Chen Shui-bian won the presidency with only 39% of the popular vote in a three-way race. The victory was a stunning defeat for the KMT and its unbroken 50-year tenure in power on Taiwan. By the narrowest of margins, President Chen was elected to a second (and final) term in March 2004, winning by only 29,518 votes out of a reported 13.25 million votes cast [9] The KMT's fall from political dominance was compounded in two subsequent legislative elections in December 2001 and December 2004. By 2004, the KMT saw its majority of 115 seats in the 225- member Legislative Yuan (LY) cut to just 79.

With neither the DPP nor the KMT having a working majority, each formed coalitions with smaller parties to gain strength. President Chen Shui-bian presided over a "Pan-Green" coalition composed of his DPP party and the Taiwan Solidarity Union; it was opposed by the "pan-Blue" coalition of the KMT and the People First Party (PFP), which together retained the barest control of Taiwan's 225-member legislature. Since the two opposing coalitions had very different political ideologies and roughly equal political strength, this split government created significant gridlock in Taiwan's political arena, and thus difficult political realities for U.S. policymakers throughout Chen's tenure.

KEY CURRENT ISSUES

Current Political Situation in Taiwan

Between the two contending political parties described above, politics in Taiwan play out against a backdrop that blends strongly held views on divisive domestic issues with a running debate over Taiwan's political status and its relations with the PRC. While much of the American press focuses on the latter issues, Taiwan's domestic political fights often are bare-knuckled affairs fraught with charges and countercharges over official corruption, nepotism, misuse of public funds, and various failures in management of the economy.

The political situation in Taiwan changed substantially in 2008 when momentum swung back behind the KMT while the DPP, struggling with growing political scandal and low voter confidence, lost power in both presidential and legislative elections. While many had expected a victory on March 22, 2008, for KMT presidential candidate Ma Ying-jeou and his running mate, Vincent Siew, the size of the party's winning margin (2.2 million votes) was a surprise to most outside observers and even to some in the party itself [10]. Emphasizing a platform of economic improvement and better relations with the PRC and the United States, Ma did respectably even in southern and rural districts heavily dominated by the DPP in the past. His ticket's wide margin of victory echoed a similarly dramatic KMT victory in the January 2008 legislative elections, where the party gained a majority of 81 seats in a newly constituted and smaller 113-seat body compared to the DPP's 27 seats [11]. When Ma assumed office on May 20, 2008, the KMT had regained solid control of the government.

The DPP's electoral fortunes in 2008 were burdened by a number of factors. These included what was widely regarded as the poor performance of the DPP incumbent President Chen Shui-bian; economic difficulties during his tenure; corruption scandals in the DPP; and Chen's increasing emphasis on a controversial pro-independence agenda. Some observers felt that the DPP missed the opportunity to make critical adjustments in its policies after public dissatisfaction with its performance became clear in 2005. Instead of becoming more moderate and moving to where the voters were, according to this view, the DPP had tried to move the voters to it, a strategy that did not serve it well in the 2008 elections [12].

Taiwan's new President, Ma Ying-jeou, of the KMT, has pursued a more conciliatory approach toward the PRC and has vowed to improve relations with the United States. Since his landslide election, however, Ma's popularity has fallen, plagued among other things by a faltering economy, tumbling stock markets, and rising energy prices as well as by concerns over his cross-strait policies and by residual domestic political tensions in Taiwan. Under Taiwan's new KMT government, then, the United States faces new challenges involving the implications of closer and more cordial ties between Taiwan and the PRC for U.S. interests, and what role, if any, Washington should play in cross-strait relations.

Resumption of Cross-Strait Talks

Many observers believe that the election of President Ma presented an opportunity to lay a new framework in Taiwan-PRC relations—one that moves toward cross-strait improvements and new understandings, and away from the more confrontational policies of the past. In the two months between his election and his inauguration on May 20, 2008, Ma spoke of his intentions to begin normalizing cross-strait ties in a "cross-strait common market," to establish direct air links with the PRC, and to ease other restrictions on cross-strait contacts. He sought to ease tensions with China by pledging adherence to what he called a "three no's" approach: no unification, no independence, and no use of force—a pledge he repeated in his inaugural address. He called for a "diplomatic truce" with China and pledged to stop using "dollar diplomacy" to win foreign country recognition [13]. These were departures from the policies of former President Chen, who while seeking to reach out to the PRC also had antagonized Beijing by emphasizing Taiwan's separate identity and independent political status.

After his inauguration, Ma moved quickly to implement improvements in cross-strait relations, expanding on the foundations that had been laid by the previous Chen administration. In a symbolic move, Taiwan in mid-May 2008 worked jointly with the PRC in providing disaster relief after the Sichuan earthquake.

After its prickly relationship with the former Chen Administration, Beijing appeared equally receptive to the idea of cross-strait improvements under the Ma Administration. By late May, the PRC had issued – and Taiwan had accepted – a PRC invitation to resume quasi-official talks for the first time since October 1998. The Taiwan and PRC governments still do not negotiate directly. In Taiwan, cross-strait talks are handled on the Taiwan side by the Straits Exchange Foundation (SEF), a nominally non-governmental organization authorized to handle such exchanges.

The corresponding body in the PRC is the Association for Relations Across the Taiwan Strait (ARATS), under the Taiwan Affairs Office of the State Council. The two rounds of cross-strait talks held to date have been conducted by these two semi-official bodies. They include:

- A first round in Beijing on June 12-13, 2008, resulting in agreements to allow weekend direct charter flights and boost PRC tourism to Taiwan.
- A second round in Taiwan on November 4-7, 2008, resulting in four agreements on direct sea transportation, air transportation, food safety, and direct postal links.

In addition to cross-strait talks, there have been other senior level encounters. The chairman of the KMT, Wu Poh-hsiung, met with PRC President Hu Jintao on May 28, 2008, the highest-level encounter between the two sides to that point since 1949 [14]. On November 21, 2008, Taiwan's Lien Chan, who in the past has served as both Taiwan's Vice-President and as Premier, met with PRC President Hu Jintao during the Asian Pacific Economic Cooperation (APEC) meeting in Peru. Although Lien currently holds no formal government positions, his stature is sufficient that this meeting was said to be the highest-level meeting between the two sides in an international forum since 1949.

Taiwan's cross-strait negotiator, P.K. Chiang, began a trip to China on January 7, 2009, visiting a number of PRC cities to discuss issues facing investors from Taiwan on the mainland. Taiwan also has undertaken a number of unilateral initiatives, including lifting caps on Taiwan investment in the PRC.

Other cross-strait initiatives are still in the discussion stage. President Ma signaled that his administration would be more flexible on the names Taiwan uses in its international engagement efforts—suggesting, for instance, that Taiwan's negotiation of Free Trade

Agreements (FTAs) would be less divisive if Taiwan used the same name it used when applying to the WTO— "separate customs territory of Taiwan, Penghu, Kinmen, and Matsu." DPP members and others in Taiwan have criticized the Ma government's new policy approach, saying that by not "properly analyzing the consequences" of easing cross-strait economic restrictions, the KMT government has jeopardized Taiwan's interests.

The opposition party also has criticized Ma's diplomatic overtures toward China as being "over-dependent on China's goodwill." [15] While President Ma himself reportedly has said that cross-strait talks should be accelerated, opponents of his new policies have criticized them as proceeding too rapidly [16]. In March 2009, the Chairman of the U.S. American Institute in Taiwan (AIT), Ray Burghardt, said that the United States was "comfortable with what's happening" in Taiwan-PRC engagement.

Bid for U.N. Membership/Participation

The Ma Administration also has been more moderate and flexible than its predecessor concerning Taiwan's annual United Nations (U.N.) bid. In its first such bid on August 14, 2008, the Ma Administration submitted a proposal to the U.N. Secretariat asking to be allowed to have "meaningful participation" in U.N. special organizations such as the World Health Organization (WHO) [17]. Because of PRC objections, a U.N. subcommittee decided on September 18, 2008 not to include Taiwan's request for "meaningful participation" in U.N. activities on the agenda for the 63rd General Assembly.

In 2009, however, there appears to be progress on Taiwan's bid to participate in the WHO. On January 13, 2009, WHO officials sent a letter to the Taiwan government stating that the island henceforth would be included in the International Health Regulations (IHR), a set of legally binding rules governing international commitment to disease surveillance, alert, and response [18]. As an IHR participant, Taiwan will be included in the Global Outbreak and Alert Response Network, receiving the latest updates on global epidemics. While welcoming the news as a positive development, a Taiwan spokesperson said that Taiwan would continue to seek observer status at the annual World Health Assembly meeting [19]. Other Taiwan observers have bristled at the suggestion that PRC officials essentially had given "permission" for Taiwan to participate by negotiating directly with the WHO to include Taiwan in the IHR [20] Taiwan's Foreign Minister, Francisco H.L. Ou, said that Taiwan will only accept an invitation extended directly by the WHO Secretariat to participate in the WHA, not one routed through Beijing [21].

Taiwan has been unsuccessful in 15 previous attempts to gain either membership or non-member status in the U.N. and its affiliates such as the WHO. Taiwan's efforts under the DPP Administration of President Chen included an application both for full U.N. membership as well as for use of either the name "Republic of China" or "Taiwan." These applications had been of particular concern to both China and the United States.

In keeping with long-standing U.S. policy, U.S. officials said that the United States would play no mediating role in Taiwan-PRC talks on the WHO issue [22] While there is support in the U.S. Congress for Taiwan's U.N. membership, [23] U.S. government officials, on record as supporting Taiwan's membership in organizations "where statehood is not an issue," [24] have been unusually blunt and outspoken in opposition to some of Taiwan's past

U.N. application efforts under President Chen. In August 2007, for instance, a senior U.S. officials said:

> We are very supportive of Taiwan on many many fronts.... However, membership in the United Nations requires statehood. Taiwan, or the Republic of China, is not at this point a state in the international community. The position of the United States government is that the ROC ... is an issue undecided, and it has been left undecided ... for many, many years [25]

Taipei also points out that it is a full member in other international organizations to which the PRC also belongs, such as the Asian Development Bank (ADB), the World Trade Organization (WTO), and the Asia Pacific Economic Cooperation (APEC) [26] In 2004, the 108th Congress enacted legislation (P.L. 108-235) requiring the Secretary of State to seek Taiwan's observer status in WHO each year at its annual meeting, the World Health Assembly (WHA). Taiwan has maintained that its "observer status" in U.N. bodies such as WHO would be an apolitical solution since other non-sovereign entities, like the Holy See and the Palestine Liberation Organization, have been given such status. The PRC has opposed Taiwan's bid for U.N. participation in the past because it suggests that Taiwan is a sovereign state. Beijing argues that since Taiwan is not a state but a part of China, it cannot separately be admitted to U.N. entities for which sovereign status is a pre-requisite for membership.

Corruption Investigations: Former Chen Administration

On December 12, 2008, former President Chen Shui-bian was indicted on charges of corruption while he served as Taiwan's president. He was arrested on those charges on November 12, 2008; his trial began on March 26, 2009.

The Taiwan government conducted broadening investigations into allegations of corruption made since 2006 against then-President Chen, his family members, and officials in his administration. New allegations of money-laundering arose in August 2008 against Chen and his family, plunging the DPP further into crisis, according to current DPP chairwoman Tsai Ing-wen [27].

The August 2008 allegations, which involve foreign government investigations and not just those of Taiwan's KMT-dominated government, also are the first in which Chen publicly admitted even partial culpability, saying that the funds were from campaign contributions, legally acquired, that he failed to report.

On August 15, 2008, Chen apologized to the DPP for causing "humiliation" and "irreparable damage" to the party for his failure to declare the campaign funds. He announced his and his wife's immediate resignations from DPP party membership [28]

Shortly after Chen stepped down as president on May 20, 2008 (thereby losing his presidential immunity), Taiwan prosecutors announced they were starting an official investigation on his potential role in the 2006 corruption and malfeasance charges. In pursuit of these allegations, President Ma on August 6, 2008 announced that he was declassifying documents, classified by Chen while he was president, that allegedly implicated Chen in the case of the special expenses fund. Chen has maintained that the funds wired to overseas accounts are undeclared campaign funds legally acquired, not government funds embezzled from the "special affairs" account while he was president or bribes associated with the 2004 financial reforms he initiated [29]. He has called the corruption investigations a "political vendetta" by the KMT against him and his family. One Taiwan press editorial has criticized recurring corruption allegations in recent years—which have involved a number of senior Taiwan politicians—suggesting they are fueled more by political partisanship than by interest in real reform [30]

Special Expense Accounts

Investigations and indictments for corruption have been a recurring feature of political life in Taiwan, particularly over the issue of how senior officials use and account for expenditures from so-called "special expense accounts." Such accounts are to be used for official expenses only, but give the controlling officials broad discretion on how the funds are spent. They operate generally with poor government oversight and are subject to vague rules that many Taiwan officials have said are confusing. Among those investigated and cleared of such charges in the past are: current President Ma Ying-jeou, former foreign minister James Huang, former economics minister Steve Chen, and current DPP chairwoman Tsai Ing-wen (investigated when she was head of the Mainland Affairs Council).

Other investigations for "special expense account" infractions include former Vice President Annette Lu, former justice minister Shi Mao-lin, former education minister Tu Cheng-sheng, former interior minister Lee Yi-yang, and former civil service minister Chu Wuhsien, among others.

Economic and Trade Relations

Taiwan's economy grew rapidly (around 10% a year) in the 1970s and 1980s. Growth declined to around 5-6% a year in the 1990s as the economy matured. But Taiwan's economy has faltered in the global financial crisis, experiencing a serious slowdown beginning in the 4th quarter of 2008. According to a March 2009 report by Taiwan's Council for Economic Planning and Development Taiwan's export-heavy economy suffered a 28.6% drop in exports from February 2008 to February 2009 [31]

Taiwan-U.S. Trade and Investment

Taiwan is the United States' ninth-largest overall trading partner, with two-way trade in 2008 valued at $61.6 billion, a slight decrease from 2007. Taiwan also is the sixth-largest destination for U.S. agricultural exports, about $2.5 billion annually. In addition to agricultural goods, Taiwan's U.S. imports include industrial raw materials and machinery and equipment; its exports to the United States are largely electronics and consumer goods. Once Taiwan's largest trading partner, the United States has been surpassed by China and Japan and is now Taiwan's third- largest trading partner, supplying 11% of Taiwan's imports and absorbing 14% of its exports. The U.S. trade deficit with Taiwan in 2008 was $11 billion.

Special 301 Watch List

Taiwan has been on the U.S. Special 301 Watch List for years because of strong U.S. concerns that it maintained insufficient protections for intellectual property rights (IPR). This changed in 2009, after Taiwan initiated a series of new laws and established institutional frameworks to assure IPR protections. On January 16, 2009, the USTR announced that Taiwan had made sufficient improvements to be removed from the list [32]

To address U.S. concerns, the Taiwan government passed more robust copyright legislation, enacted new laws targeting illegal Internet file sharing, and improved prosecution of IPR offenses through the establishment (July 1, 2008) of a specialized Intellectual Property Court [33]. The U.S. Trade Representative (USTR) had removed Taiwan from the more stringent "Priority Watch List" in 2004. But pursuant to provisions the Trade Act of 1974, Taiwan remained on the U.S. Special 301 "Watch List"—a designation of a less serious risk of IPR violations than indicated by the "Priority Watch List."

The U.S. business community was divided on whether Taiwan had made sufficient IPR improvements to merit removal from the "Watch List." For instance, in separate letters to USTR dated September 8, 2008, the U.S.-Taiwan Business Council said it "strongly supports" Taiwan's removal from the Watch List, while the U.S.-based International Intellectual Property Alliance recommended that "Taiwan remain on the Watch List" pending further IPR improvements.

Free Trade Agreement (FTA)

Taiwan for years has been seeking the economic and political benefits of a U.S.-Taiwan Free Trade Agreement (FTA), so far without success. President Ma reportedly mentioned the subject again during his August 2008 transit visit through the United States on his way to Latin America [34]. To date, U.S.-Taiwan trade discussions have been held under a 1994 Trade and Investment Framework Agreement (TIFA), a non-binding consultative mechanism the United States employs for resolving trade and investment difficulties with countries still opening their economies [35]. In some instances, a TIFA may lead to economic liberalization that is significant enough to result in a U.S. FTA with the TIFA country. Taiwan has argued that its status as a major trading partner of the United States justifies an FTA on economic grounds.

U.S. officials cite a number of obstacles to an FTA with Taiwan over the near term—not only trade matters, such as Taiwan's record on intellectual property rights (IPR), but more fundamentally, the complicated political issues involving both Taiwan's and U.S. relations with the PRC. The PRC strongly opposes a U.S.-Taiwan FTA. In the past, Taiwan's bid has had its supporters in the U.S. Congress, several of whom have introduced measures regarding an FTA for Taiwan [36].

Cross-Strait Trade and Investment

Since 1949, both Taiwan and the PRC have maintained restrictions on trade and economic investment relations across the Taiwan Strait. These have included requirements that goods and articles be transshipped via third parties and not directly; restrictions on the kinds of goods and articles that can be traded; and caps on investment levels, among others. Even with these restrictions on official trade and contacts, Taiwan businesses have invested increasingly across the strait into the mainland, although the exact figures remain unclear. Taiwan-China trade has also increased dramatically, so that China (along with Hong Kong) has surpassed the United States as Taiwan's most important trading partner. According to Taiwan's Central News Agency, Taiwan's total bilateral trade with the PRC for 2008 was $105.4 billion.

Taiwan's growing economic interconnectedness with the PRC has created increasing pressures on a succession of Taiwan governments to ease its restrictions on direct travel and investment. Since 1987, Taiwan incrementally eased long-standing restrictions on contacts with the PRC. Initiatives under President Chen and the DPP, included the start in January 2005 of the first non-stop direct charter flights flown in 55 years between the two adversaries (limited to the Lunar New Year holiday that year).

The resumption of cross-strait talks in June 2008 and the subsequent agreements signed (discussed elsewhere in this report) have already increased the potential for cross-strait trade and investment. Ma Administration officials also have talked about creating a comprehensive agreement to expand economic cooperation between Taiwan and China – with names suggested such as the Comprehensive Economic Partnership Agreement (CEPA) or the Economic Cooperation Framework Agreement (ECFA). The idea is controversial to some in Taiwan because of the economic inter-dependence they fear such an agreement could help create [37]. President Ma's willingness to significantly expand such cross-strait exchanges has concerned many DPP members and pro-independence advocates in Taiwan, who see the Ma initiatives as having overly ambitious expectations and as moving far too rapidly. These DPP observers say that cross-strait overtures need to be calibrated carefully to avoid compromising Taiwan's economic security and political autonomy.

Other Key Bilateral Issues

U.S. Arms Sales to Taiwan and Taiwan's Defense Budget

Under the Taiwan Relations Act (P.L. 9 6-8), the United States is obligated to provide Taiwan with defense articles and services for its self-defense—a commitment to which the PRC objects. In spite of the apparent warming ties with Taiwan after the March 2008 presidential election, many thought the Bush Administration delayed sending forward notifications to Congress concerning a number of long-pending U.S. arms sales to Taiwan [38]. In June 2008, some Members of the U.S. Senate wrote to President Bush expressing concern about the reports and urging the White House to act swiftly on Taiwan's arms sales requests [39]. Some speculated that the delay in arms sales notifications was related to Beijing's hosting of the 2008 Summer Olympic Games from August 8-24, 2008. One Pentagon official hinted in a public forum that the United States may have imposed a freeze on weapons sales to Taiwan [40]. A State Department spokesman at the time maintained that the pending arms sales still were being discussed in "an internal interagency process." [41]

Since then, U.S. arms sales to Taiwan have resumed. On August 25, 2008, the Pentagon announced that it was awarding the McDonnell-Douglas Corp. (owned by Boeing) a contract to provide Taiwan with 60 Harpoon missiles and associated hardware, worth $89.8 million, that Taiwan requested in 2007 [42]. On October 3, 2008, the Defense Security Cooperation Agency (DSCA) notified Congress of the possible Foreign Military Sale of six different types of defense articles and equipment, consistent with the policies of P.L. 9 6-8, which could total a maximum of approximately $6.4 billion. These included:

- upgrades of four E-2T Aircraft to the HAWKEYE 2000 configuration (est. maximum of $250 million)

- 30 AH-64D Block III APACHE Longbow Attack helicopters (est. maximum of $2.532 billion)
- 330 PATRIOT Advanced Capability (PAC-3) missiles (est. maximum of $3.1 billion)
- 32 UGM-84L Sub-Launched HARPOON Block II missiles and 2 UTM-84L HARPOON Block II Exercise missiles (est. maximum of $200 million)
- follow-on spare parts in support of F-5E/F, C-1 30H, F-1 6A/B, and Indigenous Defense Fighter IDF aircraft (est. maximum of $334 million)
- 182 JAVELIN guided missile rounds and 20 JAVELIN command launch units (est. maximum of $47 million) [43]

Visa Waiver Program (VWP)

Taiwan also has sought to qualify for coverage under the U.S. Visa Waiver Program (VWP), which eliminates some visa requirements for qualified countries, allowing their citizens to make temporary U.S. visits without first obtaining a valid visa. VWP countries must meet certain criteria—such as offering reciprocal privileges to U.S. citizens, having machine-readable passports, and having a low nonimmigrant refusal rate (defined as the formal denial of a nonimmigrant visa application by a U.S. consular official). The latter criteria appears to have been a particularly difficult one for Taiwan [44]. In 2007, Congress enacted amendments to the VWP which may provide for a waiver of the non-immigrant refusal rate [45]. With a waiver, Taiwan may meet the requirements of the program.

Although Taiwan citizens would benefit from the facilitated travel that the U.S. Visa Waiver Program affords, another key Taiwan government motive is thought to be the international stature that Taiwan would gain from being among the VWP's group of participants. In addition, participation in the program is often seen as evidence of close ties with the United States. In addition to its current failure to meet all of the program's qualifications (absent a non-immigrant refusal rate waiver), Taiwan's chances of participation in the VWP also are subject to the anticipated kinds of political difficulties involving the PRC that are aspects of other U.S.-Taiwan relations. The PRC does not qualify for the VWP.

U.S. Policy Trends

It is unclear at this point what the Taiwan policy of the Obama Administration will be. Trends since 1979 strongly suggest that the White House will maintain policy continuity, with U.S. policy remaining rooted firmly in the fundamentals of the Taiwan Relations Act and the three communiques. In a press conference in Taiwan on March 18, 2009, for example, AIT Chairman Ray Burghardt stressed that U.S. commitments under the Taiwan Relations Act will remain unchanged, and also emphasized that U.S. officials "truly are enthusiastic" about improvements in cross-strait ties [46].

Recent history on U.S. Taiwan policy indicates, however, that even within the framework of policy continuity there can be nuance. Many observers concluded in 2001 that the newly elected George W. Bush then had abandoned the long-standing U.S. policy of "strategic ambiguity" in favor of "strategic clarity" that placed a clearer emphasis on Taiwan's interests and showed less concern for PRC views. In addition to approving a major arms sales package for Taiwan in 2001, subsequent statements and actions by Bush Administration officials continued to appear more supportive of Taiwan than those of previous U.S. Administrations. This support was in keeping with growing concern in Congress in the late 1990s that the U.S. policy framework toward Taiwan had become outdated and that Taiwan's self-defense capabilities had eroded while those of the PRC had grown. A series of congressionally mandated annual reports issued by the Pentagon supported these conclusions, assessing that the military balance in the Taiwan Strait was increasingly tilting in the PRC's favor.

During its tenure, however, the Bush Administration began reshaping its own policy articulations concerning both Taiwan and the PRC. Administration officials came to see that smooth U.S.-PRC relations may be an important tool in cooperating against terrorism, maintaining stability on the Korean peninsula, and many other key U.S. strategic goals. As articulated by Vice President Cheney during his visit to Shanghai in April 2004, the White House judged that "the areas of agreement [between the United States and the PRC] are far greater than those areas where we disagree ... " [47] Also, such problems of trust developed between Taiwan's President Chen and U.S. officials that the bilateral atmosphere eroded significantly during the Bush Administration [48]. The Bush White House came to balance criticisms of China's military buildup opposite Taiwan with periodic warnings to the Taiwan government that U.S. support was not unconditional [49]. Whether such nuance will continue in the Obama Administration remains to be seen.

POLICY OPTIONS FOR CONGRESS

Given developments in U.S. relations with Taiwan since 2001, lawmakers who are concerned about current trends and the U.S. ability to meet future challenges may consider a number of various options for U.S. policy.

Maintain and Reaffirm the Current "One-China" Policy

The official U.S. policy view is that the "one-China" policy and the fundamental framework surrounding it is an important constant in an otherwise dangerously fluid and evolving U.S.- Taiwan-PRC relationship. In this view, any alteration or apparent flexibility in that policy would lead to a "disintegrating policy" damaging to U.S. interests [50]. In addition, according to this view, the current policy framework helps protect the United States and U.S. policies from becoming greater factors in the domestic Taiwan and PRC political environments. The slightest deviation from U.S. policy formulations and actions — an off-the-cuff comment, the use of different wording beyond that already approved, a visit by a more senior U.S. official — can be and has in the past been seized upon by actors from either side to further domestic political agendas, inevitably creating nettlesome diplomatic problems for U.S. policy.

Moreover, these proponents say, those who advocate scrapping the "one-China" policy and other aspects of the U.S. policy framework are recklessly discounting PRC resolve on unifying Taiwan with the mainland and irresponsibly advocating actions that well could lead to the use of U.S. military forces in a U.S.-PRC conflict. The Taiwan Relations Act and the current policy approach, according to these proponents, should be maintained and regularly reaffirmed. As the PRC itself is firmly committed to the "one-China" policy, maintaining and reaffirming the current policy would be the last disruptive to U.S.-PRC relations.

Change the "One China" Policy

A strongly held but minority view places greater emphasis on the political aspirations and democratic rights to self-determination of the people on Taiwan. According to proponents of this view, the current U.S. policy framework on Taiwan is completely out of step with the American emphasis on global democratization. They hold that as the PRC and Taiwan have evolved, the original U.S. policy framework on Taiwan has grown stultified and increasingly irrelevant. The "one-China" policy itself, they argue, originally was based on the U.S. acknowledgment that both Taiwan and the PRC held there was only one China and that Taiwan was part of it [51]. They contend that this U.S. policy has become untenable; it no longer reflects the reality in Taiwan. They say it is based on a faulty premise that perpetuates more-or-less continual deferral of a resolution to Taiwan's political status and ignores Taiwan's peaceful transition to democracy.

Therefore, they say, the "one-China" policy needs to be abandoned and replaced with a "one- China, one-Taiwan" policy in which the United States would work toward gradual normalization of relations with Taiwan.

Some who advocate this viewpoint believe that the costs of such a policy change for the United States would be minimal. They believe that PRC actions and statements on Taiwan are just "saber-rattling," and they doubt that the PRC will attack Taiwan should Taipei declare independence [52]. Even if the PRC should attack Taiwan, these proponents appear confident that for political and strategic reasons, the United States would come to Taiwan's aid [53]. To do nothing, they say, would seriously damage U.S. credibility and influence in Asia.

Others in the U.S. policy community and elsewhere stress that changing the "one-China" policy would be an about-face in the long-standing U.S. position and would involve the greatest risk to U.S.-PRC relations. Given the high priority the PRC places on the Taiwan issue, Beijing likely would view such a policy change uncompromisingly and could react strongly, to the detriment of U.S. interests. Potential PRC reactions could include a break or suspension in U.S.-China talks at many or all levels; abandonment of PRC support for important U.S. global policy initiatives; rupture of economic and perhaps even political relations; and military operations against Taiwan that could involve U.S. military forces. Some suggest also that such a move would be damaging to Taiwan's ultimate economic and political security.

Make U.S. Policy More Assertive and Transparent

Bracketed within the above two policy options is a steady but quiet flow of alternative policy suggestions. These tend to advocate various substantive changes in day-to-day U.S. relations with Taiwan that their proponents believe would remain within the boundaries of the current policy framework and within U.S. understandings with the PRC.

Another "Taiwan Policy Review"

At the very least, some say, the United States needs to consider doing another comprehensive review of its Taiwan policy in order to revisit once again the 1979-1980 "Taiwan Guidelines" that govern U.S. government interactions with Taiwan and with Taiwan officials. Reportedly, only one such review to update the guidelines has been conducted since 1979 - the 1993-1994 Taiwan Policy Review undertaken in the Clinton Administration - and that review resulted in a new approval for exchanges of high-level official visits in the economic arena [54]. But even the high-level economic visits resulting from the 1993-94 policy review were not pursued with vigor by the Bush Administration, according to these proponents [55]

Furthermore, since the 1993-94 policy review, there have been dramatic developments in Taiwan's political development. From an authoritarian, one-party government some saw as only marginally more democratic than that of the PRC, Taiwan has become a fully functioning democracy, with multiple political parties, competitive elections, and two complete, peaceful shifts in government – the DPP's victory under Chen in 2000 and the KMT's return to power under Ma in 2008.

In addition, since 1995 the PRC has undertaken a substantial military buildup along the coast opposite Taiwan, and in 2005 Beijing adopted the anti-secession law suggesting hostile intent against Taiwan. These significant developments since 1993-94, according to this view, justify another Taiwan Policy Review to make selected changes in U.S. policy. Proponents of a review believe that the importance of Taiwan for U.S. interests, and of peace and stability in the Taiwan strait, warrant such renewed policy attention. Limited changes, they argue, could result in a more rational policy process and could improve communications. Among the policy changes that have been discussed are:

- More transparent and open interactions with Taiwan at the working level, including visits between U.S. and Taiwan officials in official U.S. government buildings and invitations to Taiwan officials to attend special events such as swearing-in ceremonies;
- Higher level U.S. government visits and exchanges with Taiwan counterparts;
- Greater coordination within the U.S. government - including regular inter-departmental meetings involving the Departments of Commerce, Defense, State, and Treasury, among others - on policy and substantive issues involving Taiwan; and
- More open and active support for Taiwan's participation in international organizations for which statehood is not a requirement, and greater support for observer status for Taiwan in organizations for which statehood is a requirement (such as the United Nations and World Health Organization).

The implications of a Taiwan policy review for U.S.-PRC relations likely would depend on the nature of the policy review itself. A substantial or comprehensive public review undoubtedly would raise concerns both in the PRC and likely in Taiwan. As stated before, however, such a review is not without precedent, and could be seen by both U.S. and PRC officials as a pragmatic adjustment to current circumstances.

More Active U.S. Role on Cross-Strait Relations

Among those suggesting alternative approaches, there appears to be greater sentiment that a more active U.S. role in cross-strait matters is both justifiable within the current policy framework and warranted by changing sentiments within the PRC and Taiwan. They suggest, for instance, that there is room for U.S. involvement in trying to moderate, re-shape, or otherwise influence those contending positions of the two sides that remain major obstacles to greater stability in the Taiwan Strait. Such greater involvement would require changes in long-standing U.S. assurances to Taiwan that the United States would not become involved in a mediating role between the two sides, and long-standing objections from the PRC that the United States not "interfere" in China's internal affairs. U.S. officials maintain, however, both governments in recent years have changed the way they talk to Washington about Taiwan. U.S. officials now are under subtle and perhaps increasing pressure from both governments to become directly involved in some aspects of cross- strait issues.

According to U.S. officials, the PRC during Taiwan's Chen Administration suggested that Beijing and Washington cooperate to manage controversial Taiwan issues. This included suggestions and pressure from PRC officials that the United States pressure Chen into shelving plans for an island-wide referendum and that U.S.officials avoid sending the "wrong signals" to Taiwan couraging independence aspirations [56]. For their part, members of the Taiwan government suggested that the Taiwan Relations Act needed to be strengthened or reevaluated. They sought U.S. support for Chen's constitutional reform plans and more visible and routine U.S.-Taiwan official interaction. As a result, some observers in both Taiwan and the United States suggest that the time may be ripe for the United States to step up its rhetoric and activities to promote cross- strait dialogue.

Nevertheless, this receptivity to U.S. involvement has significant limitations—the chief of which is that each side wants U.S. involvement only on behalf of its own interests. Taiwan urges the United States to press the PRC to renounce the use of force and to agree to no preconditions for cross-strait talks. The PRC urges the United States to oppose Taiwan independence and to be more forceful in opposing unilateral changes in the status quo. According to many, U.S. involvement in such a one-sided way could help foster rather than ease cross-strait tensions. Former U.S. officials report that the United States is willing to help in a cross-strait dialogue if both sides can reach consensus on the kind of U.S. help they can accept [57]

Expert More Pressure on the PRC

Another alternate view is that the United States has become too responsive to PRC sensitivities on Taiwan, and therefore unwilling to exert more pressure on the PRC government to reduce its hostile military posture toward Taiwan. According to this view, the U.S. stake in maintaining a democratic Taiwan, along with the potential cost of a non-peaceful resolution to Taiwan's political status, is too high for the U.S. government to remain on the sidelines. The United States should use more of its considerable leverage with Beijing in an effort to bring about more conciliatory behavior and promote more cross-strait concessions. Proponents suggest that U.S. officials could pressure the PRC to reduce its missile and military buildup opposite Taiwan and to revisit China's 2005 Anti-Secession Law which specifically provides for use of force against Taiwan.

More Overt U.S. Support for Taiwan Democracy

Another set of policy suggestions supports greater U.S. support for and involvement in Taiwan's democratic institutions. According to this view, Taiwan has already transformed itself by adopting a democratic system of governance; it is in the interests of all parties to have Taiwan's government be as effective and stable as possible. In particular, Taiwan's democratic system serves as a principle barrier to a Taiwan leadership's "preemptive capitulation" to PRC initiatives [58]. But proponents of this view say that the very immaturity of Taiwan's democracy and the infrastructural weaknesses of its political institutions are hampering Taiwan governance, contributing to cross-strait tensions, and posing problems for U.S. policy. Proponents suggest that the U.S. might pursue initiatives to improve the effectiveness of Taiwan's governance, such as:

- U.S. support for limited constitutional reforms in Taiwan (such as movement to a parliamentary system or reduction in the multiple levels of government) that could contribute directly to more effective government institutions and a more workable balance of power;
- Greater dialogue and more direct contact between the U.S. Congress and Taiwan's Legislative Yuan (LY), particularly to assist the LY's current structural reform and committee structure and processes; and
- Encouragement for Taiwan to use its political strengths and resources in a non-isolating way - by de-emphasizing divisive sovereignty issues, for instance, and instead emphasizing the global role Taiwan can play in democratic capacity building - such as in vote-counting and monitoring.

In addition, say these proponents, the United States can and should be more open in offering rhetorical support for the statements and actions of Taiwan leaders, defending them as natural components of Taiwan's democratic processes [59]. The United States might feel obliged publicly to disagree with those espousing Taiwan independence aspirations, according to this view, but U.S. officials should openly support the rights of Taiwan officials to say such things as an essential part of the open debate that characterizes a democratic government.

Implications

Many consider the continued success in 2008 of the democratic process in Taiwan to be a validation of U.S. goals for the spread of democratic values. It also further emphasizes the unique and delicate challenge for U.S. policy that Taiwan continues to pose: Taiwan is our ninth largest trading partner with a vibrant and free democratic government on an island claimed by the PRC, with which the United States has no diplomatic relations but does have defense commitments, and whose independence from China U.S. officials say they do not support. With Taiwan under the KMT government, the United States will be faced with some challenges familiar from past years, including decisions on: new arms sales; how to accommodate requests for visits to the United States by President Ma and other senior Taiwan officials; the level of U.S. relations with the Ma government; and whether to pursue closer economic ties, such as through a Free Trade Agreement. In addition, Taiwan-U.S. relations under the KMT government face new challenges—notably the implications that President Ma's initiatives toward the PRC have for U.S. interests; and what role, if any, Washington should play in Taiwan-PRC relations.

For Cross-Strait Relations

President Ma's emphasis on improving relations with the PRC presents a potentially new policy environment for the United States. U.S. policy had been stressed after President Chen abandoned his early, unsuccessful olive branches to Beijing in favor of a more pro-independence approach, with U.S. officials subjected to increasing pressure from both sides to become directly involved in some aspects of cross-strait ties. PRC officials began quietly urging the United States to pressure Chen into shelving plans for an island-wide referendum, and they pressed U.S. officials to avoid sending the "wrong signals" to Taiwan. Members of the Taiwan government urged U.S. officials to give more overt support for Taiwan's democracy and to put more pressure on Beijing to lessen its hostility – efforts that some see as setting a precedent for overriding the "six assurances" to Taiwan. U.S. officials were put in the position of continually seeking to re-balance the cross-strait relationship to achieve some sort of stasis in keeping with stated U.S. policy goals.

The cross-strait policy of President Ma's government presents the United States with a different set of challenges. Ma's new approach toward the PRC would seem to be in keeping with U.S. wishes, as U.S. officials in the past have urged both sides to move toward greater conciliation and less confrontation. In 2008, a U.S. State Department spokesman spoke favorably (if somewhat tepidly, in keeping with most U.S. policy pronouncements on Taiwan issues) of the resumption of cross-strait talks under the Ma Administration, responding to a reporter's question with " ... we believe it's important for the two to work towards a peaceful resolution of the ... Cross-Strait issues." [60]

While U.S. policy favors improvements in Taiwan-PRC relations, it has been silent on what should be the speed, depth, and degree of cross-strait conciliation. Some observers worry that the KMT government may be overly responsive to economic imperatives and to pressures from influential Taiwan business interests that have substantial economic investments in China. They worry that the Ma government could reach a swift accommodation with Beijing that may complicate U.S. regional interests.

The implication for U.S. interests is only one factor President Ma will have to continue to consider in pursuing his PRC policy. Ma faces multiple balancing acts. These include efforts to improve cross-strait relations—and Taiwan's economic opportunities on the mainland—while not appearing overly eager to voters who worry that he will sell out Taiwan's political interests in pursuit of closer mainland economic ties. He also will have to strike a balance between those in the electorate who favor unification with China; those who argue for a strong defense for Taiwan and the continuation of U.S. weapons purchases; and those who urge significant improvements in Taiwan's relations with Beijing.

For U.S. Arms Sales

Relatedly, the question of U.S. arms sales to Taiwan takes on new shades of delicacy in an environment of improving Taiwan-PRC ties. While U.S. law mandating arms sales to Taiwan states that these sales shall be "based solely upon ... the needs of Taiwan," such decisions can be and have been a useful U.S. policy lever in U.S.-Taiwan-PRC relations [61].

Either the approval of a major weapons package to Taiwan or an apparent "freeze" in weapons sales can have symbolic significance for either side of the strait. U.S. policymakers will be faced with decisions on what kind of signal a specific U.S. arms sale will send under current circumstances. The PRC objects to U.S. arms sales to Taiwan and has reacted punitively in some cases, so that future U.S. arms sales to Taiwan may have significant implications for cross-strait ties. A recent news story from a Taiwan newspaper alleged that U.S. military officials are concerned that potential Taiwan-PRC military exchanges could provide Beijing with an opportunity to learn details about sensitive U.S. military technology sold to Taiwan and, therefore, could jeopardize future U.S. arms sales to Taiwan [62]

For PRC Policy and Credibility

Despite the challenges that Ma faces, many believe that his policy approach will be an important test of the PRC's stated intentions of approaching cross-strait problems by "putting aside differences and seeking a win-win result" [63] Having railed against President Chen's independence-aspirations for eight years while wooing the KMT, the PRC now is faced with the question of whether it wishes to follow through with creative initiatives if it is to capitalize on the opportunity that a KMT government presents. Rebuffing a new and, at least initially, a more conciliatory Taiwan government could damage the PRC's credibility that it wishes to pursue a peaceful and constructive solution for cross-strait ties. Any perceived PRC reluctance also could serve to revitalize U.S. and congressional opposition to the PRC's Taiwan policy—opposition which remained relatively muted for years in part because of mutual U.S.-PRC problems with former President Chen.

Observers suggest there are a number of options now for Beijing to make meaningful gestures toward Taiwan that would not impinge on PRC sovereignty claims. Beijing has appeared willing to take some guarded steps. These include willingness to restart cross-strait talks on a mutually acceptable basis; a new willingness to entertain Taiwan's aspirations to be a "meaningful participant" in the WHO; and, with the November 2008 meeting between Taiwan's Lien Chan and PRC President Hu Jintao during the APEC meeting, at least the suggestion of a halt to inflexible posturing against Taiwan in APEC and other multilateral organizations. Other such steps could include a suspension of Taiwan-focused military exercises and other military maneuvers in the strait and a meaningful drawing-down of missiles deployed opposite the Taiwan coast.

For Taiwan Democracy

Many Americans have welcomed the 2008 election results as a sign that Taiwan's democracy has continued to ripen and mature. They say Taiwan's democratic development has been validated by having passed the "Huntington test" for established democracies—having two successful, consecutive changes of government through a free and peaceful electoral process [64]. Those harboring concern about how the DPP's supporters would take such a defeat were reassured greatly by the gracious concession speech of candidate Frank Hsieh and the widespread DPP acceptance of the results of the democratic process. To some watching the March 22, 2008 election, the Taiwan electorate also appeared to have attained a new level of maturity and sophistication, apparently motivated more in its election decisions by pragmatic calculations of governmental performance than by more emotional issues involving U.N. membership or sovereignty issues [65]

Some, however, suggest that functional political pluralism in Taiwan may be in trouble over the short term. An effective democracy requires a viable opposition, and the overwhelming KMT electoral victories in 2008 left Taiwan's polity lopsided, the opposition effectively crushed. The DPP has been demoralized and decimated further by the political scandals involving former President Chen, who brought the party from a fledgling opposition party to the pinnacle of power. The scandals, wrote DPP Chairwoman Tsai Ing-wen, have brought the DPP "a kind of sadness so painful it cannot be soothed, and a kind of disappointment so grave it cannot be overcome" [66] Despite the warming U.S.-Taiwan relationship under the KMT, then, many feel that U.S. interests in having Taiwan remain a full-fledged democracy may be compromised should the opposition remain too feeble effectively to monitor and hold accountable the majority party.

LEGISLATION IN THE 111TH CONGRESS

H.Con.Res. 18 (Linder)

Expressing the sense of Congress that the United States should resume normal diplomatic relations with Taiwan. The measure calls on the President to abandon the "one-China" policy, adopt a "one-China, one-Taiwan" policy that recognizes Taiwan sovereignty, and begin establishing normal diplomatic relations with Taiwan. The measure also calls on the President to aggressively support Taiwan's membership in the U.N. and other international organizations for which statehood is a requirement. The measure was introduced on January 9, 2009, and referred to the House Foreign Affairs Committee.

H.Con.Res. 55 (Berkeley)

Recognizing the 30th anniversary of the Taiwan Relations Act. The resolution reaffirms the unwavering U.S. commitment to the Taiwan Relations Act, reaffirms strong U.S. support for Taiwan's democratic development, and supports deepening U.S.-Taiwan ties. The measure was introduced on February 23, 2009, and referred to the House Foreign Affairs Committee's Subcommittee on Asia and the Pacific, which held mark-up on March 19, 2009. The Subcommittee forwarded the bill to the full Committee, amended, by voice vote the same day.

CHRONOLOGY

03/18/09—U.S. American Institute in Taiwan (AIT) chairman Ray Burghardt said that the United States was "comfortable with what's happening" in Taiwan-PRC engagement. The same day, former President Chen Shui-bian appeared at his final pre-trial hearing before going on trial for corruption, scheduled to begin March 26, 2009.
03/17/09—The first luxury cruise ship (Ocean Mystery) to sail directly to Taiwan from the PRC (Shanghai) arrived at Keelung, reportedly carrying 1,600 PRC tourists.

03/16/09—In its first quadrennial report (QDR), Taiwan's Ministry of Defense said that Taiwan would cut its military personnel from 275,000 to 215,000 over the next five years – part of a plan to create an all-volunteer force by December 2014.

03/14/09—The Taiwan government urged the PRC to jettison its "anti-secession" law. The law, passed in March 2005, justifies the use of force to prevent Taiwan independence.

01/13/09—World Health Organization officials sent a letter to the Taiwan government stating that the island henceforth would be included in the International Health Regulations (IHR), a set of legally binding rules governing international commitment to disease surveillance, alert, and response

01/07/09—Taiwan's cross-strait negotiator, Chiang Pin-kung, began a visit to four PRC cities to discuss issues facing Taiwan investors in the mainland.

12/12/08—Former Taiwan President Chen Shui-bian was indicted on charges of corruption, having been arrested on November 12, 2008.

11/21/08 – On November 21, 2008, Taiwan's Lien Chan, a former Vice-President and Premier, met with PRC President Hu Jintao during the Asian Pacific Economic Cooperation (APEC) meeting in Peru. It was said to be the highest-level meeting between the two sides in an international forum since 1949.

10/03/08—The Defense Security Cooperation Agency notified Congress of the possible Foreign Military Sale of six different types of defense articles and equipment, totaling approximately $6.4 billion.

09/08/08—Taiwan announced that it would cancel the live-fire exercise portion of its annual five- day military exercises, in deference to warming ties between Taiwan and the PRC.

09/08/08—Taiwan's Foreign Ministry announced it would seek closer participation in the 16-member Pacific Islands Forum (PIF). Taiwan has taken part every year in the PIF since joining in 1993, but because of PRC objections has been restricted to dialoguing only with its 6 diplomatic South Pacific partners.

08/27/08—The Pentagon announced the sale of 58 Harpoon missiles as well as related support, logistics, and training equipment to Taiwan worth about $101 million.

08/19/08—Taiwan's Special Investigation Unit (SIU) announced it was inviting the Taipei-based Central Bank of China (CBC) and the cabinet-level Financial Supervisory Commission (F SC) to assist in investigating the source of $21 million in a Swiss bank account in the name of former President Chen Shui-bian's daughter-in-law, Huang Jui-ching. SIU investigators said they were looking into possible irregularities in the second-phase financial reform initiated by President Chen in 2004 as a potential source of the funds.

08/18/08—Prosecutors in Taiwan named five suspects in an alleged high-level money laundering scheme involving former President Chen Shui-bian. They included Chen Shui-bian; his wife Wu Shu-jen; Chen's son Chen Chih-chung and his wife Huang Jui-ching; and Wu's brother Wu Ching-mao.

08/17/08—Tsai Ing-wen, head of Taiwan's DPP party, said the current political crisis had come about because the DPP put too much faith and trust in Chen Shui-bian.

08/14/08—Former Taiwan President Chen Shui-bian held a press conference to resign from DPP membership. He admitted failing fully to declare campaign funds and for wiring millions of dollars overseas, and apologized for causing "humiliation" and "irreparable damage" to the party.

08/14/08—Taiwan's Ministry of Foreign Affairs (MOFA) confirmed that the Swiss Confederation's Department of Justice sought assistance from Taiwan about suspected money laundering by Chen's daughter-in-law, Huang Jui-ching.

08/14/08—Taiwan submitted a proposal to the UN Secretariat via St. Vincent and the Solomon Islands (2 of Taiwan's diplomatic relationships), asking the UN to consider permitting Taiwan to have "meaningful participation" in the organization's specialized agencies.

08/13/08—A spokesman for Taiwan's presidential office said that this year's UN bid would focus on "participation" in specialized UN agencies.

08/12/08—AIT Chairman Ray Burghardt gave a dinner for President Ma in Los Angeles. Ma also met with Members of Congress.

08/12/08—Taiwan President Ma YJ left for state visits to Paraguay and the Dominican Republic, returning on the 19th. He flew a commercial flight to the United States—a first for a Taiwan president—and transited through LA (coming) and through San Francisco (returning home).

07/27/08—Taiwan's Sports Affairs Council (SAC—a cabinet-level council) announced that several Taiwan Ministers would attend the 2008 Olympic Games at IOC invitation using National Olympic Committee ID cards. In the past, China's protests had led to the issuance of the less prestigious "Guest Card" for Taiwan officials.

07/22/08—Taiwan's SEF chairman, Chiang Pin-kung, was reported as having said he wants to study and promote the creation of a cross-strait comprehensive economic cooperation agreement (CECA).

07/17/08—Taiwan's cabinet announced it would revise regulations limiting investment by Taiwan companies in China, and that new measures would be put into place August 1. Preliminary reports said that the current investment cap would be abolished for some companies and raised to 60% of net worth for other companies.

06/12/08—The first cross-strait meetings in a decade began between China and Taiwan in Beijing at the Diaoyutai State Guest House, conducted by SEF and ARATS. The two sides reportedly agreed to set up permanent offices in each other's territory and to begin regular weekend direct charter flights.

05/26/08—KMT Chairman Wu Poh-hsiung visited China and met with PRC Party Secretary Hu Jintao at the latter's invitation in the highest-level contact between the two sides of the Taiwan Strait.

05/20/08—Ma Ying-jeou was inaugurated President of Taiwan.

05/19/08—Tsai Ing-wen, considered a moderate in the DPP Party and a former Vice-Premier, was elected chairwoman of the Party.

05/19/08—The WHO rejected Taiwan's bid for observer status.

03/22/08—KMT candidate Ma Ying-jeou was elected president of Taiwan, defeating the rival DPP ticket of Frank Hsieh.

FOR ADDITIONAL READING

CRS Report RS22853, *Taiwan's 2008 Presidential Election*, by Kerry Dumbaugh.

CRS Report RL33684, *Underlying Strains in Taiwan-U.S. Political Relations*, by Kerry Dumbaugh.

CRS Report RS22388, *Taiwan's Political Status: Historical Background and Ongoing Implications*, by Kerry Dumbaugh.

CRS Report RL30957, *Taiwan: Major U.S. Arms Sales Since 1990*, by Shirley A. Kan.

CRS Report RL30341, *China/Taiwan: Evolution of the "One China" Policy—Key Statements from Washington, Beijing, and Taipei*, by Shirley A. Kan.

REFERENCES

[1] Definitions of the "status quo" for Taiwan vary among the parties involved. Some in the United States, such as Georgetown University Professor Robert Sutter, see the "status quo" as the maintenance of balance between the two sides. The former government of Taiwan President Chen Shui-bian interpreted "status quo" to mean that Taiwan was already a fully independent, sovereign state. The current Taiwan government of President Ma Ying-jeou has described the "status quo" more as *de facto* independence. The PRC definition of the "status quo" counts Taiwan as an unalienable part of China.

[2] U.S. weapons sales to Taiwan are governed by Section 2 and Section 3(b) of the Taiwan Relations Act, P.L. 96-8:22 U.S.C., Chapter 48, Sections 3301-3316.

[3] Various participants in crafting U.S. Taiwan policy report differing versions of the "six assurances." Basically, the assurances are that the United States will not change the TRA and will not pressure Taiwan to negotiate with the PRC; or become involved as mediator in negotiations between Taiwan and the PRC. For a more thorough discussion, see CRS Report RL30341, *China/Taiwan: Evolution of the "One China" Policy—Key Statements from Washington, Beijing, and Taipei*, by Shirley A. Kan.

[4] For more detailed discussions of congressional actions at the time, see "Congress and U.S. policy in Asia: New relationships with China and Taiwan," in Congress and Foreign Policy – 1979, House Committee on Foreign Affairs, U.S. Government Printing Office, Washington D.C. 1980, pp. 54-71; Wolff, Lester L. And Simon, David L., eds., Legislative History of the Taiwan Relations Act, American Association for Chinese Studies, Jamaica, New York, 1982; Jones, DuPre, ed., China: U.S. Policy Since 1945, Congressional Quarterly Inc., 1980.

[5] See the American Institute in Taiwan (AIT) website at [http://www.ait.org.tw/en/]

[6] See CRS Report 96-246, *Taiwan: Texts of the Taiwan Relations Act, the U.S. - China Communiques, and the "Six Assurances"*, by Kerry Dumbaugh.

[7] In Chinese, the Nationalist Party is "Kuomintang" (or KMT) in Taiwan and Guomindang (or GMD) in the PRC.

[8] This particular quote is from the 1972 Shanghai Communique issued at the conclusion of President Richard Nixon's landmark trip to China. A somewhat vaguer formulation—"The [United States] acknowledges the Chinese position that there is but one China and Taiwan is part of China."—was part of the 1979 communique normalizing U.S. relations with the PRC.

[9] In this campaign, President Chen and his Vice-president, Annette Lu, were both shot and slightly wounded just before the election. KMT opponents, who believed they were on the verge of victory, called this the "shooting incident," believing it helped the DPP attain victory.

[10] Based on the author's conversations in Taiwan on March 23-24, 2008, with both KMT party officials and with foreign observers.
[11] DPP candidates received 37% of the votes in the 2008 legislative elections, which were held under new rules that favored the KMT. See CRS Report RS22791, *Taiwan's Legislative Elections, January 2008: Implications for U.S. Policy*, by Kerry Dumbaugh.
[12] Shelley Rigger, Brown Associate Professor of East Asian Politics, Davidson College, in a discussion roundtable on Taiwan, March 23, 2008.
[13] "Dollar diplomacy" (or "checkbook diplomacy") refers to the situation in which both Taiwan and the PRC have competed for official diplomatic relations by promising to and investing huge sums in countries that may be wavering in their diplomatic allegiances.
[14] On April 29, 2005, when the KMT was out of power, KMT Chairman Lien Chan met with PRC President Hu Jintao, the first time the leaders of the CCP and KMT had met since World War II.
[15] "Ma's cross-strait economic and trade policies are not ready," DPP News link, July 22, 2008, http://www.dpp.org.tw/.
[16] Wu, Sofia, "Cross-strait talks should be accelerated: president," *Central News Agency* English, June 15, 2008.
[17] According to *The China Post* of August 16, 2008, the resolution was titled "The Need to Examine the Fundamental Rights of the 23 Million People of the Republic of China (Taiwan) to Participate Meaningfully in the Activities of the U.N. Specialized Agencies."
[18] Some have suggested that there may be relevance for Taiwan's current U.N. bid in the fact that Hong Kong's Margaret Chan, a Chinese national, is currently the head of WHO. Chan, was elected to the WHO post in 2006, and presided over several previous rejections of Taiwan's U.N. application.
[19] Hsu, Jenny, "'Taipei' gets direct link to WHO unit," *Taipei Times*, January 23, 2009, p. 1.
[20] Xie Yu, "Taiwan put under WHO health rules," *China Daily*, February 12, 2009.
[21] Chen, Jian, "WHA arrangements directed by China unacceptable: foreign minister," *Central News Agency*, March 19, 2009.
[22] Chan, Rachel, "U.S. will not mediate on WHA issue: AIT chair," *Central News Agency* English, March 18, 2009.
[23] Resolutions introduced in the 110th Congress in support of Taiwan's U.N. bid include H.Con.Res. 73 and H.Con.Res. 250.
[24] A State Department spokesman, in response to a press question at the State Department press briefing of March 20, 2002.
[25] Dennis Wilder, National Security Council Senior Director for Asian Affairs, at a White House press briefing on the President's September APEC trip, August 30, 2007.
[26] Hong Kong also enjoys separate membership in these organizations from its sovereign, the PRC.
[27] DPP Chairwoman Tsai Ing-wen, quoted in "DPP chief 'shocked' by former President Chen's graft scandal," *The China Post* in English, August 17, 2008.
[28] "Former president quits DPP in disgrace," *Central News Agency* in English, August 15, 2008.

[29] After questioning by prosecutors on August 12, 2008, former President Chen was quoted as saying "I have never put any illegal income in my own or in my family's pockets. I believe the judiciary will prove me innocent." "Former President Chen professes his innocence after questioning," *Taiwan News Online*, August 13, 2008.
[30] "Does corruption stop here?" Taipei Times, August 22, 2008, p. 8.
[31] The report, issued on March 27, 2009, (Taiwan's Economic Situation and Outlook), can be found at the website: http://www.cepd.gov.tw/encontent/m1.aspx?sNo=0011655.
[32] USTR News, "USTR announces conclusion of the Special 301 Out-of-Cycle review for Taiwan," January 16, 2009, http://www.ustr.gov/assets/Document_Library/ Press_Releases/2009/January/asset_upload_file824_15293.pdf?ht=.
[33] "2008 Special 301 Report," Office of the United States Trade Representative, text at http://www.ustr.gov/assets/Document_Library/Reports_Publications/2008/2008_ Special_301_Report/asset_upload_file553_14869.pdf
[34] Lin Yi-feng and Wu, Lilian, "President Ma arrives in San Francisco," *Central News Agency* in English, August 18, 2008.
[35] Negotiations for the TIFA were conducted through the respective U.S. and Taiwan unofficial representative bodies at the time: the American Institute in Taiwan (AIT), and the Coordination Council for North American Affairs (CCNAA).
[36] S.Con.Res. 60 (Sen. Baucus), introduced on December 18, 2007; and H.Con.Res. 137 (Rep. Berkley), introduced on May 1, 2007, both express congressional support for the opening of FTA negotiations with Taiwan.
[37] The Chairman of Taiwan's Mainland Affairs Council, for instance, expressed opposition to the idea: "No CEPA to be signed with China: MAC," *The China Post*, October 17, 2008.
[38] For details on Taiwan's arms purchases, see CRS Report RL30957, *Taiwan: Major U.S. Arms Sales Since 1990*, by Shirley A. Kan.
[39] "Inhofe urges support of Taiwan," June 30, 2008 press release. For a full text, see http://inhofe.senate.gov/public/index. cfm?FuseAction=PressRoom.PressReleases& ContentRecord _id=DAB422E7-802A-23AD-4 101- 32FFB910FFE4.
[40] Admiral Timothy Keating hinted at a freeze during a briefing at the Heritage Foundation on July 16, 2008.
[41] State Department spokesman Sean McCormack, in response to a question at the Daily Briefing on July 17, 2008.
[42] U.S. Department of Defense, Office of the Assistant Secretary of Defense (Public Affairs), No. 717-08, August 25, 2008. http://www.defenselink.mil/contracts/ contract.aspx?contractid=3 848
[43] The notifications can be found on the DSCA website under "36(b) Arms Sales Notifications." http://www.dsca.mil/ PressReleases/36-b/36b_index.htm
[44] For additional information on the Visa Waiver Program, see CRS Report RL32221, *Visa Waiver Program*, by Alison Siskin.
[45] The measure was enacted in 2007 in P.L. 110-53, although the visa waiver did not become available until October 2008
[46] Chairman Raymond Burghardt, AIT Press Conference, Taipei, Taiwan, March 18, 2009, http://www.ait.org.tw/en/news/officialtext/viewer.aspx?id=200903 1901.

[47] From the Q & A session with Vice President Cheney following his speech at Fudan University in Shanghai, broadcast by Beijing CCTV in English, found in *FBIS*, April 15, 2004.
[48] See CRS Report RL33684, *Underlying Strains in Taiwan-U.S. Political Relations*, by Kerry Dumbaugh.
[49] "There are limitations with respect to what the United States will support as Taiwan considers possible changes to its constitution." Testimony of Assistant Secretary of State James A. Kelly before the House International Relations Committee, April 21, 2004.
[50] Interview with former U.S. government official, June 22, 2006.
[51] This was the formulation in the U.S.-PRC "Shanghai Communique" of 1972, which held that "The United States acknowledges that all Chinese on either side of the Taiwan Strait maintain there is but one China and that Taiwan is a part of China. The [U.S.] Government does not challenge that position." In repeating this assertion, the Joint Communique of 1979 establishing official relations with the PRC eliminated specific mention of either government: "The Government of the United States of America acknowledges the Chinese position that there is but one China and Taiwan is part of China." See CRS Report 96-246, for full texts of the Taiwan Relations Act and the three U.S.-China communiques.
[52] Coen Blaauw, of FAPA, and John Tkacik, of The Heritage Foundation, are two proponents of this view.
[53] Tkacik, John, ed. *Rethinking One China*, The Heritage Foundation, December 1, 2004.
[54] Apart from the Taiwan Policy Review, several other Clinton Administration decisions led to debates over whether the United States had changed its policy on Taiwan. In 1997-1998, the White House made statements that became known as the "three noes" - that the United States did not support a "one China, One Taiwan" policy, Taiwan independence, or Taiwan membership in international organizations requiring statehood. In 2000, the Clinton Administration made further incremental changes to U.S. rhetoric by adding the U.S. expectation that any resolution to the Taiwan issue would not only be peaceful, but decided "with the assent of the Taiwan people." For these and other U.S. policy statements, see CRS Report RL30341, *China/Taiwan: Evolution of the "One China" Policy—Key Statements from Washington, Beijing, and Taipei*, by Shirley A. Kan.
[55] The only such contact in recent years was the Taiwan visit of Deputy U.S. Trade Representative Karan Bhatia in May-June 2006.
[56] Some critics of U.S. policy suggest that the PRC's search for U.S. involvement is a "united front" tactic designed primarily to isolate Taiwan from some of its U.S. support.
[57] Former U.S. government official interviewed on July 5, 2006.
[58] Bush, Richard and Romberg, Alan, "Cross-Strait Moderation and the United States," the Brookings Institution, March 30, 2009.
[59] John Tkacik, from The Heritage Foundation, is one of the proponents of this view.
[60] Acting Deputy Spokesman Gonzalo R. Gallegos, State Department Daily Press Briefing, June 12, 2008.
[61] Arms sales to Taiwan are mandated in P.L. 96-8, the Taiwan Relations Act (TRA). Section 3302(b) of U.S.C. 22, Ch. 48, Sect. 3301-3316, enacted April 10, 1979.

[62] Lowther, William, "Pentagon wary of PRC-Taiwan ties," *Taipei Times*, January 7, 2009, p. 1.
[63] Reportedly language in a letter written to the U.N. Secretary General by the PRC's U.N. Ambassador Wang Guangya concerning Taiwan's current bid for "meaningful participation" in the U.N. "China gives U.N. bid cold shoulder," *CNA*, September 10, 2008.
[64] Samuel P. Huntington defined this process in his book *The Third Wave: Democratization in the Late Twentieth Century*, Norman and London, 1991. Taiwan qualifies by virtue of the DPP having wrested power from the KMT in 2000 and the KMT having regained power in 2008.
[65] Many U.S. and other foreign election observers were in Taiwan before and after the March 22 election, including this author. This report draws heavily on these personal observations and insights.
[66] DPP Chairwoman Tsai Ing-wen, "An open letter to DPP supporters," *Taipei Times*, August 27, 2008, p. 8.

In: Political and Economic Developments in Asia
Editor: Felix Chin

ISBN: 978-1-61209-783-1
©2011 Nova Science Publishers, Inc.

Chapter 9

U.S.-CHINA MILITARY CONTACTS: ISSUES FOR CONGRESS[*]

Shirley A. Kan

ABSTRACT

This CRS Report, updated as warranted, discusses policy issues regarding military-to-military (mil-to-mil) contacts with the People's Republic of China (PRC) and provides a record of major contacts and crises since 1993. The United States suspended military contacts with China and imposed sanctions on arms sales in response to the Tiananmen Crackdown in 1989. In 1993, the Clinton Administration re-engaged with the top PRC leadership, including China's military, the People's Liberation Army (PLA). Renewed military exchanges with the PLA have not regained the closeness reached in the 1980s, when U.S.-PRC strategic cooperation against the Soviet Union included U.S. arms sales to China. Improvements and deteriorations in overall bilateral relations have affected military contacts, which were close in 1997-1998 and 2000, but marred by the 1995-1996 Taiwan Strait crisis, mistaken NATO bombing of a PRC embassy in 1999, the EP-3 aircraft collision crisis in 2001, and aggressive naval confrontations (including in March 2009).

In early 2001, the Bush Administration continued the policy of engagement with China, but the Pentagon skeptically reviewed and cautiously resumed military-to-military contacts. Secretary of Defense Donald Rumsfeld, in 2002, resumed the Defense Consultative Talks (DCT) with the PLA (first held in 1997) and, in 2003, hosted General Cao Gangchuan, a Vice Chairman of the Central Military Commission (CMC) and Defense Minister. General Richard Myers (USAF), Chairman of the Joint Chiefs of Staff, visited China in January 2004, as the highest ranking U.S. military officer to do so since November 2000. Visiting Beijing in September 2005 as the Commander of the Pacific Command (PACOM), Admiral William Fallon sought to advance mil-to-mil contacts, including combined exercises. Secretary Rumsfeld visited China in October 2005, the first visit by a defense secretary since William Cohen's visit in 2000. Fallon invited PLA observers to the U.S. "Valiant Shield" exercise that brought three aircraft carriers to waters off Guam in June 2006. In July 2006, a CMC Vice Chairman, General Guo

---

[*] This is an edited, reformatted and augmented version of CRS Report RL32496, dated April 15, 2009.

Boxiong, made the first visit to the United States by the highest ranking PLA commander after 1998.

Issues for the 111th Congress include whether the Obama Administration has complied with legislation overseeing dealings with the PLA and has pursued a program of contacts with the PLA that advances a prioritized list of U.S. security interests. Oversight legislation includes the Foreign Relations Authorization Act for FY1990-FY1991 (P.L. 101-246); National Defense Authorization Act for FY2000 (P.L. 106-65); and National Defense Authorization Act for FY2006 (P.L. 109-163). Skeptics and proponents of military exchanges with the PRC have debated whether the contacts have significant value for achieving U.S. objectives and whether the contacts have contributed to the PLA's warfighting capabilities that might harm U.S. security interests. Some have argued about whether the value that U.S. officials have placed on the contacts overly extends leverage to the PLA. U.S. interests in military contacts with China include communication, conflict prevention, and crisis management; transparency and reciprocity; tension reduction over Taiwan; weapons nonproliferation; strategic nuclear and space talks; counterterrorism; and accounting for POW/MIAs.

Despite U.S. pursuit of mil-to-mil dialogues, U.S. defense officials have reported inadequate cooperation from the PLA, including denials of port visits at Hong Kong by U.S. Navy ships around Thanksgiving 2007. Also, the PLA has tried to use its suspensions of exchanges (the latest in October 2008) to demand cessations of U.S. arms sales to Taiwan, U.S. legal restrictions on contacts with the PLA, the Pentagon's report to Congress on PRC Military Power, etc. The PRC's aggressive harassment of U.S. surveillance ships (including the Impeccable in March 2009) have shown the limits to the value of mil-to-mil talks and PLA restraint now and the future.

OVERVIEW OF U.S. POLICY

U.S. leaders have applied military contacts as one tool and point of leverage in the broader policy toward the People's Republic of China (PRC). The first part of this CRS Report discusses policy issues regarding such military-to-military (mil-to-mil) contacts. The second part provides a record of such contacts since 1993, when the United States resumed exchanges after suspending them in response to the Tiananmen Crackdown in 1989. Congress has exercised important oversight of the military relationship with China.

Cooperation in the Cold War

Since the mid-1970s, even before the normalization of relations with Beijing, the debate over policy toward the PRC has examined how military ties might advance U.S. security interests, beginning with the imperatives of the Cold War [1]. In January 1980, Secretary of Defense Harold Brown visited China and laid the groundwork for a relationship with the PRC's military, the People's Liberation Army (PLA), intended to consist of strategic dialogue, reciprocal exchanges in functional areas, and arms sales. Furthermore, U.S. policy changed in 1981 to remove the ban on arms sales to China. Secretary of Defense Casper Weinberger visited Beijing in September 1983. In 1984, U.S. policymakers worked to advance discussions on military technological cooperation with China [2]. Between 1985 and 1987, the United States agreed to four programs of Foreign Military Sales (FMS): modernization of artillery ammunition production facilities; modernization of avionics in F-8 fighters; sale of four Mark-46 anti-submarine torpedoes; and sale of four AN/TPQ-37 artillery-locating radars [3].

Suspensions after Tiananmen Crackdown

The United States suspended mil-to-mil contacts and arms sales in response to the Tiananmen Crackdown in June 1989. (Although the killing of peaceful demonstrators took place beyond just Tiananmen Square in the capital of Beijing on June 4, 1989, the crackdown is commonly called the Tiananmen Crackdown in reference to the square that was the focal point of the nation-wide pro-democracy movement.) Approved in February 1990, the Foreign Relations Authorization Act for FY1990-FY1991 (P.L. 101-246) enacted into law sanctions imposed on arms sales and other cooperation, while allowing for waivers in the U.S. national interest. In April 1990, China canceled the program (called "Peace Pearl") to upgrade the avionics of the F-8 fighters [4].

In December 1992, President Bush decided to close out the four cases of suspended FMS programs, returning PRC equipment, reimbursing unused funds, and delivering sold items without support [5]

Re-engagement

In the fall of 1993, the Clinton Administration began to re-engage the PRC leadership up to the highest level and across the board, including the PLA. However, results were limited and the military relationship did not regain the closeness reached in the 1980s, when the United States and China cooperated strategically against the Soviet Union and such cooperation included arms sales to the PLA. Improvements and deteriorations in overall bilateral relations affected mil-tomil contacts, which had close ties in 1997-1998 and 2000, but were marred by the 1995-1996 Taiwan Strait crisis, mistaken NATO bombing of the PRC embassy in Yugoslavia in 1999, and the EP-3 aircraft collision crisis in 2001.

Re-evaluation

Since 2001, the George W. Bush Administration has continued the policy of engagement with the PRC, while the Pentagon has skeptically reviewed and cautiously resumed a program of mil-tomil exchanges. Secretary of Defense Donald Rumsfeld reviewed the mil-to-mil contacts to assess the effectiveness of the exchanges in meeting U.S. objectives of reciprocity and transparency. Soon after the review began, on April 1, 2001, a PLA Navy F-8 fighter collided with a U.S. Navy EP-3 reconnaissance plane over the South China Sea [6]. Upon surviving the collision, the EP-3's crew made an emergency landing on China's Hainan island. The PLA detained the 24 U.S. Navy personnel for 11 days. Instead of acknowledging that the PLA had started aggressive interceptions of U.S. reconnaissance flights in December 2000 and apologizing for the accident, top PRC ruler Jiang Zemin demanded an apology and compensation from the United States. Rumsfeld limited mil-to-mil contacts after the crisis, subject to case-by-case approval, after the White House objected to a suspension of contacts with the PLA as outlined in an April 30 Defense Department memo. Rumsfeld told reporters on May 8, 2001, that he decided against visits to China by U.S. ships or aircraft and against social contacts, because "it really wasn't business as usual." Deputy Secretary of Defense Paul Wolfowitz reported to Congress on June 8, 2001, that mil-to-mil exchanges for 2001 remained under review by Secretary Rumsfeld and exchanges with the PLA would be conducted "selectively and on a case-by-case basis." The United States did not transport the damaged EP-3 out of China until July 3, 2001.

The Bush Administration hosted PRC Vice President Hu Jintao in Washington in the spring of 2002 (with an honor cordon at the Pentagon) and President Jiang Zemin in Crawford, Texas, in October 2002. Afterwards, Secretary of Defense Rumsfeld, in late 2002, resumed the Defense Consultative Talks (DCT) with the PLA (first held in 1997) and, in 2003, hosted General Cao Gangchuan, a Vice Chairman of the Central Military Commission (CMC) and Defense Minister. (The CMC under the Communist Party of China (CPC) commands the PLA. The Ministry of Defense and its titles are used in contacts with foreign militaries.) General Richard Myers (USAF), Chairman of the Joint Chiefs of Staff, visited China in January 2004, as the highest ranking U.S. military officer to do so since November 2000. (see Table 1 on the PLA's high command and the summary of senior-level military visits.)

Visiting Beijing in January 2004, Deputy Secretary of State Richard Armitage met with PRC leaders, including General Cao Gangchuan. Armitage acknowledged that "the military-to-military relationship had gotten off to a rocky start," but noted that the relationship had improved so that "it's come pretty much full cycle." He said that "we're getting back on track with the military-tomilitary relationship" [7].

Resumption

Still, mil-to-mil interactions remained "exceedingly limited," according to the Commander of the Pacific Command, Admiral William Fallon, who visited China to advance mil-to-mil contacts in September 2005. He discussed building relationships at higher and lower ranks, cooperation in responding to natural disasters and controlling avian flu, and reducing tensions. Fallon also said that he would seek to enhance military-to-military contacts with China and invite PLA observers to U.S. military exercises, an issue of dispute in Washington [8]. In October 2005, Defense Secretary Donald Rumsfeld visited China, the first visit by a defense secretary since William Cohen's visit in 2000. After Rumsfeld's visit, which was long sought by the PLA for the perceived full resumption of the military relationship, General Guo Boxiong, a CMC Vice Chairman and the PLA's highest ranking officer visited the United States in July 2006, the first such visit since General Zhang Wannian's visit in 1998.

At a news conference on March 7, 2007, Defense Secretary Robert Gates said that he did not see China as a "strategic adversary" of the United States, but "a partner in some respects" and a "competitor in other respects." Gates stressed the importance of engaging the PRC "on all facets of our relationship as a way of building mutual confidence." Nonetheless, U.S. officials have expressed concerns about inadequate "transparency" from the PLA, most notably when it tested an anti-satellite (ASAT) weapon in January 2007. At a news conference in China on March 23, 2007, the Chairman of the Joint Chiefs of Staff, Marine

General Peter Pace, said the primary concern for the bilateral relationship is "miscalculation and misunderstanding based on misinformation."

Table 1. The PLA's High Command

		Central Military Commission (CMC) of the CPC	
Chairman		Hu Jintao	CPC General Secretary; PRC President
Vice Chm	General	Guo Boxiong	Politburo Member
Vice Chm	General	Xu Caihou	Politburo Member
Member	General	Liang Guanglie	Defense Minister
Member	General	Chen Bingde	Chief of General Staff (GSD)
Member	General	Li Jinai	Director of GPD
Member	General	Liao Xilong	Director of GLD
Member	General	Chang Wanquan	Director of GAD
Member	General	Jing Zhiyuan	Commander of the 2nd Artillery
Member	Admiral	Wu Shengli	Commander of the Navy
Member	General	Xu Qiliang	Commander of the Air Force

Notes: Jiang Zemin was installed as the previous chairman of the CPC's CMC in November 1989 and remained in this position after handing other positions as CPC general secretary and PRC president to Hu Jintao. Jiang had ruled as the general secretary of the CPC from June 1989 until November 2002, when he stepped down at the 16th CPC Congress in favor of Hu Jintao. Jiang concurrently represented the PRC as president from March 1993 until March 2003, when he stepped down at the 10th National People's Congress. At the 4th plenum of the 16th Central Committee in September 2004, Jiang resigned as CMC chairman, allowing Hu to complete the transition of power. At the same time, General Xu Caihou rose from a CMC member to a vice chairman, and the commanders of the PLA Air Force, Navy, and 2nd Artillery rose to be CMC members for the first time in the PLA's history, reflecting.

Table 2. Summary of Senior-Level Military Visits Since 1994

Year	Defense Secretary/ Minister	Highest Ranking Officer	Defense Consultative Talks
1994	William Perry		
1995			
1996	Chi Haotian		
1997		John Shalikashvili	1st DCT
1998	William Cohen	Zhang Wannian	2nd DCT
1999			
2000	William Cohen	Henry Shelton	3rd DCT; 4th DCT
2001			
2002			5th DCT
2003	Cao Gangchuan		
2004		Richard Myers	6th DCT
2005	Donald Rumsfeld		7th DCT
2006		Guo Boxiong	8th DCT
2007	Robert Gates	Peter Pace	9th DCT

Deputy Under Secretary of Defense Richard Lawless testified to the House Armed Services Committee on June 13, 2007, that "in the absence of adequate explanation for capabilities which are growing dynamically, both in terms of pace and scope, we are put in the position of having to assume the most dangerous intent a capability offers." He noted a lack of response from the PLA about a U.S. offer in 2006 to talk about strategic nuclear weapons.

Figure 1. Map - China's Military Regions.

In November 2007, despite various unresolved issues, Secretary Gates visited China, and the PLA agreed to a long-sought U.S. goal of a "hotline." Later in the month, despite a number of senior U.S. visits to China (particularly by U.S. Navy Admirals and Secretary Gates) to promote the milto-mil relationship, the PRC denied port calls at Hong Kong for U.S. Navy minesweepers in distress and for the aircraft carrier USS Kitty Hawk for the Thanksgiving holiday and family reunions, according to the PACOM Commander and Chief of Naval Operations (CNO), Admirals Timothy Keating and Gary Roughead. The Pentagon protested to the PLA [9]

Congressional Oversight

Congress has exercised oversight of various aspects of military exchanges with China. Issues for Congress include whether the Administration has complied with legislation overseeing dealings with the PLA and has determined a program of contacts with the PLA that advances, and does not harm, U.S. security interests.

Section 902 of the Foreign Relations Authorization Act for FY1990- FY1991 (P.L. 101-246) prohibits arms sales to China, among other stipulations, in response to the Tiananmen Crackdown in 1989. Section 1201 of the National Defense Authorization Act for FY2000 (P.L. 106-65) restricts "inappropriate exposure" of the PLA to certain operational areas and requires annual reports on contacts with the PLA. Section 1211 of the National Defense Authorization Act for FY2006 (P.L. 109-163) prohibits procurement from any "Communist Chinese military company" for goods and services on the Munitions List, with exceptions for U.S. military ship or aircraft visits to the PRC, testing, and intelligence-collection; as well as waiver authority for the Secretary of Defense. (See detailed discussion below.)

	Select Abbreviations
AMS	Academy of Military Science
CMC	Central Military Commission
COSTIND	Commission of Science, Technology, and Industry for National Defense
CPC	Communist Party of China
DCT	Defense Consultative Talks
DPMO	Defense POW/Missing Personnel Office
GAD	General Armament Department
GLD	General Logistics Department
GPD	General Political Department
GSD	General Staff Department
MR	Military Region
MMCA	Military Maritime Consultative Agreement
NDU	National Defense University
PACOM	Pacific Command
PLAAF	People's Liberation Army Air Force
PLAN	People's Liberation Army Navy

POLICY ISSUES FOR CONGRESS

Skepticism in the United States about the value of military exchanges with China has increased after the experiences in the 1990s; crises like the PLA's missile exercises targeting Taiwan in 1995-1996, mistaken bombing of the PRC embassy in Belgrade in 1999, and the F-8/EP-3 collision crisis of 2001; and changes in the U.S. policy approach. Since 2002, President Bush has pursued a closer relationship with the PRC.

As the Defense Department gradually resumes the mil-to-mil relationship in that context, policy issues for Congress include whether the Administration has complied with legislation and has used leverage effectively in its contacts with the PLA to advance a prioritized list of U.S. security interests, while balancing security concerns about the PLA's warfighting capabilities.

Congressional Oversight

One issue for Congress in examining the military relationship with the PRC is the role of Congress, including the extent of congressional oversight of the Administration's policy. Congress could, as it has in the past, consider options to:

- Host PLA delegations on Capitol Hill or meet them at other venues
- Engage with the PLA as an aspect of visits by Codels to China
- Receive briefings by the Administration before and/or after military visits
- Hold hearings on related issues
- Investigate or oversee investigations of prisoner-of-war/missing-in-action (POW/MIA) cases (once under the specialized jurisdiction of the Senate Select Committee on POW/MIA Affairs)
- Write letters to Administration officials to express congressional concerns
- Require reports from the Pentagon, particularly in unclassified form
- Review interactions at the Asia-Pacific Center for Security Studies of the Pacific Command (PACOM) in Hawaii
- Fund or prohibit funding for certain commissions or activities
- Pass legislation on sanctions and exchanges with the PLA
- Assess the Administration's adherence to laws on sanctions, contacts, and reporting requirements
- Obtain and review the Department of Defense (DOD)'s program for upcoming mil-to-mil contacts, particularly proposed programs already discussed with the PLA.

Arms Sales

Congress has oversight of sanctions imposed after the Tiananmen Crackdown that were enacted in Section 902 of the Foreign Relations Authorization Act for FY1 990 and FY1 991 (P.L. 101- 246). The sanctions continue to prohibit the issuance of licenses to export Munitions List items to China, including helicopters and helicopter parts, as well as crime control equipment. The President has waiver authority.

Related to views of the U.S. ban on arms sales is the European arms embargo. In January 2004, the European Union (EU) decided to reconsider whether to lift its embargo on arms sales to China. On January 28, 2004, a State Department spokesman acknowledged that the United States has held "senior-level" discussions with France and other countries in the EU about the issue of whether to lift the embargo on arms sales to China. He said, "certainly for the United States, our statutes and regulations prohibit sales of defense items to China. We believe that others should maintain their current arms embargoes as well. We believe that the U.S. and European prohibitions on arms sales are complementary, were imposed for the same reasons, specifically serious human rights abuses, and that those reasons remain valid today" [10] At a hearing of the House International Relations Committee on February 11, 2004, Representative Steve Chabot asked Secretary of State Colin Powell about the EU's reconsideration of the arms embargo against China, as supported by France. Powell responded that he raised this issue with the foreign ministers of France, Ireland, United Kingdom, and Germany, and expressed opposition to a change in the EU's policy at this time in light of the PLA's missiles arrayed against Taiwan, the referendums on sensitive political issues then planned in Taiwan, and China's human rights conditions [11].

Joint Defense Conversion Commission

In China in October 1994, Secretary of Defense William Perry and PLA General Ding Henggao, Director of the Commission of Science, Technology, and Industry for National Defense (COSTIND), [12] set up the U.S.-China Joint Defense Conversion Commission. Its stated goal was to facilitate economic cooperation and technical exchanges and cooperation in the area of defense conversion.

However, on June 1, 1995, the House National Security Committee issued H.Rept. 104-131 (for the National Defense Authorization Act for FY1996) and expressed concerns that this commission led to U.S. assistance to PRC firms with direct ties to the PLA and possible subsidies to the PLA. The committee inserted a section to prohibit the use of DOD funds for activities associated with the commission. The Senate's bill had no similar language. On January 22, 1996, conferees reported in Conference Report 104-450 that they agreed to a provision (Section 1343 in P.L. 104-106) to require the Secretary of Defense to submit semi-annual reports on the commission. They also noted that continued U.S.-PRC security dialogue "can promote stability in the region and help protect American interests and the interests of America's Asian allies." Nonetheless, they warned that Congress intends to examine whether that dialogue has produced "tangible results" in human rights, transparency in military spending and doctrine, missile and nuclear nonproliferation, and other important U.S. security interests. Then, in the National Defense Authorization Act for FY1997 (P.L. 104-201), enacted in September 23, 1996, Congress banned DOD from using any funds for any activity associated with the commission until 15 days after the first semi-annual report is received by Congress. In light of this controversy, Secretary Perry terminated the commission and informed Congress in a letter dated July 18, 1996.

Past Reporting Requirement

Also in 1996, the House National Security Committee issued H.Rept. 104-563 (for the National Defense Authorization Act of FY1997) that sought a "full accounting and detailed presentation" of all DOD interaction with the PRC government and PLA, including technology-sharing, conducted during 1994-1996 and proposed for 1997-1998, and required a classified and unclassified report by February 1, 1997. DOD submitted the unclassified report on February 21, 1997, and did not submit a classified version, saying that the unclassified report was comprehensive and that no contacts covered in the report included the release of classified material or technology sharing.

Programs of Exchanges

Certain Members of Congress have written to the Secretary of Defense to express concerns that mil-to-mil exchanges have not adequately benefitted U.S. interests. In early 1999, under the Clinton Administration, the Washington Times disclosed the existence of a "Gameplan for 1999 U.S.-Sino Defense Exchanges," and Pentagon spokesperson Kenneth Bacon confirmed that an exchange program had been under way for years [13]. Representative Dana Rohrabacher wrote a letter to Secretary of Defense William Cohen, saying that "after reviewing the 'Game Plan,' it appears evident that a number of events involving PLA logistics, acquisitions, quartermaster and chemical corps representatives may benefit PLA modernization to the detriment of our allies in the Pacific region and, ultimately, the lives of own service members." He requested a detailed written description of various exchanges [14]

In December 2001, under the Bush Administration, Senator Bob Smith and Representative Dana Rohrabacher wrote to Secretary of Defense Donald Rumsfeld, expressing concerns about renewed military contacts with the PRC. They contended that military exchanges failed to reduce tensions (evident in the EP-3 crisis), lacked reciprocity, and provided militarily-useful information to the PLA. They charged that the Clinton Administration "largely ignored" the spirit and intent of legislation governing military exchanges with the PLA, including a "violation" of the law by allowing the PLA to visit the Joint Forces Command in August 2000, and, as initiators of the legislation, they "reminded" Rumsfeld of the congressional restrictions [15].

Restrictions in the FY2000 NDAA

Enacted on October 5, 1999, the FY2000 National Defense Authorization Act (NDAA) set parameters to contacts with the PLA. Section 1201 of the NDAA for FY2000 (P.L. 106-65) prohibits the Secretary of Defense from authorizing any mil-to-mil contact with the PLA if that contact would "create a national security risk due to an inappropriate exposure" of the PLA to any of the following 12 operational areas (with exceptions granted to any search and rescue or humanitarian operation or exercise):

- Force projection operations
- Nuclear operations
- Advanced combined-arms and joint combat operations
- Advanced logistical operations
- Chemical and biological defense and other capabilities related to weapons of mass destruction
- Surveillance and reconnaissance operations
- Joint warfighting experiments and other activities related to transformations in warfare
- Military space operations
- Other advanced capabilities of the Armed Forces
- Arms sales or military-related technology transfers
- Release of classified or restricted information
- Access to a DOD laboratory.

The Secretary of Defense—rather than an authority in Congress or outside of the Defense Department—is also required to submit an annual written certification by December 31 of each year as to whether any military contact with China that the Secretary of Defense authorized in that year was a "violation" of the restrictions.

At a hearing of the House Armed Services Committee on March 9, 2006, Admiral Fallon, Commander of the Pacific Command, raised with Representative Victor Snyder the issue of whether to modify this legislation to relax restrictions on contacts with the PLA [16]. Skeptics say that it is not necessary to change or lift the law to enhance exchanges, while the law contains prudent parameters that do not ban all contacts. A third option would be for

Congress or the Secretary of Defense to clarify what type of mil-to-mil contact with the PLA would "create a national security risk due to an inappropriate exposure." At a hearing of the House Armed Services Committee on June 13, 2007, Deputy Under Secretary of Defense Richard Lawless contended that limitations in the law should not change. The PLA objects to the U.S. law, claiming that it restricts the military-to-military relationship.

Required Reports and Classification

Section 1201(f) of the NDAA for FY2000 required an unclassified report by March 31, 2000, on past military-to-military contacts with the PRC. The Office of the Secretary of Defense submitted this report in January 2001.

Section 1201(e) requires an annual report, by March 31 of each year starting in 2001, from the Secretary of Defense on the Secretary's assessment of the state of mil-to-mil exchanges and contacts with the PLA, including past contacts, planned contacts, the benefits that the PLA expects to gain, the benefits that DOD expects to gain, and the role of such contacts for the larger security relationship with the PRC. The law did not specify whether the report shall be unclassified and/or classified. In the report submitted in January 2001 (on past mil-to-mil exchanges), the Pentagon stated that "as a matter of policy, all exchange activities are conducted at the unclassified level. Thus, there is no data included on the section addressing PLA access to classified data as a result of exchange activities." On June 8, 2001, Deputy Secretary of Defense Paul Wolfowitz signed and submitted an unclassified report on the mil-to-mil exchanges in 2000 under the Clinton Administration and did not provide a schedule of activities for 2001, saying that the 2001 program was under review by the Secretary of Defense.

However, concerning contacts with the PLA under the Bush Administration, Secretary of Defense Donald Rumsfeld submitted reports on military exchanges with China in May 2002, May 2003, and May 2005 (for 2003 and 2004) that were classified "Confidential" and not made public [17]. In July 2006, Secretary of Defense Donald Rumsfeld submitted an unclassified report on contacts in 2005 [18] Secretary of Defense Robert Gates submitted an unclassified report in June 2007 for 2006 [19]. In March 2008, Deputy Defense Secretary Gordon England submitted an unclassified report to Congress for 2007 [20].

Procurement Prohibition in FY2006 NDAA

Section 1211 of the National Defense Authorization Act for FY2006 (signed into law as P.L. 109- 163 on January 6, 2006) prohibits procurement from any "Communist Chinese military company" for goods and services on the Munitions List, with exceptions for U.S. military ship or aircraft visits to the PRC, testing, and intelligence-collection; as well as waiver authority for the Secretary of Defense. Original language reported by the House Armed Services Committee in H.R. 1815 on May 20, 2005, would have prohibited the Secretary of Defense from any procurement of goods or services from any such company. S. 1042 did not have similar language. During conference, the Senate receded after limiting the ban to goods and services on the U.S. Munitions List; providing for exceptions for procurement in connection with U.S. military ship or aircraft visits, testing, and intelligence-collection; and authorizing waivers. The House passed the conference report (H.Rept. 109-360) on December 19, 2005, and the Senate agreed to it on December 21, 2005.

Leverage to Pursue U.S. Security Objectives

Objectives

At different times, under the Clinton and Bush Administrations, DOD has pursued exchanges with the PLA to various degrees of closeness as part of the policy of engagement in the bilateral relationship with China. The record of the mil-to-mil contacts in over ten years can be used to evaluate the extent to which those contacts provided tangible benefits to advance U.S. security goals.

The Pentagon's last East Asia strategy report issued by Secretary of Defense Cohen in November 1998 placed "comprehensive engagement" with China in third place among nine components of the U.S. strategy. It said that U.S.-PRC dialogue was "critical" to ensure understanding of each other's regional security interests, reduce misperceptions, increase understanding of PRC security concerns, and build confidence to "avoid military accidents and miscalculations." While calling the strategic non-targeting agreement announced at the summit in June 1998 a "symbolic" action, it asserted that the action "reassured both sides and reaffirmed our constructive relationship." The report further pointed to the presidential hotline set up in May 1998, Military Maritime Consultative Agreement (MMCA), and Defense Consultative Talks (DCT) as achievements in engagement with the PLA [21]

Under the Bush Administration, in a report to Congress on June 8, 2001, required by the NDAA for FY2000, P.L. 106-65, Deputy Secretary of Defense Paul Wolfowitz wrote that military exchanges in 2000 sought to:

- foster an environment conducive to frank, open discussion
- complement the broader effort to engage the PRC
- reduce the likelihood of miscalculations regarding cross-strait issues.

Deputy Secretary of Defense Paul Wolfowitz told reporters on May 31, 2002, that "we believe that the contact between American military personnel and Chinese military personnel can reduce misunderstandings on both sides and can help build a better basis for cooperation when opportunities arise. So we'd like to enhance those opportunities for interaction but we believe that to be successful we have to have principles of transparency and reciprocity. It's very important that there's mutual benefit to both sides.... The more each country knows about what the other one is doing, the less danger is there, I believe, of misunderstanding and confrontation" [22].

In agreeing to discuss a resumption of mil-to-mil contacts, Secretary of Defense Donald Rumsfeld told reporters on June 21, 2002, that Assistant Secretary of Defense Peter Rodman would talk to the PLA about the principles of transparency, reciprocity, and consistency for milto-mil contacts that Rumsfeld stressed to Vice President Hu Jintao at the Pentagon in May 2002.

After the fifth DCT in December 2002, Under Secretary of Defense for Policy Douglas Feith said that if contacts are structured property, "they will serve our interests, they will serve our common interests. And the principal interest is in reducing the risks of mistake, miscalculation, and misunderstanding. If these military-to-military exchanges actually lead to our gaining insights into Chinese thinking and policies and capabilities and the like, and they can gain insights into ours, then it doesn't mean we'll necessarily agree on everything, but it at least means that as we're making our policies, we're making them on the basis of accurate information" [23].

In March 2008, Deputy Secretary of Defense Gordon England defined these principal U.S. objectives in the annual report to Congress on contacts with the PLA:

- support the President's overall policy goals regarding China;
- prevent conflict by clearly communicating U.S. resolve to maintain peace and stability in the Asia-Pacific region;
- lower the risk of miscalculation between the two militaries;
- increase U.S. understanding of China's military capabilities and intentions;
- encourage China to adopt greater openness and transparency in its military capabilities and intentions;
- promote stable U.S.-China relations;
- increase mutual understanding between U.S. and PLA officers;
- encourage China to play a constructive and peaceful role in the Asia-Pacific region; to act as a partner in addressing common security challenges; and to emerge as a responsible stakeholder in the world.

Debate

U.S. security objectives in mil-to-mil contacts with China have included gaining insights about the PLA's capabilities and concepts; deterrence against a PLA use of force or coercion against Taiwan or U.S. allies; reduction in tensions in the Taiwan Strait; strategic arms control; weapons nonproliferation in countries such as like North Korea, Iran, and Pakistan; closer engagement with top PRC leaders; freedom of navigation and flight; preventing dangers to U.S. military personnel operating in proximity to the PLA; minimizing misperceptions and miscalculations; and accounting for American POW/MIAs.

Skeptics of U.S.-PRC mil-to-mil contacts say they have had little value for achieving these U.S. objectives. Instead that they contend that the contacts served to inform the PLA as it builds its warfighting capability against Taiwan and the United States, which it views as a potential adversary, and seemed to reward belligerence. They oppose rehabilitation of PLA officers involved in the Tiananmen Crackdown. They question whether the PLA has shown transparency and reciprocated with equivalent or substantive access, and urge greater attention to U.S. allies over China. From this perspective, the ups and downs in the military relationship reflect its use as a tool in the bilateral political relationship, in which the PRC at times had leverage over the United States. Thus, they contend, a realistic appraisal of the nature of the PLA threat would call for caution in military contacts with China, perhaps limiting them to exchanges such as strategic talks and senior-level policy dialogues, rather than operational areas that involve military capabilities.

A former U.S. Army Attache in Beijing wrote in 1999 that under the Clinton Administration, military-to-military contacts allowed PLA officers "broad access" to U.S. warships, exercises, and even military manuals. He argued that "many of the military contacts between the United States and China over the years helped the PLA attain its goals [in military modernization]." He called for limiting exchanges to strategic dialogue on weapons proliferation, Taiwan, the Korean peninsula, freedom of navigation, missile defense, etc. He urged policymakers not to "improve the PLA's capability to wage war against Taiwan or U.S.

friends and allies, its ability to project force, or its ability to repress the Chinese people" [24]. He also testified to Congress in 2000 that the PLA conceals its capabilities in exchanges with the United States. For example, he said, the PLA invited General John Shalikashvili, Chairman of the Joint Chiefs of Staff, to see the capabilities of the 15th Airborne Army (in May 1997), but it showed him a highly scripted routine. Furthermore, the PLA allowed Secretary of Defense Cohen to visit an Air Defense Command Center (in January 1998), but it was "a hollow shell of a local headquarters; it was not the equivalent of America's National Command Center" that was shown to PRC leaders [25]

In 2000, Randy Schriver, a former official in the Office of the Secretary of Defense, discussed lessons learned in conducting military exchanges during the Clinton Administration and argued for limiting such exchanges. Schriver assessed senior-level talks as exchanges of talking points rather than real dialogue, but nonetheless helpful. He considered the MMCA a successful confidence-building measure (not knowing the EP-3 aircraft collision crisis would occur less than one year later in April 2001). He also said it was positive to have PLA participation in multilateral fora and to expose younger PLA officers to American society. However, Schriver said that the United States "failed miserably" in gaining a window on the PLA's modernization, gaining neither access as expected nor reciprocity; failed to shape China's behavior while allowing China to shape the behavior of some American "ardent suitors"; and failed to deter the PLA's aggression while whetting the PLA's appetite in planning against a potential American adversary. He disclosed that the Pentagon needed to exert control over the Pacific Command's contacts with the PLA, with the Secretary of Defense issuing a memo to set guidelines. He also called for continuing consultations with Congress [26].

Warning of modest expectations for military ties and that such exchanges often have been suspended to signal messages or retaliate against a perceived wrong action, former Deputy Assistant Secretary of Defense Kurt Campbell contended in late 2005 that security ties can only follow, not lead, the overall bilateral relationship [27]. After serving as Deputy Assistant Secretary of State for East Asian and Pacific Affairs in the Bush Administration, Randy Schriver observed in 2007 that military engagement with China has continued to pursue the "same modest, limited agenda that has been in place for close to 20 years," despite a high-level visit by Secretary of Defense Robert Gates in November 2007 [28].

Proponents of military exchanges with the PRC point out that contacts with the PLA cannot be expected to equal contacts with allies in transparency, reciprocity, and consistency. They argue that the mil-to-mil contacts nonetheless promote U.S. interests and allow the U.S. military to gain insights into the PLA, including its top leadership, that no other bilateral contacts provide. U.S. military attaches, led by the Defense Attache at the rank of brigadier general or rear admiral, have contacts at levels lower than the top PLA leaders and are subject to strict surveillance in China. In addition to chances for open intelligence collection, the military relationship can minimize miscalculations and misperceptions, and foster pro-U.S. leanings and understanding, particularly among younger officers who might lead in the future. Proponents caution against treating China as if it is already an enemy, since the United States seeks China's cooperation on international security issues. There might be benefits in cooperation in military medicine to prevent pandemics of diseases, like avian flu. During the epidemic of SARS (severe acute respiratory syndrome) in 2003, it was a PLA doctor, Dr. Jiang Yanyong, who revealed the PRC leadership's coverup of SARS cases at premier PLA hospitals [29]. Since the early 1990s, Congress and the Defense Department have viewed

China as the key to getting information to resolve the cases of POW/MIAs from the Korean War.

Citing several exchanges in 1998 (Commander of the Pacific Command's visit that included the first foreign look at the 47th Group Army, a U.S. Navy ship visit to Shanghai, and naval consultative talks at Naval Base Coronado), the U.S. Naval Attache in Beijing wrote that "the process of mutual consultation, openness, and sharing of concerns and information needed to preclude future misunderstandings and to build mutual beneficial relations is taking place between the U.S. and China's armed forces, especially in the military maritime domain." He stressed that "the importance of progress in this particular area of the Sino-American relationship cannot be overestimated" [30].

Two former U.S. military attaches posted to China maintained in a report that "regardless of whether it is a high-level DoD delegation or a functional exchange of medical officers, the U.S. military does learn something about the PLA from every visit." They advocated that "the United States should fully engage China in a measured, long-term military-to-military exchange program that does not help the PLA improve its warfighting capabilities." They said, "the most effective way to ascertain developments in China's military and defense policies is to have face-to-face contact at multiple levels over an extended period of time." Thus, they argued, "even though the PLA minimizes foreign access to PLA facilities and key officials, the United States has learned, and can continue to learn, much about the PLA through its long-term relationship" [31]

Another former U.S. military attache in Beijing (from 1992 to 1995) acknowledged that he saw many PLA drills and demonstrations by "showcase" units and never any unscripted training events. Nonetheless, he noted that in August 2003, the PLA arranged for 27 military observers from the United States and other countries to be the first foreigners to observe a PLA exercise at its largest training base (which is in the Inner Mongolia region under the Beijing Military Region). He wrote that "by opening this training area and exercise to foreign observers, the Chinese military leadership obviously was attempting to send a message about its willingness to be more 'transparent' in order to 'promote friendship and mutual trust between Chinese and foreign armed forces" [32] However, in a second PLA exercise opened to foreign observers, the "Dragon 2004" landing exercise at the Shanwei amphibious operations training base in Guangdong province in September 2004, only seven foreign military observers from France, Germany, Britain, and Mexico attended, with no Americans (if invited) [33].

A retired PACOM Commander, Dennis Blair, co-chaired a task force on the U.S.-China relationship. Its report of April 2007 recommended a sustained high-level military strategic dialogue to complement the "Senior Dialogue" started by the Deputy Secretary of State in 2005 and the "Strategic Economic Dialogue" launched by the Secretary of Treasury in 2006 [34].

Perspectives

The Center for Naval Analyses found in a study that U.S. and PRC approaches to military exchanges are "diametrically opposed," thus raising tensions at times. While the United States has pursued a "bottom-up" effort starting with lower-level contact to work toward mutual understanding and then strategic agreement, the PRC has sought a "trickle-down" relationship in which agreement on strategic issues results in understanding and then allows for specific activities later. The study said that "the PLA leadership regards the military relationship with the U.S. as a political undertaking for strategic reasons—not a freestanding set of military initiatives conducted by military professionals for explicitly military reasons. Fundamentally, the military relationship is a vehicle to pursue strategic political ends." While recognizing that using the military relationship to enhance military modernization is extremely important to the PLA, the study contended that "it is not the key motive force driving the PLA's engagement with DOD." The report also argued that because the PLA suspects the United States uses the military relationship for deterrence, intelligence, and influence, "it seems ludicrous for them to expose their strengths and weaknesses to the world's 'sole superpower'." It noted that using "reciprocity" as a measure of progress "is sure to lead to disappointment" [35].

U.S. Security Interests

With lessons learned, a fundamental issue in overall policy toward China is how to use U.S. leadership and leverage in managing a prudent program of military contacts that advances, and does not harm, a prioritized list of U.S. security interests. The Pentagon could pursue such a program with focused control by the Office of the Secretary of Defense; with consultation with Congress and public disclosures; and in coordination with allies and friends in the region, such as Japan, South Korea, Australia, and Singapore. Such a program might include these objectives.

Communication, Conflict Avoidance, and Crisis Management

Crises

The various crises of direct confrontation between the U.S. military and PLA might call for greater cooperation with China to improve communication, conflict avoidance, and crisis management. Analysts in China have studied the government's strengths and weaknesses in crisis management in light of the EP-3 crisis in 2001 [36]. Nonetheless, the crisis over the EP-3 aircraft collision and subsequent confrontations have shown the limits in benefits to the United States of pursuing personal relationships with PLA leaders, the consultations under the Military Maritime Consultative Agreement (MMCA), as well as the presidential hotline. From the beginning of the crisis, PRC ruler Jiang Zemin pressed the United States with a hard-line stance, while PLA generals followed without any greater inflammatory rhetoric [37]. (See the Appendix for text boxes that summarize the major bilateral tensions in crises or confrontations.)

Telephones

During his second visit to China as PACOM Commander in December 1997, Admiral Prueher said that "I remember wishing I had your telephone number," in response to a PLA naval officer's question about Prueher's thinking during the Taiwan Strait crisis in 1995-1996 [38] After becoming ambassador to China in December 1999, Prueher was nonetheless frustrated when the Ministry of Foreign Affairs and the PLA would not answer the phone or return phone calls in the immediate aftermath of the EP-3 collision crisis in April 2001 [39].

Still, some continue to believe there could be benefits in fostering relationships with PLA officers, both at the senior level and with younger, future leaders. While in Beijing in January 2004, the Chairman of the Joint Chiefs of Staff, General Myers, said that "it's always an advantage to be able to pick up a telephone and talk to somebody that you know fairly well. The relationship that I have with General Liang [Chief of General Staff], the relationship that Defense Secretary Rumsfeld has with his counterpart, General Cao, is going to be helpful in that regard" [40] Likewise, visiting Beijing in September 2005, Admiral William Fallon, Commander of the Pacific Command, referred to the value for his regional responsibilities to "pick up the telephone and call someone I already know" [41].

MMCA

The MMCA, initialed at the first DCT in December 1997 and signed by Secretary Cohen in Beijing in January 1998, only arranged meetings to discuss maritime and air safety (i.e., to talk about talking). There was no agreement on communication during crises or rules of engagement. Despite the 2001 crisis, the Defense Department encountered difficulties with the PLA in discussions under the MMCA, including simply setting up meetings and PLA objections to U.S. activities in China's claimed 200-nautical mile exclusive economic zone (EEZ) (even beyond the territorial sea up to 12 nautical miles from the coast) [42]

DPCT

In early 2005, U.S. defense and PLA officials held a Special Policy Dialogue to discuss policy disputes and end an impasse in talks over safety and operational concerns under the MMCA. The separate discussions continued in the Defense Policy Coordination Talks (DPCT) held in Washington in December 2006. The first combined exercise held under the MMCA, a search and rescue exercise (SAREX), did not take place until the fall of 2006, after eight years of discussions. By 2007, the MMCA's status and value were in greater doubt, and no MMCA working groups or plenary meetings took place that year.

On February 25-26, 2008, in Qingdao, PACOM's Director for Strategic Planning and Policy (J-5), USMC Major General Thomas Conant, and PLA Navy Deputy Chief of Staff Zhang Leiyu led an annual meeting under the MMCA, the first since 2006. The PLA sought to amend the MMCA. The U.S. side opposed PLA proposals to discuss policy differences at the MMCA meetings and to plan details of future military exercises [43]. The PLA and U.S. military have clashed over the PRC's disputes with foreign countries over the freedom of navigation in the high seas.

INCSEA

For his nomination hearing to be the PACOM Commander on March 8, 2007, Admiral Timothy Keating responded to questions from the Senate Armed Services Committee by claiming that a dangerous incident similar to the EP-3 crisis would be "less likely." He also proposed negotiating with the PLA an "Incidents at Sea" (INCSEA) protocol, like the agreement with the Soviet Union (signed in 1972).

After the Pentagon reported in March 2009 that PRC ships were aggressively harassing U.S. ocean surveillance ships (including the USNS Impeccable) in the Yellow Sea and South China Sea, some observers raised again the issue of whether to agree with the PLA on an INCSEA. For example, retired Rear Admiral Eric McVaden suggested that an INCSEA could compel China's top leaders to agree to avoid collisions or escalations of tensions, as well as provide rules and a safety valve. However, skeptics said that the question was not whether there was an agreement or dialogue. For example, former Deputy Assistant Secretary of State Randy Schriver pointed out that the MMCA would have been called an INCSEA (but the United States wanted to avoid "Cold War connotations") and that the MMCA had limited usefulness because China has more interest in stopping U.S. reconnaissance than any interest in the agreement that it had signed. Thus, he contended that the MMCA already has provided the mechanism for dealing with incidents at sea. The problem has been that the PLA is not interested in a "rules-based, operator-to-operator approach to safety on the high seas" [44].

Hotline

After staff-level preliminary discussions in 2003, Under Secretary of Defense Douglas Feith formally proposed a hotline for crisis management and confidence building with the PLA at the DCT in February 2004. However, the PLA did not give a positive signal until a defense ministerial conference in Singapore in June 2007, when Lt. General Zhang Qinsheng, Deputy Chief of General Staff, said that the PLA would discuss such a hotline. During Secretary of Defense Robert Gates' visit to China in November 2007, the PLA agreed in principle to set up a defense telephone link (DTL) with the Pentagon. The two sides signed an agreement in February 2008. Then, in May 2008, PACOM's Commander, Admiral Keating, used the hotline in its first operational use to communicate with PLA Deputy Chief of General Staff Ma Xiaotian about the U.S. Air Force's dispatch of two C-17 transport aircraft to deliver relief supplies to Sichuan province after an earthquake. However, during the confrontation in March 2009 when PRC ships aggressively harassed the U.S. surveillance ship USNS Impeccable, Secretary of Defense Robert Gates told reporters on March 18, 2009, that he did not use the hotline.

ATC

Another area for possible improved communication and prevention of accidents is air traffic control in China, which is controlled by the PLA Air Force. In December 2006, the PLA suddenly shut down the busy Pudong International Airport near Shanghai and at least three other airports under the Nanjing Military Region, ostensibly for training [45]

Sanya Initiative

For dealing with a possible crisis, Admiral Keating revealed in 2007 that he used a network of retired Admirals who had commanded PACOM and had met with PLA commanders [46]. Possibly related to this reference, a "Sanya Initiative" (a dialogue first held at the Sanya resort on Hainan island) began in February 2008. Xiong Guangkai (President of the China Institute for International Strategic Studies and former Deputy Chief of General Staff in charge of intelligence) led the PLA side. Bill Owens (retired admiral and former Vice Chairman of the Joint Chiefs of Staff) led the U.S. side. The PLA side asked the U.S. participants to help with PRC objections: namely the Pentagon's report to Congress on PRC Military Power and legal restrictions on military contacts in the National Defense Authorization Act for FY2000 [47]. A second meeting was scheduled for March 2009 at PACOM in Hawaii. While some believe that more dialogue is useful to avoid conflict, others oppose the use of such unofficial channels.

Transparency, Reciprocity, and Information-Exchange

Critics of military exchanges with China have charged that the United States gained limited information about the PLA, while granting greater access to the PLA than the access we received. A related question in the debate has concerned the extent to which the issues of reciprocity and transparency should affect or impede efforts to increase mutual understanding with the PLA.

According to the Pentagon's report submitted to Congress in January 2001, in 1998, the PLA denied requests by the U.S. Air Force Chief of Staff, General Ryan, to fly in an SU-27 fighter, see integration of the SU-27s into units, and see progress in development of the F-10 fighter. Also in 1998, the PLA denied a U.S. request for Secretary of Defense Cohen to visit China's National Command Center. Still, the PLA requested access to U.S. exercises showing warfighting capabilities, with two cases of denial by the Pentagon in 1999: PLA requests to send observers to the U.S. Army's premier National Training Center (NTC) at Fort Irwin in California and to the Red Flag air combat training exercise at Nellis Air Force Base in Nevada (see Table 2 on PLA delegation's visit in March 1999).

Regarding controversial access to the U.S. Army's NTC, visits by PLA delegations in the 1990s included those in November 1994 and December 1997 [48]. Then, in December 1998, the U.S. Army reportedly resisted a PLA request for greater, unprecedented access to the NTC in 1999, because the PLA asked for access greater than that granted to other countries, the PLA would gain information to enhance its warfighting, and the PLA was unlikely to reciprocate with similar access for the U.S. military. The PLA wanted to observe, with direct access, the 3rd Infantry Division (Mechanized) and the 82nd Airborne Division in a training exercise. Army officials reportedly felt pressured by Admiral Prueher at PACOM and Secretary Cohen to grant the request. In the end, the Pentagon announced on March 17, 1999, that it denied the PLA's request [49].

The Defense Department's 2003 report to Congress on PRC military power charged that "since the 1980s, U.S. military exchange delegations to China have been shown only 'showcase' units, never any advanced units or any operational training or realistic exercises" [50] However, a Rand study in 2004 argued that the DOD's statement "appears to be inaccurate." Rand reported that between 1993 and 1999, U.S. visitors went to 51 PLA units. (PLA delegations visited 71 U.S. military units between 1994 and 1999.) The report recommended that "the best way of dealing with the reciprocity and transparency issue is to remove it as an issue." It called for proper planning and a focus on educational exchanges [51].

In 2005, the PRC did not allow U.S. forces to observe the major combined PLA-Russian military exercise, "Peace Mission 2005," and prohibited U.S. participation in the multilateral humanitarian exercise in Hong Kong, to which U.S. forces had joined for years in the past [52]. Still, PACOM Commander, Admiral Fallon, invited PLA observers to the U.S. "Valiant Shield" exercise that brought three aircraft carriers to waters off Guam in June 2006. In August 2007, the U.S. observers were not invited to monitor the PRC-Russian combined exercise "Peace Mission 2007."

Nonetheless, U.S. participants in contacts with the PLA have reported gaining insights into PLA capabilities and concepts. The record of military contacts since 1993 (in the next part of this CRS Report) shows some instances when the PLA allowed U.S. officials to be first-time foreign visitors with "unprecedented access:"

- Satellite Control Center in Xian (1995)
- Guangzhou Military Region headquarters (1997)
- Beijing Military Region's Air Defense Command Center (1998)
- 47th Group Army (1998)
- Armored Force Engineering Academy (2000)
- Training base in Inner Mongolia (2003), with multinational access
- Zhanjiang, homeport of the PLAN's South Sea Fleet (2003)
- Beijing Aerospace Control Center (2004)
- 2nd Artillery (missile corps) headquarters (2005)
- 39th Group Army (2006)
- FB-7 fighter at 28th Air Division (2006)
- Su-27 fighter and T-99 tank (2007)
- Jining Air Force Base (2007).

Tension Reduction over Taiwan

Tensions over Taiwan have continued to flare since the mid-1990s, with many observers fearing the possibility of war looming between the United States and China—two nuclear powers. The Bush Administration maintains that it has managed a balanced policy toward Beijing and Taipei that preserves peace and stability. Nonetheless, in April 2004, Assistant Secretary of State James Kelly testified to Congress that U.S. efforts at deterring China's coercion "might fail" if Beijing becomes convinced that it must stop Taiwan from advancing on a course toward permanent separation from China [53]. Kelly also noted that the PRC leadership accelerated the PLA buildup after 1999.

The Pentagon reported to Congress in May 2004 that the PLA has "accelerated" modernization, including a missile buildup, in response to concerns about Taiwan [54].

Under the Taiwan Relations Act (TRA), P.L. 9 6-8, that has governed U.S. policy toward Taiwan since 1979, Congress has oversight of the President's management of the cross-strait situation under the rubric of the "one China" policy [55]. While considering contacts with the PLA, the United States, after the 1995-1996 Taiwan Strait Crisis, has increased arms sales to and ties with Taiwan's military [56].

Policy considerations include offering arms sales and cooperation to help Taiwan's self-defense; securing leverage over Beijing and Taipei; deterring aggression or coercion; discouraging provocations from Beijing or Taipei; and supporting cross-strait dialogue and confidence-building measures. In educational exchanges with the PLA, questions have concerned whether to allow PLA officers to attend U.S. military academies, colleges, or universities, and how that change could affect attendees from Taiwan's military; and whether to allow attendees from Taiwan at PACOM's Asia-Pacific Center for Security Studies (APCSS).

Concerning the APCSS courses in Honolulu, the Bush Administration's policy change to allow attendance from Taiwan has affected the PLA's attendance and interactions among the U.S., PRC, and other Asian militaries. In November 2001, the Department of Defense directed APCSS to allow people from Taiwan to participate in courses and conferences. Acknowledging the potential difficulty for continuing participation by the PLA, the policy called for alternating invitations to the PRC and Taiwan. In the summer of 2002, three fellows from Taiwan attended the Executive Course, the first time that Taiwan sent students to

APCSS. Dissatisfied with alternating attendance with Taiwan's representatives, the PLA stopped sending representatives to APCSS courses and conferences by 2004 [57].

While the Mutual Defense Treaty of 1954 terminated at the end of 1979 and the TRA does not commit the United States to defend Taiwan, the TRA states that it is U.S. policy, among other points:

- to consider any non-peaceful efforts to determine the future of Taiwan, including boycotts or embargoes, a threat to the peace and security of the Western Pacific region and of "grave concern" to the United States;
- to provide Taiwan with arms of a defensive character (making available to Taiwan such defense articles and defense services in such quantity as may be necessary to enable Taiwan to maintain a sufficient self-defense capability);
- to maintain the U.S. capacity to resist any resort to force or other forms of coercion that would jeopardize the security, or the social or economic system, of the people on Taiwan.

There is a question about the extent of the U.S. role in supporting cross-strait dialogue. In Shanghai in July 2000, visiting Secretary of Defense Cohen said that the Clinton Administration viewed the newly-elected President Chen Shui-bian of Taiwan as offering hope for cross-strait reconciliation. Cohen stepped out of the narrow mil-to-mil context and met with Wang Daohan, chairman of the PRC's Association for Relations Across the Taiwan Strait (ARATS).

This meeting raised questions about the U.S. role in more actively encouraging cross-strait talks. Cohen said that Chen showed flexibility after becoming president and that there was a window of opportunity for changes [58]. In contrast, in Beijing in February 2004, visiting Under Secretary of Defense Feith said he did not discuss the contentious issue raised by PLA leaders "at length" concerning referendums in Taiwan—an issue over which the PRC threatened to use force. Feith said he did not discuss the issue because it was not defense-related [59].

There are complications in consideration of the question of Taiwan in the U.S.-PRC military relationship. Not discussing Taiwan leaves the primary dispute subject to misperception or miscalculation. However, linking the Taiwan question can raise tensions and frustrations over a disagreement that military exchanges cannot solve. A 2007 study co-authored by former PACOM Commander Dennis Blair called for discussion of the PLA's missile buildup against Taiwan and greater efforts to reduce tensions across the Taiwan Strait [60].

The PLA has suspended military exchanges in retaliation for steps in U.S. policy toward Taiwan, especially continued arms sales. However, even as the PLA signaled its displeasure and urged U.S. cooperation in "peace and stability" in the Taiwan Strait, suspensions of military exchanges have played a counter-productive role by raising U.S.-PRC tensions. Moreover, the PRC's implicit linkage has targeted the U.S. Navy in particular, precisely the service advocating engagement with the PLA.

After Taiwan's President Chen Shui-bian proposed in June 2007 that Taiwan hold a referendum on membership in the U.N. under the name "Taiwan" on the day of the next presidential election (scheduled for March 22, 2008), Beijing opposed it as a step toward

Taiwan's de jure independence. While joining the PRC in opposing the referendum, the Bush Administration continued the U.S. policy of providing some security assistance to Taiwan.

After notifications to Congress of arms sales to Taiwan in September and November 2007, the PRC protested by refusing to hold military-to-military exchanges, including an annual MMCA meeting scheduled for October 2007. The PRC also denied port visits at Hong Kong in November 2007 by U.S. Navy minesweepers in distress (USS Patriot and USS Guardian) and by the carrier group led by the USS Kitty Hawk for the Thanksgiving holiday and family reunions, leading to official protests by the Pentagon to the PLA.

After sailing away from the denied port call in Hong Kong toward Japan, the USS Kitty Hawk sailed through the Taiwan Strait, raising objections in China with claims in PRC media of the strait as China's "internal waterway." When asked at a news conference in Beijing on January 15, 2008, visiting PACOM Commander, Admiral Keating said, "we don't need China's permission to go through the Taiwan Strait. It's international water. We will exercise our free right of passage whenever and wherever we choose as we have done repeatedly in the past and we'll do in the future."

Two days later, when asked whether ships need the PRC's permission to sail through the Taiwan Strait, China's foreign ministry spokesperson did not reject the idea of permission from Beijing while claiming the strait as a "highly sensitive area."

After the Bush Administration notified Congress of some pending arms sales to Taiwan on October 3, 2008, the PLA suspended some but not all military exchanges and nonproliferation talks. The Defense Department spokesman said that the PRC canceled or postponed several meetings in "continued politicization" of the military-to-military exchanges [61].

After tentative support in 2008 in both Beijing and Taipei for cross-strait confidence building measures (CBMs), PACOM's Admiral Keating raised the question of a U.S. role when he offered in February 2009 to host talks between the PLA and Taiwan's military [62]. However, Reagan's Six Assurances to Taiwan in 1982 included one of not mediating between Beijing and Taipei.

Weapons Nonproliferation

Despite past engagement with the PLA to seek cooperation in weapons nonproliferation, the United States continues to have concerns about PRC entities and has repeatedly imposed sanctions. Secretary of Defense Cohen visited China and urged its commitment to weapons nonproliferation. China did not join in the U.S.-led Proliferation Security Initiative (PSI) announced by President Bush in May 2003 (to interdict dangerous shipments).

There is a debate about the policy of the Bush Administration in engaging China—and the PLA— in a multilateral effort to achieve the dismantlement of North Korea's nuclear weapons and nuclear programs. In April 2003, China hosted trilateral talks among the United States, China, and North Korea. Then, China hosted the first round of six-nation talks in August 2003 that also included Japan, South Korea, and Russia. The following month, PLA units replaced paramilitary People's Armed Police (PAP) units along China's border with North Korea, apparently to signalto Pyongyang the seriousness of the tensions and warn against provocative actions. Beijing has hosted additional rounds of Six-Party Talks. After the third round, PRC leaders hosted North Korea's defense minister in July 2004. There have been questions about whether China has been adequately assertive in using its economic and political leverage over North Korea and whether China shares the U.S. priority of the complete, verifiable, and irreversible dismantlement—not just a freeze—of North Korea's nuclear weapons programs. China, nonetheless, has stated the common goal of a nuclear-free Korean peninsula and demonstrated its displeasure with North Korea after its missile and nuclear tests in 2006, including during CMC Vice Chairman Guo Boxiong's visit in the United States in 2006 [63]

Strategic Nuclear and Space Talks

As for a strategic nuclear dialogue, the Clinton Administration had included nuclear forces as a priority area for expanded military discussions, including during the visits to China in 1998 of Secretary of Defense Cohen and President Clinton. In his visit to China in 1998, President Clinton announced a bilateral agreement not to target strategic nuclear weapons against each other, but it was symbolic and lacked implementation.

Since then, concerns have increased about China's modernizing strategic nuclear force and its "No First Use" policy, including whether it is subject to debate. In July 2005, PLA Major General Zhu Chenghu, a dean at the PLA's National Defense University, told western journalists in Beijing that "if the Americans draw their missiles and position-guided ammunition into the target zone on China's territory, I think we will have to respond with nuclear weapons," and he included the PLA's naval ships and fighters as China's "territory." Zhu added that if the United States is determined to intervene in a Taiwan scenario, "we will be determined to respond, and we Chinese will prepare ourselves for the destruction of all cities east of Xian [an ancient capital city in north- central China]. Of course, the Americans will have to be prepared that hundreds of, or two hundreds of, or even more cities will be destroyed by the Chinese." Zhu also dismissed China's "No First Use" policy, saying that it applied only to non-nuclear states and could be changed [64]. China's experts argued that Zhu's comments reflected China's concerns about the challenges presented by U.S. defense policy and nuclear strategy for China's policy [65]

When Defense Secretary Rumsfeld visited China in October 2005, the PLA accorded him the honor of being the first foreigner to visit the Second Artillery's headquarters. Its commander, General Jing Zhiyuan, assured Rumsfeld that China would not be the first to use nuclear weapons [66]. General Jing later hosted the chairman of the House Armed Services Committee, Representative Ike Skelton, at the Second Artillery's headquarters in August 2007 [67].

The Bush Administration invited General Jing to visit the U.S. Strategic Command (STRATCOM), as discussed during a summit between Bush and Hu Jintao in Washington in April 2006. Two months later, Assistant Secretary of Defense Peter Rodman visited Beijing for the DCT and discussed the invitation to the 2nd Artillery Commander. In October 2006, the STRATCOM commander, General James Cartwright (USMC), expressed interest in engaging with the PLA on space issues, including ways in which the two countries can avoid and handle collisions or interference between satellites, and perceptions of attacks on satellites [68]. However, General Jing declined to schedule a visit [69]. On January 11, 2007, the PLA conducted its first successful direct ascent anti-satellite (ASAT) weapons test by launching a missile with a kinetic kill vehicle to destroy a PRC satellite [70]. On June 13, 2007, Deputy Under Secretary of Defense Richard Lawless testified to the House Armed Services Committee that the PLA would not set a date to hold a dialogue on nuclear policy, strategy, and doctrine. Lawless said that PLA strategic forces have improved the capability to target the U.S. mainland [71]. General Jing Zhiyuan has traveled outside of China, but not to the United States, including a trip to Sweden and Bulgaria in November 2007.

The PLA took some modest steps in December 2007, when the PLA delegation to the 9th DCT included 2nd Artillery Deputy Chief of Staff Yang Zhiguo. In April 2008, the PLA and the Defense Department held talks in Washington on nuclear strategy at the "experts" level. The PLA proposed to change the Pentagon-PLA defense policy talks into a "Strategic Dialogue," that would include nuclear policy. In early 2009, the National Security Council's Senior Director for Asia, Dennis Wilder, said that the PLA was intentionally being mysterious to have an advantage and expressed concerns about miscalculation and doubts China would engage in arms control [72]. General Jing Zhiyuan visited Tanzania and Uganda in October 2008, but not the United States.

Counterterrorism and Olympic Security

The PRC's cooperation in counterterrorism after the attacks on September 11, 2001, has not included military cooperation with the U.S. military. The U.S. Commanders of the Central and Pacific Commands, General Tommy Franks and Admiral Dennis Blair, separately confirmed in April 2002 that China did not provide military cooperation (nor was it requested) in Operation Enduring Freedom against Al Qaeda in Afghanistan (e.g., basing, staging, or overflight) and that China's shared intelligence was not specific enough. Also, the Pentagon issued a report in June 2002 on the international coalition fighting terrorism and did not include China among the countries providing military contributions. China has provided diplomatic support, cited by the State Department. U.S.-PRC counterterrorism cooperation has been limited, while U.S. concerns have increased about the PRC's increased influence in the Shanghai Cooperation Organization (SCO) and its call for U.S. withdrawals from Central Asia, and about PRC-origin small arms and anti-aircraft missiles found in Afghanistan and Iraq [73].

Some have urged caution in military cooperation with China on this front, while others see benefits for the U.S. relationship with China and the war on terrorism. Senator Bob Smith and Representative Dana Rohrabacher wrote Secretary of Defense Rumsfeld in late 2001, to express concerns about renewed military contacts with China. In part, they argued that "China is not a good prospect for counterterrorism cooperation," because of concerns that China has practiced internal repression in the name of counterterrorism and has supplied technology to rogue regimes and state sponsors of terrorism [74]. In contrast, a report by Rand in 2004 urged a program of security management with China that includes counterterrorism as one of three components [75].

As preparations intensify for the summer Olympics in Beijing in 2008, a policy issue concerns the extent to which the United States, including the U.S. military, should support security at the games to protect U.S. citizens and should cooperate with the PLA and the paramilitary PAP. With concerns about internal repression by the PRC regime in the Tiananmen Crackdown of June 1989 and after, U.S. sanctions (in Section 902 of the Foreign Relations Authorization Act for FY1990- FY1 991, P.L. 101-246) have denied the export to China of defense articles/services, including helicopters, as well as crime control equipment. Presidential waivers are authorized. A precedent was set in 2004, when various U.S. departments, including the Department of Defense, provided security assistance for the Olympic games in Athens, Greece, in 2004. On June 22, 2006, at a hearing of the House Armed Services Committee, Brigadier General John Allen, the Principal Director for Asian and Pacific Affairs at the Office of the Secretary of Defense, testified that the Pentagon started discussions with China regarding security cooperation for the 2008 Olympics. However, Deputy Under Secretary of Defense Richard Lawless testified to the House Armed Services Committee on June 13, 2007, that China has not accepted offers from the Defense Department to assist in Olympic security.

Accounting for POW/MIAs

For humanitarian reasons or to advance the broader U.S.-PRC relationship, the PLA has been helpful in U.S. efforts to resolve POW/MIA cases from World War II, the Vietnam War, and the Cold War. In February 2001, the Defense Department characterized PRC assistance to the United States in recovering remains from World War II as "generous," citing the missions in 1994 in Tibet and in 1997-1999 in Maoer Mountain in southern China [76].

However, for 16 years—even as the survivors of those lost in the Korean War were aging and dying—the United States faced a challenge in securing the PLA's cooperation in U.S. accounting for POW/MIAs from the Korean War. Despite visits by the Director of the Defense POW/MIA Office and other senior U.S. military leaders to China and improved bilateral relations, the United States was not able to announce progress in obtaining cooperation from the PLA until 2008.

In April 1992, a military official in Eastern Europe supplied a report to then Secretary of Defense Dick Cheney, alleging that "several dozen" American military personnel captured in the Korean War (1950-1953) were sent to a camp in the Northeastern city of Harbin in China where they were used in psychological and medical experiments before being executed or dying in captivity [77]. In May 1992, the State Department raised the issue of POW/MIAs with the PRC, saying it was a "matter of the highest national priority," and in June 1992, the Senate Select Committee on POW/MIA Affairs received information from the Russian government indicating that over 100 American POWs captured in the Korean War were interrogated by the Soviet Union and possibly sent to China [78]. The United States also presented to the PRC a list of 125 American military personnel still unaccounted for since the Korean War, who were believed to have been interrogated in the Soviet Union and then sent to China. China responded to the United States that it did not receive anyone on that list from the former Soviet Union [79]. But that response apparently did not address whether China received American military personnel from North Korea or China itself transferred them.

Upon returning from North Korea and Southeast Asia in December 1992, Senator Robert Smith, Vice Chairman of the Select Committee on POW/MIA Affairs, disclosed that officials in Pyongyang admitted that "hundreds" of American POWs captured in the Korean War were sent to China and did not return to North Korea. According to Smith, North Korean officials said that China's PLA operated POW camps in North Korea during the Korean War and the Cold War and detained Americans in China's northeastern region. Moreover, North Korean officials told Smith that some American POWs could have been sent to the Soviet Union for further interrogations. Smith advocated that the U.S. government press the PRC government for information on POWs rather than accept the PRC's denials that it had POWs or information about them, saying "this is where the answers lie" [80] (The Senate created the Select Committee on POW/MIA Affairs in August 1991, chaired by Senator John Kerry. It concluded in December 1992, after gaining "important new information" from North Korea on China's involvement with U.S. POWs [81])

Secretary of Defense Cohen visited China in 1998 and stressed cooperation on POW/MIA cases one of four priorities in relations with the PLA. After visiting China in January 1999 to seek the PLA's cooperation in opening its secret archives on the Korean War, the Director of the Defense POW/MIA Office (DPMO), Robert Jones, said that "we believe that Chinese records of the war may hold the key to resolving the fates of many of our missing servicemen from the Korean War." The office's spokesman, Larry Greer, reported that the PRC agreed to look into the U.S. request to access the archives [82].

In March 2003, DPMO Director Jerry Jennings visited China and said that PRC records likely hold "the key" to resolving some POW/MIA cases from the Korean War [83]. Just days after the Chairman of the Joint Chiefs of Staff, General Myers, visited Beijing in January 2004, PRC media reported on January 19, 2004, that the government declassified the first batch of over 10,000 files in its archives on the PRC's foreign relations from 1949 to 1955. However, this step apparently excluded wartime records, and General Myers did not announce cooperation by China in providing information in its archives related to American POW/MIAs from the Korean War [84]. The PRC later announced in July 2004 the declassification of a second batch of similar files. In February 2005, DPMO acknowledged that PRC cooperation on Korean War cases remained the "greatest challenge" [85].

Visiting Beijing with Secretary of Defense Donald Rumsfeld in October 2005, Pentagon officials again raised the issue of access to China's Korean War archives believed to hold documents on American POWs [86]. In July 2006, General Guo Boxiong (the top PLA commander) visited the United States and agreed to open PLA archives on the Korean War. However, in his June 2007 report to Congress on military contacts, Defense Secretary Robert Gates reported that the PLA's cooperation "yielded mixed results." PLA cooperation with DPMO was "limited" in 2006, despite General Guo's promise.

There was some progress in February 2008, when China finally agreed to allow access to the PLA archives on the Korean War. However, the PLA did not grant direct access to the records, as asked by the Defense Department. The DPMO would have to request searches done by PRC researchers at the archives and the PLA would control and turn over acceptable records. The two sides would have to also negotiate the frequency, amount, and expenses of the searches [87]. Deputy Assistant Secretary of Defense for POW/MIA Affairs Charles Ray signed a Memorandum of Understanding in Shanghai on February 29, 2008 [88].

Despite the PRC's refusal to cooperate for many years, a PRC Foreign Ministry spokesman said China agreed out of "humanitarianism" [89]. On July 10, 2008, the House Armed Services Subcommittee on Military Personnel held a hearing on POWs and MIAs, with discussion of POW/MIAs taken to China during the Korean War, including Sergeant Richard Desautels who was buried in China in 1953.

APPENDIX: MAJOR MILITARY CONTACTS SINCE 1993

The scope of this record of mil-to-mil contacts focuses on senior-level visits, strategic talks, functional exchanges, agreements, commissions, and training or exercises. This compiled chronology does not provide a detailed list of all mil-to-mil contacts (that also include confidence building measures, educational exchanges that include visits by students at U.S. military colleges and the U.S. Capstone educational program for new general/flag officers, the numerous port calls in Hong Kong that continued after its hand-over from British to PRC control in July 1997, disaster relief missions, multilateral conferences, "track two" discussions sponsored by former Defense Secretary William Perry, etc.). There is no security assistance, as U.S. sanctions against arms sales have remained since 1989. Sources include numerous official statements, reports to Congress, documents, U.S. and PRC news stories, interviews, and observations. Specific dates are provided to the extent possible, while there are instances in which just the month is reported. Text boxes summarize major bilateral tensions in crises or confrontations as a context for the alternating periods of enthusiastic and skeptical contacts.

1993

In July 1993, the Clinton Administration suspected that a PRC cargo ship, called the Yinhe, was going to Iran with chemicals that could be used for chemical weapons and sought to inspect its cargo. In an unusual move, on August 9, China first disclosed that it protested U.S. "harassment" and finally allowed U.S. participation in a Saudi inspection of the ship's cargo on August 26, 1993. Afterward, the State Department said that the suspected chemicals were not found on the ship at that time. The PRC has raised this Yinhe incident as a grievance against the United States and the credibility of U.S. intelligence in particular.

November 1-2	Assistant Secretary of Defense for International Security Affairs Chas Freeman visited China, renewing mil-to-mil ties for the first time since the Tiananmen Crackdown in June 1989. Freeman met with General Liu Huaqing (a Vice Chairman of the CMC), General Chi Haotian (Defense Minister), Lieutenant General Xu Huizi (Deputy Chief of General Staff), and Lieutenant General Huai Guomo (Vice Chairman of the Commission of Science, Technology, and Industry for National Defense, or COSTIND).

1994

January 17-21	Lieutenant General Paul Cerjan, President of the National Defense University (NDU), visited China to advance professional military exchanges with the PLA's NDU. Cerjan visited the Nanjing Military Region and saw the 179th Infantry Division.
March 11-14	Under Secretary of Defense for Policy Frank Wisner visited China, along with Secretary of State Warren Christopher.
July 6-8	Commander of the Pacific Command (PACOM), Admiral Charles Larson, visited China and held talks with PLA Deputy Chief of General Staff, General Xu Huizi.
August 15-18	The Director of the PRC's National Bureau of Surveying and Mapping (NBSM) visited the United States and signed an agreement for a cooperative program with the Defense Mapping Agency, the predecessor of the National Imagery and Mapping Agency (NIMA), regarding the global positioning system (GPS). The agreement refers to the "Protocol for Scientific and Technical Cooperation in Surveying and Mapping Studies Concerning Scientific and Technical Cooperation in the Application of Geodetic and Geophysical Data to Mapping, Charting, and Geodetic (MC&G) Programs."
August	PLA Deputy Chief of General Staff, General Xu Huizi, visited the

15-25	United States and met with Defense Secretary William Perry and General John Shalikashvili, Chairman of the Joint Chiefs of Staff, in Washington, DC, and PACOM Commander, Admiral Richard Macke, in Hawaii.
September 7-29	In a POW/MIA operation, a U.S. Army team traveled to Tibet with PLA support to recover the remains of two U.S. airmen whose C-87 cargo plane crashed into a glacier at 14,000 feet in Tibet on December 31, 1944, during a flight over the "hump" back to India from Kunming, China, in World War II.
September 19-24	Chief of Staff of the U.S. Air Force, General Merrill McPeak, visited China and met with PLA Air Force Commander, General Cao Shuangming.
October 16-19	Secretary of Defense William Perry visited China and met with Generals Liu Huaqing (CMC Vice Chairman) and Chi Haotian (Defense Minister). On October 17, Perry and PLA General Ding Henggao, Director of COSTIND, conducted the first meeting of the newly-established U.S.-China Joint Defense Conversion Commission. They signed the "U.S.-China Joint Defense Conversion Commission: Minutes of the First Meeting, Beijing, October 17, 1994."

In a confrontation in the Yellow Sea on October 27-29, 1994, the U.S. aircraft carrier battle group led by the USS Kitty Hawk discovered and tracked a Han-class nuclear attack submarine of the PLA Navy. In response, the PLA Air Force sent fighters toward the U.S. aircraft tracking the submarine. Although no shots were fired by either side, China followed up the incident with a warning, issued to the U.S. Naval Attache over dinner in Beijing, that the PLA would open fire in a future incident.

November 5-10	The Director of the Defense Intelligence Agency (DIA), Lieutenant General James Clapper, visited China. He met with the GSD's Second Department (Intelligence) and the affiliated China Institute for International Strategic Studies (CIISS), saw the 179th Division in Nanjing, and received a briefing on tactical intelligence.
November 11-15	The Administrator of the Federal Aviation Administration, David Hinson, and the Defense Department's Executive Director of the Policy Board on Federal Aviation, Frank Colson, visited China to formulate the "U.S.-China 8-Step Civil-Military Air Traffic Control Cooperative Plan" agreed to during establishment of the Joint Defense Conversion Commission.
November 19-26	The PLA sent a delegation of new general and flag officers to the United States (similar to the U.S. Capstone program), led by Lieutenant General Ma Weizhi, Vice President of the NDU. They visited: Fort Irwin (including the National Training Center); Nellis Air Force Base (and observed a Red Flag exercise); Washington, DC (for meetings at NDU and Pentagon, including with the Vice Chairman of the Joint Chiefs of Staff, Admiral William Owens); and Norfolk Naval Base (and toured an aircraft carrier).
December	A delegation from NIMA visited China to sign a GPS survey plan and discuss provision of PRC data on gravity for a NIMA/NASA project on gravity modeling and establishment of a GPS tracking station near Beijing.
December 10-13	Assistant Secretary of Defense for Strategy and Requirements Ted Warner visited China to conduct briefings on the U.S. defense

strategy and budget as part of a defense transparency initiative, based on an agreement between Secretary Perry and General Chi Haotian in October 1994.

1995

January 28-February 10	PLA Major General Wen Guangchun, Assistant to the Director of the General Logistics Department (GLD), visited the United States at the invitation of the Office of the Under Secretary of Defense for Acquisition and Technology. The U.S. military provided briefings on logistics doctrine and systems and allowed the PLA visitors to observe U.S. military logistics activities and installations.
February 6-10	U.S. Air Force Deputy Chief of Staff for Plans and Operations, Lieutenant General Joseph Ralston, led a delegation of officials from the Department of Defense, Federal Aviation Administration, and Department of Commerce to visit China. They studied the PRC's civil-military air traffic control system and discussed futurecooperation.

In early February 1995, the PLA Navy occupied Mischief Reef in the Spratly Islands in the South China Sea, although Mischief Reef is about 150 miles west of the Philippines' island of Palawan but over 620 miles southeast of China's Hainan island off its southern coast. China seized a claim to territory in the South China Sea against a country other than Vietnam for the first time and challenged the Philippines, a U.S. treaty ally. Some Members of Congress introduced resolutions urging U.S. support for peace and stability. Three months later, on May 10, 1995, the Clinton Administration issued a statement opposing the use or threat of force to resolve the competing claims, without naming China.

February 24-March 7	President of the PLA's NDU, Lieutenant General Zhu Dunfa, visited the United States. Zhu visited West Point in New York; U.S. NDU and Pentagon in Washington, DC; Maxwell Air Force Base in Alabama; Naval Air Station North Island, Marine Recruit Depot, and Camp Pendleton Marine Corps Base in California; and PACOM in Hawaii.
March 22-24	The USS Bunker Hill (Aegis-equipped, Ticonderoga-class cruiser) visited Qingdao, in the first U.S. Navy ship visit to China since 1989. The senior officer aboard, Rear Admiral Bernard Smith, Commander of Carrier Group Five, met with Vice Admiral Wang Jiying, Commander of the PLA Navy (PLAN)'s North Sea Fleet.
March 25-28	A Deputy Director of COSTIND, Lieutenant General Huai Guomo, visited Washington to meet with officials at the Department of Commerce, Department of Defense, and people in the private sector to discuss possible projects for the Joint Defense Conversion Commission.
March 26-April 2	Lieutenant General Xiong Guangkai, PLA Assistant Chief of General Staff (with the portfolio of military intelligence), visited the United States, reciprocating for Assistant Secretary of Defense for Strategy and Requirements Ted Warner's visit to Beijing in December 1994. Xiong provided briefings on the PLA's defense strategy and budget, and the composition of the armed forces, and received briefings on U.S. national and global information infrastructures.
March 28-April 4	A delegation from the PRC's National Bureau of Surveying and Mapping visited the United States to hold discussions with NIMA and release PRC gravity data for analysis.

April 19	Vice Minister of the PRC's General Administration of Civil Aviation (CAAC) Bao Peide visited the United States to meet with the Federal Aviation Administration and U.S. companies. U.S. Air Force Deputy Chief of Staff for Plans and Operations, Lieutenant General Ralph Eberhart, briefed the PRC delegation on U.S. Air Force air traffic control programs.
April 25-30	PACOM Commander, Admiral Richard Macke, visited China, hosted by PLA Deputy Chief of General Staff, General Xu Huizi.
May 17-22	PLA Air Force Commander, Lieutenant General Yu Zhenwu, visited the United States, hosted by the U.S. Air Force Chief of Staff. Originally scheduled to last until May 27, the PLA terminated the visit on May 22 to protest the Clinton Administration's decision to grant a visa to Taiwan's President Lee Teng-hui to visit his alma mater, Cornell University.

On July 21-28, 1995, after the Clinton Administration allowed Taiwan's President Lee Teng-hui to make a private visit to give a speech at Cornell University on June 9, the PLA launched M-9 short-range ballistic missiles in "test-firings" toward target areas in the East China Sea. The PLA held other exercises directed against Taiwan until November.

On August 3, 1995, China expelled two U.S. Air Force attaches stationed in Hong Kong who traveled to China and were detained. China accused them of collecting military intelligence in restricted military areas along the southeastern coast.

August 31-September 2	PLA Commander of the Guangzhou Military Region, Lieutenant General Li Xilin, visited Hawaii to participate in a ceremony to commemorate the 50th anniversary of victory in the Pacific in World War II. Li met with Secretary of Defense Perry, Chairman of the Joint Chiefs of Staff, General Shalikashvili, and PACOM Commander, Admiral Macke.
September 7-16	Two NIMA teams visited China to establish GPS satellite tracking stations and discuss plans for a GPS survey in China in 1996.
October 15-25	Lieutenant General (USAF) Ervin Rokke, President of the NDU, visited China and held talks with Lieutenant General Xing Shizhong, President of the PLA's NDU, about professional military educational exchanges. The PLA arranged for Rokke to visit the 196th Infantry Division under the Beijing Military Region, the Satellite Control Center in Xian (the first U.S. access), the Guilin Army Academy in Guilin, and the Guangzhou Military Region.
November 14-18	Assistant Secretary of Defense for International Security Affairs Joseph Nye visited Beijing and met with General Chi Haotian. Nye said that "nobody knows" what the United States would do if the PLA attacked Taiwan.

1996

On January 19, 1996, China expelled the U.S. Assistant Air Force Attache and the Japanese Air Force Attache, after detaining them while they were traveling in southern China.

January 20-27	The Deputy Chief of Staff for Plans and Operations of the U.S. Air Force, Lieutenant General Ralph Eberhart, visited China as head of

	a delegation of representatives of the Department of Defense, Federal Aviation Administration, and Department of Commerce, as part of the Air Traffic Control Cooperative Program.
January 31-February 4	The USS Fort McHenry, a dock-landing ship, visited Shanghai, under the command of Rear Admiral Walter Doran.
February 6	Visiting PRC Vice Foreign Minister Li Zhaoxing met with Under Secretary of Defense for Policy Walter Slocombe at the Pentagon.
March 7	Secretary of Defense Perry, along with National Security Advisor Anthony Lake, attended a dinner meeting hosted by Secretary of State Christopher at the State Department for PRC Foreign Affairs Office Director Liu Huaqiu. Perry warned Liu that there would be "grave consequences" should the PLA attack Taiwan.

On March 8-15, 1996, the PLA launched four M-9 short-range ballistic missiles into waters close to the two ports of Keelung and Kaohsiung in Taiwan. Leading up to Taiwan's first democratic presidential election on March 23, the PLA conducted live fire exercises in the Taiwan Strait on March 12-25.

On March 10-11, 1996, the United States announced that it would deploy two aircraft carriers, the USS Independence and USS Nimitz, to waters near the east coast of Taiwan.

March 9-17	Assistant Secretary of Defense for Health Affairs Stephen Joseph visited China to advance bilateral military medical relations. Joseph and a Deputy Director of the GLD, Lieutenant General Zhou Youliang, signed a "Memorandum of Medical Exchange and Cooperation"
April 5-13	Geodesy and geophysical staff from NIMA visited China to hold discussions with the PRC's National Bureau of Surveying and Mapping.
May 4-20	A geodesy and geophysical survey team from NIMA visited China to perform a cooperative GPS survey.
June 25-28	Under Secretary of Defense for Policy Walter Slocombe visited China.
July 11-August 31	The PRC's National Bureau of Surveying and Mapping visited the United States to hold discussions with NIMA on cooperative projects and computation of results for the GPS China survey.
September 2-8	PACOM Commander, Admiral Joseph Prueher, visited China, hosted by a PLA Deputy Chief of General Staff, Lieutenant General Xiong Guangkai.
September 10	The Office for Defense Procurement/Foreign Contracting of the Under Secretary of Defense for Acquisition and Technology hosted Vice Chairman of the State Planning Commission She Jianming at the Pentagon and provided a briefing on the Defense Department's procurement system.
September 16-18	NIMA participated in the 9th meeting of the U.S.-PRC Joint Working Group for Scientific and Technical Cooperation in Surveying in Beijing.

September 17-29	A Deputy Director of the GLD, Lieutenant General Zhou Youliang, visited the United States to advance bilateral military medical relations, as the reciprocal visit for that of the Assistant Secretary of Defense for Health Affairs to China in March 1996. Both sides discussed cooperation between military hospitals, such as PLA 301 Hospital and Walter Reed Army Medical Center.
September 17	At the Pentagon, Deputy Assistant Secretary of Defense for Asian and Pacific Affairs Kurt Campbell met with the vice president of the Chinese Institute for Contemporary International Relations (CICIR), which is associated with the Ministry of State Security.
September 21-27	A team from NIMA visited China to perform maintenance on the GPS tracking station and discuss cooperative plans on gravity data.
October 4-17	Lieutenant General Xing Shizhong, President of the PLA's NDU, visited the United States. He and Lieutenant General Ervin Rokke, President of the U.S. NDU, signed a "Memorandum on Cooperation and Reciprocal Relations" between the two NDUs. They agreed to undertake reciprocal interaction on a broad range of issues relevant to professional military education, including military art, the evolution of strategy and doctrine, strategic assessment, the impact of technological advance on the nature of warfare, library science, and publishing.
October 11-17	The Surgeon General of the U.S. Air Force, Lieutenant General Edgar Anderson, led a U.S. military medical delegation to participate in the XXXI International Congress on Military Medicine held in Beijing.
October 20	At the Pentagon, Deputy Assistant Secretary of Defense for Asian and Pacific Affairs Kurt Campbell met with a delegation from the Chinese Institute of International Strategic Studies (CIISS), which is associated with the PLA.
November 11-19	The Director of DIA, Lieutenant General Patrick Hughes, visited China.
December 5-18	General Chi Haotian, a Vice Chairman of the CMC and Minister of Defense, visited the United States, to reciprocate for Defense Secretary Perry's visit to China in October 1994. Perry announced that General Chi's visit allowed for discussions of global and regional security issues as well as the future of mil-to-mil relations. While in Washington, General Chi met with President William Clinton. A controversy arose when General Chi gave a speech at NDU at Fort McNair and defended the PLA's crackdown on peaceful demonstrators in Beijing in 1989 (during which he was the PLA's Chief of General Staff) and claimed—apparently in a narrow sense—that no one died in Tiananmen Square itself. DOD provided a draft proposal for a bilateral military maritime cooperative agreement. The two sides agreed to continue U.S. port calls to Hong Kong after its hand-over from British to PRC control on July 1, 1997; to allow PLA ship visits to Hawaii and the U.S. west coast; to institutionalize Defense Consultative Talks; to hold senior-level visits; and to allow U.S. repatriation of the remains of the crew of a B-24 bomber that crashed in southern China in World War II (after General Chi presented dog tags found at the crash site). After Washington, Perry arranged for General Chi to travel to Air Force and Navy facilities in

Norfolk, Virginia; the Air University at Maxwell Air Force Base in Alabama; Army units at Fort Hood, Texas; the Cooperative Monitoring Center at the Sandia National Laboratory in Albuquerque, New Mexico (for discussion of technology that could be used to verify the Comprehensive Test Ban Treaty); and PACOM in Hawaii headed by Admiral Joseph Prueher.

1997

January 13-17	A Defense POW/MIA team went to Maoer Mountain in Guangxi province (in southern China) to recover the remains of a "Flying Tigers" crew whose B-24 bomber crashed into the mountain in 1944 after bombing Japanese forces near Taiwan during World War II.
January 15	At the Pentagon, Assistant Secretary of Defense for International Security Affairs Frank Kramer met with Wang Daohan, president of the PRC's Association for Relations Across the Taiwan Strait (ARATS).
February 21-March 6	Lieutenant General Kui Fulin, a Deputy Chief of General Staff, visited the United States, hosted by the Chief of Staff of the U.S. Army, General Dennis Reimer. General Kui visited the Pentagon, West Point in New York, U.S. Army Forces Command in Georgia, Fort Benning in Georgia, and PACOM in Hawaii.
February 24-27	The Principal Assistant Deputy Under Secretary of Defense for Environmental Security, Gary Vest, visited Beijing to participate in the 1997 China Environment Forum and met with PLA leaders to discuss environmental security issues.
March 9-25	PLA Naval ships (the Luhu-class destroyer Harbin, the Luda-class destroyer Zhuhai, and the oiler Nanchang) visited Pearl Harbor, HI (March 9-13) and San Diego, CA (March 21-25), in the PLA Navy (PLAN)'s second ship visit to Pearl Harbor and first port call to the U.S. west coast. As part of the occasion, Vice Admiral He Pengfei (a PLAN Deputy Commander) and Vice Admiral Wang Yongguo (PLAN South Sea Fleet Commander) visited the United States.
April	Major General John Cowlings, Commandant of the Industrial College of the Armed Forces of the U.S. NDU, visited China.
May 12-15	The Chairman of the Joint Chiefs of Staff, General John Shalikashvili, visited China, hosted by the PLA's Chief of General Staff, General Fu Quanyou. On May 14, 1997, Shalikashvili gave a speech at the PLA's NDU, in which he called for mil-to-mil contacts that are deeper, more frequent, more balanced, and more developed, in order to decrease suspicion, advance cooperation, and prevent miscalculations in a crisis. He called for a more equal exchange of information, confidence building measures (CBMs), military academic and functional exchanges, the PLA's participation in multinational military activities, and a regular dialogue between senior military leaders. He also urged the completion of the military maritime and air cooperative agreement. However, Shalikashvili reportedly got only a limited view of the PLA during a visit to the 15th Airborne Army (in Hubei province).
July	Lieutenant General Xu Qiliang, Chief of Staff of the PLA Air Force, led an education and training delegation to the United States.
July	Lieutenant General Wu Quanxu, a Deputy Chief of General Staff of the PLA, visited PACOM in Hawaii.

August 5-13	General Fu Quanyou, PLA Chief of General Staff, visited the United States. Secretary of Defense William Cohen and General John Shalikashvili welcomed Fu at the Pentagon with a 19-gun salute. General Fu also visited West Point in New York, Fort Bragg in North Carolina, Norfolk Naval Base in Virginia, Langley Air Force Base in Virginia, and PACOM in Hawaii. General Fu boarded a U.S. nuclear attack submarine and the USS Blue Ridge, the 7th Fleet's amphibious command ship.
September 11-15	An Arleigh Burke-class destroyer, the USS John S. McCain, visited Qingdao. As part of the occasion, Commander of the U.S. Pacific Fleet, Admiral Archie Clemins, visited China and met with the Commander of the PLAN North Sea Fleet, Rear Admiral Zhang Dingfa.
September 14-21	The Judge Advocate General of the U.S. Army, Major General Walter Huffman, visited China, including the Jinan Military Region, to discuss military law.
September 22-26	The U.S. Army's Chief of Staff, General Dennis Reimer, visited China, along with the Army's Deputy Chief of Staff for Intelligence, Lieutenant General Claudia Kennedy. They met with Generals Chi Haotian and Fu Quanyou, and visited the 6th Tank Division and an engineering regiment in the Beijing Military Region, and an artillery unit in the Nanjing Military Region. They also paid the first U.S. visit to the command headquarters of the Guangzhou Military Region.
October 6	The Chief of Naval Operations, Admiral Jay Johnson, visited China and met with General Chi Haotian, General Fu Quanyou, and Admiral Shi Yunsheng, PLAN Commander.
October	Lieutenant General He Daoquan, a Vice President of the PLA's NDU, led a delegation to the United States (similar to the U.S. Capstone program for new general/flag officers).
October 29	Jiang Zemin, General Secretary of the Communist Party of China, CMC Chairman, and PRC President, visited Washington for a summit with President Clinton. Among a number of agreements, they agreed to strengthen mil-to-mil contacts to minimize miscalculations, advance transparency, and strengthen communication. In the "U.S.-PRC Joint Statement," the Administration reiterated that it adheres to the "one China" policy and the principles in the three U.S.-PRC Joint Communiques, but did not mention the Taiwan Relations Act (TRA), the law governing U.S. relations with Taiwan (including security assistance for its self-defense).
November	Continuing a POW/MIA mission, a team from the U.S. Army's Central Identification Laboratory Hawaii (CILHI) returned to Maoer Mountain in southern China to recover additional remains from a B-24 bomber that crashed in 1944.
December 8-19	PACOM Commander, Admiral Joseph Prueher, visited China and met with PRC leader Jiang Zemin, General Zhang Wannian, General Chi Haotian, General Fu Quanyou, among others. Prueher enjoyed what the PLA considered the broadest access ever granted to a visiting military official during one trip. Prueher visited the Jinan, Nanjing, and Guangzhou Military Regions. He visited the PLA Air Force Flight Test and Development Center in Cangzhou in Jinan,

	where he saw a static display of aircraft, after poor weather conditions apparently precluded a flight demonstration of F-7 and F-8 fighters. Prueher visited the 179th Infantry Division at the Nanjing Military Region, watched a live-fire assault demonstration, and toured a farm run by the PLA. At Zhanjiang, Prueher visited the PLA Navy's South Sea Fleet, where he observed a demonstration by the 1st Marine Brigade, saw a new air-cushioned landing craft, and toured the destroyer Zhuhai. Prueher stressed future PLA-PACOM cooperation in peacekeeping and disaster relief training.
December 11-12	Lieutenant General Xiong Guangkai, a PLA Deputy Chief of General Staff, visited the Pentagon to hold the 1st U.S.-PLA Defense Consultative Talks (DCT) with Under Secretary of Defense for Policy Walter Slocombe. During their summit in October, Presidents Clinton and Jiang had agreed to hold regular rounds of DCT. The two sides initialed the Military Maritime Consultative Agreement (MMCA) ("Agreement Between the Department of Defense of the United States of America and the Ministry of National Defense of the People's Republic of China on Establishing a Consultation Mechanism to Strengthen Military Maritime Safety").
December	The U.S. Air Force and Coast Guard conducted search-and-rescue exercises in Hong Kong (with its Civil Aviation Department), after the British hand-over of Hong Kong to PRC sovereignty in July 1997. At a news briefing on July 7, 1998, the Pentagon said that the PLA observed this exercise.
December	A PLA training delegation visited the U.S. Army's premier National Training Center (NTC) at Fort Irwin in California.

1998

January 17-21	Secretary of Defense William Cohen, accompanied by Admiral Prueher (PACOM Commander), visited China. Cohen signed the "Military Maritime Consultative Agreement (MMCA)," intended to set up a framework for dialogue on how to minimize the chances of miscalculation and accidents between U.S. and PLA forces operating at sea or in the air. He said that Jiang Zemin and General Chi Haotian promised that China did not plan to transfer to Iran additional anti-ship cruise missiles. The PLA allowed Cohen to be the first Western official to visit the Beijing Military Region's Air Defense Command Center, a step that Cohen called important and symbolic. However, the PLA denied Cohen's request to visit China's National Command Center. Cohen gave a speech at the PLA's Academy of Military Science (AMS) and called for expanded mil-to-mil contacts on: (1) defense environmental issues; (2) strategic nuclear missile forces; (3) POW/MIA affairs; and (4) humanitarian operations (as part of shifting contacts from those that build confidence to those that advance real-world cooperation). Cohen asked the PLA to allow U.S. access to PRC archives to resolve questions about the fate of U.S. POW/MIAs in the Korean War who might have been in prison camps in China.
February 16-20	For the first time, the PLA attended the Pacific Area Special Operations Conference (PASOC) in Hawaii.
March 14-24	A U.S. Army training delegation from the Training and Doctrine Command (TRADOC) based at Fort Monroe, VA, visited China. The

	Deputy Chief of Staff for Training, Major General Leroy Goff and Assistant Deputy Chief of Staff for Personnel, Major General David Ohle, led the delegation. They saw the PLA's training base in Anhui province under the Nanjing Military Region (similar to the NTC).
March 29-April 10	General Wang Ke, Director of the GLD of the PLA, visited the United States, hosted by the Under Secretary of Defense for Acquisitions and Technology. General Wang visited West Point in New York, Aberdeen Proving Ground in Maryland, the Pentagon, Warner-Robins Air Logistics Center in Georgia, the Defense Logistics Agency's Defense Supply Center in Richmond, the USS Abraham Lincoln aircraft carrier at Naval Air Station North Island (San Diego) in California, and PACOM in Hawaii. At the Pentagon, DOD provided briefings on: organizations for the DOD Logistics Systems, Logistics Modernization Initiatives, Joint Logistics/Focused Logistics, DOD Outsourcing Process and Experiences, DOD Military Retirement Systems, and the Army's Integrated Training Area Management Program.

In April 1998, the New York Times disclosed that the Justice Department had begun a criminal investigation into whether U.S. satellite manufacturers, Loral Space and Communications Ltd. and Hughes Electronics Corporation, violated export control laws. They allegedly provided expertise that China could use to improve its ballistic missiles, when the companies shared their technical findings with China on the cause of a PRC rocket's explosion while launching a U.S.-origin satellite in February 1996. The House set up the "Cox Committee" to investigate the allegations of corporate misconduct and policy mistakes. The Senate set up a task force. Congress passed legislation to control satellite exports to China

April 6-10	The PLA went to PACOM's Military Operations and Law Conference, organized by the Judge Advocate's office.
April 29-30	The Defense Department and PLA held pre-talks on the Military Maritime Consultative Agreement (MMCA).
May 3-5	Assistant Secretary of Defense for International Security Affairs Franklin Kramer visited Beijing.
May 4-9	The Chief of Staff of the U.S. Air Force, General Michael Ryan, visited China. The PLA Air Force gave him a tour of Foshan Air Base and allowed him to fly an F-7 fighter and view an air-refuelable version of an FA-2. However, the PLA Air Force denied General Ryan's requests to fly in a SU-27 fighter, to see integration of the SU-27s into the units, and to see progress on development of the F-10 fighter.
May	A PLA delegation on military law visited the United States.
June 25-July 3	President Clinton traveled to China to hold his second summit with Jiang Zemin, following the summit in October 1997. They announced that the United States and China: have a direct presidential "hot line" that was set up in May 1998; will not target strategic nuclear weapons under their respective control at each other; will hold the first meeting under the MMCA; will observe exercises of the other based on reciprocity (meaning the PLA would also issue invitations to U.S. observers); will cooperate in humanitarian assistance; and will cooperate in military environmental security. However, China only agreed to study

whether to join the Missile Technology Control Regime (MTCR) and did not agree to open archives to allow U.S. research on POW/MIAs from the Korean War. In Shanghai on June 30, Clinton stated the so-called "Three Noes" of non-support for Taiwan's independence; non-support for two Chinas or one China and one Taiwan; and non-support for Taiwan's membership in international bodies requiring statehood.

July 9-24	At U.S. invitation, the PLA sent two observers to Cope Thunder 98-4, a multinational air exercise held at Eielson and Elmendorf Air Force Bases in Alaska. The air forces of the United States, United Kingdom, Australia, Japan, and Singapore participated in the exercise, which was designed to sharpen air combat skills, exchange air operational tactics, and promote closer relations. Pilots flew a variety of aircraft in air-to-air and air-to-ground combat missions, and combat support missions against a realistic set of threats. Russia, Brunei, Malaysia, Thailand, and the Philippines also sent military observers.
July 14-15	In Beijing, the DOD and PLA held the first plenary meeting under the MMCA.
July 15-20	At U.S. invitation, the PLA Navy sent two observers to RIMPAC 1998, the first time the PLA observed this multinational naval exercise based in Hawaii in the Pacific Ocean. The naval forces of the United States, Australia, Canada, Chile, Japan, and South Korea participated in the exercise, which was designed to enhance their tactical capabilities in maritime operations. During part of the exercise, the U.S. Navy hosted the PLA Navy's representatives on board the USS Coronado (the 3rd Fleet's command ship), the USS Carl Vinson aircraft carrier, the USS Paul Hamilton (an Arleigh Burke-class destroyer), and the USS Antietam (a Ticonderoga-class cruiser).
July 20-26	PLA Deputy Chief of General Staff, Lieutenant General Qian Shugen, visited the United States.
July	A PRC civilian and military delegation visited the United States, including Pensacola, FL, to discuss air traffic control with the Federal Aviation Administration, Departments of Commerce and Defense, and the U.S. Air Force.
August 2-6	The command ship of the 7th Fleet, USS Blue Ridge, and a destroyer, USS John S. McCain, visited Qingdao. As part of the occasion, Vice Admiral Robert Natter, Commander of the 7th Fleet, visited and met with Vice Admiral Shi Yunsheng, PLAN Commander, and Vice Admiral He Pengfei, a PLAN Deputy Commander.
August 16-23	The Commandant of the Army War College, Major General Robert Scales, and the U.S. Army's Chief of Military History, Brigadier General John Mountcastle, visited Beijing, Tianjin, and Nanjing, and discussed the PLA's historical campaigns.
September 12-20	NDU President, Lieutenant General Richard Chilcoat, visited China, including Hong Kong, Beijing, Xian, and Dalian.
September 14-24	General Zhang Wannian, a Vice Chairman of the CMC and highest ranking PLA officer, visited the United States. However, with General Shalikashvili's disappointment with the lack of transparency and reciprocity shown to him by the PLA during his trip to China in May 1997, Secretary of Defense William Cohen

invoked the "Shali Prohibitions" in restricting General Zhang's exposure to the U.S. military during his visits to the Pentagon, Fort Benning in Georgia, and Nellis Air Force Base in Nevada. President Clinton met with General Zhang at the White House. At a news conference on September 15, 1998, Secretary Cohen announced that he and General Zhang signed an agreement on cooperation in environmental security ("Joint Statement on the Exchange of Information by the United States Department of Defense and the Chinese Ministry of National Defense on Military Environmental Protection"); discussed weapons proliferation and international terrorism; and agreed to conduct sand table exercises on disaster relief and humanitarian assistance in 1999, to have a ship visit by the PLA Navy in 1999, to conduct a seminar on maritime search and rescue, to allow each other to observe specific military exercises, to exchange military students, and to allow a PRC delegation to visit the Cooperative Monitoring Center at the Sandia National Laboratory. However, Cohen did not announce any progress in following up on U.S. concerns about Korean War POW/MIA cases, non-targeting of strategic nuclear forces (involving the Strategic Command (STRATCOM) and the PLA's Second Artillery), PLA threats against Taiwan, or weapons nonproliferation. General Zhang cited President Clinton's statements in China in June about the U.S. "one China" policy and the "Three Noes," while Secretary Cohen stressed peaceful resolution and said that Clinton reiterated commitment to the Taiwan Relations Act.

October 20-21   Under Secretary of Defense for Policy Walter Slocombe visited Beijing for the 2nd DCT and met with Generals Zhang Wannian and Chi Haotian (CMC Vice Chairmen), and Lieutenant General Xiong Guangkai. They discussed global and regional security issues, defense relations in the Asia-Pacific region, military strategy and modernization, and mil-to-mil contacts in 1999 ("Gameplan for 1999 U.S.-Sino Defense Exchanges"). The PLA raised objections to the U.S. plan to field theater missile defense systems.

November 1   Secretary of Defense Cohen visited Hong Kong (on his way to South Korea and Japan) to underscore the U.S. determination to continue its defense involvement there, including ship visits, after its hand-over to PRC rule.

November 9-14   PACOM Commander, Admiral Joseph Prueher, visited China, along with Lieutenant General Carl Fulford (Commander of U.S. Marine Forces Pacific) and Major General Earl Hailston (Director for Strategic Planning and Policy). They met with General Zhang Wannian (a CMC Vice Chairman), General Fu Quanyou (Chief of General Staff), General Wang Ke (GLD Director), and Lieutenant General Xiong Guangkai (a Deputy Chief of General Staff). The PLA arranged for visits to the 47th Group Army based near Xian and a subordinate air defense brigade, in granting the first foreign military access to these two commands. Admiral Prueher also visited the PLA Air Force's 28th Air Attack Division in Hangzhou and observed ordnance loading of A-5 bombers and a live-fire demonstration of an air-to-ground attack by A-5s. He then toured a Jiangwei-class frigate of the PLA Navy in Shanghai.

December 1-4	U.S. and PLA military forces participated in an annual search and rescue exercise (HK SAREX 98) held by Hong Kong's Civil Aviation Department.
December 4	PACOM Commander, Admiral Joseph Prueher, visited Hong Kong and met with Major Generals Zhou Borong and Xiong Ziren, Deputy Commander and Political Commissar of PLA forces there.
December 4-8	A U.S. Navy frigate, the USS Vandegrift, visited Shanghai. As part of the port call, Rear Admiral Harry Highfill, Commander of the U.S. 7th Fleet's Amphibious Force, met with Rear Admiral Hou Yuexi, Commander of the Shanghai Naval Base. The PLAN arranged for Admiral Highfill to tour the PLAN's Jiangwei-class frigate, the Anqing.
December 9-11	Military maritime consultative talks (under the MMCA) between the U.S. Navy and PLAN took place near San Diego, CA. The PLAN delegation, led by Captain Shen Hao, Director of the PLAN Operations Department, stayed at the Naval Amphibious Base at Coronado and toured a U.S. destroyer (USS Stetham) and the U.S. Navy's Maritime Ship Handling Simulator at the San Diego Naval Station.

1999

At the end of 1998 and start of 1999, the New York Times and Wall Street Journal disclosed that the Cox Committee was looking at the Clinton Administration's investigation that began in 1995 into whether China obtained secret U.S. nuclear weapons data, in addition to missile technology associated with satellite launches. On April 21, 1999, the Director of Central Intelligence confirmed that "China obtained by espionage classified U.S. nuclear weapons information that probably accelerated its program to develop future nuclear weapons." However, it was uncertain whether China obtained documentation or blueprints, and China also benefitted from information obtained from a wide variety of sources, including open sources (unclassified information) and China's own efforts.

January 19-26	The Director of the Defense POW/MIA Office, Deputy Assistant Secretary of Defense Robert Jones, visited China to seek the PLA's cooperation in accounting for U.S. POW/MIAs from the Korean War, specifically seeking U.S. access to PLA archives, veterans, and a film with information about POW camps in China.
March	President of the PLA's NDU, General Xing Shizhong, visited Washington and gave a speech at the U.S. NDU at Fort McNair on March 18, 1999. The Pentagon arranged for General Xing to visit Norfolk Naval Base in Virginia, receive a briefing on the U.S. Navy's "Network Centric Warfare" in Rhode Island, visit Fort Hood in Texas and receive a briefing on Task Force XXI (an experimental warfighting force in the Army), and see the Air Warfare Center at Nellis Air Force Base in Nevada. However, the Defense Department denied the PLA delegation's access to observe the Red Flag combat training exercise at Nellis Air Force Base.

In April 1999, under congressional pressure, the Clinton Administration approved a potential sale of long-range early warning radars to Taiwan.

On May 7, 1999, U.S.-led NATO forces bombed the PRC's embassy in Belgrade, Yugoslavia, having mistakenly targeted it as a military supply facility belonging to Yugoslav President Slobodan Milosevic whose Serbian forces attacked Kosovo.

Despite President Clinton's apology, the PRC angrily suspended mil-to-mil contacts, allowed protesters to attack violently U.S. diplomatic facilities in China, and denied ship visits to Hong Kong by the U.S. Navy until September 1999. In July 1999, the United States agreed to pay $4.5 million in compensation for PRC casualties. In FY2001 legislation, Congress appropriated $28 million to compensate for damages to China's embassy.

May	A U.S. Navy working group under the MMCA visited Qingdao to discuss international standards of communication at sea.
May 9-20	A PRC delegation that included PLA officers visited the United States to discuss air traffic control. On May 18, 1999, they visited Edwards Air Force Base in California and received a briefing on daily planning, integration, and control of civilian and military operations.

In May 1999, as required by the National Defense Authorization Act for FY1999 (P.L. 105-261), Secretary of Defense Cohen submitted the unclassified version of the "Report to Congress on Theater Missile Defense Architecture Options for the Asia-Pacific Region." Congress required a report on theater missile defense systems that could be transferred to Japan, South Korea, and Taiwan, which the conference report called "key regional allies."

On July 9, 1999, Taiwan President Lee Teng-hui characterized the cross-strait relationship as "special state-to-state ties," sparking military tensions with the PLA. The Clinton Administration responded that Lee's statement was not helpful and reaffirmed the "one China" policy. The PLA flew fighters across the "center" line of the Taiwan Strait and conducted exercises along the coast opposite Taiwan. In early September, CMC Vice Chairman General Zhang Wannian personally directed a major, joint landing exercise. A tragic earthquake in Taiwan on September 21 defused the tensions

November 19-21	Deputy Assistant Secretary of Defense for Asian and Pacific Affairs Kurt Campbell and Major General (USMC) Michael Hagee, PACOM's Director for Strategic Planning and Policy (J5), visited Beijing to discuss resuming military contacts.
December 1-4	U.S. military and PLA forces participated in Hong Kong's annual search and rescue exercise.

2000

January 24-26	Resuming contacts, Lieutenant General Xiong Guangkai (a Deputy Chief of General Staff) visited Washington to hold the 3rd DCT with Under Secretary of Defense for Policy Slocombe. They discussed the program for mil-to-mil contacts in 2000, international security issues, U.S. strategy in Asia, the PLA's missile buildup, Taiwan, missile defense, weapons proliferation, and North Korea. Xiong met with Secretary of Defense Cohen, Chairman of the Joint Chiefs General Henry Shelton, Deputy National Security Advisor James Steinberg, Under Secretary of State Thomas Pickering, and State Department Senior Advisor John Holum.
February 17-18	Deputy Secretary of State Strobe Talbott, Under Secretary of Defense for Policy Walter Slocombe, Vice Chairman of the Joint Chiefs of Staff General Joseph Ralston, and Deputy National Security Advisor James Steinberg visited Beijing (after visiting

Tokyo) for a strategic dialogue. They met with CMC Vice Chairman General Zhang Wannian, who raised the Taiwan issue, including U.S. arms sales to Taiwan.

On February 21, 2000, ahead of Taiwan's presidential election on March 18, 2000, the PRC issued its second Taiwan White Paper, which declared a threat to use force against Taiwan if a serious development leads to Taiwan's separation from China in any name, if there is foreign invasion or occupation of Taiwan, or if Taiwan's government indefinitely refuses to negotiate national unification (called the "Three Ifs"). Under Secretary of Defense Slocombe, who was just in Beijing but was given no indication that the PRC would issue the White Paper and the threat, responded forcefully on February 22 by warning that China would face "incalculable consequences" if it used force against Taiwan.

February 27-March 2	PACOM Commander, Admiral Dennis Blair, visited China and discussed tensions over Taiwan with Chief of General Staff, General Fu Quanyou, and General Chi Haotian.
March 10-12	Secretary of Defense William Cohen visited Hong Kong and discussed issues such as port calls by the U.S. Navy and the prevention of trans-shipments of advanced U.S. technology to mainland China.
March 27-29	A working group under the MMCA held a planning meeting in China.
April 14-22	PLAN Commander, Admiral Shi Yunsheng, visited the United States, coinciding with an annual round of U.S.-Taiwan arms sales talks in Washington. Admiral Shi met with Secretary of Defense Cohen, Vice Chairman of the Joint Chiefs of Staff General Richard Myers, and Chief of Naval Operations Admiral Jay Johnson.

In April 2000, during a round of annual arms sales talks, the Clinton Administration approved a request from Taiwan's military to purchase AIM-120 Advanced Medium-Range Air-to-Air Missiles (AMRAAMs).

May 28-June 3	PACOM in Hawaii hosted the second plenary meeting under the MMCA. PACOM's Director for Strategic Planning and Policy (J5), Major General Michael Hagee (USMC), and the PLA's Deputy Chief of Staff, Rear Admiral Wang Yucheng, led the proceedings. They reviewed a mutually-produced document, "A Study on Sino-U.S. Maritime Navigational Safety, Including Communications."
June 13-14	Assistant Secretary of Defense for International Security Affairs Frank Kramer visited Beijing and met with Major General Zhan Maohai, Lieutenant General Xiong Guangkai, and General Chi Haotian to plan Secretary of Defense Cohen's visit to China.
June 13-21	Superintendent of the U.S. Military Academy (West Point), Lieutenant General Daniel Christman, visited China. He met with General Chi Haotian and visited the PLA's Armored Force Engineering Academy, where he was the first American to have access to a PLA Type-96 main battle tank.
June 18-23	Nanjing Military Region Commander Liang Guanglie led a PLA delegation to visit PACOM in Hawaii and met with Admiral Dennis Blair.

On July 10, 2000, responding to objections from the Clinton Administration and Congress, Israeli Prime Minister Ehud Barak told PRC ruler Jiang Zemin in a letter that Israel canceled the nearly completed sale of the Phalcon airborne early warning system to the PLA. Prime Minister Barak informed President Clinton the next day during peace talks at Camp David, MD.

July 11-15	Secretary of Defense William Cohen visited Beijing and Shanghai. Cohen met with President Jiang Zemin and Generals Chi Haotian, Zhang Wannian, and Fu Quanyou. Cohen did not visit any PLA bases. Cohen referred to the promise made by PRC President Jiang Zemin during Cohen's previous visit to China in January 1998 and said that the PRC has abided by that agreement not to ship cruise missiles to Iran. Cohen and General Chi signed an "Agreement on the Exchange of Environmental Protection Research and Development Information" and discussed the need for cross-strait dialogue, weapons nonproliferation, and regional stability. The PRC objected to U.S. plans for missile defense and pressure on Israel to cancel the sale of the Phalcon airborne early warning system to the PLA, concerning which Israel notified China just before Cohen's visit. Cohen offered to fund PLA students at PACOM's APCSS in Honolulu. Regarding Taiwan, General Chi said that China would adopt a wait and see posture toward the leader of Taiwan (referring to Chen Shui-bian of the Democratic Progressive Party, who won the presidential election on March 18, 2000, bringing an end to the Kuomintang (KMT)'s 55 years of rule in Taiwan). Cohen said that the Administration viewed Chen as offering hope for cross-strait reconciliation. In Shanghai, Cohen stepped out of the narrow mil-to-mil context and met with Wang Daohan, chairman of the PRC's Association for Relations Across the Taiwan Strait (ARATS). Cohen said that Chen showed flexibility after becoming president and that there was a window of opportunity for changes.
July 23-August 4	A delegation of the PLA Medical Department visited the United States.
July 31-August 5	Admiral Thomas Fargo, Commander of the U.S. Pacific Fleet, visited Beijing and Qingdao in conjunction with the visit of the U.S. Navy's guided-missile cruiser USS Chancellorsville in Qingdao (August 2-5).
August 21-September 2	President of the PLA's Academy of Military Sciences (AMS), General Wang Zuxun, visited the United States. There is no counterpart in the U.S. military with which to set up reciprocal exchanges. The AMS delegation included the Directors of the Departments of Strategic Studies, Operational and Tactical Studies, and Foreign Military Studies. They visited the Pentagon; Joint Forces Command in Norfolk, Virginia; West Point in New York; Army War College in Pennsylvania; Army's Training and Doctrine Command (TRADOC) at Fort Monroe in Virginia; and PACOM in Hawaii. The Joint Forces Command provided unclassified tours of its Joint Training Directorate (J-7) and Joint Training Analysis Simulation Center, but not the Joint Experimentation Battle Lab.
September 5-18	PLA Navy ships (the Luhu-class destroyer Qingdao and Fuqing-class oiler Taicang) visited Pearl Harbor, HI (September 5-8) and Naval Station Everett, near Seattle, WA (September 14-18). In Hawaii, the visitors toured the U.S. destroyer USS O'Kane.
October	For the first time, the PLA invited two U.S. military personnel to

	attend the one-month International Security Symposium at the NDU in Beijing. (Subsequent invitations dropped required fees.)
October 10-18	The PLA participated in a visit to the United States by a Humanitarian Disaster Relief Sandtable Planning Team.
October 12-13	Secretary of the Navy Richard Danzig visited Shanghai, in the first visit by a U.S. Secretary of the Navy to China. His visit was curtailed because of the attack on the USS Cole in a Yemeni harbor on October 12, 2000.
October 24-November 4	CMC Member and Director of the General Political Department (GPD)—the top political commissar, General Yu Yongbo, visited the United States. He was hosted by Under Secretary of Defense for Readiness Bernard Rostker. General Yu's delegation visited the Pentagon and met with Secretary of Defense Cohen; West Point in New York; Bolling Air Force Base in Washington, DC; Fort Jackson in South Carolina; Patrick Air Force Base in Florida; and PACOM in Hawaii.
November 2-6	Chairman of the Joint Chiefs of Staff, General Henry Shelton, visited China, at the invitation of PLA Chief of General Staff, General Fu Quanyou. The PLA allowed General Shelton to observe a brigade exercising at the PLA's Combined Arms Training Center in the Nanjing Military Region. Shelton stressed the peaceful resolution of the Taiwan question.
November 2-12	A Deputy Chief of Staff of the PLA Navy, Rear Admiral Zhang Zhannan, led a delegation from the Naval Command Academy (in Nanjing) to visit Newport News, RI (Naval War College); Washington, DC (including a meeting with the Secretary of the Navy); Monterey, CA (Naval Post-Graduate School); and Honolulu, HI (Pacific Command, including a tour aboard an Aegis-equipped cruiser).
November 12-19	A PLA NDU delegation (similar to the U.S. Capstone program) visited the United States.
November 28-December 2	Under Secretary of Defense for Policy Walter Slocombe visited Beijing to hold the 4th DCT with PLA Deputy Chief of General Staff Xiong Guangkai. Slocombe also met with Generals Chi Haotian and Fu Quanyou and visited the PLA Navy's North Sea Fleet in Qingdao. The U.S. and PRC sides discussed sharp differences over Taiwan and missile defense, the program for mil-to-mil contacts in 2001, Korea, and weapons proliferation.
December 3-9	A Working Group under the MMCA held its second meeting (in China).
December 5-8	U.S. military and PLA forces participated in Hong Kong's annual search and rescue exercise and worked together in a demonstration.

At the end of December 2000 in New York, PLA Senior Colonel Xu Junping, who closely handled U.S.-PRC military relations, defected to the United States and presented an intelligence loss for the PLA (reported Far Eastern Economic Review, April 5, 2001).

2001

February 9-23	Major General Wang Shouye, Director of the GLD's Capital Construction and Barracks Department, led a delegation on military

	environmental protection matters to the United States. They visited Washington, DC; Fort Pickett in Virginia; Fort Bliss in Texas; the "boneyard" at Davis-Monthan Air Force Base in Arizona; Las Vegas in Nevada; and PACOM in Hawaii.
March 14-17	PACOM Commander, Adm. Dennis Blair, visited Beijing, Nanjing, and Shanghai. PACOM said that Blair's trip was intended to discuss military activities and plans of the PLA and PACOM, exchange views and enhance mutual understanding, discuss Taiwan, and stress the inclusion rather than exclusion of China in multilateral activities.
March 23-26	The command ship of the 7th Fleet, the USS Blue Ridge, made a port call to Shanghai. In conjunction with the ship visit, Vice Admiral James Metzger, Commander of the 7th Fleet, visited Shanghai and met with Vice Admiral Zhao Guojun, Commander of the PLAN's East Sea Fleet.

On March 24, 2001, in the Yellow Sea near South Korea, a PLA Navy Jianghu III-class frigate passed as close as 100 yards to a U.S. surveillance ship, the USS Bowditch, and a PLA reconnaissance plane shadowed it. The PLA's harassment of the USS Bowditch continued for months.

On April 1, 2001, a PLA Navy F-8 fighter collided with a U.S. Navy EP-3 reconnaissance plane over the South China Sea. Upon surviving the collision, the EP-3's crew made an emergency landing on China's Hainan island. The PLA detained the 24 U.S. Navy personnel for 11 days. Instead of acknowledging that the PLA had started aggressive interceptions of U.S. reconnaissance flights in December 2000 and apologizing for the accident, top PRC ruler Jiang Zemin demanded an apology and compensation from the United States. The United States did not transport the damaged EP-3 out of China until July 3.

On April 24, 2001, during arms sales talks in Washington, President Bush approved a request from Taiwan's military to purchase weapons systems including diesel-electric submarines; P-3 anti-submarine warfare aircraft; and destroyers (approving four Kidd-class destroyers). The Bush Administration also decided to brief Taiwan on the PAC-3 missile defense missile. The next day, the President said in an interview that if the PRC attacked Taiwan, he has an obligation to do "whatever it took to help Taiwan defend herself."

September 14-15	DOD and the PLA held a special meeting under the MMCA (in Guam) to discuss how to avoid clashes like the one involving the EP-3. The Commander of U.S. Naval Forces Marianas, Rear Admiral Tom Fellin, led the U.S. delegation. The issues for U.S. side were: principles of safe flight and navigation for military activities conducted on the high seas, international airspace, and EEZs; and safety of ships and aircraft exercising the right of distressed entry. The Deputy Director of the Foreign Affairs Office, Major General Zhang Bangdong, led the PLA delegation.
December 5-7	A Working Group under the MMCA met in Beijing.

2002

April 10-12	The third plenary meeting under the MMCA was held in Shanghai. PACOM's Director for Strategic Planning and Policy (J5), Rear Admiral William Sullivan, and the PLA Navy's Deputy Chief of Staff, Rear Admiral Zhou Borong, led the delegations.
April 27-May 1	PRC Vice President Hu Jintao visited PACOM and was

	welcomed by Admiral Dennis Blair. In Washington, Secretary of Defense Rumsfeld welcomed Hu with an honor cordon at the Pentagon. PRC media reported that Rumsfeld and Hu reached a consensus to resume military exchanges, but the Pentagon's spokeswoman said that they agreed to have their representatives talk about how to proceed on mil-to-mil contacts, which were still approved on a case-by-case basis. Vice President Hu also met with President Bush and Vice President Dick Cheney.
May 14-28	The PLA sent observers to Cobra Gold 2002 in Thailand, a combined exercise involving forces of the United States, Thailand, and Singapore.
June 26-27	Assistant Secretary of Defense for International Security Affairs Peter Rodman visited Beijing to discuss a resumption of military exchanges. He met with General Xiong Guangkai and General Chi Haotian, who said that the PRC was ready to improve military relations with the United States. Secretary Rumsfeld told reporters on June 21, 2002, that Rodman would discuss the principles of transparency, reciprocity, and consistency for mil-to-mil contacts that Rumsfeld stressed to Vice President Hu Jintao.
July 15-29	In the first POW/MIA mission in China on a Cold War case, a team from the Army's Central Identification Laboratory in Hawaii (CILHI) went to northeastern Jilin province to search for, but did not find, the remains of two CIA pilots whose C-47 plane was shot down in 1952 during the Korean War.
August 6-8	The PLA and DOD held a meeting under the MMCA in Hawaii.
August-September	In a POW/MIA recovery mission, a team from the Army's Central Identification Laboratory in Hawaii (CILHI) recovered remains of the crew of a C-46 cargo plane that crashed in March 1944 in Tibet while flying the "Hump" route over the Himalaya mountains back to India from Kunming, China, during World War II. The two-month operation excavated a site at 15,600 ft.
October 8-14	The President of NDU, Vice Admiral Paul Gaffney, visited Beijing, Xian, Hangzhou, and Shanghai. He met with CMC Vice Chairman and Defense Minister Chi Haotian, Deputy Chief of General Staff Xiong Guangkai, and NDU President Xing Shizhong.
October 25	President Bush held a summit with PRC President Jiang Zemin at his ranch in Crawford, TX. Concerning security issues, President Bush said they discussed "the threat posed by the Iraqi regime," "concern about the acknowledgment of the Democratic People's Republic of Korea of a program to enrich uranium," counterterrorism (calling China an "ally"), weapons proliferation, Taiwan, and a "candid, constructive, and cooperative" relationship with contacts at many levels in coming months, including "a new dialogue on security issues." Jiang offered a vague proposal to reconsider the PLA's missile buildup in return for restraints in U.S. arms sales to Taiwan.
November 24	In the first U.S. naval port call to mainland China since the EP-3 crisis, the destroyer USS Paul F. Foster visited Qingdao.
November 30-December 8	Lieutenant General Gao Jindian, a Vice President of the NDU, led a Capstone-like delegation to the United States.

December 4-6	The Maritime and Air Safety Working Group under the MMCA met in Qingdao. The U.S. team toured the destroyer Qingdao.
December 9-10	Following a two-year hiatus after the previous Defense Consultative Talks (DCT) in December 2000, the Pentagon held the 5th DCT (the first under the Bush Administration) and kept U.S. representation at the same level as that under the Clinton Administration. Under Secretary of Defense for Policy Douglas Feith met with General Xiong Guangkai, a Deputy Chief of General Staff, at the Pentagon. The PLA played up the status of Xiong and the DCT, calling the meeting "defense consultations at the vice ministerial level." At U.S. urging, Xiong brought a proposal for mil-to-mil exchanges in 2003. Feith told reporters that he could not claim progress in gaining greater reciprocity and transparency in the exchanges, although they had a discussion of these issues. They did not discuss Jiang's offer on the PLA's missile buildup. Feith also said that DOD had no major change in its attitude toward the PLA since the EP-3 crisis. Secretary Rumsfeld did not meet with Xiong. Deputy Secretary of Defense Wolfowitz and National Security Advisor Condoleezza Rice met with Xiong on December 10.
December 12-17	PACOM Commander, Admiral Thomas Fargo, visited Chengdu, Nanjing, Ningbo, Beijing, and Shanghai. The PLA showed him a live-fire exercise conducted by a reserve unit of an infantry division in Sichuan. General Liang Guanglie (Chief of General Staff) met with Admiral Fargo.

2003

March 25-29	The Director of the Defense POW/MIA Office (DPMO), Deputy Assistant Secretary of Defense Jerry Jennings, visited China and met with officials of the PLA, Ministry of Foreign Affairs, and Red Cross Society of China. Jennings said that the PRC has records that may well hold "the key" to helping DOD to resolve many of the cases of American POWs and MIAs from the Vietnam War, the Korean War, and the Cold War. While the PRC has been "very cooperative" in U.S. investigations of losses from World War II and Vietnam, Jennings said both sides suggested ways to "enhance cooperation" on Korean War cases and acknowledged that there is limited time. Jennings sought access to information in PRC archives at the national and provincial levels, assistance from PRC civilian researchers to conduct archival research on behalf of the United States, information from the Dandong Museum relating to two F-86 pilots who are Korean War MIAs, and resumption of contact with PLA veterans from the Korean War to build on information related to the PRC operation of POW camps during the war.
April 9-11	In Hawaii, in the fourth plenary meeting under the MMCA, PACOM's Director for Strategic Planning and Policy (J5), Rear Admiral William Sullivan, met with PLA Navy's Deputy Chief of Staff, Rear Admiral Zhou Borong.
April 25-May 4	The Commandant of the PLA's NDU, Lieutenant General Pei Huailiang, led a delegation to visit the U.S. Naval Academy in Annapolis, MD; U.S. NDU in Washington, DC; Marine Corps

	Recruit Depot in San Diego, CA; and PACOM in Honolulu, HI.
May 15-29	The PLA sent observers to Cobra Gold 2003 in Thailand, a combined exercise involving the armed forces of the United States, Thailand, and Singapore.
August 19-21	The Military Maritime and Air Safety Working Group under the MMCA met in Hawaii. The PLA delegation met with PACOM's Chief of Staff for the Director for Strategic Planning and Policy, Brigadier General (USAF) Charles Neeley, and toured the U.S. Aegis-equipped cruiser USS Lake Erie.
August 25	The PLA arranged for 27 military observers from the United States and other countries to be the first foreign military observers to visit China's largest combined arms training base (in the Inner Mongolia Autonomous Region) and watch an exercise that involved elements of force-on-force, live-fire, and joint operational maneuvers conducted by the Beijing Military Region.
September 22-26	In the first foreign naval ship visit to Zhanjiang, the cruiser USS Cowpens and frigate USS Vandegrift visited this homeport of the PLAN's South Sea Fleet. Its Chief of Staff, Rear Admiral Hou Yuexi, welcomed Rear Admiral James Kelly, Commander of Carrier Group Five, who also visited.
October 22-25	The PLAN destroyer Shenzhen and supply ship Qinghai Lake visited Guam.
October 24-November 1	CMC Vice Chairman and PRC Defense Minister, General Cao Gangchuan, visited PACOM in Hawaii, West Point in New York, and Washington, DC, where he met with Secretary of Defense Donald Rumsfeld and Secretary of State Colin Powell. General Cao stressed that Taiwan was the most important issue. The PLA sought the same treatment for General Cao as that given to General Chi Haotian when he visited Washington as defense minister in 1996 and was granted a meeting with President Clinton. In the end, President Bush dropped by for five minutes when General Cao met with National Security Advisor Rice at the White House. Rumsfeld did not attend the PRC Embassy's banquet for Cao. At PACOM, Cao met with Admiral Thomas Fargo, toured the cruiser USS Lake Erie.
November 12-19	Nanjing Military Region Commander, Lieutenant General Zhu Wenquan, visited PACOM where he met with Admiral Thomas Fargo and boarded the destroyer USS Russell. LTG Zhu also visited San Diego, where he toured the carrier USS Nimitz and the Marine Corps Recruit Depot. He also stopped in Washington, DC, and West Point in New York.

On November 18, 2003, a PRC official on Taiwan affairs who is a PLA major general, Wang Zaixi, issued a threat to use force against the perceived open promotion of Taiwan independence. Campaigning for re-election on March 20, 2004, Taiwan's President Chen Shui-bian was calling for controversial referendums and a new Taiwan constitution. On the eve of his visit to Washington, PRC Premier Wen Jiabao threatened that China would "pay any price to safeguard the unity of the motherland." On December 3, PRC media reported the warnings of a PLA major general and a senior colonel at AMS, who wrote that Chen's use of referendums to seek independence will push Taiwan into the "abyss of war." They warned that China would be willing to pay the costs of war, including boycotts of the 2008 Olympics in Beijing, drops in foreign investment, setbacks in foreign relations, wartime damage to the southeastern coast, economic costs, and PLA casualties. Appearing with Premier Wen at the White House on December 9, 2003, President Bush criticized Chen, saying that "we oppose any unilateral decision by either China or Taiwan to change the status quo. And the comments and actions made by the leader of Taiwan indicate that he may be willing to make decisions unilaterally to change the status quo, which we oppose."

2004

January 13-16	The Chairman of the Joint Chiefs of Staff, General (USAF) Richard Myers, visited Beijing, the first visit to China by the highest ranking U.S. military officer since November 2000. General Myers met with Generals Guo Boxiong and Cao Gangchuan (CMC Vice Chairmen) and General Liang Guanglie (PLA Chief of General Staff). CMC Chairman Jiang Zemin met briefly with Myers, echoing President Bush's brief meeting with General Cao. The PLA generals and Jiang stressed Taiwan as their critical issue. General Myers stressed that the United States has a responsibility under the TRA to assist Taiwan's ability to defend itself and to ensure that there will be no temptation to use force. Myers pointed to the PLA's missile buildup as a threat to Taiwan. The PLA allowed Myers to be the first foreign visitor to tour the Beijing Aerospace Control Center, headquarters of its space program. Myers discussed advancing mil-to-mil contacts, including search and rescue exercises, educational exchanges, ship visits, and senior-level exchanges (including a visit by General Liang Guanglie). Myers also indicated a U.S. expectation of exchanges between younger officers, saying that interactions at the lower level can improve mutual understanding in the longer run.
February 10-11	Under Secretary of Defense for Policy Douglas Feith visited Beijing to hold the 6th DCT with General Xiong Guangkai, a meeting which the PLA side claimed to be "defense consultations at the vice ministerial level." Feith met with General Cao Gangchuan (a CMC Vice Chairman and Defense Minister), who raised extensively the issue of Taiwan and the referendums. Feith said he discussed North Korean nuclear weapons, Taiwan, and maritime safety. He stressed that avoiding a war in the Taiwan Strait was in the interests of both countries and that belligerent rhetoric and the PLA's missile buildup do not help to reduce cross-strait tensions. The PRC's Foreign Ministry said that the two sides discussed a program for mil-to-mil contacts in 2004. The Department of Defense proposed a defense telephone link (DTL), or "hotline," with the PLA.
February 24-28	The USS Blue Ridge, the 7th Fleet's command ship, visited Shanghai. In conjunction with the port call, Vice Admiral Robert Willard, Commander of the 7th Fleet, met with Rear Admiral Zhao Guojun, Commander of the East Sea Fleet.
March 9-11	The Maritime and Air Safety Working Group under the MMCA met in Shanghai. The U.S. visitors met with Rear Admiral Zhou Borong, Deputy Chief of Staff of the PLAN, and toured the frigate Lianyungang.
May 3-June 29	A team from the Joint POW/MIA Accounting Command (JPAC) traveled to northeastern city of Dandong near China's border with North Korea on an operation to recover remains of a pilot whose F-86 fighter was shot down during the Korean War. In following up

	on an initial operation in July 2002 on a Cold War case, the U.S. team also went to northeastern Jilin province to recover remains of two CIA pilots whose C-47 transport plane was shot down in 1952.
July 21-25	PACOM Commander, Admiral Thomas Fargo, visited China and met with General Liu Zhenwu (Guangzhou Military Region Commander), Foreign Minister Li Zhaoxing, General Liang Guanglie (Chief of General Staff), and General Xiong Guangkai (a Deputy Chief of General Staff), who opposed U.S. arms sales and defense cooperation with Taiwan. Fargo said that policy on Taiwan has not changed.
August-September	DPMO sent a team to Tibet to recover wreckage from a site where a C-46 aircraft crashed during World War II.
September 24-27	The USS Cushing, a destroyer with the Pacific Fleet, visited Qingdao for a port visit.
October 24-30	Reciprocating General Myers' visit to China, PLA Chief of General Staff, General Liang Guanglie, visited the United States, including the Joint Forces Command and Joint Forces Staff College at Norfolk; the carrier USS George Washington and the destroyer USS Laboon at Norfolk Naval Base; Air Combat Command at Langley Air Force Base; Joint Task Force-Civil Support at Fort Monroe; Army Infantry Center at Fort Benning; Washington, D.C.; and Air Force Academy in Colorado Springs. In Washington, General Liang held meetings with National Security Advisor Condoleezza Rice, Secretary of State Colin Powell, and General Richard Myers, Chairman of the Joint Chiefs of Staff. Secretary of Defense Rumsfeld saw General Liang briefly. Talks covered military exchanges, the Six-Party Talks on North Korea, and Taiwan.
November 22-23	DPMO held Technical Talks in Beijing on POW/MIA recovery operations in 2005.

2005

January 30-February 1	Deputy Under Secretary of Defense Richard Lawless visited Beijing to hold a Special Policy Dialogue for the first time, as a forum to discuss policy problems separate from safety concerns under the MMCA. Meeting with Zhang Bangdong, Director of the PLA's Foreign Affairs Office, Lawless tried to negotiate an agreement on military maritime and air safety. He also discussed a program of military contacts in 2005, the U.S. proposal of February 2004 for a "hotline," Taiwan, the DCTs, PLA's buildup, and a possible visit by Secretary Rumsfeld. Lawless also met with General Xiong Guangkai.
February 23-25	Deputy Assistant Secretary of Defense for POW/MIA Affairs Jerry Jennings visited Beijing and Dandong to discuss China's assistance in resolving cases from the Vietnam War and World War II. He also continued to seek access to China's documents related to POW camps that China managed during the Korean War. At Dandong, Jennings announced the recovery of the remains of a U.S. Air Force pilot who was missing-in-action from the Korean War.
April 29-30	General Xiong Guangkai, Deputy Chief of General Staff, visited Washington to hold the 7th DCT with Under Secretary of Defense

	Douglas Feith. They continued to discuss the U.S. proposal for a "hotline" and an agreement on military maritime and air safety with the PLA and also talked about military exchanges, international security issues, PLA modernization, U.S. military redeployments, and energy. Xiong also met with Deputy Secretary of Defense Paul Wolfowitz, National Security Advisor Stephen Hadley, and Under Secretary of State Nicholas Burns.
July 7-8	The Department of Defense and the PLA held an annual MMCA meeting in Qingdao, to discuss unresolved maritime and air safety issues under the MMCA.
July 18-22	General Liu Zhenwu, Commander of the PLA's Guangzhou Military Region, visited Hawaii, as hosted by Admiral William Fallon, Commander of the Pacific Command. Among visits to parts of the Pacific Command, General Liu toured the USS Chosin, a Ticonderoga-class cruiser.
September 6-11	Admiral William Fallon, Commander of the Pacific Command, visited Beijing, Shanghai, Guangzhou, and Hong Kong at the invitation of General Liu Zhenwu, Guangzhou Military Region Commander. As Admiral Fallon said he sought to deepen the "exceedingly limited military interaction," he met with high-ranking PLA Generals Guo Boxiong (CMC Vice Chairman) and Liang Guanglie (Chief of General Staff). Fallon discussed military contacts between junior officers; PLA observers at U.S. exercises; exchanges with more transparency and reciprocity; cooperation in disaster relief and control of avian flu; and reducing tensions.
September 13-16	The destroyer USS Curtis Wilbur visited Qingdao, hosted by the PLA Navy's North Sea Fleet.
September 27	U.S. and other foreign military observers (from 24 countries) observed a PLA exercise ("North Sword 2005") at the PLA's Zhurihe training base in Inner Mongolia in the Beijing MR.
October 18-20	Defense Secretary Donald Rumsfeld visited Beijing, China. He met with General Cao Gangchuan (including a visit to the office in the August 1st [Bayi] Building of this CMC Vice Chairman and Defense Minister), General Guo Boxiong (a CMC Vice Chairman), General Jing Zhiyuan (commander of the Second Artillery, or missile corps, in the first foreign visit to its headquarters), and Hu Jintao (Communist Party General Secretary, CMC Chairman, and PRC president). General Jing introduced the Second Artillery and repeated the PRC's declared "no first use" nuclear weapons policy. Rumsfeld's discussions covered military exchanges; greater transparency from the PLA, including its spending; China's rising global influence; Olympics in Beijing in 2008; and China's manned space program. Rumsfeld also held round-tables at the Central Party School and Academy of Military Science. The PLA denied a U.S. request to visit its command center in the Western Hills, outside Beijing, and continued to deny agreement on a "hot line." The PLA did not agree to open archives believed to hold documents on American POWs in the Korean War, an issue raised by Assistant Secretary of Defense Peter Rodman and Deputy Under Secretary of Defense Richard Lawless.

November 13-19	The PLA sent its first delegation of younger, mid-ranking brigade and division commanders and commissars to the United States. Led by Major General Zhang Wenda, Deputy Director of the GSD's General Office, they visited units of the Pacific Command in Hawaii and Alaska.
December 8-9	Deputy Under Secretary of Defense Lawless visited Beijing to discuss the military exchange program in 2006 and military maritime security. He met with the Director of the PLA's Foreign Affairs Office, Major General Zhang Bangdong, and Deputy Chief of General Staff, General Xiong Guangkai.
December 12-15	A delegation from the PLA's NDU, led by Rear Admiral Yang Yi, Director of the Institute for Strategic Studies, visited Washington (NDU, Pentagon, and State Department).
December 13	Following up on Rumsfeld's visit, a DPMO delegation visited Beijing to continue to seek access to China's archives believed to contain information on American POWs during the Korean War. The delegation also discussed POW/MIA investigations and recovery operations in China in 2006.

2006

January 9-13	PLA GLD delegation representing all military regions visited PACOM (hosted by Col. William Carrington, J1) to discuss personnel management, especially U.S. vs. PLA salaries.
February 27-28	A PACOM military medical delegation visited China.
March 13-18	To reciprocate the PLA's first mid-ranking delegation's visit in November 2005, PACOM's J5 (Director for Strategic Planning and Policy), Rear Admiral Michael Tracy, led a delegation of 20 O-5 and O-6 officers from PACOM's Army, Marines, Navy, and Air Force commands to Beijing, Shanghai, Nanjing, Hangzhou, and Ningbo.
April 9-15	NDU President Lt. Gen. Michael Dunn and Commandant of the Industrial College of the Armed Forces (ICAF) Maj. Gen. Frances Wilson visited Beijing, Nanjing, and Shanghai.
May 9-15	PACOM Commander, Admiral William Fallon, visited Beijing, Xian, Hangzhou, and cities close to the border with North Korea, including Shenyang. He met with a CMC Vice Chairman, General Cao Gangchuan, and a Deputy Chief of General Staff, General Ge Zhenfeng, and discussed issues that included the U.S.-Japan alliance and real PLA spending. Fallon was the first U.S. official to visit the 39th Group Army, where he saw a showcase unit (346th regiment). At the 28th Air Division near Hangzhou, he was the first U.S. official to see a new FB-7 fighter. He invited the PLA to observe the U.S. "Valiant Shield" exercise in June near Guam.
May 15-26	A PLA delegation observed "Cobra Gold," a multilateral exercise hosted by Thailand and PACOM.
June 8	Assistant Secretary of Defense Peter Rodman visited Beijing for the 8th DCT, the first time at this lower level and without Xiong

	Guangkai. He talked with Major General Zhang Qinsheng, Assistant Chief of General Staff, about exchanges, weapons nonproliferation, counterterrorism, Olympics, invitation to the Second Artillery commander to visit, etc.
June 16-23	A PLA and civilian delegation of 12, led by Rear Admiral Zhang Leiyu, a PLAN Deputy Chief of Staff and submariner, observed the U.S. "Valiant Shield" exercise that involved three carrier strike groups near Guam. They boarded the USS Ronald Reagan and visited Guam's air and naval bases.
June 27-30	USS Blue Ridge (7th Fleet's command ship) visited Shanghai.
July 16-22	The highest ranking PLA commander, CMC Vice Chairman Guo Boxiong, visited San Diego (3rd Marine Aircraft Wing and carrier USS Ronald Reagan), Washington, and West Point, at Defense Secretary Rumsfeld's invitation. General Guo agreed to hold a combined naval search and rescue exercise (a U.S. proposal for the past two years in the context of the MMCA talks) and to allow U.S. access to PLA archives with information on U.S. POW/MIAs from the Korean War (a U.S. request for many years). Guo personally gave Rumsfeld information on his friend, Lt. j.g. James Deane, a Navy pilot who was shot down by the PLA Air Force in 1956. Guo also had meetings with Representatives Mark Steven Kirk and Rick Larsen (co-chairs of the U.S.-China Working Group), Secretary of State Condoleezza Rice, and National Security Advisor Stephen Hadley, and President Bush briefly dropped by during the latter. During the meetings and an address at the National Defense University, General Guo discussed North Korea's July 4 missile tests, critically citing the U.N. Security Council resolution condemning the tests (remarks not reported by PRC press). In contrast to the meeting in Beijing with General Myers in January 2004, Taiwan was not a heated issue in General Guo's talks with Rumsfeld and the Chairman of the Joint Chiefs of Staff, General Peter Pace.
August 7-11	MMCA plenary and working group meetings held in Hawaii. The two sides established communication protocols, planned communications and maneuver exercises, and scripted the two phases of the planned search and rescue exercise.
August 21-23	PACOM Commander, Admiral Fallon, visited Harbin.
September 6-20	The PLAN destroyer Qingdao visited Pearl Harbor (and held the first U.S.-PLA basic exercise in the use of tactical signals with the U.S. Navy destroyer USS Chung-Hoon) and San Diego (and held the first bilateral search and rescue exercise (SAREX), under the MMCA, with the destroyer USS Shoup).
September 10-21	In the second such visit after the first in 1998, a large, 58-member PLA Air Force delegation, with its own PLAAF aircraft, visited Elmendorf AFB (saw an F-15C fighter) in Alaska, Air Force Academy and Air Force Space Command in Colorado, Maxwell AFB and Air War College in Alabama, Andrews AFB in Maryland, the Pentagon in D.C., McGuire AFB in New Jersey, Philadelphia, and New York.
September 20-30	DPMO Team visited China to discuss POW/MIA concerns.

September 26	USS Chancellorsville made a port visit to Qingdao.
September 26-28	Principal Deputy Under Secretary of Defense for Policy, Ryan Henry, visited Beijing and Xian. He briefed PLA General Ge Zhenfeng, Deputy Chief of General Staff, on the Quadrennial Defense Review (QDR) of February 2006.
October 8-13	A U.S. delegation from the Office of the Deputy Under Secretary of Defense for Installations and Environment visited China to discuss military environmental issues.
October 20-27	A delegation of NDU operational commanders visited the United States.

On October 26, 2006, a PLAN Song-class diesel electric submarine approached undetected to within five miles of the aircraft carrier USS Kitty Hawk near Okinawa. PACOM Commander Admiral Fallon argued that the incident showed the need for military-to-military engagement to avoid escalations of tensions.

October 30-November 4	PLA mid-level, division and brigade commanders (senior colonels and colonels) visited Honolulu, toured the destroyer USS Preble in San Diego, and observed training at Camp Pendleton Marine Base. They were denied requests to have closer looks at an aircraft carrier and Strykers.
November 12-19	Commander of the Pacific Fleet, Adm. Gary Roughead, visited Beijing, Shanghai, and Zhanjiang, overseeing second phase of bilateral search and rescue exercise (involving the visiting amphibious transport dock USS Juneau and destroyer USS Fitzgerald), and the first Marine Corps visit to the PRC.
December 7-8	Stemming from the MMCA-related Special Policy Dialogue of 2005, the Deputy Assistant Secretary of Defense held Defense Policy Coordination Talks (DPCT) in Washington with the director of the PLA's Foreign Affairs Office to discuss a dispute over EEZs.

2007

On January 11, 2007, the PLA conducted its first successful direct-ascent anti-satellite (ASAT) weapons test by launching a missile with a kinetic kill vehicle to destroy a PRC satellite at about 530 miles up in space.

January 28-February 9	Deputy Chief of General Staff, General Ge Zhenfeng led a PLA delegation to visit PACOM in Honolulu, Washington, Fort Monroe, Fort Benning, and West Point. The U.S. Chief of Staff of the Army (CSA) hosted Ge, who also met with the Deputy Secretary of Defense and Vice Chairman of the Joint Chiefs of Staff in the Pentagon. However, the PLA declined to attend the Pacific Armies' Chiefs' Conference in August and a reciprocal visit by the CSA.
January 30-31	DPMO/JPAC delegation visited China to discuss POW/MIA cooperation.
February 23-28	Commander of Combined Forces Command-Afghanistan, Lt. General Karl Eikenberry, visited China.
March 22-25	Chairman of the Joint Chiefs of Staff, Marine Corps General Peter Pace, was hosted in China by Chief of General Staff Liang Guanglie

	and also met with CMC Vice Chairmen Guo Boxiong and Cao Gangchuan. Pace visited Beijing, Shenyang, Anshan, Dalian, and Nanjing, including the Academy of Military Sciences, Shenyang MR (where he was the first U.S. official to sit in a PLAAF Su-27 fighter and a T-99 tank), and the Nanjing MR command center.
April 1-7	PLA Navy Commander Wu Shengli visited Honolulu and Washington, where he met with the PACOM Commander Keating, Pacific Fleet Commander Roughhead, Chief of Naval Operations (CNO) Mullen, Deputy Secretary of Defense England, Chairman of the Joint Chiefs of Staff Pace, and Navy Secretary Winter. The CNO, Admiral Michael Mullen, discussed his "1,000-ship navy" maritime security concept with Vice Admiral Wu. He also toured the Naval Academy at Annapolis, the cruiser USS Lake Erie in Honolulu, and aircraft carrier USS Harry Truman and nuclear attack submarine USS Montpelier at Norfolk Naval Base. Wu also went to West Point.
April 15-22	General Counsel of the Defense Department William Haynes II visited Beijing and Shanghai, and met with GPD Director Li Jinai. Haynes sought to understand the rule of law in China.
April 21-28	U.S. mid-level officers' visit to China, led by RAdm Michael Tracy (PACOM J-5). The delegation visited Beijing, Qingdao, Nanjing, and Shenyang, including the East Sea Fleet Headquarters, a Su-27 fighter base, and 179th Brigade.
May 12-16	PACOM Commander Admiral Timothy Keating visited Beijing, meeting with CMC Vice Chairman Guo Boxiong and questioning the ASAT weapon test in January. Keating also met with PLA Navy Commander Wu Shengli and heard interest in acquiring an aircraft carrier. Keating visited the Nanjing Military Region (including the Nanjing Naval Command, Nanjing Polytechnic Institute, and 179th Brigade). At a press conference in Beijing on May 12, Keating suggested U.S. "help" if China builds aircraft carriers.
June 15-25	In the third such visit and nominally under its Command College, the PLAAF sent a 20-member delegation (U.S. limit reduced from 58 members in September 2006). They visited New York, McGuire AFB (saw KC-135 Stratotanker) in New Jersey, the Pentagon in D.C., Maxwell AFB and Air War College in Alabama, Lackland AFB and Randolph AFB (Personnel Center) in Texas, and Los Angeles.
July 23-29	Pacific Air Forces Commander, General Paul Hester, visited Beijing and Nanjing. He met with PLAAF Commander Qiao Qingchen and Deputy Chief of General Staff Ge Zhenfeng. Hester visited Jining Air Base (as the first U.S. visitor) and Jianqiao Air Base. He was denied access to the J-10 fighter.
August 17-23	After nomination to be Chairman of Joint Chiefs of Staff, the CNO, Adm. Michael Mullen, visited Lushun, Qingdao, Ningbo, and Dalian Naval Academy. He met with PLAN Commander Wu Shengli and two CMC Vice Chairmen, Generals Guo Boxiong and Cao Gangchuan. After postponing his reciprocal visit (for hosting PLAN Commander Wu Shengli in April) due to inadequate substance and access given by the PLA, Mullen got unprecedented observation of an exercise, boarding a Song-class sub and Luzhou-class destroyer.

November 4-6	Defense Secretary Robert Gates visited China (then South Korea and Japan). Defense Minister Cao Gangchuan finally agreed to the U.S. proposal to set up a defense telephone link (hotline). Gates also sought a dialogue on nuclear policy and broader exchanges beyond the senior level. Gates also met with CMC Vice Chairmen Guo Boxiong and Xu Caihou, and Chairman Hu Jintao.

In November 2007, the PRC disapproved a number of port calls at Hong Kong by U.S. Navy ships, including two minesweepers in distress (USS Patriot and USS Guardian) seeking to refuel in face of an approaching storm, and the aircraft carrier USS Kitty Hawk and accompanying vessels planning on a holiday and family reunions for Thanksgiving. In response, on November 28, President Bush raised the problem with the PRC's visiting Foreign Minister, and Deputy Assistant Secretary of Defense David Sedney lodged a demarche to the PLA. When the Kitty Hawk left Hong Kong, it transited the Taiwan Strait, raising PRC objections. In Beijing in January 2008, Adm. Keating asserted that the strait is international water and PRC permission is not needed.

December 3	9th DCT was held in Washington. PLA Deputy Chief of General Staff Ma Xiaotian and Under Secretary of Defense for Policy Eric Edelman led discussions that covered PLA objections to U.S. arms sales to Taiwan and U.S. law restricting military contacts, military exchanges in 2008, nuclear proliferation in North Korea and Iran (including the just-issued U.S. National Intelligence Estimate on Iran's nuclear program), lower-ranking exchanges, hotline, PLA's suspension of some visits and port calls in Hong Kong, and U.S. interest in a strategic nuclear dialogue. The PLA delegation included PLAN Deputy Chief of Staff Zhang Leiyu and 2nd Artillery Deputy Chief of Staff Yang Zhiguo. They also met: Deputy Defense Secretary Gordon England, Vice Chairman of the Joint Chiefs of Staff James Cartwright, Deputy National Security Advisor James Jeffrey, and Deputy Secretary of State John Negroponte.

2008

January 13-16	In his 2nd visit as PACOM Commander, Adm. Timothy Keating, visited Beijing, Shanghai, and Guangzhou, before Hong Kong. He visited AMS and Guangzhou MR, and met with PLA Chief of General Staff, General Chen Bingde; CMC Vice Chairman, General Guo Boxiong, who demanded an end to U.S. arms sales to Taiwan. Keating discussed planned exchanges with a new invitation to the PLA to participate in the Cobra Gold multilateral exercise in May, the PRC's strategic intentions, denied port calls in Hong Kong, etc. (But the PLA only observed Cobra Gold in Thailand in May 2008.)
February 25-26	PACOM's Director for Strategic Planning and Policy (J-5), USMC Major General Thomas Conant, and PLA Navy Deputy Chief of Staff Zhang Leiyu led an annual meeting under the MMCA in Qingdao, the first since 2006. The U.S. delegation visited the frigate Luoyang. The U.S. side opposed PLA proposals to discuss policy differences and plan details of naval exercises at the MMCA meetings.
February 25-29	Deputy Assistant Secretary of Defense for POW/MIA Affairs Charles Ray signed a Memorandum of Understanding in Shanghai

	on February 29, 2008, gaining indirect access to PLA archives on the Korean War in an effort to resolve decades-old POW/MIA cases.
February 26-29	Deputy Assistant Secretary of Defense David Sedney met with PLA Assistant Chief of General Staff, Major General Chen Xiaogong, in Beijing. Sedney also led another meeting of the DPCT in Shanghai. Sedney and Major General Qian Lihua, Director of the PLA's Foreign Affairs Office, signed an agreement to set up a hotline.

Days before Taiwan's presidential election on March 22, 2008, in a sign of U.S. anxiety about PRC threats to peace and stability, the Defense Department had two aircraft carriers (including the Kitty Hawk returning from its base in Japan for decommissioning) positioned east of Taiwan to respond to any provocative situation.

March 8-15	PACOM's Deputy Director for Strategic Planning and Policy, Brigadier General Sam Angelella, led a 19-member delegation of mid-level officers to Beijing, Zhengzhou, and Qingdao.
March 30-April 4	The U.S. Marine Corps Commandant, General James Conway, visited Beijing, as hosted by PLA Navy Commander Wu Shengli. Conway met with Defense Minister Liang Guanglie and spoke at NDU. The PLAN allowed Conway to board an amphibious ship, a destroyer, and an expeditionary fighting vehicle. In meeting Guangzhou MR Commander, Lt. Gen. Zhang Qinsheng, Conway apparently discussed deploying forces together in disaster relief operations.
April 21-22	The first discussion on nuclear weapon strategy and policy was held in Washington, DC, at the "experts" level.
May 18	After the earthquake in China on May 12, PACOM sent two C-17 transport aircraft to Chengdu to deliver disaster relief supplies. PACOM Commander Keating used the Pentagon's hotline to discuss that aid with PLA Deputy Chief of General Staff Ma Xiaotian.
June 16-21	Air Force Command Chief Master Sgt James Roy from PACOM led the first U.S. NCO delegation to China. The group of senior NCOs visited the PLA's 179th Infantry Battalion in Nanjing and the Second Artillery (Missile Force) Academy's NCO training school in Wuhan.
July 5-17	PLA Lieutenant General Zhang Qinsheng, Guangzhou Military Region Commander, led a delegation to Hawaii. He met with Admiral Robert Willard, Commander of the Pacific Fleet, at his headquarters and with Rear Adm. Joe Walsh, Submarine Force Commander, during a tour of the attack submarine USS Santa Fe. The PLA delegation also was able to observe the RIMPAC exercise. PACOM Commander, Admiral Timothy Keating, agreed with Zhang about planning for two humanitarian aid exercises, the first combined land-based ones, to "push the envelope." The PLA delegation also visited Alaska, Washington, D.C., and New York. In Washington, Zhang met with U.S. officials of the Marine Corps, Departments of Defense and State, and NSC, including Deputy Secretary of Defense Gordon England.
October 1-2	The PLA sent its first "NCO" delegation to PACOM supposedly to reciprocate the U.S. NCO visit in June. However, the PLA delegation was led by Major General Zhong Zhiming, and only 3

	out of 13 members in the group were enlisted.
December 17-19	After the PLA suspended some military exchanges in response to notifications to Congress of arms sales to Taiwan on October 3, Deputy Assistant Secretary of Defense David Sedney visited Beijing to try without success to resume exchanges. He met with PLA Assistant Chief of General Staff Chen Xiaogong.

2009

January	The PLA Navy and U.S. Navy coordinated anti-piracy operations off Somalia.
February 27-28	Deputy Assistant Secretary of Defense David Sedney again visited Beijing to resume military exchanges after suspension in October 2008. He held a round of the DPCT, met with Deputy Chief of General Staff Ma Xiaotian, and then called his meetings "the best set of talks" he has experienced. However, results were limited, and the PLA made demands, including cessations to U.S. arms sales to Taiwan, U.S. legal restrictions on military contacts, and reports on PRC Military Power.

On March 4-8, 2009, Y-12 maritime surveillance aircraft, a PLAN frigate, PRC patrol and intelligence collection ships, and trawlers coordinated in increasingly aggressive and dangerous harassment of unarmed U.S. ocean surveillance ships, the USNS Victorious and USNS Impeccable, during routine operations in international waters in the Yellow Sea and South China Sea (75 miles south of Hainan island). The PRC ships risked collision. On March 10, China sent its largest "fishery patrol" ship (converted from a PLAN vessel) to "safeguard sovereignty" in the South China Sea. U.S. press reported the next day that the destroyer USS Chung-Hoon, already deployed in the area, provided armed escort to continuing U.S. surveillance operations. On March 10, Director of National Intelligence (DNI) Dennis Blair (also retired admiral and former PACOM commander) testified to the Senate Armed Services Committee that this crisis is the most serious since the EP-3 crisis of 2001, China has been even more aggressive in the South China Sea in the past two years, and there is still a question as to whether China will use its increasingly powerful military "for good or for pushing people around." (For years, China has tried to stake sovereign claims to Exclusive Economic Zones (EEZs) (up to 200 miles from the coast) beyond territorial waters (up to 12 miles from the coast), while the United States and other countries assert access and freedom of navigation in and flight over the high seas.) On March 12, President Obama stressed military dialogue to avoid future incidents with visiting PRC Foreign Minister Yang Jiechi.

ACKNOWLEDGMENTS

This CRS study was originally written at the request of the House Armed Services Committee in the 108th Congress and is updated and made available for general congressional use.

REFERENCES

[1] Michael Pillsbury, "U.S.-Chinese Military Ties?", *Foreign Policy*, Fall 1975; Leslie Gelb, "Arms Sales," *Foreign Policy*, Winter 1976-77; Michael Pillsbury, "Future

Sino-American Security Ties: The View from Tokyo, Moscow, and Peking," *International Security*, Spring 1977; and Philip Taubman, "U.S. and China Forging Close Ties; Critics Fear That Pace is Too Swift," *New York Times*, December 8, 1980.

[2] Deputy Assistant Secretary of Defense for East Asian and Pacific Affairs James Kelly, Testimony before the House Foreign Affairs Subcommittee on Asian and Pacific Affairs, "Defense Relations with the People's Republic of China," June 5, 1984.

[3] Department of State and Defense Security Assistance Agency, "Congressional Presentation for Security Assistance, Fiscal Year 1992."

[4] *Jane's Defense Weekly*, May 26, 1990.

[5] Department of State, "Presidential Decision on Military Sales to China," December 22, 1992.

[6] CRS Report RL30946, *China-U.S. Aircraft Collision Incident of April 2001: Assessments and Policy Implications*, by Shirley A. Kan et al.

[7] Department of State, "Deputy Secretary of State Richard 's Media Round Table," Beijing, China, January 30, 2004.

[8] U.S. Pacific Command, Adm. William J. Fallon, press conference, Hong Kong, September 11, 2005; and author's discussions with Pentagon officials.

[9] "Navy: China 'Not Helpful' on Thanksgiving," *Associated Press*, November 28, 2007; White House press briefing, November 28, 2007; *Washington Post*, November 29, 2007.

[10] Department of State, press briefing by Richard Boucher, spokesman, January 28, 2004.

[11] See CRS Report RL32870, *European Union's Arms Embargo on China: Implications and Options for U.S. Policy*, by Kristin Archick, Richard F. Grimmett, and Shirley A. Kan.

[12] CRS Report 96-889, *China: Commission of Science, Technology, and Industry for National Defense (COSTIND) and Defense Industries*, by .

[13] Bill Gertz, "Military Exchanges with Beijing Raises Security Concerns," *Washington Times*, February 19, 1999.

[14] Dana Rohrabacher, letters to William Cohen, March 1, 1999 and March 18, 1999.

[15] Bob Smith and Dana Rohrabacher, letter to Donald Rumsfeld, December 17, 2001.

[16] House Armed Services Committee, hearing on the FY2007 Budget for PACOM, March 9, 2006. Adm. Fallon also discussed a consideration of modifying the law in an interview: Tony Capaccio, "Fallon Wants to Jumpstart Military Contacts between U.S., China," *Bloomberg*, March 13, 2006.

[17] Bill Gertz and Rowan Scarborough, "Inside the Ring," *Washington Times*, May 17, 2002; author's discussions with the Defense Department and Senate Armed Services Committee.

[18] Secretary of Defense, "Report to Congress Pursuant to Section 1201(e) of the FY2000 National Defense Authorization Act (P.L. 106-65)," July 19, 2006.

[19] Secretary of Defense, "Report to Congress Pursuant to Section 1201(e) of the FY2000 National Defense Authorization Act (P.L. 106-65)," June 22, 2007.

[20] Deputy Secretary of Defense, "Report to Congress Pursuant to Section 1201(e) of the FY 2000 National Defense Authorization Act (P.L. 106-65)," March 31, 2008.

[21] Secretary of Defense, *The United States Security Strategy for the East Asia-Pacific Region*, 1998.

[22] Department of Defense, "Deputy Secretary Wolfowitz's Interview with Phoenix Television," May 31, 2002.
[23] Department of Defense, "Under Secretary Feith's Media Roundtable on U.S.-China Defense Consultative Talks," December 9, 2002.
[24] Larry Wortzel, "Why Caution is Needed in Military Contacts with China," Heritage Foundation Backgrounder, December 2, 1999.
[25] Larry Wortzel, Director of the Asian Studies Center at the Heritage Foundation, testimony on "China's Strategic Intentions and Goals" before the House Armed Services Committee, June 21, 2000.
[26] Randy Schriver, former Country Director for China in the Office of the Secretary of Defense during the Clinton Administration, and later Deputy Assistant Secretary of State for East Asian and Pacific Affairs during the Bush Administration, discussed military contacts with China at an event at the Heritage Foundation on July 27, 2000. See Stephen Yates, Al Santoli, Randy Schriver, and Larry Wortzel, "The Proper Scope, Purpose, and Utility of U.S. Relations with China's Military," *Heritage Lectures*, October 10, 2000.
[27] Kurt Campbell (Deputy Assistant Secretary of Defense for East Asia and the Pacific in 1995-2000) and Richard Weitz, "The Limits of U.S.-China Military Cooperation: Lessons From 1995-1999," *Washington Quarterly*, Winter 2005-2006.
[28] Randall Schriver, "The Real Value in Gates' Asia Trip," *Taipei Times*, November 16, 2007.
[29] John Pomfret, "Doctor Says Health Ministry Lied About Disease," *Washington Post*, April 10, 2003; "Feature: A Chinese Doctor's Extraordinary April in 2003," *People's Daily*, June 13, 2003.
[30] Captain Brad Kaplan, USN, "China and U.S.: Building Military Relations," *Asia-Pacific Defense Forum*, Summer 1999.
[31] Kenneth Allen and Eric McVadon, "China's Foreign Military Relations," Stimson Center, October 1999.
[32] Dennis Blasko, "Bei Jian 0308: Did Anyone Hear the Sword on the Inner Mongolian Plains?" *RUSI Chinese Military Update*, October 2003.
[33] Xinhua, September 2, 2004; *Liberation Army Daily*, September 3, 2004; *Jane's Defense Weekly*, September 22, 2004.
[34] Dennis Blair and Carla Hills, Task Force of the Council on Foreign Relations, "U.S.-China Relations: An Affirmative Agenda, A Responsible Course," April 10, 2007.
[35] David Finkelstein and John Unangst, "Engaging DoD: Chinese Perspectives on Military Relations with the United States," *CNA* Corporation, October 1999.
[36] Author's discussions with government-affiliated research organizations in China in 2002.
[37] CRS Report RL30946, *China-U.S. Aircraft Collision Incident of April 2001: Assessments and Policy Implications*, by Shirley A. Kan et al.
[38] LTC Frank Miller (USA), "China Hosts Visit by the U.S. Commander in Chief, Pacific," *Asia Pacific Defense Forum*, Spring 1998. The article ended by saying that "perhaps the most important result of Adm. Prueher's December 1997 trip to China is that, should there be another crisis like the March 1996 Taiwan Strait Missile Crisis, Adm. Prueher now has the phone number."

[39] John Keefe, "Anatomy of the EP-3 Incident, April 2001," Center for Naval Analyses report, January 2002.
[40] Jim Garamone, "China, U.S. Making Progress on Military Relations," American Forces Press Service, January 15, 2004.
[41] U.S. Pacific Command, Adm. William J. Fallon, "Roundtable at Embassy PAS Program Room," Beijing, China, September 7, 2005. Adm. Fallon also said he consulted "extensively" with retired Adm. Prueher, former Commander of the Pacific Command.
[42] Chris Johnson, "DOD Will Urge China to Conduct Joint Search and Rescue Exercise," *Inside the Navy*, March 13, 2006.
[43] Major General Thomas Conant and Rear Admiral Zhang Leiyu, "Summary of Proceedings of the Annual Meeting Under the Agreement Between the Ministry of National Defense of the People's Republic of China and the Department of Defense of the United States of America on Establishing a Consultative Mechanism to Strengthen Military Maritime Safety," Qingdao, February 26, 2008.
[44] Quoted in the "Nelson Report," March 11, 2009.
[45] Bruce Stanley, "China's Congested Skies," *Wall Street Journal*, February 16, 2007.
[46] Forum on "Evolving and Enhancing Military Relations," George Bush U.S.-China Relations Conference 2007, Washington, DC, October 24, 2007.
[47] *People's Daily*, February 24, 2008; Sanya Initiative, "Key Outcomes and Summary Report," March 2008; Jennifer Harper, "Retired U.S. Brass to Defend Chinese Military," *Washington Times*, April 4, 2008; CSIS, "A Briefing on the Sanya Initiative," June 6, 2008; author's consultations, March 2009.
[48] The PLA's visit to the NTC in November 1994 was not the first time that the PLA observed U.S. military training at Fort Irwin. In August 1985, the United States allowed the PLA to observe military training at Fort Benning, GA; Fort Bragg, NC; and Fort Irwin, CA. See Colonel Jer Donald Get, "What's With the Relationship Between America's Army and China's PLA?" Army War College monograph, September 15, 1996.
[49] Sean Naylor, "Chinese Denied Full Access to the NTC," *Army Times*, March 29, 1999.
[50] Department of Defense, "Report on PRC Military Power," July 2003.
[51] Kevin Pollpeter, "U.S. China Security Management: Assessing the Military-to-Military Relationship," RAND Corporation, 2004.
[52] Assistant Secretary of Defense Peter Rodman, remarks to the U.S.-China Economic and Security Review Commission, March 16, 2006.
[53] Testimony at a hearing on "The Taiwan Relations Act: The Next 25 Years," before the House International Relations Committee, April 21, 2004.
[54] Defense Department, "Annual Report on PRC Military Power," May 29, 2004.
[55] See CRS Report RL30341, *China/Taiwan: Evolution of the "One China" Policy—Key Statements from Washington, Beijing, and Taipei*, by Shirley A. Kan.
[56] See CRS Report RL30957, *Taiwan: Major U.S. Arms Sales Since 1990*, by Shirley A. Kan.
[57] Author's discussions at the Biennial Conference at APCSS on July 16-18, 2002; interview with former PACOM staff.
[58] Department of Defense, "Secretary Cohen's Press Conference at the Shanghai Stock Exchange," Shanghai, China, July 14, 2000.

[59] Joe McDonald (AP), "Feith Voices Concern Over Chinese Missiles," *Army Times*, February 11, 2004.
[60] Dennis Blair and Carla Hills, co-chairs of a task force at the Council on Foreign Relations, "U.S.-China Relations: An Affirmative Agenda, A Responsible Course," April 10, 2007.
[61] Statement quoted in "China Cancels Military Contacts with U.S. in Protest," AP, October 6, 2008.
[62] Quoted in "Optimism Grows for U.S.-China Military Talks," *New York Times*, February 19, 2009.
[63] CRS Report RL31555, *China and Proliferation of Weapons of Mass Destruction and Missiles: Policy Issues*, by Shirley A. Kan.
[64] Jason Dean, "Chinese General Lays Nuclear Card on U.S.' Table," *Wall Street Journal*, July 15, 2005; Danny Gittings, "General Zhu Goes Ballistic," *Wall Street Journal*, July 18, 2005.
[65] World Security Institute China Program, "Opening the Debate on U.S.-China Nuclear Relations," *China Security*, Autumn 2005.
[66] General Jing's reiteration of the "no first use" pledge was cited by one official PRC media report: "Rumsfeld Visits China; The Chinese Side Reiterates It Will Not Use Nuclear Weapons First," *Zhongguo Tongxun She [New China News Agency]*, October 20, 2005.
[67] *Xinhua* and *Associated Press*, August 27, 2007.
[68] Jeremy Singer, "Cartwright Seeks Closer Ties with China, Russia," *Space News*, October 16, 2006.
[69] Bill Gertz, "Chinese General's U.S. Visit for Nuke Talks Deferred," *Washington Times*, January 15, 2007.
[70] See CRS Report RS22652, *China's Anti-Satellite Weapon Test*, by Shirley A. Kan.
[71] House Armed Services Committee, hearing on China: Recent Security Developments, June 13, 2007.
[72] Quoted in "Bush Official Urges China to Lift Nuclear Secrecy," *AP,* January 14, 2009.
[73] See CRS Report RL33001, *U.S.-China Counterterrorism Cooperation: Issues for U.S. Policy*, by Shirley A. Kan.
[74] Senator Bob Smith and Representative Dana Rohrabacher, letter to Secretary of Defense Donald Rumsfeld, December 17, 2001.
[75] Rand, "U.S.-China Security Management: Assessing the Military-to-Military Relationship," July 2004.
[76] Department of Defense, news release, "China Provides World War II U.S. Aircraft Crash Sites," February 8, 2001.
[77] Melissa Healy, "China Said to Have Experimented on U.S. POWs," *Los Angeles Times*, July 4, 1992.
[78] Mark Sauter, "POW Probe Extends to Korea, China," *Tacoma News-Tribune*, June 21, 1992.
[79] "No U.S. POWs in China," *Beijing Review*, July 27-August 2, 1992.
[80] Carleton R. Bryant, "N. Korea: POWs Sent to China: Senator Says U.S. Must Prod Beijing," *Washington Times*, December 23, 1992.

[81] Report of the Select Committee on POW/MIA Affairs, S.Rept. 103-1U.S. Senate, Report 103-1, January 3, 1993. Also see CRS Report RL33452, *POWs and MIAs: Status and Accounting Issues*, by Charles A. Henning.
[82] Sue Pleming, "U.S. Asks China for Access to Korean POW Files," *Reuters*, February 4, 1999.
[83] Department of Defense, "U.S., China Agree to Enhanced Cooperation on POW/MIA Matters," March 29, 2003.
[84] Confirmed in discussions with DPMO officials, January 29, 2004.
[85] Defense POW/Missing Personnel Office, "Personnel Accounting Progress in China as of February 4, 2005," February 2005.
[86] Robert Burns, "Pentagon Seeking Access to Chinese Records on War MIAs," *AP/Arizona Republic*, October 23, 2005; and author's discussions with DPMO.
[87] "Pentagon Cites MIA Deal With China," *Associated Press*, February 25, 2008, quoting DPMO spokesman Larry Greer.
[88] Defense Department, "U.S. and China Sign POW/ MIA Arrangement," February 29, 2008.
[89] "PRC Will Continually Help Look for Remains of U.S. Soldiers Killed in Korean War," *Xinhua*, February 28, 2008.

INDEX

#

9/11, 27, 75
9/11 Commission, 75

A

A(H1N1), 157
abolition, 23, 77
Abraham, 244
abuse, 114
access, viii, xiii, 7, 17, 24, 29, 31, 32, 33, 37, 38, 39, 41, 46, 50, 51, 53, 54, 55, 61, 64, 65, 70, 71, 74, 81, 83, 102, 110, 124, 143, 148, 149, 162, 164, 170, 172, 219, 221, 222, 223, 227, 228, 234, 238, 242, 243, 246, 247, 249, 254, 257, 259, 260, 262, 263, 265
accommodation, 58, 198
accountability, 142
accounting, xv, 38, 51, 59, 142, 157, 210, 217, 221, 233, 247
accuracy, 18, 92, 98
achievement, vii, 1, 6, 58
acquisitions, 218
activism, 62
acute, 66
additives, 42
adjustment, 124, 144, 195
administration, 64
administrative, 11, 52, 57, 63, 64
advancement, 90
adverse effects, 56
adverse event, 141
advisory body, 50
advocacy, 142
Afghanistan, 105, 232, 261

Africa, 26
age, 11, 25, 26, 40, 67
ageing, 38
agencies, xiv, 3, 62, 81, 86, 87, 89, 92, 93, 141, 142, 155, 162, 170, 172, 179, 202
aggregate demand, 123, 124
aggression, 222, 228
aging, 51, 65
agricultural, 19, 23, 24, 31, 32, 34, 36, 37, 38, 39, 41, 42, 69, 70, 71
agricultural commodities, 32, 39
agricultural exports, 32, 39, 71, 135, 145, 189
agricultural market, 36
agriculture, 7, 30, 31, 32, 39, 40, 71, 145
aid, 24, 45, 81, 82, 84, 86, 90, 91, 97, 108, 112
AIDS, 17, 105
air, 60, 76, 108, 109
Air Force, 213, 215, 226, 227, 228, 236, 237, 238, 240, 241, 242, 243, 244, 245, 246, 247, 248, 251, 257, 259, 260, 262, 264
air traffic control system, 237
aircraft collision crisis, xiv, 209, 211, 222
airports, 6, 17, 226
Al Qaeda, 17, 232
Alabama, 73, 78
Alaska, 92, 245, 259, 260, 264
Alberta, 114
alien smuggling, 110
allies, 31
allocative efficiency, 38
alternative, vii, 1, 2, 7, 106
aluminum, 147
ambiguity, 192
ambivalence, 9
amendments, viii, 29, 30, 58, 64
amphetamine, 107
analog, 76

analysts, 3, 59, 69, 103, 104, 105, 106, 108, 109, 111, 113
animals, 108
Animals, 115
annual rate, 41
Antarctic, 77
antidumping, xii, 50, 51, 56, 57, 128, 132, 145, 149
Antidumping Agreement, 56
ants, 96
anxiety, 93, 264
APEC, vii, viii, 1, 2, 3, 4, 5, 6, 7, 8, 9, 10, 11, 12, 13, 14, 15, 16, 17, 18, 19, 20, 21, 22, 23, 24, 25, 26, 27, 28, 57, 76
APEC leaders, vii, 1, 2, 4, 9, 23
apparel, 34, 35, 47, 48, 49, 64, 137, 144, 153, 158, 159
apparel industry, 48
apparel products, 153, 159
appendix, 26
appetite, 222
applications, 187
appointments, 6
appropriations, 18, 111
Appropriations Act, 116, 149, 164, 168, 169, 174, 175, 178
Arabia, 26
arbitration, 60
Argentina, 26, 127, 175
argument, 38, 67
armed forces, 103, 106, 223, 237, 255
armed groups, 103
arms control, 221, 232
arms sales, xiii, xiv, xv, 179, 180, 182, 183, 191, 192, 197, 198, 209, 210, 211, 215, 216, 228, 229, 230, 235, 248, 249, 252, 253, 257, 263, 265
arms trafficking,, 109
Army, 96, 103, 109
arrest, 47, 158
ASEAN, vii, 1, 2, 11, 16, 21, 24, 25, 27, 65, 78, 111, 112, 114, 133
Asia, i, iii, v, vii, viii, ix, x, xiii, 1, 2, 3, 7, 8, 9, 11, 12, 14, 15, 16, 17, 18, 19, 20, 21, 22, 24, 25, 26, 27, 28, 30, 32, 37, 65, 66, 86, 94, 97, 98, 101, 104, 105, 106, 110, 113, 114, 115, 116, 124, 125, 134, 173, 176, 177, 179, 188, 194, 200, 203, 216, 220, 221, 228, 232, 233, 246, 248, 266, 267
Asia Pacific Economic Cooperation, v, vii, 1, 2, 18, 20, 26, 188
Asia Pacific Economic Cooperation (APEC), v, vii, 1, 2, 18, 26, 188
Asian, vii, 1, 2, 7, 9, 12, 14, 19, 21, 22, 23, 24, 27, 28, 37, 65, 67, 104, 108, 111, 114
Asian countries, 67, 121, 124, 138

Asian crisis, 125
aspiration, 199
assault, 242
assessment, 44, 64, 102, 219, 240
assessment procedures, 44, 64
assets, xi, 81, 120, 123, 125, 129, 138, 140, 143, 144, 155, 205
Association of Southeast Asian Nations, vii, 1, 2, 24, 65, 114, 133
Association of Southeast Asian Nations (ASEAN), vii, 1, 2, 65, 114, 133
atmosphere, 193
atomic weapon, ix, 79, 85, 86, 94
attacks, 12, 16, 23, 27, 231, 232
attitudes, viii, 2
attractiveness, 122
Australia, 6, 8, 9, 17, 20, 22, 24, 25, 26, 27, 65, 68, 167, 175, 224, 245
autarky, 109
authentication, 64
authorities, 76, 110, 117, 151
authority, viii, 5, 20, 29, 30, 56, 82, 164, 168, 169, 176, 183, 215, 216, 218, 219
authors, 177
automakers, 43, 74
Automobile, 71
automobiles, 36, 72
automotive sector, 46, 49
autonomy, xiv, 102, 179, 191
availability, 53, 154
avian, 17, 24, 212, 222, 258
avian flu, 24
avian influenza, 17
avoidance, 224

B

back, 43, 45, 63, 83, 86, 108
background, 182
backlash, 10
bacteria, 157
balance of payments, 123, 144
ballistic missile, x, 80, 90, 91, 92, 98, 109
ballistic missiles, 91, 98, 109, 238, 239, 244
ban, viii, 30, 67, 105, 106, 154, 210, 216, 218, 219
Bangladesh, 104, 117
bank account, 104
Bank of Korea, 36
banking, 36, 53, 59, 110, 121, 144, 145, 146
banking industry, 36
banking sector, 110
banks, 9, 104, 110, 116, 122, 138, 146
bargaining, 77

Index

barrier, 15, 16
barriers, vii, xii, 1, 8, 9, 14, 15, 20, 31, 32, 33, 34, 36, 37, 39, 44, 46, 49, 50, 53, 63, 64, 69, 72, 74, 131, 145, 151, 154
base, xii, 11, 44, 59, 69, 72, 87, 90, 97, 104, 108, 124, 141, 147, 150, 161, 162, 165, 175, 223, 228, 243, 255, 258, 262, 264
bauxite, 147
BEA, 139, 156
beef, viii, ix, 30, 31, 32, 38, 39, 40, 42, 64, 66, 67, 68, 71, 78, 143, 147
beef sector, 39
behavior, 196, 222
Beijing, xv, 129, 151, 175, 176, 180, 182, 186, 187, 188, 191, 194, 195, 196, 198, 199, 202, 203, 206, 209, 210, 211, 212, 221, 223, 225, 228, 229, 230, 231, 232, 234, 236, 237, 238, 239, 240, 241, 242, 243, 244, 245, 246, 248, 249, 250, 251, 252, 253, 254, 255, 256, 257, 258, 259, 260, 261, 262, 263, 264, 265, 266, 268, 269
Belarus, 127
benchmarks, viii, 29, 30, 65
beneficiaries, 123
benefits, 31, 32, 39, 45, 47, 53, 55, 94, 109, 122, 125, 150, 158, 190, 219, 220, 222, 224, 225, 232
Best Practice, 24
betrayal, 66
Big Three, 45, 47, 73
bilateral relations, 10, 55, 70
bilateral relationship, 70, 213, 220, 222
bilateral trade, viii, 14, 15, 29, 30, 35, 50, 55
binding, 164, 167, 187, 190, 201
biodiversity, 108
biological weapons, 163
bipartisan, 61, 77
Bipartisan Trade Promotion Act of 2002, viii, 29, 30, 64
birds, 24
black market, 102, 111
blame, 141
blends, 185
blocks, 15
blood, 141
board members, 165
Bogor Goals, vii, 1, 3, 4, 6, 8, 9, 11, 12, 22, 25, 27
bomb, 87, 88, 93, 94, 98, 99
bonds, 126
bone, 32, 40, 67, 68
border control, 111
borrowers, 123
bovine, 67
bovine spongiform encephalopathy, 67
branching, 91

Brazil, 26, 68, 136
bribes, 150, 188
Britain, 223
broadcaster, 109
Buddhist, 103
budget deficit, x, xi, xii, 119, 123, 124, 131, 139, 140
building blocks, 15
Bulgaria, 232
Bureau of Economic Analysis, 36, 75, 76
Bureau of Labor Statistics, 128
bureaucracy, 103
Burma, v, vii, x, 25, 101, 102, 103, 104, 105, 106, 107, 108, 109, 110, 111, 112, 113, 114, 115, 116, 117
burn, 142
Bush administration, 82
Bush Administration, vii, viii, ix, 1, 2, 18, 21, 29, 30, 56, 61, 63, 64, 65, 66, 79, 80, 81, 82, 83, 84, 85, 86, 89, 95, 97
Bush, George W., viii, 7, 30, 73, 192, 211
Bush, President, 8, 9, 10, 26, 39, 46, 55, 75, 77, 82, 95, 165, 191, 211, 215, 230, 252, 253, 255, 256, 260, 263
Bush, President George W., 7, 73
Business Roundtable, 74
businesses, 104, 154, 190
buyers, 109, 123
Byrd Amendment, 75

C

CAFTA, 38
Cambodia, 25, 78, 104
Camp David, 250
campaign funds, 188, 201
campaigns, 245
Canada, 6, 8, 22, 23, 24, 25, 26, 27, 41, 68, 69, 113, 132, 133, 136, 175, 245
candidates, 65, 204
CAP, 6
capacity building, 17, 23, 197
capital flows, 123, 124
capital goods, 46, 49, 50
capital inflow, 123, 124
Capitol Hill, 39, 216
caps, 46, 54
carbon, 154
carrier, 183, 214, 230, 236, 244, 245, 255, 257, 260, 261, 262, 263
cash, 106, 109, 147, 164, 176
cast, 184
catalyst, 22
catfish, 141

cattle, 32, 38, 40, 67, 68
ceasefire, 105, 106, 114
cease-fire, 102
censorship, 151
Census, 36, 137
Census Bureau, 36
Central America, 38
Central Asia, 232
central bank, 120, 123, 126
Central Intelligence Agency, 90, 93, 114
Central Military Commission (CMC), xv, 209, 212, 213
CEO, 27
certification, 33, 44, 88, 143, 218
challenges, xiv, 9, 153, 180, 185, 193, 197, 198, 199, 221, 231
Chamber of Commerce, 74
channels, 109, 226
character, 229
chemical, 142, 147, 163, 218, 235
chemicals, 35, 59, 141, 156, 235
Cheney, Dick, 233, 252
chicken, 154, 157
Chief of Staff, 225, 227, 232, 236, 237, 238, 241, 242, 243, 244, 249, 251, 252, 254, 255, 256, 260, 261, 263
child labor, 77
children, 108, 142, 157
Chile, vii, 1, 2, 6, 21, 24, 25, 27, 65, 66, 175, 245
Chinese domestic market, xi, 131
Chinese firms, 122, 128, 143, 145, 146, 147, 150
Chinese government, xi, xii, 88, 120, 122, 125, 126, 127, 128, 131, 136, 142, 143, 144, 146, 147, 149, 150, 151, 152, 156, 181
Chrysler, 43, 45, 46, 47, 69, 72, 73
CIA, 87, 88, 90, 92, 94, 97, 253, 256
cigarettes, 109
cities, 186, 201, 231, 259
citizens, 82, 123, 167, 192, 232
citrus, 33, 41
civil service, 189
civil war, 181, 184
civilian, 17, 50
clarity, 192
clean energy, 20, 154
climate, 8, 9, 25, 76, 153, 155
climate change, 8, 9, 25, 153, 155
Clinton Administration, xiv, 80, 88, 92, 195, 206, 209, 211, 217, 218, 219, 221, 222, 229, 231, 235, 237, 238, 247, 248, 249, 250, 254, 267
Clinton, Hillary Rodham, 65
Clinton, William, 240
clothing, 14

CMC, xv, 209, 212, 213, 215, 231, 235, 236, 240, 242, 245, 246, 248, 251, 253, 255, 256, 258, 259, 260, 261, 262, 263
CNN, 115
Co, vii, 1, 2, 4, 5, 15, 18, 19, 20, 26, 28, 36, 55, 61, 114
coal, 146
Coast Guard, 243
codes, 18
coercion, 183, 221, 228, 229
coke, 147
Cold War, 210, 226, 233, 253, 254, 256
collaboration, ix, 80, 81, 89, 90, 91, 94
Collaboration, ix, 80, 82, 89
collective bargaining, 77
colleges, 228, 234
collisions, 226, 231
collusion, x, 101, 103
Colombia, 67
command economy, 146, 150
commerce, 5, 64, 108
Commerce Department, 42, 50
commercial, xii, xiii, 31, 48, 55, 63, 64, 67, 132, 136, 138, 141, 151, 179, 202
commercial ties, xii, xiii, 132, 138, 179
commodities, 32, 39, 105
commodity, 42, 70, 71
communication, xv, 143, 178, 210, 224, 225, 226, 242, 248, 260
Communist Party, 88, 212, 215, 242, 258
communities, 103, 108
community, viii, 30, 170, 171, 188, 190, 194
community support, viii, 30
comparative advantage, 43
compensation, 57, 60, 211, 247, 252
competition, 33, 37, 38, 45, 50, 56, 64, 65, 142
competition policy, 50
competitive advantage, 144, 147
competitiveness, 8, 38, 65, 68, 146
competitor, 22, 68, 69, 212
competitors, 52
complement, 2, 3, 11, 19, 220, 223
compliance, 46, 64, 102, 146, 149
complications, 184, 229
components, ix, 14, 49, 80, 81, 89, 93, 94, 124, 134, 135, 155, 156, 197, 220, 232
composition, 58, 85, 86, 120, 124, 155, 237
Comprehensive Test Ban Treaty, 240
computation, 239
computer, 49, 50, 137, 138
conciliation, 198
concrete, 66, 91, 104, 153
conditioning, 108

conference, 80, 93, 192, 201, 212, 219, 226, 230, 245, 248, 262, 266
Conference Report, 217
confidence, 33, 68, 185, 212, 220, 222, 226, 228, 230, 234, 241, 243
configuration, 191
conflict, xv, 10, 26, 31, 183, 193, 210, 221, 224, 226
conflict avoidance, 224
conflict prevention, xv, 210
conformity, 44, 64
confrontation, 4, 198, 220, 224, 226, 236
Congressional Budget Office, 169, 176
consensus, 3, 4, 6, 11, 16, 25, 94, 196, 252
consent, 83
Consolidated Appropriations Act, 174, 178
constituents, 4
construction, ix, 18, 19, 20, 80, 85, 87, 89, 91, 165
consumer electronics, 14, 37, 50
consumer goods, 14, 146, 189
Consumer Product Safety Improvement Act, 157
consumer protection, 142
consumers, x, 40, 64, 68, 119, 122, 123, 141, 146
consumption, xii, 122, 123, 126, 131
Continued Dumping and Subsidy Offset Act, 75
continuity, 192
contracts, 43, 62, 104
control, x, 58, 69, 92, 99, 102, 103, 105, 111, 119, 139, 146, 171, 184, 185, 216, 222, 224, 226, 232, 234, 235, 238, 240, 244, 245, 248, 258
controversial, 14, 38, 163, 185, 191, 196, 227, 255
Convention on International Trade in Endangered Species, 77
conversations, 177, 204
conversion, 217
cooperation, xiv, xv, 4, 5, 6, 9, 11, 16, 17, 18, 23, 32, 49, 57, 64, 66, 82, 88, 90, 97, 98, 142, 143, 154, 164, 166, 170, 173, 174, 191, 202, 209, 210, 211, 212, 217, 220, 222, 224, 228, 229, 230, 232, 233, 234, 240, 241, 242, 243, 245, 247, 254, 257, 258, 261
coordination, 17, 195, 224
copyright, 61, 151, 190
copyright law, 151
corn, 35
corporate social responsibility, 8, 9
corporations, 14, 62
corruption, x, 9, 24, 101, 102, 103, 104, 108, 113, 142, 143, 180, 185, 188, 189, 200, 201, 205
cost, x, 36, 41, 44, 59, 62, 91, 119, 121, 124, 128, 140, 144, 147, 150, 151, 156, 158, 163, 169, 176, 196
costs, 17, 23, 24, 32, 52, 66, 151, 165, 168, 194, 255
cotton, 135

counterbalance, 32
counterfeit, 61, 109
counterfeiting, 104, 110
countermeasures, 110, 116
counter-terror, 17
counterterrorism, xv, 17, 23, 153, 210, 232, 253, 259
covering, 32, 68, 92, 143
CPC, 212, 213, 215
CR, 9
crack, 143
credibility, 194, 199, 235
credit, 37, 122, 148, 155
crime, x, 101, 102, 103, 104, 110, 111, 116, 117, 216, 232
crimes, x, 101
criminal activity, x, 101, 102
crises, xiv, 209, 215, 224, 225, 235
crisis management, xv, 210, 224, 226
critical period, vii, 1
critical points, 51
criticism, 23, 126
cronyism, 103
crops, 104
cross-border, 53
CRS report, 182
cruise missiles, 243, 250
Cuba, 178
cultivation, 104, 105, 106, 107, 111
culture, x, 101, 153, 184
currency, vii, x, xi, xii, 51, 59, 104, 109, 110, 119, 120, 121, 122, 123, 125, 126, 127, 128, 129, 131, 132, 139, 141, 143, 144, 152, 155, 158, 171
currency manipulation, x, 51, 119, 144
current account, 123, 144
current account deficit, 123
current account surplus, 144
customers, 51
Customs and Border Protection, 150
CVD, 50, 51, 56, 57, 76
cyclone, 102, 104, 108
Czech Republic, 175

D

Daewoo, 47, 69
dairy, 40
dairy products, 40
damages, 247
danger, 12, 24, 142, 220
database, 171
dating, 45, 83
death, 177
deaths, 105, 141

debt, xi, xii, 120, 122, 126, 131, 139, 140, 144, 152, 156
decisions, ix, xiv, 3, 4, 5, 6, 34, 52, 53, 58, 63, 66, 68, 80, 83, 86, 147, 170, 172, 180, 197, 198, 199, 206, 255
defense, xiv, xv, 19, 90, 180, 183, 191, 193, 197, 198, 201, 209, 210, 212, 216, 217, 218, 221, 223, 225, 226, 228, 229, 230, 231, 232, 236, 237, 242, 243, 246, 248, 250, 251, 252, 254, 255, 256, 257, 263
Defense Authorization Act, 2, 18, 19
deficiencies, 74
deficit, x, xi, xii, 42, 43, 50, 72, 119, 121, 123, 124, 125, 128, 129, 132, 134, 138, 140, 141, 144, 189
definition, 203
delivery, 53, 64, 94, 167, 168, 172
Delta, 94
democracy, 110, 112, 194, 195, 197, 198, 199, 200, 211
democratic elections, 184
democratization, xiv, 179, 194
demonstrations, 223
denial, 192, 227
Department of Agriculture, 67, 70, 154, 163
Department of Commerce, 36, 73, 75, 76, 159, 237, 238
Department of Defense, 169, 205, 216, 228, 232, 237, 238, 243, 245, 256, 258, 267, 268, 269, 270
Department of Energy, 88, 164, 176
Department of Health and Human Services, 143
Department of Homeland Security, 75
Department of Justice, 110, 202
Department of State, 3, 25, 28, 47, 97, 113, 114, 115, 116
deployments, 31
depository institutions, 139
deposits, 108
depreciation, xi, 120, 126, 140
depth, 198
destruction, 24, 61, 102, 218, 231
detection, 93
deterrence, 149, 221, 224
devaluation, 125
development assistance, 174
development banks, 9
deviation, 193
dialogues, xv, 153, 210, 221
diamonds, 113
diesel, 33, 44
diplomacy, vii, 15, 186, 204
diplomatic efforts, 19
direct funds, 146
direct investment, 36, 54, 59, 122, 127, 138

directives, 146
directors, 4, 60
disabled, ix, 79, 95
disappointment, 41, 77, 147, 151, 200, 224, 245
disaster, 9, 18, 174, 186, 235, 242, 245, 258, 264
disaster relief, 174, 186, 235, 242, 245, 258, 264
discounting, 193
discrimination, 4, 37, 64, 77
discriminatory, 15, 16, 31, 33, 44, 60
diseases, 17, 222
dismantlement, 85, 86, 96, 97, 162, 165, 166, 167, 169, 176, 230, 231
displacement, 33, 44
disposition, 169
dispute resolution, xii, 56, 132, 147, 148, 158
dispute settlement, 42, 45, 61, 63, 75
disputes, 36, 37, 42, 56, 60, 63
dissatisfaction, 185
distortions, 126
distress, 214, 230, 263
distribution, 145, 146, 148, 151, 172
divergence, 12
division, 254, 259, 261
Doha, 6, 14, 15, 16, 21, 23, 24, 27, 41, 56, 67, 145
domestic industry, 34, 48, 57
domestic issues, 185
dominance, 184
Dominican Republic, 38, 202
donations, xiii, 161, 164, 169, 170, 171, 172, 173
donors, xiii, 162, 170
doors, 36, 91
draft, viii, 29, 30, 64, 82, 240
drawing, 199
Drug Enforcement Administration, 104, 114
Drug Enforcement Administration (DEA), 104
drug manufacturers, 53
drug safety, 142
drug trafficking, 104, 105, 110
drug use, 105
drug-related, 104, 113
drugs, x, 51, 53, 101, 102, 103, 105, 106, 108, 109, 111, 143, 157
dumping, 75, 76, 128, 145, 149, 155
duties, 45, 48, 49, 51, 56, 57, 64, 148, 152, 154, 158
duty free, 33, 48
duty-free access, 70, 71
duty-free treatment, 46, 48, 49

E

early warning, 247, 250
earnings, 45, 103, 104
earthquake, 18

Index

East Asia, 2, 11, 16, 19, 21, 27, 28, 32, 37, 66, 86, 106, 114, 121, 124, 175, 177, 204, 220, 222, 266, 267
East China Sea, 238
East Sea, 252, 256, 262
East Timor, 23
Eastern Europe, 233
echoing, 256
e-commerce, 64
economic activity, 11, 40
economic change, 38
economic cooperation, 18, 166, 191, 202, 217
economic crisis, xi, xii, 9, 40, 68, 69, 119, 121, 131, 144
economic development, vii, 2, 121, 146
economic fundamentals, 124
economic growth, xi, xii, 3, 7, 14, 38, 119, 122, 126, 131, 132, 135, 136, 141
economic growth rate, 14
economic integration, 2, 8, 9, 15, 22, 24, 25
economic liberalization, 190
economic policy, 144
economic problem, 11
economic reform, xiii, 37, 121, 135, 141, 144, 152, 162
economic reforms, xiii, 37, 121, 135, 141, 144, 152, 162
economic relations, xi, xii, 31, 32, 37, 38, 59, 131, 132
Economic Research Service, 70, 71
economic transformation, 182
economic well-being, 123
economics, 189
ecstasy, 108
education, 5, 18, 38, 129, 153, 189, 240, 241
Education, 18
educational exchanges, 227, 228, 234, 238, 256
educational programs, 57
election, 37, 65, 66, 184, 185, 191, 199, 203, 207, 229, 239, 249, 250, 255, 264
electric power, 88
elephants, 108
e-mail, 177
embargo, 216
embassy, xiv, 209, 211, 215, 247
emergency, 164, 170, 172, 174, 211, 252
Emergency Assistance, 177
emigration, 155
emission, 46
employees, 47, 59, 62, 155
employment, 35, 54, 60, 61, 77, 121, 122, 124, 128, 154
encephalopathy, 67

endangered species, 105
energy, ix, xii, 5, 8, 20, 25, 79, 84, 86, 94, 153, 154, 155, 161, 162, 164, 165, 166, 167, 168, 173, 175, 185, 257
energy efficiency, 154
energy prices, 185
enforcement, 3, 12, 51, 61, 102, 111, 117, 128, 141, 145, 146, 148, 149, 150, 151, 153
engagement, xv, 2, 19, 66, 180, 186, 187, 200, 209, 211, 220, 221, 222, 224, 225, 229, 230, 261
engineering, 242
England, 115, 219, 221, 262, 263, 264
enterprise, 102
entrapment, 142
environment, 5, 11, 21, 35, 58, 60, 63, 66, 77, 153, 154, 198, 220
environmental issues, 243, 261
environmental protection, 251
environmental standards, 21, 63, 128
EP-3, 211, 215, 218, 222, 224, 225, 252, 253, 254, 265, 268
epidemic, 222
epidemics, 53
equipment, 34, 35, 37, 46, 49, 50, 90, 91, 123, 137, 138, 143, 146, 147, 156, 158, 166, 168, 169, 174, 189, 191, 201, 211, 216, 232
equities, 139, 140, 156
equity, 51
espionage, 247
estimating, 34
ethnic groups, 103, 106
EU, 31, 88, 147, 216
Europe, 3, 14, 45, 72, 233
European Free Trade Association, 65
European Union, 16, 24, 26, 28, 31, 65, 111, 133, 134, 165, 169, 175, 216, 266
evidence, 17, 83, 88, 89, 93, 103, 124, 151, 170, 171, 192
evolution, 27, 240
excess demand, 120
exchange rate, xii, 120, 121, 122, 124, 125, 126, 128, 132, 143, 144
exchange rate policy, 122, 126, 144
exchange rate target, 144
exclusion, 38, 41, 252
executive branch, 93, 164, 183
Executive Branch, vii, 1, 2
Executive Order, x, 101, 116
exercise, xv, 24, 164, 169, 201, 209, 218, 223, 225, 227, 230, 236, 243, 245, 247, 248, 251, 253, 254, 255, 258, 259, 260, 261, 262, 263, 264
exile, 98
expenditures, 53, 189

expertise, 169, 244
exploitation, 105, 108, 111
explosions, 91
export control, 155, 244
export market, xi, 36, 41, 120, 126, 131, 132, 134, 135, 136
export subsidies, 24, 145, 147, 148
exporters, xi, 36, 37, 39, 40, 41, 42, 49, 63, 67, 68, 72, 124, 131
export-oriented manufacturing facilities, xi, 131
exports, viii, x, xii, 2, 12, 13, 14, 29, 31, 32, 34, 36, 39, 40, 41, 42, 43, 45, 46, 47, 48, 49, 50, 51, 65, 67, 69, 71, 72, 105, 108, 111, 119, 121, 122, 124, 125, 126, 127, 131, 132, 134, 135, 137, 141, 143, 144, 145, 149, 153, 154, 155, 158, 180, 189, 244
exposure, 18, 215, 218, 219, 245
extremists, 17
eyes, 66

F

fabric, 48
factories, 58, 122
failure, xi, xii, 31, 32, 38, 52, 64, 66, 67, 80, 92, 94, 131, 132, 141, 142, 146, 188, 192
faith, 201
false alarms, 18
families, 104, 113, 171
family, 188, 189, 205, 214, 230, 263
family members, 188
famine, 169, 172, 177
Far East, 113
farmers, 38, 39, 104, 106, 157, 171
farming, 40
fast-track trade authority, viii, 29, 30
fatigue, 170
FBIS, 206
FDA, 75, 141, 143, 156
FDI, 36, 59, 122, 125, 138, 140, 155, 156
fear, 16, 122, 144, 191
fears, 147
February, ix, 17, 28, 31, 33, 37, 41, 43, 47, 56, 59, 65, 70, 71, 72, 73, 78, 79, 80, 81, 83, 87, 91, 92, 93, 94, 96, 97, 98, 99, 104, 114
federal law, 20
Federal Register, 74, 113
Federal Reserve, 71
Federal Reserve Bank, 71
fees, 53, 59, 104
feet, 40, 87, 236
fertilizer, 109
fibers, 48, 134, 135
fights, 185

filament, 135
films, 59, 150
finance, 5, 16, 90, 124, 139
financial, x, 3, 7, 8, 9, 10, 11, 12, 14, 16, 17, 18, 19, 20, 22, 23, 27, 37, 53, 54, 55, 59, 60, 81, 86, 101, 103, 104, 110, 111, 116, 122, 125, 134, 144, 145, 148, 149, 150, 153, 157, 175, 189, 201
financial aid, 81, 86
financial capital, 60
Financial Crimes Enforcement Network, 110, 115
financial crisis, 7, 8, 9, 10, 11, 12, 14, 27, 37, 59, 122, 125, 134, 144, 150, 153, 189
financial institution, 16, 17, 54, 103, 104, 110, 116
financial institutions, 16, 17, 54, 103, 104, 110, 145
financial markets, 8
financial sector, 9, 110, 144
financial support, 3, 18, 19, 20, 22, 157, 175
financing, 19, 115, 146
fines, 21
fire, 102
fires, 102
firms, x, xi, xii, 36, 37, 38, 53, 54, 58, 62, 63, 65, 68, 104, 119, 122, 123, 124, 128, 131, 142, 143, 145, 146, 147, 150, 152, 154, 157, 158, 217
fish, 71, 116, 157
Fish and Wildlife Service, 114
fission, 92
flexibility, 4, 24, 56, 174, 193, 229, 250
flight, 202, 221, 236, 242, 252, 265
flights, xiv, 27, 179, 186, 191, 202, 211, 252
float, 121, 143, 144
floating, xi, xii, 120, 121, 124, 125, 131, 132, 143
flood, 147
floods, 172
flow, ix, x, 8, 23, 30, 47, 97, 101, 105, 111, 113
fluid, 40, 193
focusing, vii, 1, 22, 94
food, xii, xiii, xiv, 8, 9, 27, 32, 39, 40, 42, 70, 71, 106, 141, 142, 143, 155, 156, 161, 162, 163, 164, 169, 170, 171, 172, 173, 174, 179, 186
food additives, 42
food products, 39, 40, 70
food safety, xiv, 8, 27, 42, 179, 186
food security, 8, 9, 106, 172
footwear, 34, 137
force, viii, xiii, 6, 9, 14, 29, 30, 34, 48, 54, 55, 58, 61, 63, 86, 103, 179, 180, 186, 196, 201, 221, 222, 223, 224, 229, 231, 237, 244, 247, 249, 255, 256, 269
forced labor, 77, 108
Ford, 45, 46, 47, 69, 73, 137
foreign assistance, x, 101, 102, 110, 117, 162
foreign companies, 36, 46, 62, 69, 125

foreign direct investment, 36, 54, 59, 122, 127, 138
foreign exchange, x, xi, 119, 120, 127, 129, 144
foreign firms, 36, 138, 146, 148, 158
foreign investment, xi, 31, 34, 53, 59, 60, 63, 76, 119, 122, 147, 255
foreign policy, 2, 15, 65
Foreign Relations Committee, 88, 93
forests, 105, 108
forgiveness, 152
formation, 15, 164, 184
formula, 46, 141
Fort Hood, 240, 247
foundations, 186
France, 26, 95, 97, 98, 114, 116, 136, 176, 216, 223
free market conditions, x, 119
free trade, vii, 1, 4, 8, 10, 15, 19, 21, 23, 30, 38, 47, 70, 128
free trade agreement, vii, 1, 8, 10, 15, 19, 23, 30, 38
freedom, 77, 155, 163, 221, 225, 265
freezing, xii, 161, 162
freight, 53
friction, 65
friendship, 223
FTA, viii, 10, 15, 29, 30, 31, 32, 33, 34, 35, 36, 37, 38, 39, 40, 42, 43, 44, 45, 46, 47, 48, 49, 50, 51, 52, 53, 54, 55, 56, 57, 58, 59, 60, 61, 62, 63, 64, 65, 66, 67, 68, 69, 70, 71, 72, 73, 74, 75, 76, 77
FTAs, 8, 9, 14, 15, 16, 21, 24, 27, 31, 38, 42, 46, 49, 55, 56, 57, 60, 61, 63, 65, 66, 67, 76, 77
fuel, ix, xii, 7, 79, 81, 87, 89, 93, 122, 161, 162, 165, 166, 167, 168, 169, 176
fulfillment, 22
full employment, 124
funding, viii, xi, 2, 18, 20, 24, 111, 120, 126, 146, 147, 164, 176, 183, 216
funds, x, 23, 28, 94, 98, 101, 146, 164, 168, 169, 171, 175, 176, 185, 188, 189, 201, 211, 217
furniture, 144

G

G20 commitment, vii, 1
gas, 90, 111, 113
gasoline, 33, 44
GATT, 56, 62, 145
GDP, 34, 35, 37, 124, 150
General Agreement on Tariffs and Trade, 56, 62, 145
General Motors, 26, 45, 69, 73, 137
generation, 88, 146
generators, 49
generic drug, 51, 52
generic drugs, 51
Geneva, 14

Georgia, 10, 26, 241, 244, 245
Germany, 26, 68, 136, 216, 223
gestures, 199
girls, 108
global demand, 125
global economy, 11, 111
global supply chain, 14, 27
global trade, viii, xi, 2, 14, 131
Globalization, 28
goals, 3, 4, 5, 6, 16, 22, 37, 59, 65, 136, 193, 197, 198, 220, 221
goods and services, 15, 20, 24, 62, 123, 136, 154, 215, 219
governance, 197
government funds, 188
government intervention, 158
government procurement, 50, 62, 146
governments, viii, ix, xiii, 30, 37, 51, 57, 58, 60, 62, 68, 79, 85, 92, 94, 102, 162, 163, 186, 191, 196
governor, xi, 120, 127
GPA, 62
GPS, 235, 236, 238, 239, 240
grains, 135
grants, 152, 154
graphite, 165
grass, 40
gravity, 236, 237, 240
Greece, 232
greed, 32, 34, 40, 52, 54, 88, 149, 210, 234, 247
gross domestic product, 37, 124, 150
groups, viii, x, 4, 5, 6, 22, 24, 28, 30, 39, 42, 45, 101, 102, 103, 105, 106, 108, 114, 134, 142, 149, 150, 153, 183, 260
growth, viii, xi, xii, 2, 3, 7, 8, 12, 13, 14, 15, 16, 27, 38, 71, 119, 121, 122, 124, 126, 131, 132, 135, 136, 141, 144
growth rate, 12, 14, 71
Guam, 92
Guangdong, 223
Guangzhou, 228, 238, 242, 257, 258, 263, 264
guidelines, 24, 42, 147, 183, 195, 222
Guinea, 25
guns, 102

H

H5N1, 17
hair, 6
harassment, xv, 210, 235, 252, 265
hard currency, 59
hardwoods, 111
harm, xii, xv, 32, 131, 210, 215, 224
harmonization, 44

harvest, 41
Hawaii, 92, 216, 226, 235, 237, 238, 240, 241, 242, 243, 244, 245, 249, 250, 251, 253, 254, 255, 258, 259, 260, 264
hazards, 142, 154
health, xi, xii, 17, 32, 38, 42, 52, 53, 64, 65, 131, 132, 141, 142, 143, 146, 153, 157, 174, 204
Health and Human Services, 143
health information, 141
health insurance, 52
health problems, 17
hearing, 31
heart, 105
heat, 35
heavy oil, 84, 85, 166
heroin, 105, 106
Heroin, 105
heterogeneous, 15
Hezbollah, 82, 91
HHS, 143
high enriched uranium, x, 80
high-level, 39, 103, 108
highways, 62
hip, 70, 256
hips, 50
history, 12, 163, 175, 192, 213
HIV, 17, 53, 105
HIV/AIDS, 17
HK, 109
Homeland Security, 75
honey, 32, 39
Hong Kong, xv, 3, 22, 25, 26, 27, 115, 127, 138, 190, 204, 210, 214, 227, 230, 234, 238, 240, 243, 245, 246, 247, 248, 249, 251, 258, 263, 266
hospitals, xiii, 162, 174, 222, 240
host, vii, 1, 3, 7, 11, 23, 230
hostilities, 103
hostility, 198
House, 2, 3, 8, 9, 10, 28, 46, 47, 68, 72, 73, 75, 77, 82, 83, 90, 95, 96, 115, 176, 177, 183, 184, 191, 192, 193, 200, 202, 203, 204, 206, 211, 213, 216, 217, 218, 219, 231, 232, 234, 244, 245, 255, 265, 266, 267, 268, 269
House of Representatives, 73, 90, 115
household, 68, 106
households, 106
housing, 123
Housing and Urban Development, 154
hub, 15, 37
HUD, 154
human, x, 2, 5, 8, 16, 18, 19, 21, 23, 32, 38, 58, 101, 105, 108, 110, 111, 153, 163, 216, 217
human health, 32, 38

human resources, 5
human right, x, 2, 5, 19, 58, 101, 105, 110, 153, 163, 216, 217
human rights, x, 2, 5, 19, 58, 101, 105, 110, 153, 163, 216, 217
human security, 8, 16, 18, 21
humanitarian, 102, 110, 112
humanitarian aid, 112, 170, 174, 264
humanitarianism, 234
humans, x, 24, 101, 102, 104, 111
Hunter, 176
hybrid, 45
hybrids, 45
Hyundai, 42, 43, 45, 62, 69, 72, 73, 78

I

IAEA, 88, 93, 98
IAP, 6, 23
Iceland, 78
id, viii, 27, 29, 32, 38, 76, 82, 89
identity, 32, 39, 40, 52, 184, 186
idiosyncratic, 44
illegal drugs, 105, 108
ILO, 77
images, 97
IMF, 25, 27, 36
immigration, 6
immunity, 102, 188
implementation, viii, ix, 8, 29, 30, 42, 47, 52, 53, 57, 63, 64, 67, 79, 80, 83, 84, 103, 146, 149, 168, 231
import controls, 141
import penetration, 46, 69
import prices, 121
imported products, 158
importer, 39
imports, viii, x, xi, xii, xiii, 2, 12, 13, 14, 30, 32, 33, 34, 36, 37, 39, 40, 41, 42, 43, 44, 45, 46, 47, 48, 49, 50, 53, 55, 56, 57, 64, 67, 69, 72, 75, 101, 119, 121, 122, 123, 124, 125, 126, 131, 132, 134, 137, 138, 141, 142, 144, 145, 146, 147, 148, 152, 153, 154, 155, 157, 158, 159, 162, 172, 189
imprisonment, 62
improvements, 50, 164, 170, 173, 181, 185, 186, 190, 192, 198
inauguration, 186
incentive, 82
incentives, 43, 86, 146
inclusion, 63, 86, 164, 252
income, 38, 58, 106, 174, 205
incompatibility, 15
increased access, 31, 38, 54
increased competition, 37, 38, 65

Index

independence, 180, 184, 185, 186, 191, 194, 196, 197, 198, 199, 201, 203, 206, 230, 244, 255
Independence, 239
India, 26, 65, 68, 103, 104, 112, 117, 155, 236, 253
Indian, 18
Indian Ocean, 18
indication, 10, 104, 249
individuals, 5, 89, 108, 110, 158
Indonesia, 3, 6, 18, 22, 23, 25, 26, 78, 104, 127, 175
industrial, 7, 31, 34, 36, 38, 45, 57, 58, 69
industrial policies, xi, 131, 141, 146
industrialized countries, 65
industries, xii, 31, 36, 38, 49, 50, 53, 55, 56, 65, 121, 122, 131, 136, 139, 141, 144, 146, 148, 152, 153
industry, x, 33, 34, 36, 41, 42, 43, 45, 46, 47, 48, 49, 50, 51, 53, 55, 57, 67, 68, 69, 74, 76, 77, 101, 111, 146, 147, 149, 150, 153, 155, 157
infectious, 17
infectious disease, 17
infectious diseases, 17
inflation, x, xi, 119, 120, 122, 126, 140
influenza, 17, 21, 24, 157
information sharing, 57, 143
Information System, 73
information technology, 50
Information Technology, 22, 50
infrastructure, 18, 23, 88, 104, 126, 136
ingredients, 141
initiation, ix, 50, 57, 79
injection, 51, 105
injury, 34, 48, 55, 56, 75
innocence, 205
insertion, 87
inspection, ix, 80, 83
inspections, ix, 79, 82, 83, 84, 85, 95, 142, 143
inspectors, ix, 79, 80, 82, 83, 143, 165
instability, 112
institutions, 16, 17, 54, 103, 104, 110, 138, 145, 197
instruments, 35, 126
insurance, 52, 53, 54, 145, 148, 154
insurance companies, 54
insurgency, 109
integration, vii, 1, 2, 8, 9, 11, 15, 21, 22, 24, 25, 58, 227, 244, 248
intellectual property, xi, xii, xiv, 8, 49, 50, 59, 60, 61, 76, 131, 132, 141, 180, 189, 190
intellectual property rights, xi, xii, xiv, 8, 49, 60, 61, 76, 131, 132, 141, 180, 189, 190
intelligence, 80, 81, 87, 88, 89, 90, 91, 92, 93, 94, 109, 215, 219, 222, 224, 226, 232, 235, 236, 237, 238, 251, 265
intelligence estimates, 80, 81, 88, 92, 93

Intelligence Reform and Terrorism Prevention Act, 19
intentions, 186, 199, 221, 263
interaction, 36, 196, 217, 220, 240, 258
interactions, 181, 183, 195, 212, 216, 228, 256
Inter-American Development Bank, 9
interdependence, 3
interest groups, 164
interest rates, x, 119, 123, 144
interference, 103, 231
intermediate range ballistic missile, x, 80, 91
International Atomic Energy Agency, 83, 84, 91, 94
international financial institutions, 110
international investment, 4
international law, 60
International Monetary Fund, xi, 9, 11, 36, 81, 86, 120, 127
International Narcotics Control, 113, 114, 115, 116
international standards, 8, 43, 248
international terrorism, 245
international trade, vii, 1, 2, 3, 6, 7, 12, 14, 23, 63, 144
International Trade, 12, 27, 31, 35, 44, 70, 71, 73, 74, 75, 77
International Trade Administration, 71
international trade and investment in Asia, vii, 1, 2
International Trade Commission, 31, 35, 44, 70, 73, 77
internet, 61, 96, 97, 98, 99
Internet, 64, 67
interrogations, 233
intervention, 121, 158
interview, 72, 93, 252, 266, 268
interviews, 76, 83
intrusions, 81
inventories, 68
investigative, 57
investment, vii, viii, xi, xiv, 1, 2, 3, 4, 6, 11, 12, 14, 15, 16, 22, 23, 29, 30, 31, 34, 36, 38, 47, 53, 54, 59, 60, 61, 63, 76, 81, 119, 122, 123, 124, 126, 127, 129, 131, 138, 140, 145, 147, 166, 179, 186, 190, 191, 202, 255
investments, 59, 60, 123, 138, 198
investors, 36, 54, 59, 60, 76, 122, 156, 186, 201
IP, 108
IPR, xii, 59, 60, 61, 74, 132, 141, 145, 146, 148, 149, 150, 151, 158, 189, 190
Iran, ix, 80, 81, 82, 86, 89, 90, 91, 92, 97, 98, 99, 178, 221, 235, 243, 250, 263
Iraq, 23, 31, 232
Ireland, 216
iron, 35
isolation, 111

Israel, ix, 20, 80, 89, 97, 250
Italy, 26
ITC, 72, 74

J

Jamaica, 203
Japan, vii, ix, xii, 1, 3, 6, 9, 11, 14, 15, 16, 22, 25, 26, 27, 28, 36, 37, 45, 57, 67, 68, 69, 72, 76, 79, 80, 82, 83, 84, 92, 93, 96, 109, 111, 124, 131, 133, 134, 136, 138, 139, 140, 161, 163, 165, 166, 167, 169, 175, 176, 189, 224, 230, 245, 246, 248, 259, 팸263, 264
Japanese, 14, 22, 37, 45, 65, 82, 84, 88, 90, 91, 92, 93, 94, 98
job creation, 38
jobs, x, 43, 47, 55, 111, 119, 122, 141, 144, 150, 157
joining, 2, 9, 21
joint ventures, 54, 155
journalists, 231
judge, ix, 30
judges, 149
judiciary, 31, 205
jurisdiction, 216
justice, 189

K

kidnapping, 82
kill, 231, 261
killing, 211
Korean government, ix, 40, 46, 52, 58, 59, 60, 68, 69, 79, 80, 84, 93
Korean War, 81
Kosovo, 247
Kuomintang, 10

L

labor, viii, 21, 30, 34, 36, 47, 58, 61, 62, 63, 66, 76, 77, 108, 121, 124, 137, 168
Labor Advisory Committee, 62, 77
labor market, 36, 62
labor markets, 62
LAC, 62, 77
land, 264
Landscape, 181
language, 20, 61, 77, 164, 168, 169, 176, 207, 217, 219
Laos, 25, 78, 104, 114, 117
Latin America, 190
laundering, 103, 104, 109, 110, 115
law, x, 12, 20, 51, 54, 57, 60, 82, 86, 101, 102, 111, 117
law enforcement, 12, 51, 102, 111, 117, 149, 153
laws, 22, 47, 50, 52, 55, 56, 57, 61, 62, 64, 103, 108, 123, 128, 142, 146, 148, 149, 150, 151, 152, 154, 183, 190, 216, 244
laws and regulations, 52, 64, 146
lawyers, 54
layoffs, xi, 119, 125
LC, 73
lead, xi, 15, 35, 48, 63, 119, 142, 143, 147, 190, 193, 220, 222, 224
leadership, xiv, 6, 22, 65, 90, 107, 197, 209, 211, 222, 223, 224, 228
leather, 34
Lebanon, 91
legislation, viii, xv, 2, 3, 12, 20, 29, 30, 64, 174, 183, 188, 190, 210, 214, 215, 216, 218, 244, 247
liberalization, vii, viii, xii, 1, 2, 3, 4, 6, 11, 12, 13, 14, 15, 16, 22, 23, 30, 35, 43, 66, 132, 190
license fee, 53
licenses, 110, 216
licensing, 54
lien, 110
lift, viii, 30, 82, 94
light, 15, 40, 42, 45, 69, 85, 86, 111, 146, 152, 157, 165, 166, 168, 181, 183, 217, 224, 242
light trucks, 45, 69
likelihood, 81, 93, 220
limitations, 61
Lincoln, Abraham, 244
line, 125, 224, 244, 248, 258
linkage, 52, 86, 170, 229
links, xiv, 97, 102, 104, 179, 186
livestock, 35
living standards, xi, 119, 126, 132, 136
loans, x, 101, 110, 122, 147, 152, 158
local government, 142, 148, 150
logistics, 146, 183, 201, 218, 237
London, 98, 108
Los Angeles, 98
lower prices, 147
LTC, 267

M

Macau, 22, 94
machinery, 34, 35, 36, 49, 122, 146, 156, 189
macroeconomic policy, 124
mad cow disease, 32, 38, 67, 147
magnesium, 147
magnets, 142

Index

maintenance, 181, 203, 240
major issues, 146
majority, 31, 44, 60, 65, 147, 184, 185, 200
malaria, 53
Malaysia, 6, 23, 25, 37, 66, 78, 103, 104, 127, 138, 140, 245
malfeasance, 188
management, xv, 17, 47, 156, 185, 210, 224, 226, 228, 232, 259
mandates, 54, 183
manganese, 147
manipulation, x, 51, 119, 144
manufactured goods, 30, 37, 38, 142
manufacturer, 52, 69, 142
manufacturing, x, xi, 14, 58, 59, 60, 68, 69, 73, 90, 107, 119, 121, 123, 128, 131, 138, 139, 141, 144, 147, 154, 156
Marine Corps, 237, 254, 255, 261, 264
maritime security, 259, 262
market, viii, ix, x, xi, 7, 23, 24, 29, 30, 31, 33, 36, 37, 38, 39, 40, 41, 42, 43, 44, 45, 46, 47, 51, 52, 53, 54, 55, 56, 59, 60, 62, 64, 65, 67, 68, 69, 71, 72, 78, 102, 119, 120, 121, 124, 126, 128, 131, 132, 134, 135, 136, 137, 143, 144, 145, 146, 147, 148, 149, 150, 151, 152, 154, 158, 186
market access, viii, 7, 24, 29, 31, 37, 38, 46, 54, 64, 65, 71, 148, 149
market economy, 145, 152, 154
market opening, 126
market share, 33, 40, 42, 43, 68, 72
market value, 56, 60
marketing, 43, 52
marketplace, 147, 151
markets, xiii, 8, 31, 34, 36, 37, 43, 45, 47, 51, 62, 105, 109, 111, 121, 132, 135, 136, 144, 147, 153, 158, 162, 171
martial law, 184
Maryland, 244, 260
mass, 24, 218
materials, x, 33, 67, 83, 88, 89, 97, 119, 122, 124, 147, 149, 189
matter, 40, 42, 61, 151, 219, 233
measures, xii, 8, 9, 15, 16, 17, 22, 23, 24, 26, 42, 53, 56, 60, 68, 75, 76, 80, 85, 94, 111, 126, 132, 146, 149, 152, 165, 167, 168, 190, 202, 228, 230, 234, 241
meat, 39, 68, 135
media, 89, 105, 108, 109, 142, 157, 230, 234, 252, 255, 269
medical, 17, 34, 37, 38, 51, 52, 53, 143, 162, 174, 223, 233, 239, 240, 259
medicine, 222
megawatt, 81, 88, 93

membership, 2, 13, 18, 21, 25, 145, 187, 188, 199, 200, 201, 204, 206, 229, 244
memory, 50
men, 62
merchandise, 4, 124, 134
messages, 222
metals, 146, 156
metaphors, 15
methamphetamine, 104, 105, 106, 107
Methamphetamine, 106, 114
methodology, 33, 44, 145
metric, 40, 46, 106
metric tons (MT), xiii, 40, 161, 163, 169
Mexico, 6, 8, 23, 24, 25, 26, 68, 69, 133, 136, 138, 140, 223, 240
middle class, 132
Middle East, 82
migrant, 108
migrants, 108
military, vii, x, xiv, xv, 10, 53, 83, 84, 85, 86, 88, 91, 92, 96, 98, 101, 102, 103, 104, 108, 109, 111, 146, 166, 171, 180, 181, 182, 183, 193, 194, 195, 196, 199, 201, 209, 210, 211, 212, 214, 215, 216, 217, 218, 219, 220, 221, 222, 223, 224, 225, 226, 227, 228, 229, 230, 231, 232, 233, 234, 235, 237, 238, 239, 240, 241, 242, 244, 245, 246, 247, 248, 249, 250, 251, 252, 253, 255, 256, 257, 258, 259, 261, 263, 265, 267, 268
military contacts, vii, xiv, xv, 209, 210, 212, 218, 219, 221, 224, 226, 227, 232, 234, 248, 257, 258, 263, 265, 267
military exchanges, xiv, xv, 199, 209, 210, 214, 215, 218, 219, 220, 222, 223, 227, 229, 230, 235, 252, 253, 257, 258, 263, 265
military exercises, 199, 201, 212, 225, 245
military junta, x, 101, 102
military spending, 217
military-to-military, xiv, xv, 85, 209, 210, 212, 219, 220, 221, 223, 230, 261
militia, 103
milk, 32, 39, 40, 141
mil-to-mil, xiv, xv, 209, 210, 211, 212, 215, 216, 217, 218, 219, 220, 221, 222, 229, 234, 235, 240, 241, 242, 243, 246, 247, 248, 251, 252, 253, 254, 256
minerals, 108
mining, x, 101, 108, 109, 139
minorities, 108
minority, 194
minors, 108
mirror, 38
missiles, x, 80, 82, 90, 91, 92, 94, 98, 99, 109
mission, 17, 20, 22, 242, 253

missions, 154, 233, 235, 245
misunderstanding, 213, 220
misuse, 185
mobile phone, 136
modeling, 236
models, 2, 11, 15, 35, 42
modernization, 210, 218, 221, 222, 224, 228, 246, 257
modifications, 116
momentum, 4, 185
money, 17, 94, 103, 104, 110, 115, 122, 127, 164, 188, 201, 202
money laundering, 103, 104, 110, 115, 201, 202
money supply, 122
Mongolia, 223, 228, 255, 258
Moon, 76
moratorium, 92
morning, 10
Moscow, 266
motives, 82
mountains, 102, 114, 253
movement, 17, 47, 104, 121, 138, 197, 211
multilateral, 3, 6, 9, 16, 21, 23, 33, 41, 46, 50, 56, 63, 67, 77, 112
multinational corporations, 14, 122
muscle, 32, 40, 71
music, 146, 149, 150
Myanmar, x, 25, 78, 101, 110, 113, 115, 116

N

NAFTA, viii, 29
NAM, 74
naming, 237
narcotics, 103, 104, 105, 110, 111, 117
nation, 18, 53, 60, 128, 132, 146, 211, 230
National Association of Manufacturers, 74
National Defense Authorization Act, xv, 2, 18, 19, 175, 176, 210, 215, 217, 218, 219, 226, 248, 266
National Intelligence Estimate, 263
National Party, 31, 65
national security, 32, 65, 113, 218, 219
National Security Council, 2, 91, 204, 232
National Security Strategy, 113
nationality, 60
NATO, xiv, 209, 211, 247
natural, 18, 90, 108, 111
natural disaster, 18, 212
natural disasters, 18, 212
natural gas, 90, 111
natural resources, 108
naval confrontations, xiv, 209
NEA, 50

needles, 105
negative effects, 150
negotiating, ix, 15, 31, 32, 39, 40, 47, 56, 57, 65, 66, 80, 82, 84, 85, 86, 94, 187, 225
negotiation, 24, 85, 87, 186
neoliberal, 16
net exports, 127
Netherlands, 136
network, 14, 15, 55, 104, 136, 226
neutral, 45, 46, 47
New York, 96, 97, 98, 99, 113
New York Times, 96, 97, 98, 99, 113
New Zealand, vii, 1, 2, 3, 6, 21, 22, 23, 25, 27, 28, 66, 167, 175
NGOs, xiii, 161, 163, 170, 172, 173, 174
Nixon, Richard, 203
nodes, 108
non-governmental organizations (NGOs), xiii, 161, 163, 172
non-human, 110
non-nuclear, 93
nontariff barriers, 20, 69, 154
non-tariff barriers, 46
non-tariff barriers, 50
non-tariff barriers (NTBs), 46
normal, 40
normalization, ix, 80, 82, 84, 86
norms, 2, 19, 58
North America, viii, 3, 29, 30, 135, 137, 155, 205
North American Free Trade Agreement, viii, 29, 30
North Korea, v, vii, ix, xii, xiii, 24, 31, 34, 37, 51, 58, 63, 65, 66, 79, 80, 81, 82, 83, 84, 85, 86, 87, 88, 89, 90, 91, 92, 93, 94, 95, 96, 97, 98, 99, 109, 115, 161, 162, 163, 164, 165, 166, 167, 168, 169, 170, 171, 172, 173, 174, 175, 176, 177, 178, 221, 230, 233, 248, 256, 257, 259, 260, 263
North Sea, 237, 242, 251, 258
Northeast, 37, 66
Northeast Asia, 37, 66
Norway, 78
nose, 91
NPT, 165, 168
NSA, 168
NTBs, 46
nuclear, ix, 24, 49, 79, 80, 81, 82, 83, 84, 85, 86, 87, 88, 89, 90, 91, 92, 93, 94, 95, 96, 97, 98, 99, 109
nuclear material, 83, 97
Nuclear Nonproliferation Treaty, 165
nuclear program, ix, xii, 79, 80, 81, 82, 86, 90, 91, 93, 94, 95, 97, 98, 161, 162, 165, 166, 170, 174, 175, 230, 263
nuclear reactor, ix, 50, 79, 80, 85, 86, 89
nuclear talks, 83, 84, 85, 86, 170

nuclear technology, 88, 90
nuclear threat, ix, 80, 85, 86
nuclear warhead that, x, 80, 94
nuclear weapons, vii, ix, 24, 79, 80, 82, 84, 85, 86, 87, 88, 89, 90, 92, 93, 94, 99, 109, 162, 166, 174, 175, 214, 230, 231, 244, 247, 256, 258

O

Obama, viii, ix, xi, xii, xiv, xv, 2, 11, 20, 21, 29, 30, 61, 63, 65, 68, 80, 81, 84, 86, 87, 119, 126, 132, 144, 153, 164, 180, 192, 193, 210, 265
Obama Administration, viii, ix, xi, xii, xiv, xv, 2, 11, 20, 21, 29, 30, 61, 63, 65, 68, 80, 81, 84, 86, 87, 119, 126, 132, 144, 164, 180, 192, 193, 210
Obama, President, 153, 265
objectives, xv, 210, 211, 221, 224
obligation, 81, 252
obligations, 56, 64, 80, 81
observations, 88, 207, 235
obstacles, 149, 190, 196
OECD, 36, 46, 61, 70, 77
OFAC, 110, 114
Office of Foreign Assets Control, 110
Office of Foreign Assets Control (OFAC), 110
Office of the U.S. Trade Representative, 74
Office of the United States Trade Representative, 34, 75, 205
oil, ix, xii, 79, 84, 85, 90, 146, 161, 162, 165, 166, 167, 168, 176
online, 23, 27, 28, 89
on-line, 23
openness, 46, 221, 223
Operation Enduring Freedom, 232
operations, 3, 14, 54, 69, 85, 86, 104, 109, 149, 164, 165, 170, 172, 173, 194, 218, 223, 243, 245, 248, 257, 259, 264, 265
operator, 226
opinion polls, 65
opium, 103, 104, 105, 106, 107, 111, 114
opportunities, viii, ix, 19, 29, 30, 31, 41, 49, 51, 55, 76, 124, 198, 220
opposition, viii, 4, 30, 40, 45, 47, 59, 65, 91, 98
opposition parties, 40, 65, 184
order, 121, 122, 124, 126, 127, 143, 144, 147, 153, 172, 195, 223, 241
organ, 98
organized crime, x, 101, 102, 103, 104
orientation, 11, 42
oversight, x, 3, 18, 19, 101, 102, 110, 189, 210, 214, 216, 228
over-the-air, 76
ownership, 44, 55, 116, 139, 145, 147, 156

oxalate, 88
Ozone, 77

P

Pacific, v, vii, xv, 1, 2, 3, 11, 15, 18, 19, 20, 21, 22, 25, 26, 27, 28, 66, 114, 115, 175, 176, 177, 186, 188, 200, 201, 209, 212, 215, 216, 218, 221, 222, 223, 225, 228, 229, 232, 233, 235, 238, 240, 242, 243, 245, 246, 248, 250, 251, 257, 258, 259, 261, 262, 264, 266, 267, 268
packaging, 169
Pakistan, 88, 92, 94, 99, 221
Pakistani, 88
Panama, 67
pandemic, 21, 24
Papua New Guinea, 25
Paraguay, 202
parallel, 32
parameters, 218
paramilitary, 105
participants, 192, 203, 226, 227
partnership, 172
passenger, 17, 33, 34, 43, 44, 69
passports, 26
patents, 53
PATRIOT Act, 116
peace, 87, 181, 195, 221, 228, 229, 237, 242, 250, 264
peace treaty, 87
peacekeepers, 23
peacekeeping, 242
pegging, 120
penalties, 61, 108, 142
penalty, 45, 50, 51
Pentagon, xv, 12, 16, 23, 27, 191, 193, 201, 207, 209, 210, 211, 212, 214, 216, 217, 219, 220, 222, 224, 225, 226, 227, 228, 230, 232, 233, 234, 236, 237, 239, 240, 241, 242, 243, 244, 245, 247, 250, 251, 252, 254, 259, 260, 261, 262, 264, 266, 270
per capita, 37
per capita income, 174
perceptions, 58, 66, 231
performance, 158, 185, 199
performers, 61, 77
permission, 52, 53, 187, 230, 263
permit, 12, 54
personal relations, 224
personal relationship, 224
Peru, v, vii, 1, 6, 7, 8, 10, 25, 26, 186, 201
petroleum, 121
Petroleum, 133, 134
pharmaceutical, 51, 52, 53, 60

pharmaceuticals, 34, 37, 51, 52, 53
Philadelphia, 260
Philippines, 6, 22, 25, 78, 237, 245
phosphorus, 147
photographs, 88, 89, 91
piracy, 61, 149, 150, 151, 158, 265
pirated, 61
planning, 98, 172, 222, 227, 248, 249, 263, 264
plants, 73, 87, 147, 165, 166, 176
plastics, 144
platform, 57, 125, 184, 185
play, 2, 21, 31, 67, 112
playing, 16, 112
pleasure, 55
pluralism, 200
plutonium, ix, xii, 79, 80, 81, 82, 83, 84, 85, 86, 87, 89, 90, 93, 94, 95, 96, 97, 99, 161, 162, 165, 169, 175
plutonium reprocessing plant, ix, 79, 81, 82, 87, 89
PM, 97, 114
Poland, 175
polarization, 38
police, 12, 62, 103, 113
policy choice, 182
policy initiative, 194
policy issues, xiv, 19, 209, 210, 215
policy makers, 111
policy options, 194
policy problems, 257
policymakers, xii, 37, 66, 67, 121, 131, 140, 141, 143, 144, 182, 184, 199, 210, 221
political crisis, 201
political ideologies, 184
political leaders, 16
political opposition, 184
political parties, 185, 195
political pluralism, 200
politicians, 12, 31, 66
politics, viii, 15, 30, 185
pollution, 142
poor, 104, 126, 141, 142, 149, 170, 172, 185, 189, 242
poor performance, 185
poppy cultivation, 104, 105, 106, 111
popular vote, 184
population, xi, 17, 39, 51, 103, 104, 131, 136, 172, 184
pork, 39
pornography, 109
port of entry, 6
portability, 55
portfolio, 36, 237
ports, 239

postal service, 27
posture, 196, 250
potatoes, 32, 39
potential benefits, 39
poultry, 17, 39, 149
poverty, 104
poverty line, 104
powder, 88
powders, 32, 39
power, xiv, 15, 28, 40, 49, 88, 146, 166, 168, 179, 184, 185, 195, 197, 200, 204, 207, 213, 227
power generation, 88, 146
power lines, 88
power plants, 166
powers, 36
precedent, 183, 195, 198, 232
precedents, 51, 183
predicate, 167
preference, 40
preferential treatment, 31, 48, 54, 58, 64
preparation, 18
preparedness, 9
preservation, 56, 181
presidency, 184
president, xiv, 10, 26, 31, 47, 179, 188, 202, 203, 204, 213, 229, 240, 241, 250, 258
President Bush, 8, 9, 10, 26, 39, 46, 55, 75, 77, 82, 95
President Clinton, 23, 88, 92, 125, 175, 231, 242, 244, 245, 247, 250, 255
President Lee Myung-bak, viii, 9, 30, 174
President Obama, 153, 265
presidential campaign, 30, 65
press, 2, 8, 10, 41, 85, 87, 89, 93, 94, 96, 97
pressure, xi, xii, 23, 37, 47, 65, 68, 82, 105, 112, 119, 123, 132, 144, 151, 181, 196, 198, 203, 247, 250
prestige, 22
prevention, xv, 210, 226, 249
price index, 121
prices, 52, 53, 56, 105, 109, 152, 185
principles, 4, 83, 146, 181, 220, 242, 252, 253
private banks, 110
private sector, 17, 68, 237
private-sector, 33, 54
PRK, 162, 178
producers, 35, 37, 39, 42, 44, 49, 51, 52, 61, 68, 69, 77, 105, 107, 123, 142, 145, 147, 148, 149, 151, 152, 153
production, ix, 14, 36, 40, 44, 45, 47, 68, 69, 79, 80, 81, 88, 89, 93, 96, 97, 105, 106, 111, 121, 122, 123, 124, 128, 134, 138, 143, 145, 147, 148, 149, 150, 152, 157, 158, 174, 210

Index

productivity, 65, 124
productivity growth, 124
professionals, 224
profit, 69
profit margin, 69
profits, 104, 109
program, ix, xiii, xv, 4, 8, 17, 18, 24, 38, 43, 52, 55, 67, 80, 81, 83, 86, 87, 88, 89, 90, 91, 92, 93, 94, 97, 98, 99, 162, 163, 164, 165, 169, 170, 172, 173, 174, 175, 192, 210, 211, 215, 216, 217, 219, 223, 224, 232, 234, 235, 236, 242, 247, 248, 251, 253, 256, 257, 258, 259
programming, 61, 117
project, 59, 85, 86, 88, 89, 91, 98, 222, 236
proliferation, 15, 81, 86, 142, 153, 221, 245, 248, 251, 253, 263
property rights, xi, xii, xiv, 8, 49, 52, 60, 61, 76, 131, 132, 141, 150, 180, 189, 190
proposed regulations, 63
prosperity, 3
protection, xi, xii, 8, 21, 32, 39, 41, 49, 50, 52, 59, 60, 61, 69, 74, 76, 104, 109, 131, 132, 141, 142, 145, 149, 251
protectionism, 125
protocol, 82, 83, 108, 147, 225
prototype, 92
public, 12, 18, 26, 33, 40, 53, 55, 56, 60, 61, 62, 68, 75, 76, 105, 109
public concern, 40, 68, 171
public concerns, 40, 68
public education, 18
public health, 53
public interest, 76
public policy, 26
publishing, 240
pulp, 157
purchasing power, 40, 123, 136
Pyongyang, 80, 83, 84, 85, 86, 87, 91, 92, 94, 95, 96, 97

Q

qualifications, 192
questioning, 205, 262
quotas, 32, 34, 39, 41, 59, 71, 147, 152, 153

R

race, 184
random, 50
random access, 50
range, viii, x, 8, 10, 21, 29, 30, 34, 43, 44, 45, 49, 76, 80, 84, 88, 91, 92, 93, 98, 99, 127, 169, 171, 238, 239, 240, 247
rat, 39
ratification, 31
raw material, 89
raw materials, 89, 122, 124, 147, 189
reactions, 16, 194
Reagan, Ronald, 260
reality, 40, 194
reason, 124, 171, 173
rebel, 102, 105
rebel groups, 102, 105
recall, 142, 156
recession, 11, 22, 23
reciprocity, xv, 51, 54, 210, 211, 218, 220, 222, 224, 227, 244, 245, 253, 254, 258
recognition, 3, 21, 31, 64, 77, 84, 148, 186
recommendations, 5, 34, 152
reconciliation, 229, 250
reconstruction, 104
recovery, vii, 1, 9, 17, 126, 253, 257, 259
refineries, 106
reform, 9, 24, 65, 126, 128, 144, 189, 196, 197, 201
Reform, 19, 177
Reform Act, 19
reforms, x, xii, xiii, 36, 37, 59, 75, 119, 122, 125, 132, 135, 141, 144, 146, 152, 162, 189, 197
refugees, 108
region, 125, 176, 217, 218, 221, 223, 224, 229, 233, 246
regional, x, 2, 8, 9, 14, 15, 16, 17, 18, 19, 21, 24, 25, 64, 67, 101, 109, 112
regionalism, 3, 11, 14, 25, 67
regions of the world, 102
regular, 16, 61
regulation, 52, 110
regulations, 4, 33, 34, 36, 44, 51, 52, 53, 61, 63, 64, 76, 141, 142, 146, 147, 148, 202, 216
regulatory agencies, 141, 142
regulatory framework, 141
regulatory systems, 36, 63
rehabilitation, 221
reimbursement, 34, 52, 53
rejection, 67
relationship, xii, 31, 32, 37, 59, 66, 70, 90, 131, 138, 141, 162, 186, 193, 198, 200, 210, 211, 212, 214, 215, 216, 219, 220, 221, 222, 223, 225, 229, 232, 233, 248, 253
relatives, 110
relevance, 11, 183, 204
relief, 55, 56, 108, 152, 154, 158, 164, 174, 186, 226, 235, 242, 245, 258, 264

remittances, 110
renewable energy, 154
Renewed military exchanges, xiv, 209
renminbi (RMB), xi, 119, 120, 128, 143
reporters, 212, 220, 226, 253, 254
repression, 232
reprocessing, ix, 79, 81, 82, 83, 87, 88, 89, 176
reptiles, 108
Republican, 90
reputation, 62
requirements, xiv, 40, 42, 46, 54, 57, 59, 60, 145, 146, 147, 157, 158, 164, 180, 190, 192, 216
Requirements, 236, 237
resale, xiii, 162, 171
researchers, 234, 254
reserve currency, xi, 120, 127
reserves, x, xi, 40, 119, 120, 121, 127, 129, 144
resins, 134
resistance, 59, 102
resolution, xii, 20, 56, 63, 82, 132, 147, 148, 158, 183, 194, 196, 198, 200, 204, 206, 245, 251, 260
resources, 5, 88, 108, 122, 150, 169, 170, 197
respect, 206, 212
response, xiv, 3, 8, 11, 17, 18, 32, 40, 52, 66, 102, 110, 111, 141, 162, 170, 174, 175, 187, 201, 204, 205, 209, 210, 211, 214, 215, 224, 228, 233, 236, 263, 265
restrictions, xiii, xv, 12, 37, 38, 39, 40, 54, 55, 59, 62, 111, 142, 143, 145, 146, 147, 148, 151, 152, 157, 162, 168, 170, 172, 174, 186, 187, 190, 191, 210, 218, 226, 265
restructuring, 144
retail, 59
retaliation, 229
returns, 40, 124, 129
revaluation, 121
revenue, 59, 111, 113, 150
Revolutionary Guard, 82, 90
rewards, 147
rhetoric, 196, 206, 224, 256
rhino, 116
rice, 32, 33, 35, 38, 39, 40, 41, 71, 113, 141
Rice, Condoleezza, 7, 83, 254, 257, 260
Rice, Secretary of State Condoleezza, 7, 83, 260
rights, x, xi, xii, xiv, 2, 5, 8, 19, 21, 47, 49, 50, 52, 53, 56, 58, 60, 61, 76, 77, 101, 105, 110, 131, 132, 141, 145, 146, 148, 150, 151, 153, 163, 172, 180, 189, 190, 194, 197, 217
risk, 9, 15, 16, 33, 64, 67, 102, 110, 122, 172, 190, 194, 218, 219, 221
risks, 108, 220
rods, 81, 87, 89, 90, 93, 166, 167
root, 103

roots, 39
routes, 102, 105, 108
rowing, 104
royalties, 53
RTA, 15
rubber, 134, 135
rule of law, x, 20, 101, 102, 262
rule of origin, 48
rules, xii, 15, 39, 42, 50, 51, 56, 59, 62, 63, 64, 67, 74, 132, 145, 146, 148, 151, 187, 189, 201, 204, 225, 226
rules of origin, 51, 64
rural, 39, 65, 104, 108
rural areas, 104, 122
Russia, ix, xii, 9, 10, 16, 23, 26, 28, 68, 79, 80, 83, 93, 161, 163, 165, 166, 167, 168, 175, 230, 245, 269
Russian, 25, 89, 93

S

sadness, 200
safe haven, 113
safe havens, 113
safeguard, 32, 34, 40, 46, 48, 56, 57, 71, 75
safeguards, 71, 75
safety, xi, xii, xiv, 8, 17, 27, 33, 40, 42, 44, 52, 62, 64, 67, 126, 128, 131, 132, 140, 141, 142, 143, 146, 154, 157, 179, 186, 225, 226, 252, 256, 257, 258
salaried workers, 62
sales, xiii, xiv, xv, 32, 39, 40, 41, 42, 43, 51, 53, 64, 67, 68, 69, 73, 78, 109, 157, 179, 180, 182, 183, 191, 192, 197, 198, 203, 206, 209, 210, 211, 215, 216, 218, 228, 229, 230, 235, 248, 249, 252, 253, 257, 263, 265
sample, 88
sampling, ix, 79, 80, 83, 84, 85
sanctions, ix, x, xiv, 6, 21, 63, 74, 79, 82, 84, 92, 94, 95, 96, 101, 102, 104, 109, 110, 111, 113, 116, 149, 164, 166, 168, 209, 211, 216, 230, 232, 235
SARS, 17, 24, 28, 222
satellite, xiii, 84, 91, 92, 98, 161, 168, 212, 231, 238, 244, 247, 261
Saudi Arabia, 26
savings, 41, 129
savings rate, 129
scaling, 83, 173
scandal, 185, 204
school, 264
science, 5, 147, 153, 240
SCO, 232
scope, 47, 50, 54, 83, 214, 234

Index

seafood, 108, 138, 141
search, 206, 218, 225, 243, 245, 247, 248, 251, 253, 256, 260, 261
searches, 234
Seattle, 4, 23
secret, 80, 88, 90, 91, 94, 97, 98
Secretary of Agriculture, 164
Secretary of Defense, xv, 205, 209, 210, 211, 212, 213, 215, 217, 218, 219, 220, 221, 222, 224, 226, 227, 229, 230, 231, 232, 233, 234, 235, 236, 237, 238, 239, 240, 241, 242, 243, 244, 245, 246, 247, 248, 249, 250, 251, 252, 253, 254, 255, 256, 257, 258, 259, 261, 262, 263, 264, 265, 266, 267, 268, 269
Secretary of State, 7, 65, 83, 86, 91, 94, 95, 114
Secretary of the Treasury, 104, 110, 154
securities, x, xi, xii, 119, 120, 123, 125, 127, 131, 138, 139, 140, 144, 155, 156
security, x, xiii, xiv, xv, 2, 5, 8, 9, 12, 16, 17, 18, 19, 21, 24, 31, 60, 65, 70, 101, 103, 106, 113, 146, 165, 172, 174, 179, 182, 191, 194, 210, 215, 217, 218, 219, 220, 221, 222, 224, 229, 230, 232, 235, 240, 241, 242, 244, 245, 246, 248, 253, 257, 259, 262
security assistance, 230, 232, 235, 242
Security Council, 2, 28, 91, 115
seismic, 18
seizure, 61
semiconductor, 35, 36, 148
semiconductors, 36, 50, 134, 148
seminars, 18
Senate, 20, 28, 31, 70, 73, 77, 88, 93, 116, 154, 175, 176, 178, 191, 216, 217, 219, 225, 233, 244, 265, 266, 270
Senate Finance Committee, 31, 77
Senate Foreign Relations Committee, 88, 93, 175, 178
separation, 228, 249
September 11, 12, 143, 232, 266
series, 5, 17, 33
service industries, 38
service provider, 53, 54
services, 6, 7, 15, 19, 20, 24, 27, 30, 31, 32, 34, 35, 37, 38, 53, 54, 55, 59, 60, 62, 65, 123, 128, 136, 139, 146, 148, 151, 154, 155, 175, 182, 183, 191, 215, 219, 229, 232
severance pay, 36, 62
severe acute respiratory syndrome, 222
sewing thread, 49
sex, 108
Shanghai, 16, 23
Shanghai Cooperation Organization, 232
shape, 196, 222

shaping, 67
shareholders, 36
shares, 37, 47, 55, 69, 103, 230
sharing, 17, 37, 57, 190, 217, 223
shipping, 17, 27
shock, 158
short run, 123
shortage, 59
shortages, 106
shortfall, xiii, 162
short-term, 21, 55
showing, 89, 91, 227
shrimp, 141
sign, 11, 24, 77
signaling, 10
signals, 61, 196, 198, 260
silicon, 147
simulation, 42, 45, 49
simulations, 72
Singapore, vii, 1, 2, 4, 6, 11, 12, 21, 22, 23, 25, 27, 65, 66, 78, 80, 81, 83, 95, 104, 114, 138, 140, 224, 226, 245, 253, 255
siphon, 14
sites, 82, 83
Six-Party Talks, xii, 161, 162, 164, 165, 167, 168, 170, 172, 175, 176, 230, 257
skills, 76, 245
skin, 109
slaves, 105
smugglers, 102
smuggling, 103, 108, 109, 110
Smuggling, 114
social responsibility, 8, 9
society, 123, 222
software, 150
Solomon I, 202
solution, 33, 41, 183, 188, 199
Somalia, 103, 265
South Africa, 26
South China Sea, 211, 225, 237, 252, 265
South Korea, v, vii, viii, ix, xii, xiii, 6, 9, 22, 24, 26, 27, 28, 29, 30, 31, 32, 33, 34, 35, 36, 37, 38, 39, 40, 41, 42, 43, 44, 45, 46, 47, 48, 49, 50, 51, 52, 53, 54, 55, 56, 57, 58, 59, 60, 61, 62, 63, 64, 65, 66, 67, 68, 69, 70, 71, 72, 73, 74, 75, 76, 77, 79, 80, 83, 85, 86, 87, 89, 92, 93, 104, 124, 127, 136, 161, 162, 163, 165, 166, 167, 168, 169, 170, 172, 173, 174, 175, 224, 230, 245, 246, 248, 252, 263
South Pacific, 201
Southeast Asia, vii, x, 1, 2, 24, 65, 101, 104, 105, 111, 113, 114, 115, 133, 233
sovereign state, 188, 203
sovereignty, 182, 197, 199, 200, 243, 265

Soviet Union, xiv, 88, 89, 169, 209, 211, 225, 233
soybeans, 32, 39, 135
space, xv, 210, 218, 231, 256, 258, 261
specialists, 90, 91
species, 105
speculation, 7, 99, 109, 181
speech, 27, 47, 199, 206, 238, 240, 241, 243, 247
speed, 198
spelling, 39
spending, 123, 124, 126, 217, 258, 259
spent nuclear fuel, 87
Spratly Islands, 237
Spring, 266, 267
SSA, 103
stability, xiv, 121, 125, 144, 158, 179, 181, 193, 195, 196, 217, 221, 228, 229, 237, 250, 264
staffing, 183
stages, 31, 38, 41
stainless steel, 56
standardization, 6
standards, xi, 8, 19, 21, 33, 42, 43, 44, 46, 54, 58, 61, 63, 64, 68, 72, 102, 108, 131, 141, 142, 143, 145, 146
Standards, 23, 44
stasis, 198
state, ix, 4, 9, 22, 26, 54, 60, 64, 67, 79, 81, 82, 83, 85, 86, 93, 94, 95, 102, 104, 108, 110, 121, 144, 146, 168, 171, 175, 176, 188, 202, 203, 219, 232, 248
state control, 171
State Department, 18, 20, 21, 28, 83, 88, 90, 96, 102, 103, 104, 105, 107, 108, 110, 111, 117
State Peace and Development Council (SPDC), x, 101, 102
statehood, 187, 188, 195, 200, 206, 244
state-owned, 54
state-owned enterprises, 121, 144, 146
states, 2, 3, 5, 23, 42, 43, 45, 53, 71, 103, 107, 108, 157, 167, 175, 183, 198, 229, 231
statistics, 12, 69, 75
statute, 165
statutes, 50, 61, 76, 216
steel, viii, 30, 35, 49, 50, 51, 56, 57, 74, 75, 144, 146, 147, 148, 149, 157, 158, 166, 168
steel industry, 49, 50, 51, 57, 74, 147
stimulus, 126, 146, 156
stock, 11, 37, 59, 68, 123, 185
stock exchange, 37
stock markets, 185
stockpile, ix, 79, 83, 84, 85, 86, 93
storage, 93
strategic cooperation, xiv, 209
Strategic Economic Dialogue, xii, 132, 153, 223

strategy, 162, 163, 185, 220, 231, 232, 236, 237, 240, 246, 248, 264
streams, 59
strength, 184
stress, 194, 252
strikes, 62
structure, 3, 5, 38, 87, 102, 197
students, 228, 234, 245, 250
style, 45, 150
submarines, 252
subsidies, 24, 57
subsidy, 76, 122, 123, 146, 152, 158
substitutes, 106
succession, 191
summaries, 10
summer, 81, 88, 151, 173, 174, 228, 232
Sun, v, 101
Sunday, 115
supervision, 142
supplemental, 83
supplier, 138, 142, 153
suppliers, 36, 45, 49, 62, 138, 142, 148
supply, x, 14, 27, 49, 69, 90, 119, 120, 122, 175, 247, 255
supply chain, 14, 27, 49
suppression, 102
surplus, 49, 50, 120, 144
surrogates, 92
surveillance, xv, 187, 201, 210, 222, 225, 226, 252, 265
survival, 65
surviving, 69
survivors, 233
suspects, 201, 224
suspensions, xv, 210, 229
Sweden, 232
Switzerland, 78
syndrome, 222
synthetic fiber, 135
Syria, ix, 80, 81, 82, 86, 89, 97, 98, 178

T

tactics, 245
Taiwan, v, vii, xiii, xiv, xv, 3, 4, 10, 11, 16, 22, 25, 26, 27, 66, 116, 124, 138, 145, 179, 180, 181, 182, 183, 184, 185, 186, 187, 188, 189, 190, 191, 192, 193, 194, 195, 196, 197, 198, 199, 200, 201, 202, 203, 204, 205, 206, 207, 209, 210, 211, 215, 217, 221, 224, 228, 229, 230, 231, 238, 239, 241, 242, 244, 245, 247, 248, 249, 250, 251, 252, 253, 255, 256, 257, 260, 263, 264, 265, 267, 268
Taiwan Relations Act (TRA), 206, 228, 242

Index

Taiwan Strait, 11, 66
Taiwan Strait crisis, xiv, 209, 211, 224
takeover, 31
tangible benefits, 220
Tanzania, 232
target, vii, 1, 3, 24, 43, 94, 143, 172, 231, 232, 238, 244
target zone, 231
targets, 92, 173
tariff, 15, 20, 32, 33, 34, 39, 40, 41, 42, 43, 45, 46, 48, 49, 50, 69, 70, 71, 72, 74, 145, 148, 154, 158
tariffs, 7, 30, 32, 33, 34, 37, 38, 39, 40, 41, 43, 44, 46, 47, 48, 49, 50
task force, 5, 6
tax breaks, 152, 158
tax cuts, 146
tax policy, 46, 149
tax system, 44
taxation, 38, 43, 44, 46
taxes, 33, 44, 45, 104, 147
teams, 168, 238
technical assistance, xiii, 17, 42, 161, 162, 167
technicians, 83
techniques, 17, 110
technological advances, 93
technology, 5, 23, 37, 38, 45, 50, 84, 88, 90, 92, 98, 137, 145, 146, 147, 150, 153, 154, 155, 163, 166, 199, 217, 218, 232, 240, 247, 249
technology transfer, 145, 147, 218
Tehran, 91, 98
telecommunications, 5, 36, 50, 53, 55, 146
telecommunications services, 53, 55
telephone, 224, 225, 226, 256, 263
tension, xv, 105, 210
tensions, 65, 66, 102, 141, 168, 182, 185, 186, 196, 197, 212, 218, 221, 223, 224, 226, 229, 230, 235, 248, 249, 256, 258, 261
tenure, 37, 173, 184, 185, 193
territorial, 225, 265
territory, 52, 55, 59, 63, 64, 77, 187, 202, 231, 237
terrorism, ix, 9, 16, 17, 19, 28, 79, 81, 82, 83, 86, 94, 95, 97, 110, 193, 232, 245
terrorist, 17, 24, 115
terrorist groups, 24
terrorists, 17, 23, 113
Terrorists, 113
testimony, 47, 71, 72, 73, 88, 93
testing, 88, 90, 92, 97, 157, 215, 219
textile, 34, 35, 48, 111
textile industry, 111
textiles, 14, 32, 34, 47, 48, 49, 137, 144, 146, 153, 158
Thai, 105, 109, 114, 115

Thailand, 6, 22, 24, 25, 37, 66, 78, 103, 104, 105, 106, 108, 109, 112, 114, 117, 245, 253, 255, 259, 263
theft, 47
thinking, 220, 224
third party, 52
thoughts, 11
threat, ix, 17, 18, 24, 34, 66, 80, 85, 86, 103, 163, 169, 221, 229, 237, 249, 253, 255, 256
threatened, 55
threatening, 107
threats, xiii, 17, 24, 109, 158, 179, 245, 264
threshold, 64, 75, 151, 156
thresholds, 151
Tiananmen Crackdown, xiv, 209, 210, 211, 215, 216, 221, 232, 235
Tibet, 233, 236, 253, 257
Tier 3, 108, 110
tiger, 109, 116
timber, x, 101, 102, 104, 108, 113
timing, 68, 170
Title I, 113, 155, 165
Title II, 165
Title IV, 155
Tokyo, 98
tourism, 17, 186
toys, 14, 137, 141, 142, 143
TPA, viii, 29, 30, 34, 56, 64
tracking, 143, 236, 238, 240
tracks, 153
Trade Act, 74, 75, 113, 116
trade agreement, vii, viii, 1, 4, 8, 10, 14, 15, 19, 23, 29, 30, 38, 65, 132, 149
Trade and Investment Framework (TIFA), xiv, 180
trade deficit, x, xi, xii, 119, 121, 123, 124, 128, 129, 131, 132, 134, 138, 141, 144, 189
trade diversion, 14
trade liberalization, xii, 3, 4, 6, 13, 66, 132
trade policies, viii, 2, 16, 36
trade policy, ix, 2, 3, 30, 32, 43, 56, 67
Trade Policy Staff Committee, 74
trade promotion authority (TPA),, viii, 29, 30
Trade Representative, viii, 2, 3, 29, 30, 34, 40, 57, 70, 74, 75, 76, 77
trade union, 38
trademarks, 61
trade-off, 181
Trade-Related Aspects of Intellectual Property Rights, 60
Trade-Related Aspects of Intellectual Property Rights (TRIPS), 60

trading, viii, xi, 4, 16, 23, 29, 30, 36, 37, 56, 63, 67, 120, 124, 131, 132, 134, 135, 146, 147, 148, 151, 189, 190, 197
trading bloc, 4
trading partners, xi, 37, 56, 67, 120
Trading with the Enemy Act, 81, 82, 95, 96
Trading With the Enemy Act sanctions, ix, 79
tradition, 7
traffic, 226, 238, 245, 248
Trafficked drugs, x, 101
trafficking, 102, 103, 104, 105, 107, 108, 109, 110, 111, 174
trafficking in persons, 102, 108, 110
Trafficking in Persons, 108, 110, 114, 115
training, 4, 18, 60, 82, 89, 117, 143, 149, 174, 201, 223, 226, 227, 234, 241, 242, 243, 247, 255, 258, 261, 264, 268
transaction costs, 23, 24
transactions, 23, 110, 111, 116, 143
transfer, 55, 60, 94, 99, 110
transformation, 17, 150
transformations, 182, 218
transition, 39, 71, 146, 194, 213
transition period, 39, 71
transnational, x, 101, 102, 103, 104, 105, 110, 111
Trans-Pacific Strategic Economic Partnership Agreement (TPP), an, vii, 1
transparency, xv, 4, 6, 24, 34, 36, 52, 53, 61, 62, 63, 64, 110, 146, 164, 210, 211, 212, 217, 220, 221, 222, 227, 236, 242, 245, 253, 254, 258
transparent, 44, 51, 53, 57
transport, 176, 212, 226, 252, 256, 261, 264
transportation, xiv, 5, 34, 53, 104, 156, 179, 186
travel, 49, 53, 55
Treasury, x, xi, xii, 96, 101, 104, 110, 111, 114, 115, 119, 123, 126, 127, 128, 131, 138, 139, 140, 144, 153, 154, 155, 156, 157, 159, 195, 223
Treasury Department, 96
Treasury Secretary, 153
treaties, 105, 183
treatment, 31, 37, 46, 48, 50, 53, 54, 58, 59, 61, 64, 76, 132, 145, 148, 255
trends, 127, 193
Triads, 103
trial, 116, 180, 188, 200
tribunals, 60, 61
TRIPS, 53, 60
trucks, 33, 42, 43, 45, 46, 68, 69
trust, 193, 201, 223
Tse-tung, Mao, 181
tsunami, 18
Tsunami, 18
tuberculosis, 53

Turkey, 26
turtles, 108
two-way, 36

U

U.N. Security Council, 115, 166, 260
U.S. assistance, 110, 111, 174, 217
U.S. Department of Agriculture, 67, 70
U.S. Department of Commerce, 36, 73, 75, 76
U.S. Department of the Treasury, 114
U.S. economy, x, xi, 34, 35, 119, 120, 124, 126, 140
U.S. military, 53, 85, 92
U.S. policy, viii, x, xii, xiii, xiv, 2, 43, 66, 67, 101, 102, 111, 121, 131, 140, 141, 143, 164, 179, 180, 181, 182, 183, 184, 187, 192, 193, 194, 195, 197, 198, 203, 206, 210, 215, 228, 229, 230
U.S. Treasury, x, 96, 110, 119, 123, 127, 139, 144, 153, 156, 159
U.S.-South Korea Free Trade Agreement (KORUS FTA), v, vii, 29
UK, 97
UN, 103, 202
uncertainty, 3, 94
unclassified, 97
unemployment, 124
unification, 186, 198, 249
union representatives, 62
unions, viii, 30, 62, 73
unit cost, 44
United Kingdom, 26, 136, 216, 245
United Nations, xiii, 28, 84, 103, 105, 106, 108, 114, 161, 187, 188, 195
universities, 228
uranium, ix, 80, 81, 86, 88, 89, 90, 94, 113, 162, 165, 174, 175, 253
uranium enrichment, 81, 86, 88, 94
urban, 39, 104, 108, 136
urban areas, 136
urban centers, 108
urban population, 39
USA PATRIOT Act, 116
USDA, 41, 71
USS Cole, 251
Uzbekistan, 175

V

validation, 197
values, 64
valve, 226
VAT, 148

Index

vegetables, 138
vehicles, 33, 34, 42, 43, 44, 45, 46, 47, 51, 59, 63, 68, 69, 78, 112, 137, 143
venue, 42
vessels, 263
Vice President, 189, 193, 206, 212, 220, 236, 242, 252, 253
victims, 105, 111
Victims of Trafficking and Violence Protection Act, 113, 116
Vietnam, 6, 13, 23, 24, 25, 27, 37, 78, 104, 233, 237, 254, 257
violence, 17, 23, 62, 111
visa, 6, 21, 26, 55
Visa, 26, 55, 75
Visa Waiver Program, xiv, 26, 75, 180, 192, 205
visas, 26, 55
vision, 4
voice, 156, 200
vote, viii, 30, 31, 64, 65, 184, 197, 200
voters, 185, 198
voting, 55, 139
VWP, 55, 75

W

wage structure, 59
wages, 58, 59, 62, 128, 144
waiver, 164, 168, 176, 192, 205, 215, 216, 219
Wall Street Journal, 98
war, 105, 181, 184, 216, 221, 228, 232, 234, 254, 255, 256
warning systems, 18
Washington, xiv, 4, 7, 8, 47, 70, 76, 88, 90, 93, 94, 95, 96, 97, 98, 99, 113, 157, 165, 173, 177, 180, 182, 185, 196, 198, 203, 206, 212, 217, 225, 231, 232, 235, 236, 237, 240, 242, 247, 248, 249, 251, 252, 254, 255, 257, 259, 260, 261, 262, 263, 264, 266, 267, 268, 269
Washington Post, 88, 94, 95, 96, 97, 98, 99, 113
Washington, George, 257
waste, 134
water, 85, 86, 165, 166, 230, 263
weapons, vii, ix, xv, 24, 79, 80, 82, 84, 85, 86, 87, 88, 89, 90, 92, 93, 94, 98, 99, 109, 162, 163, 165, 166, 174, 175, 182, 191, 198, 199, 203, 210, 214, 218, 221, 230, 231, 235, 244, 245, 247, 248, 250, 251, 252, 253, 256, 258, 259, 261
weapons of mass destruction, 24, 218
Weapons of Mass Destruction, 95
weapons-grade plutonium, ix, 79, 89, 94
wearing apparel, 35, 48
web, 11, 15, 25, 26, 31
well-being, 123
Western Hemisphere, 19
wheat, 35, 141
White House, 2, 3, 8, 9, 10, 68, 75, 82, 83, 95, 96, 183, 184, 191, 192, 193, 204, 206, 211, 245, 255, 266
wholesale, 59, 139
wildlife, x, 101, 102, 104, 109, 111, 116
Wilson, Woodrow, 96
winning, 184, 185
winter, 173
WMD, 166, 168
women, 111
wood, 148
worker rights, 47
workers, xii, 47, 56, 58, 61, 62, 122, 131, 165
workforce, 38, 60, 62, 65
working groups, 5, 6, 22, 143, 225
workplace, 17
World Bank, 9, 81, 86
World Food Programme (WFP), xiii, 161, 169
World Health Organization (WHO), 187, 195, 201
World Trade Center, 12, 16, 23, 27
World Trade Organization, xi, xii, WTO, xi, xii, 3, 4, 6, 14, 15, 16, 22, 23, 24, 34, 41, 42, 53, 56, 60, 62, 64, 67, 70, 71, 75, 128, 131, 132, 141, 145, 146, 147, 148, 149, 151, 152, 153, 155, 157, 158, 187, 188
World War I, 181, 204, 233, 236, 238, 240, 241, 253, 254, 257, 269
worldwide, 69
worry, 198
writing, 15, 43

Y

yang, 189
yarn, 48, 49
yield, 92
Yongbyon, ix, xii, 79, 80, 81, 82, 83, 84, 85, 86, 87, 88, 89, 93, 94, 96, 161, 162, 165, 166, 167, 168, 169, 176
yuan, xi, 119, 120, 121, 122, 123, 124, 125, 126, 127, 128, 143, 158
Yugoslavia, 211, 247

Z

zinc, 147